# EUROPE
# AND THE JEWS

*Let not the foot of pride come against me, and let not the hand of the wicked remove me.*

PSALM XXXVI: 11

# EUROPE AND THE JEWS

*The Pressure of Christendom on the*
*People of Israel for 1900 years*

## By Malcolm Hay

### Introduction by Thomas Sugrue

Academy
Chicago
Publishers

Published in 1992 by
Academy Chicago Publishers
213 West Institute Place
Chicago, Illinois 60610

*Cover design by Julia Anderson-Miller*

*So I considered again all the oppressions that are done under*
*    the sun;*
*And beheld the tears of such as were oppressed, and they had*
*    no comforter;*
*And on the side of the oppressors there was power,*
*But they had no comforter.*

*Wherefore I praised the dead that are already dead*
*More than the living that are yet alive;*
*But better than they both is he that hath not yet been,*
*Who hath not seen the evil that is done under the sun.*

ECCLESIASTES IV: 1–3

To

Alice Ivy Hay

# Contents

OTHER BOOKS BY MALCOLM HAY

*Wounded and a Prisoner of War*    1916
*A Chain of Error in Scottish History*    1927
*The Blairs Papers (1603-1660)*    1929
*The Jesuits and the Popish Plot*    1934
*Winston Churchill and James II*    1934
*The Enigma of James II*    1938

# Introduction

It is thirty-six years now since in the late summer of 1914 Captain Malcolm Vivian Hay of Seaton, Aberdeen, crossed the English Channel with the 1st Gordon Highlanders and followed the country roads of France to a place called Mons. He knew France well, and in the villages where the troops paused to rest he talked with farmers and shopkeepers in their own language. They seemed undisturbed by the idea of battle; their primary interest was in "le kilt." They felt the cloth, looked at the sporran and apron, and said, "Mais en hiver ça doit être terrible!"

Near Mons the Highlanders turned left into a beet field. They were told to dig a trench; while they worked a man in the next field planted cabbages. When they were finished and had settled in, patches of gray appeared at the edge of the wood they faced; the slim British Expeditionary Force had walked into the swinging right arm of the German field army. For a long day and a longer night the 3rd Division, of which the Highlanders were a part, held off the German advance. The odds against them in manpower were ten to one; in artillery, seven to one.

He stood at the parapet, watching the battle through field glasses until, as he recalled it later, a machine gun in the village of Bethancourt started to play up and down the trench. "The bullets began to spray too close to my left ear, and laying my glasses on the parapet, I was about to sit down for a few minutes' rest, and indeed had got halfway to the sitting position, when the machine-gun found its target . . . I knew instantly what had happened. The blow might have come from a sledgehammer, except that it seemed to carry with it an impression of speed. I saw for an instant in my mind's eye the battlefield at which I had been gazing through my glasses the whole day. Then the vision was hidden by a scarlet circle, and a voice said, 'Mr. Hay has got it.' Through the red mist of the scarlet circle I looked at my watch (the movement to do so had begun in my mind before I was hit); it was spattered with blood; the hands showed five minutes to four. The voice which had spoken before said, 'Mr. Hay is killed.'"

He began to lose consciousness then, and he thought, "Is this the end?" The answer was immediately in his mind— "Not yet." He was unconscious for a while, and then revived, feeling pains in his legs. Private Sinclair, the man who had pronounced him dead, saw that he was breathing and laid him on the straw which covered the bottom of the trench, putting a bandage on his wounded head and trying to give him a drink from his water bottle. Captain Hay tapped the breast pocket of his jacket, where he carried a flask of old brandy. The Red Cross book stated that brandy was the worst possible thing for a head wound, but Private Sinclair poured the entire contents of the flask down his captain's throat. He regained consciousness and felt better, and when Private Sinclair and another soldier attempted to remain with him after the battalion began its retreat he ordered them away.

After a night in the beet field Captain Hay was found by the Germans and turned over to members of the French Red Cross, who took him to a hospital at Caudry. There he again heard himself pronounced dead, and received, being a Roman Catholic, Extreme Unction, the last sacrament. "There is between life and death," he later wrote, "a period when the normal process of thought comes to an end—a new mode of consciousness is taking the place of the old—the soul, standing on the threshold, looks back at the body lying helpless. During the night, in that little room in Caudry . . . I was slowly discovering another self, distinct from the body lying on the bed, and yet connected with it in mist and shadow; and this was the shadow of death."

He rallied from this crisis and began to convalesce, discovering that as a result of his wound he was partially paralyzed. He was moved to the civil hospital at Cambrai, where the Germans were in occupation. There on Saint Andrew's Day his French nurse, knowing the occasion was important to a Scotsman, brought him a delicacy, a dish of snails. He had to eat them, and he liked them. Soon afterward the Germans took him from the French and sent him to Würzburg, to the fortress prison of Marienburg. There he and other prisoners of the allied forces were treated badly; he saw the German mind— the mind that a generation later produced Nazism—at work: "We lived in the very midst of an organization which moved as one for one purpose—the destruction of European civilization and the substitution of Teutonic conceptions."

In February of 1915 he was exchanged, being judged unfit for military duty, and returned to England. In London he fought his paralysis and learned to walk with the aid of a cane; he entered the intelligence service, organized a group of young university men for cryptographic work, and made a contribution to the war effort which would have irritated the jailers of Marienburg had they known of it. He also set down his experiences as a soldier and prisoner, and the story appeared in *Blackwood's Magazine*; Captain Hay preferred to remain anonymous, and identified himself in the narrative as Mr. H. In 1916 the story was published as a book: *Wounded and a Prisoner of War*, "By an Exchanged Officer." It was well received by the critics and became a best seller; it was the first of the many worthwhile books written by soldiers of the 1914–18 war. Its style, form, and clarity were praised, and this rather astonished Captain Hay, who had not fancied himself as a writer or thought of writing as a career. When the fighting stopped and he went back to Scotland the idea of writing as a career went with him; he found it an excellent companion for a man faced with the problem of permanent semi-invalidism, and he accepted it as such.

His home was at Seaton, an estate near Aberdeen which had been bought in the middle of the eighteenth century by his great-grandfather, Mr. Forbes, of Forbes and Company, Bombay. In 1813 Mr. Forbes' only child, Elizabeth, married Lord James Hay, second son of the seventh Marquis of Tweeddale, who was aide-de-camp to Wellington at Waterloo, and afterwards Military Governor of Paris. It is interesting to recall that Lord James was for a short time in command of the Grenadier Guards when they were stationed at Cambrai in the winter of 1815—almost exactly a hundred years before his grandson occupied a bed in a hospital of that city.

Malcolm Hay resumed his supervision of the estate's farms, but he also set about a task which, through a combination of literary talent and skillful historical research, produced during the next twenty years four remarkable and important books: *A Chain of Error in Scottish History, The Blairs Papers, The Jesuits and the Popish Plot,* and *The Enigma of James II.* Three of the volumes were concerned basically with the same problem—the infiltration into history books of contemporaneous misunderstandings, prejudices, libels, slanders, and simple mistakes, and the perpetuation of these distortions by historians too slipshod or unconcerned to check their sources and work on the original material of their studies. As an example of the problem Malcolm Hay chose the Catholic role in Scottish and English religious and political life during and after the Reformation; his first target was a belief firmly embedded in Scottish popular and historical "knowledge"—the notion that the Celtic Church of the sixth and seventh centuries was consciously free of Rome and was a "forerunner" of Protestantism. In *A Chain of Error in Scottish History* he traced the notion to its sources, followed it through the historians who accepted it without question—Gibbon and Skene and Sir Walter Scott among them—and demolished it with documentary evidence, in particular a letter from Saint Columbanus to Pope Boniface IV in which the loyalty of the Celtic Church to the Holy See was unequivocally declared, though its right to criticize the See's conduct in certain matters and to offer advice in others (a right unhappily unexercised by any portion of the Church in these parlous times) was as unequivocally claimed.

It was 1927 when the book was published; the careful and precise documentation, the gathering of evidence, the arrangement of the case, had taken eleven years. Its effect was explosive. *The Times Literary Supplement* published a review which peevishly expressed annoyance with the author. A learned professor, writing in *The Scottish Historical Review*, said that "the violently partisan and abusive character of the book precludes any serious notice in a review of this nature."

But a young priest named Ronald Knox wrote that, "were I a millionaire I would send it to every manse in Scotland . . . for the better instruction of its inhabitants." It was the author's sharp wit, vigorous style, and lively metaphors which precipitated much of the adverse criticism and a good deal of the enthusiastic praise of the book; the evidence it presented was actually unassailable. The editor of the *Scottish Historical Review* published in a subsequent issue the fact that he had received from many distinguished scholars—among them Professor John Fraser, of Jesus College, Oxford—protests against the unreasonable violence of the reviewer. Competent scholars agreed, stated the editor, that the author of *A Chain of Error in Scottish History*, "has shown beyond the possibility of quibbling that a number of documents of the greatest importance for early Scottish history have been consistently misrepresented by historians."

Two years later when *The Blairs Papers* appeared there was no fuss and no adverse criticism; the reviews referred to "Mr. Hay the historian" and *The Times Literary Supplement* applauded the book as a contribution to historical accuracy.

The following volumes were received with like respect and appreciation, though *The Times* continued to remark on the laird of Seaton's style, which it apparently considered too gay and satirical for the serious subjects it discussed.

*The Blairs Papers* was a preliminary study of certain records brought from the Scots College in Paris to Saint Mary's College at Blairs, Aberdeen, the Roman Catholic seminary for Scotland. The records, largely letters, revealed the effort of the Catholic clergy to save their faith from extinction in Scotland during the triumphant years of the Reformation; those presented in the book dealt with the period from 1603 to 1660, and through them considerable information was exposed on the period of Cromwell's rule in Scotland, on the Catholic secular clergy's jealousy of the Jesuits, and on Charles II's abandonment of the Catholic cause.

The unfortunate feelings of certain secular priests toward certain Jesuits formed the basis of the next volume in the series, *The Jesuits and the Popish Plot*, which appeared in 1934. In it Mr. Hay presented the theory, supported by documentary evidence, that a disappointed and embittered secular priest named John Sergeant, annoyed with the Society of Jesus, became a confederate of Titus Oates and Shaftesbury and a spy in the king's service, carrying out a work of spite and vengeance which culminated in the "Plot" of 1678.

It was a natural step from this book to *The Enigma of James II*, published in 1938, which rescued the reputation of England's last Catholic king from the canards of such historians as Gilbert Burnet and Macaulay. James was a tactless man and a poor judge of people, Mr. Hay admitted, but he was honorable, he was not a coward, his record as Duke of York was outstanding, and his Declaration of Indulgence, giving religious freedom to Catholics and Dissenters, was the act of a liberal man, not a device for delivering England to Rome. He was, in fact, in Mr. Hay's opinion, a man ahead of his time; a considerable period passed before the religious tolerance in which he believed was acceptable to the people of England. The "Bloodless Revolution" of 1688 which deposed him was caused by the birth of his son, a male heir who would continue Catholicism on the throne; the politicians and the people could not trust themselves to such a succession.

This was the end of the "chain of error" which the semi-invalid had chosen for a test of his skill and talent. He had set right—incontestably right—the Catholic side of the Reformation story in Scotland and England. Malcolm Hay had become, in twenty years, a historian of stature and a writer of power and depth.

During the Second World War, Mr. Hay organized on behalf of the Red Cross a service for prisoners of war; he founded and edited a monthly periodical which was delivered, in spite of many difficulties, to most of the prison camps in Germany and in Italy. At this time, appalled by reports of wholesale massacre which came from Germany, he turned his attention to Jewish history. After a day's work at the office of his POW service he went to bed with a Hebrew dictionary and the Bible, teaching himself the language which the Jews in Palestine had revived and were speaking. He met, when they visited England, the Zionist leaders—Weizmann, Ben Gurion, Shertok. He began to see another "chain of error" in history.

. After the war he visited Palestine; he was there in 1947 when all British civilians not in the armed forces or civil service were ordered to leave the country. Instead of complying he "went underground," and lived at Rehovot as "Rabbi Hai." On his return to Scotland he began to write *The Foot of Pride*, a book he felt had to be done, and done by a Christian; a book admitting, exposing, examining, analyzing, and condemning the "chain of error" in Christian theology and Christian ethics which is called anti-Semitism. He had gone, in his research, to original sources, to the roots of

---

* *Europe and the Jews* was first published in 1950 by the Beacon Press, under the title *The Foot of Pride*.

the evil mistake which has poisoned Christian society for eighteen hundred years; he presented his evidence with the skill, the wit, the careful scholarship, and the strong love of justice which had marked his quartet of books on the "chain of error" in Scottish and English history.

When in 1949 he visited the new state of Israel he took the manuscript with him. I met him in Tel Aviv, and when he told me of the book I asked if I might read it; when I had done so I urged him to submit it to an American publisher.

We met on the balcony of my third-floor room in a seaside hotel. I did not then know of his physical disability and allowed him to walk the stairs alone. It must have been a slow and painful journey, but he stepped into the room smiling, leaning on a stout cane and swinging his paralyzed leg with vigor. He was dressed in tweeds and was spare and trim, with a fine Scottish face, blue eyes, red cheeks, greying blond hair, and a trim moustache. When we were settled so that we could see each other and at the same time watch the Mediterranean, I discovered gradually the amazing richness of his mind and its perfect integration with a personality that glistened through a steady mist of humor. Friendship, I suppose, depends for its depth and its latitude on the areas of thought in which two people find their minds are agreeable companions, sharing interest, concern, understanding, and appreciation; it is therefore pleasantly beyond the ego, along the rim of magnanimity, though always in danger from the possibility of union at a lower level, where egos mate in prejudice and frustration and become accomplices. In a few hours Mr. Hay and I were fast friends; we had joined in our opposition to hatred and injustice and had become partners in a plan to bring *The Foot of Pride* to American readers.

In so doing it is the opinion of Mr. Hay, of the publisher, and of myself that a message of warning is necessary for those Americans who read the book. Mr. Hay has never been to America, and he has not included in his book any material on anti-Semitism in the United States. A reader might therefore be tempted to believe that none exists here, and to congratulate himself upon the restraint and tolerance of his countrymen, who have never ordered the Jews to leave their homes, never confiscated their goods, never accused them of ritual murders, never burned them at the stake. Such temptation should be resisted. Americans are as anti-Semitic as the Gentiles of other nations; they have thus far expressed their anti-Semitism less violently than the Germans and Russians of this century and the French and Spaniards and British of other centuries, but only because it has irritated them less. As Christians they are naturally infected with the notion that the Jews bear a holy guilt and are living in a state of penance, doomed to a miserable "difference" and deservedly burdened with discrimination and segregation. The discrimination and segregation are politely arranged in the United States, and are carried out by the "Gentleman's Agreement" so effectively publicized by Laura Z. Hobson's recent novel of that name; but they are not less real or effective because of the manners which attend them. It is not, after all, the degree to which anti-Semitism is expressed which is important; where it exists at all it is engaged in murder—the murder not of Jews, but of Christians. An anti-Semite is a dead Christian; his prejudice has strangled his faith.

The Jews themselves have tried to measure anti-Semitism in the United States. Through the Anti-Defamation League of B'nai B'rith they have made a study of such observable manifestations as the Ku Klux Klan, the rabble-rousing race bigots who peddle hate and fear to simpletons and paranoids, the "quota" system in colleges and professional schools, and the political and editorial comments which infiltrate anti-Semitism into opinions on Communism, Displaced Persons, and the new Jewish State of Israel. The Anti-Defamation League itself has attempted to extend this information by testing for anti-Semitism with polls and questionnaires. Some of the results obtained were disclosed recently in a book by Arnold Forster,

*A Measure of Freedom.* They present, I fear, too hopeful a
picture; they reveal the good-natured, fair-minded American's
theoretical feelings about Jews, but they hide his actual feelings. They must, in fact, hide his actual feelings, since these
feelings are generally unknown to him until he finds himself
faced by a "Jewish situation." He can say, in answer to a
question, that he would not mind if his sister married a Jew,
but since his sister is not about to marry a Jew his answer
is meaningless. As a matter of fact he might find himself
faced with a sister's proposed marriage to a Jew, and be un-
bothered by it; what would bother him might come later,
when his Jewish brother-in-law was successful in business and
he himself was not. Then his frustration, his anger at himself, would turn naturally against his brother-in-law, who
would become, suddenly, not a brighter or more energetic
or even a luckier fellow than himself, but a "damned Jew."
The Jews, he would reflect, have everything; they are everywhere; you can't keep them out; they make money while
honest folk sleep; they are taking over the country like a
swarm of ants. Thus his anti-Semitism, always present but
previously latent, would become active. As a successful man,
on the other hand, he might go through the whole of his life
without expressing more than a casual distaste for "the Hebes,"
even remarking, from time to time, along with other passive
anti-Semites, "Some of my best friends are Jews."

Nothing can be done about anti-Semitism until something
is done about Christianity. It is as illogical for a follower of
Jesus to persecute a Jew as it is for him to commit any other
sin of hate; the process by which he rationalizes his anti-
Semitism should be identical with the process by which he
rationalizes his other breaches of the code according to which
his religion orders him to live. The fact that the two processes
are not identical is the essence of the matter; the fact that a
Christian is able to feel that anti-Semitism is not a sin, and indeed may be a virtue, a participation in the divine chastisement

of a race of God-killers, is the evil which spreads and maintains and strengthens this Christian violation of the law of love. As long as so cool and Luciferian an assumption is resident in Christian thinking, the Jew is a marked man, with a yellow patch on the arm of his identity.

Religious toleration in America is legal, but in practice it is a well-mannered fraud; bigotry and prejudice are in abeyance only, they are not diminished or dead; they can be stirred as easily as the waters of a pond. One need only praise the Jews to a Gentile to see the flicker of anti-Semitism; the Gentile's brow knits and his eyes cloud, and he begins to demur: "Well, some of them, yes . . . but dash it, the Jews just don't seem to be able to resist [fill in blank with appropriate vice]." He cannot accept the Jews as a people who have among them some sinners and some saints, along with a mass of men and women composed of a portion of good and a portion of evil; the Jews to him are a folk filled with cunning, stained with greed, adept in money, fond of cheating, and desirous of power. He does not realize that this portrait, which he places over the face of every Jew, is actually the image of his own darker self, a picture of the Judas in his soul who betrays the Christ within him again and again. He does not understand that it is not the Jew he sees before him whom he dislikes and distrusts, but the Judas within himself, whom he projects into the Jew, thus exorcising the betrayer from himself. When the betrayer is firmly fixed in the Jew, then, by destroying the Jew, by cursing and despising and loathing him, the betrayer is also destroyed. That this practice should be considered theologically sound is the horror of anti-Semitism, the horror which Malcolm Hay has chronicled and documented in *The Foot of Pride*.

Every word of this infamous and unsavory story is as applicable to American Gentiles as it is to those living Germans and those dead Spaniards and Frenchmen and Englishmen and other Europeans whose deeds blow through the pages

which follow like a mistral, chilling the blood and constrict-
ing the heart. We are as infected as were they, because we
are no better Christians than they were; we are only more
comfortable with our conscience, and less in need, at the moment, of a scapegoat for our sins.

By now the reader of this Introduction will realize that
Malcolm Hay has spent twenty years trying to set the
Protestants straight about the Catholics, and will therefore
appreciate the integrity and deep sincerity behind his record-
ing of Christian behavior, both Catholic and Protestant,
towards the people of Israel.

I have just read this book for the third time; and I like it
more than ever. It is a splendid book, a great and courageous
work, and I rejoice that its first place of publication is in the
United States of America.

THOMAS SUGRUE

# History and Honesty

WHY DO SOME BOOKS move us so deeply that we never forget them? It is hard to give a general answer to this question, but when we stop to think about it we realize that for most of us the list of such books is not very long: it is likely to include the Bible, a few plays, more biographies and novels, possibly a few works by philosophers (Plato would appear on many lists, and Spinoza and Nietzsche on some) — and very little else. Few readers indeed would include anything from the natural or social sciences, and — this comes as a surprise — hardly any books by historians would appear on such lists.

Herodotus and Thucydides, some Roman historians, and Gibbon have written classics that are still widely read and honored, but not many readers are deeply moved either by the historians of the past or by their present-day successors. In fact, it is widely assumed today that history is at best entertaining but more often myopic and pedestrian, and that the only way for a historian to achieve something of genuine significance is to abandon historiography in an attempt to offer something infinitely more ambitious, comprehensive, and unsound: an all-inclusive system and predictions. Short of that, most people think, history is not really important but at most diverting; and in any case a historian is not supposed to be capable of moving us as much as a good novelist.

Malcolm Hay's book gives the lie to these implausible assumptions. He shows how moving and important a straightforward history can be. He does not forsake the standards of his craft to stun us with intriguing but ill-founded schemes;

he does not make the world his stage; and instead of regaling us with countless anecdotes he sticks to a single story. To establish its significance, he begins with a problem that is relevant to our time and lives. Then, when he studies it historically, we find that he illuminates it and deepens our understanding of men and events. In the process he does something to us, as a historian should: he corrects scores of important false impressions and beliefs and makes us see the past, the present, and ourselves in a new light.

Hay begins with the Nazis' systematic liquidation of about six million Jews. Drawing on official records and on eye-witness accounts, he brings to life in seven pages what the grim statistics have quite failed to get across. The style is terse, sometimes sarcastic, never sentimental. "The shooting of about two million people, whose bodies could not be left lying about, presented a difficult problem owing to the shortage of labor." But then an eye-witness offers a detailed description, a page later: ". . . Everything was spattered with blood and brains." And another witness describes in some detail how a family went to its execution. Throughout, Hay writes as a historian, not as a novelist who speculates about what people may have thought or felt at various points.

These opening pages only set the stage. Hay agrees with a Jew who survived Auschwitz that the responsibility for these six million deaths does not lie with Germany alone. He is not one of the false prophets who tell the public what it wants to hear, who place the blame where everybody puts it, and who ooze and multiply self-righteousness. He heeds the historian's noblest calling, which is to recall the past to us, reminding us of what we had gladly forgotten and informing us of what we had never permitted ourselves — or other writers had never allowed us — to realize.

For years before they were at long last liquidated by the Germans, hundreds of thousands of Jews tried to leave Ger-

many and did not succeed — not because the Germans would
not let them leave, but because other countries closed their
borders to them. Nor is this all. After the war, Americans
considered it hypocrisy, evasion, and dishonesty when many
Germans claimed that they had never realized what had happened in the concentration camps during the thirties, and that
the systematic killing of six million Jews during the war was
news to them. Yet in Germany no books about the concentration camps had been permitted, and the prisoners who were
released were warned that, if they talked in any way about
their treatment, they would be interned again without hope
of release. Outside Germany, on the other hand, many memoirs were published by ex-inmates, escaped from Germany,
and thousands of others who did not go into print talked
freely to all Westerners who cared to listen. Non-Germans
therefore had much less excuse for their purported ignorance
of concentration camp atrocities than did most Germans.

When wholesale liquidation began during the war, Hitler
withheld the news from the German public, and it was dangerous in Germany to ask and answer questions on such
matters. But the Western world did not find out about it
because Western governments who knew the facts felt that
it would be frightfully inconvenient — to cite an official of
the British Foreign Office — " if the Germans should offer to
dump a million Jews on us." And officials of the U. S. State
Department, too, " procrastinated when concrete rescue
schemes were placed before them, and even suppressed information about atrocities in order to prevent an outraged public
opinion from forcing their hands."

Between the first chapter, in which some executions are
described, and the Epilogue, from which these last quotations
come, the book attempts to show how such things could have
happened in countries that call themselves, or until recently
did call themselves, Christian countries. Hay goes back to the

Gospels and relates one of the most instructive, fascinating, and upsetting stories ever told — that of " The Pressure of Christendom on the People of Israel for 1900 Years."

The book tells a single story, based on about five hundred footnotes in the back. The scholarship is not obtrusive: it appears in the form of events and quotations that, but for the footnote references, would probably be shrugged off as incredible. The book is easily as gripping as the most exciting novel, but at no point can we say to ourselves that, after all, it is *only* a story.

The book deals with Europe and the Jews — not with the contributions which the Jews had made to European science, literature, philosophy, religion, art, and politics, but with the sufferings inflicted on the Jews; and it singles out the Christian contribution to this suffering. Indeed, the book might have been called " The Christian Roots of Anti-Semitism "; but the author feels that in the title it is better not to call a spade a spade (everywhere else he does) because he does not care to preach to the converted only, and he thinks that people stained by anti-Semitism might not read his book if they were told too clearly what it is about.

In a sense, then, the topic of this book is narrower than the title indicates. But there is also a sense in which the topic is much larger. Beyond Europe, Jews, and Christians, Hay's book is concerned with honesty.

Of course, Hay is highly selective and does not come anywhere near telling " the whole truth." Nobody could tell the whole truth about the sufferings of even a single victim of Auschwitz in just over 300 pages; much less the whole truth about nineteen centuries of persecution. Those who identify honesty with telling the whole truth define honesty out of existence and assure us that dishonesty is quite inevitable and therefore all right. Selectivity *is* inevitable, but there is a difference between selectivity and selectivity.

A historian can propose a daring thesis and, to back it up, select solely what fits, ignoring both the facts that contradict his thesis and rival interpretations of the data which he uses. This method, which involves a staggering abandonment of all standards of scholarship, is no bar to enormous popularity in the United States, where advertising, politicians, and religious spokesmen have combined to inculcate a frightening tolerance of unabashed dishonesty.

There are few things about which most men are less honest than they are about their attitude toward honesty. A charge involving lying or dishonesty is still considered heinous. But in advertising, which permeates our national life, gross misrepresentations are taken for granted and so little resented that it seldom occurs to anyone *not* to buy a product just to register a protest.

In politics, one can be elected to very high office even if it is known that one has quite deliberately mouthed untruths in one public address after another; while an avowal of agnosticism would ruin any man's political ambitions. Our statesmen, once elected, frequently deny in cold blood true reports, and nobody minds greatly if within a day it turns out that they were not honest. One forgives them readily if, although unbelievers, they profess in public to believe, while an honest failure to avow beliefs one does not have is ruinous. Yet one simply cannot understand how it is possible that the Soviet leaders doubt the honesty of our statesmen and, quite naturally, often disbelieve them on occasions when, in fact, they mean exactly what they say.

Children and fools are suffered to speak truth; priests and ministers, as men engaged in politics and advertising, are suffered to speak untruth. Like parents who deceive their children about Santa Claus, the men of God enjoy a dispensation to deceive their folds for their own good — it is not always clear whose good. Publicly, the shepherds give every appearance of believing what in conversations with philosophers they claim, of course, not to believe at all. Many, no doubt, are not too clear in their own minds about just what they do and don't believe, but that is not considered a good reason for appearing one whit less convinced in public.

For all that, honesty is possible; and Malcolm Hay's book, though selective, represents a rare triumph of honesty. He does not try to vindicate a new hypothesis, much less a system, and he does not attempt to impress us with vague, oracular predictions. He wants to bring to our attention words and deeds that both historians and the world at large have swept under the rug. He is not trying to blacken Christianity or some specific version of it. He happens to be a Roman Catholic and in his earlier works tried to show how anti-Catholic historians have significantly falsified some episodes in British history. He tried to set the record straight, in the name of honesty. The same concern dominates this book.

Hay never obtrudes anything that relates to his own person, and one might read his book without realizing that the author is a Catholic. But it is well to know that these unflattering vignettes of great saints, popes, and some of the most celebrated Christians, these terrible quotations from their writings, and the unforgettable sketches of the Crusades were not drawn by an exultant rationalist but by a true heir of the Hebrew prophets who, without the comfort of the least delight, accuses, spurred by honesty, his own fold and whatever it holds sacred — and does it in the name of standards that are publicly professed but shamefully belied in worship and in action.

To those of us who are not Catholics one of the most disturbing things about Catholicism is the lack in it of an articulate and prominent continuation of its ancient prophetic tradition. In that respect ancient and modern Judaism and Protestantism present a more inspiring record. Catholicism has to its credit great marvels of architecture, both in words and stone; but it has a less impressive record when it comes to radically honest criticism. Malcolm Hay confronts us as a heartening exception, a true heir of Amos and Hosea.

Hay never pretends to give us well-rounded portraits of the celebrated Christians whom he quotes. He introduces only what is relevant to his story; but in the process he raises — and deliberately so — questions about their saintliness and, indeed, their humanity. Others may try to answer these questions, though most readers will probably remember mainly the indictments of the men for whom they never cared in any case, forgetting how this story affects all of us. But this book does not merely raise questions about dozens of revered names. It stands as a major contribution to our understanding of humanity: although it does not venture new suggestions, it adduces facts that almost everybody has ignored; and suggestions that ignore such facts as these need not be taken seriously.

If there is one thing that keeps this book from being utterly depressing, it is the author's exhilarating honesty. If most priests and ministers resembled Malcolm Hay, I should still feel that Christianity is intellectually, and today emotionally, too, a failure; but I should not feel, as I do now, that it is such a dismal moral failure.

This book, then, deals with honesty in two ways. It is one of the most gripping indictments ever written of dishonesty. It exposes the dishonesty of great religious figures, the dishonesty of generations of historians, the dishonesty of statesmen, the dishonesty of millions in our time. It almost makes one despair of honesty and humanity by showing how rare and difficult they are. But for all that the book is not predominantly negative. It stands as a monument of honesty, humanity, and, for that reason, hope.

WALTER KAUFMANN

# EUROPE
# AND THE JEWS

*Suffer no man and no cause to escape
the undying penalty which history
has the power to inflict on wrong.*

LORD ACTON

# 1

..................................

# The Golden Mouth

MEN ARE NOT BORN with hatred in their blood. The infection
is usually acquired by contact; it may be injected deliberately
or even unconsciously, by parents, or by teachers. Adults, unless protected by the vigor of their intelligence, or by a rare
quality of goodness, seldom escape contagion. The disease
may spread throughout the land like the plague, so that a
class, a religion, a nation, will become the victim of popular
hatred without anyone knowing exactly how it all began; and
people will disagree, and even quarrel among themselves,
about the real reason for its existence; and no one foresees the
inevitable consequences.

For hatred dealeth perversely, as St. Paul might have said
were he writing to the Corinthians at the present time, and is
puffed up with pride; rejoiceth in iniquity; regardeth not the
truth. These three things, therefore, corrupt the world: disbelief, despair, and hatred—and of these, the most dangerous
of all is hatred.

In the spring of 1945, three trucks loaded with eight to nine
tons of human ashes, from the Sachsenhausen concentration
camp, were dumped into a canal in order to conceal the high
rate of Jewish executions. When a German general was asked
at Nuremberg how such things could happen, he replied:
"I am of the opinion that when for years, for decades, the
doctrine is preached that Jews are not even human, such an

outcome is inevitable." [1] This explanation, which gets to the
root of the matter, is, however, incomplete. The doctrine
which made such deeds inevitable had been preached, not
merely for years or for decades, but for many centuries; more
than once during the Middle Ages it threatened to destroy the
Jewish people. "The Jews," wrote Léon Bloy, "are the most
faithful witnesses, the most authentic remainders, of the candid
Middle Ages which hated them for the love of God, and so
often wanted to exterminate them." In those days the excuse
given for killing them was often that they were "not human,"
and that, in the modern German sense, they were "non-
adaptable"; they did not fit into the mediaeval conception of
a World State.

The German crime of genocide—the murder of a race—has
its logical roots in the mediaeval theory that the Jews were
outcasts, condemned by God to a life of perpetual servitude,
and it is not, therefore, a phenomenon completely discon-
nected from previous history. Moreover, responsibility for
the nearly achieved success of the German plan to destroy a
whole group of human beings ought not to be restricted to
Hitler and his gangsters, or to the German people. The plan
nearly succeeded because it was allowed to develop without
interference.

"It was an excellent saying of Solon's," wrote Richard
Bentley, "who when he was asked what would rid the world
of injuries, replied: 'If the bystanders would have the same
resentment with those that suffer wrong.'" The responsibility
of bystanders who remained inactive while the German plan
proceeded was recognized by one European statesman, by the
least guilty of them all, Jan Masaryk, who had helped to rescue many thousands from the German chambers of death.
Masaryk said:

> I am not an expert on the Near East and know practically
> nothing about pipe-lines. But one pipe-line I have watched

---

[1] References are to the Notes at the end of the book.

with horror all my life; it is the pipe-line through which, for centuries, Jewish blood has flowed sporadically, and with horrible, incessant streams from 1933 to 1945. I will not, I cannot, forget this unbelievable fact, and I bow my head in shame as one of those who permitted this greatest of wholesale murders to happen, instead of standing up with courage and decision against its perpetrators before it was too late.

Even after the Nuremberg Laws of 1935, every frontier remained closed against Jews fleeing from German terror, although a few were sometimes allowed in by a back door. Bystanders from thirty-two countries attended a conference at Evian, in 1938, to discuss the refugee problem; they formed a Permanent Intergovernmental Department in London to make arrangements for the admission of Jewish immigrants from Germany. The question of saving Jewish children by sending them to Palestine was not on the agenda of the Committee for assistance to refugees. "Up to August, 1939, the Committee had not succeeded in discovering new opportunities of immigration, though negotiations were proceeding with San Domingo, Northern Rhodesia, the Philippines and British Guiana." [2]

An American writer asked in 1938:

> What is to be done with these people, with the millions who are clawing like frantic beasts at the dark walls of the suffocating chambers where they are imprisoned? The Christian world has practically abandoned them, and sits by with hardly an observable twinge of conscience in the midst of this terrible catastrophe. The Western Jews, still potent and powerful, rotate in their smug self-satisfied orbits, and confine themselves to genteel charity.[3]

Until Germany obtained control of the greater part of Western Europe her policy had been directed mainly to compulsory Jewish emigration. But victories in 1940 had opened up new possibilities; and the Jews were therefore driven into ghettos in Poland and neighboring areas, where arrangements

were being made for the "final solution," which was proclaimed in 1942, and put into action throughout all Germany
and German-occupied territories. "What should be done with
them," asked Hans Frank, governor general of occupied
Poland, on December 16th, 1941. The German answer was no
longer a secret. "I must ask you, gentlemen," said the governor, "to arm yourselves against all feelings of pity. We
must annihilate the Jews wherever we find them." [4]

Hitler, in 1941, was still waiting to see what the Christian
world was going to do. Had the Allies opened their doors
wide, even then, at least a million people, including hundreds
of thousands of children, could have been saved. But no doors
anywhere were widely opened. Few hearts anywhere were
deeply moved. In Palestine, in the corner secured to Jews by
the decision of the League of Nations, the entries by land and
by sea were guarded by British soldiers and British sailors.
Great numbers, especially in Poland, would have fled from
the impending terror: "*If only they could*," wrote Jacques
Maritain in 1938, "if only other countries would open their
frontiers." The German government at that time, and even
after, was not always unwilling, and in 1939 and 1940, was
still prepared to let them go on certain conditions. "The Allies
were told that if the Jews of Germany were to receive certificates to Palestine, or visas for any other country, they could
be saved. Although for Jews to remain in Germany meant
certain death, the pieces of paper needed to save human lives
were not granted." [5]

These pieces of paper were not provided, even to save the
lives of children. In April, 1943, the Swedish government
agreed to ask the German government to permit twenty
thousand children to leave Germany for Sweden, provided
that Sweden should be relieved of responsibility for them after
the war. These children would have been saved had the British
government given them certificates for Palestine. But even
to save twenty thousand children from being slaughtered

by the Germans, "it was not possible," said a British minister in the House of Commons, "for His Majesty's Government to go beyond the terms of policy approved by Parliament." [6]

About the same time, in 1943, the Germans were considering an offer by the Red Cross and the British to evacuate seventy thousand children from Rumania to Palestine. Negotiations dragged on with the usual lack of vigor. And the Germans were persuaded by the Mufti of Jerusalem and Raschid Ali Gailani, prime minister of Iraq, who at the time were living, at German expense, in Berlin, to reject the plan. [7] So the seventy thousand children were sent to the gas chambers.

More than a million children, including uncounted thousands of newborn infants, were killed by the Germans; most of them could have been saved had the countries of the world been determined to save them. But the doors remained closed. The children were taken away from their parents and sent, crowded in the death trains, and alone, to the crematoria of Auschwitz and Treblinka, or to the mass graves of Poland and Western Russia. [8]

The German method of burying people in communal pits was a great improvement on the old system, once considered to be inhuman, of making each condemned man dig his own grave. The shooting of about two million people, whose bodies could not be left lying about, presented a difficult problem owing to the shortage of labor. Jewish women and children, weakened by torture and by long internment in concentration camps, were physically incapable of digging; and the men, when put on the list for "special treatment," were, as a rule, reduced to such a condition by hard labor on meager rations that they could hardly walk. The mass grave was an obvious necessity; but the German stroke of genius was the idea of making their victims get into the grave before they were shot, thus saving the labor of lifting two million dead bodies and throwing them in. Many hundreds of these

death pits were dug in Central Europe until the Germans
began to apply to extermination their well-known scientific efficiency. One of the largest pits, at Kerch, was examined in
1942 by officials of the Russian army:

> It was discovered that this trench, one kilometer in length,
> four meters wide, and two meters deep, was filled to over-
> flowing with bodies of women, children, old men, and boys
> and girls in their teens. Near the trench were frozen pools
> of blood. Children's caps, toys, ribbons, torn off buttons,
> gloves, milkbottles, and rubber comforters, small shoes,
> galoshes, together with torn off hands and feet, and other
> parts of human bodies, were lying nearby. Everything was
> spattered with blood and brains.[9]

What happened at Dulmo, in the Ukraine, reported by a
German witness, Hermann Graebe, is one of the grimmest
short stories that has ever been told in the bloody record of
inhuman history. Graebe was manager of a building con-
tractor's business at Dulmo. On October 5, 1942, he went as
usual to his office and there was told by his foreman of terrible
doings in the neighborhood. All the Jews in the district, about
five thousand of them, were being liquidated. About fifteen
hundred were shot every day, out in the open air, at a place
nearby where three large pits had been dug, thirty meters long
and three meters deep. Graebe and his foreman, who was in-
tensely agitated, got into a car and drove off to the place.
They saw a great mound of earth, twice the length of a cricket
pitch and more than six feet high—a good shooting range.
Near the mound were several trucks packed with people.
Guards with whips drove the people off the trucks. The
victims all had yellow patches sewn onto their garments, back
and front—the Jewish badge. From behind the earth mound
came the sound of rifle shots in quick succession. The people
from the lorries, men, women and children of all ages, were
herded together near the mound by an SS man armed with
a dog whip. They were ordered to strip. They were told to

put down their clothes in tidy order, boots and shoes, top clothing and underclothing.

Already there were great piles of this clothing, and a heap of eight hundred to a thousand pairs of boots and shoes. The people undressed. The mothers undressed the little children, "without screaming or weeping," reported Graebe, five years after. They had reached the point of human suffering where tears no longer flow and all hope has long been abandoned. "They stood around in family groups, kissed each other, said farewells, and waited." They were waiting for a signal from the SS man with a whip, who was standing by the pit. They stood there waiting for a quarter of an hour, waiting for their turn to come, while on the other side of the earth mound, now that the shots were no longer heard, the dead and dying were being packed into the pit. Graebe said:

> I heard no complaints, no appeal for mercy. I watched a family of about eight persons, a man and a woman both about fifty, with their grown up children, about twenty to twenty-four. An old woman with snow-white hair was holding a little baby in her arms, singing to it and tickling it. The baby was cooing with delight. The couple were looking at each other with tears in their eyes. The father was holding the hand of a boy about ten years old and speaking to him softly; the boy was fighting his tears . . .

Then suddenly came a shout from the SS man at the pit. They were ready to deal with the next batch. Twenty people were counted off, including the family of eight. They were marched away behind the earth mound. Graebe and his fore-man followed them. They walked round the mound and saw the tremendous grave, nearly a hundred feet long and nine feet deep. "People were closely wedged together and lying on top of each other so that only their heads were visible. Nearly all had blood running over their shoulders from their heads." They had been shot, in the usual German way, in the back of the neck. "Some of the shot people were still moving. Some were lifting their arms and turning their heads to show that they were still alive."

The pit was already nearly full; it contained about a thousand bodies. The SS man who did the shooting was sitting on the edge of the pit, smoking a cigarette, with a tommy gun on his knee. The new batch of twenty people, the family of eight and the baby carried in the arms of the woman with snow-white hair, all completely naked, were directed down steps cut in the clay wall of the pit, and clambered over the heads of the dead and the dying. They lay down among them. "Some caressed those who were still alive and spoke to them in a low voice." Then came the shots from the SS man, who had thrown away his cigarette. Graebe looked into the pit "and saw the bodies were twitching, and some heads lying already motionless on top of the dead bodies that lay under them."

The Jews who died in this manner at Dulmo were the most fortunate ones. They were spared torture in laboratory tests carried out by German doctors in order to find out how much agony the human body can endure before it dies; they were spared the choking terror of death in the gas chamber where hundreds of people at a time, squeezed together as tightly as the room could hold them, waited for the stream of poison to be turned on, while members of the German prison staff stood listening for ten or fifteen minutes until the screaming ceased, until all sounds had ceased, and they could safely open the door to the dead. And when the door was opened, the torture was not yet over. Four young Jews, whose turn would come perhaps with the next batch, dressed in a special sanitary uniform, with high rubber boots and long leather gauntlets, and provided with grappling irons, were compelled to drag out the pale dead bodies; and another group of young men was waiting to load the bodies onto a cart and drive them to the crematorium; and they knew that their turn, too, would soon come.

Responsibility for these deeds which have dishonored humanity does not rest solely with Hitler and the men who sat in the dock at Nuremberg. Another tribunal will judge the bystanders, some of them in England, who watched the murderous beginnings, and then looked away and in their hearts secretly approved. "The Jewish blood shed by the Nazis," writes J.–P. Sartre, "is upon the heads of all of us." [10]

As Maxim Gorky said more than thirty years ago, one of the greatest crimes of which men are guilty, is indifference to the fate of their fellow men. This responsibility of the indifferent was recognized by Jacques Maritain a few years before the final act of the tragedy. "There seems to be a spirit," he said in 1938, "which, without endorsing excesses committed against Jews . . . and without professing anti-Semitism, regards the Jewish drama with the indifference of the rational man who goes coldly along his way." [11] It was this spirit of indifference, this cold aloofness of the bystanders, which made it possible for Hitler to turn Europe into a Jewish cemetery. Christian responsibility has, however, been recognized by one English bystander who for many years had never failed "to have the same resentment with those that suffer wrong": "In our own day, and within our own civilization," writes Dr. James Parkes, "more than six million deliberate murders are the consequence of the teachings about Jews for which the Christian Church is ultimately responsible, and of an attitude to Judaism which is not only maintained by all the Christian Churches, but has its ultimate resting place in the teaching of the New Testament itself." [12]

Repressing the instinct to make excuses, read the following words written by a survivor of Auschwitz:

German responsibility for these crimes, however overwhelming it may be, is only a secondary responsibility, which has grafted itself, like a hideous parasite, upon a secular tradition, which is a Christian tradition. How can one forget that Christianity, chiefly from the eleventh century, has employed against Jews a policy of degradation and of pogroms, which has been extended—among certain Christian people—into contemporary history, which can be observed still alive to-day in most Catholic Poland, and of which the Hitlerian system has been only a copy, atrociously perfected.[13]

Even in countries where pogroms are unknown, it was the coldness, the indifference of the average man which made the Jewish drama in Europe possible. "I am convinced," wrote Pierre van Paassen, "that Hitler neither could nor would have done to the Jewish people what he has done . . . if we had not actively prepared the way for him by our own unfriendly attitude to the Jews, by our selfishness and by the anti-Semitic teaching in our churches and schools."[14]

The way was prepared by a hatred which has a long history. The inoculation of the poison began long ago in the nurseries of Christendom.

Millions of children heard about Jews for the first time when they were told the story of how Christ was killed by wicked men; killed by the Jews; crucified by the Jews. And the next thing they learned was that God had punished these wicked men and had cursed the whole of their nation for all time, so that they had become outcasts and were unfit to associate with Christians. When these children grew up, some of them quarreled among themselves about the meaning of the word of Christ and about the story of his life, death and resurrection; and others were Christians only in name; but most of them retained enough Christianity to continue hating the perfidious people, the Christ-killers, the deicide race.

Although the popular tradition that "the Jews" crucified Christ goes back to the beginnings of the Christian Church, no justification for it can be found in the New Testament. St. Matthew, St. Mark and St. Luke all took special care to impress upon their readers the fact that the Jewish people, their own people, were not responsible for, and were for the most part ignorant of, the events which led up to the apprehension, the trial and the condemnation of Christ. St. Matthew's account of what happened does not provide any opportunity for people to differ about his meaning. He states quite clearly in his twenty-sixth chapter that "the Jews" had nothing to do with the plot against Christ. He explains who the conspirators were, and why they had to do their work in secret. "Then were gathered together the Chief Priests and the Ancients of the people into the court of the High Priest who is called Caiphas. And they consulted together that by subtlety they might apprehend Jesus and put him to death." Secrecy was essential to the plans of the plotters because they "feared the multitude" (Matthew XXI:46). They were afraid that "the Jews" might find out what was brewing and start a riot.

The plot which ended on Calvary began to take shape for the first time at that gathering in the court of Caiphas. These men were engaged upon an enterprise which they knew would not meet with public approval. They had no mandate from the Jewish people for what they were about to do. They did not represent the two or three million Jews who at that time lived in Palestine, or another million who lived in Egypt, or the millions more who were scattered all over the Roman Empire.[15] At least three-quarters of all these people lived and died without ever hearing the name of Christ.

The conspirators did not even represent the wishes of the Jewish population in and around Jerusalem. They were afraid, explained Matthew, of arresting Jesus "on the festival day, lest there should be a tumult among the people."

They had to act promptly; they had to avoid publicity. They employed the crowd of idlers and ruffians which can be always collected for an evil purpose, to provide a democratic covering for what they proposed to do. This crowd formed a majority of the people present at the trial; these were the men who, when Pilate, the pioneer of appeasement, tried to save Christ from their fury, replied with the fateful words which Matthew recorded in the twenty-seventh chapter of his

Gospel: "And the whole people answering said: 'His blood be upon us and upon our children.'" Although "the whole people," as Matthew explained, meant only the people present "who had been persuaded by the High Priest and the Ancients" (XXVII:20), his text has been used for centuries by countless Christian preachers as a stimulant to hate and an excuse for anti-Jewish pogroms. "O cursed race!" thundered Bossuet from his pulpit, "your prayer will be answered only too effectively; that blood will pursue you even unto your remotest descendants, until the Lord, weary at last of vengeance, will be mindful, at the end of time, of your miserable remnant." [16]

St. Mark, also, records that the Jewish people had nothing to do with the plot and that if they had known about it they would have expressed violent disapproval. "The Chief Priests and the Pharisees sought how they might destroy him. For they feared him because the whole multitude was in admiration of his doctrine" (XI:18). "They sought to lay hands upon him, but they feared the people" (XII:12). They sought to lay hold on him and kill him, but they said, "not on the festival day, lest there should be a tumult among the people" (XIV:2).

St. Luke tells the same story with the same emphasis. "And the Chief Priests and the Scribes, and the rulers of the people, sought to destroy him. And they found not what to do to him; for all the people were very attentive to hear him" (XIX:47, 48). "The Chief Priests and the Scribes sought to lay hands on him . . . but they feared the people" (XX:19). "And the Chief Priests and the Scribes sought how they might put Jesus to death; but they feared the people" (XXII:2).

This Christian tradition, which made "the Jews" responsible for the death of Christ, first took shape in the Fourth Gospel. St. John deals with the historical beginnings of the Christian Church even more fully than with the ending of the era which preceded the foundation of Christianity. Unlike the other evangelists, he wrote as one outside the Jewish world, as one hostile to it. He was already disassimilated. His Gospel contains the first hint of hostility, the first suggestion of a religious Judaeophobia. He almost invariably employs the phrase "the Jews" when the context shows, and the other evangelists confirm, that he is referring to the action or to the opinions of the High Priests and the Ancients.

Whereas Matthew, Mark and Luke all wrote as if they had foreseen, and were trying to refute in advance, the accusation which would be brought against their fellow-countrymen, John, by his repeated use of the phrase "the Jews," puts into the mind of his readers the idea that they were all guilty. Although Matthew, for instance, says that when Jesus healed the man with a withered hand on the Sabbath, "the Pharisees made a consultation how they might destroy him," John, reporting a similar incident, indicts, not the Pharisees, but "the Jews": "*The Jews* therefore said to him that was healed: it is not lawful for thee to take up thy bed . . . therefore did *the Jews* persecute Jesus because he did these things on the Sabbath" (V:10, 16).

When John tells the story of the blind man, he begins by relating what the Pharisees said, but after the man received his sight his parents are reported to have "feared *the Jews*," although it is obvious from the context that they feared the Pharisees. In the same chapter, John wrote that "*the Jews* had agreed among themselves that if any man should confess him to be the Christ, he should be put out of the synagogue." This agreement had been reached, not by the Jews, but by the Chief Priests and the Ancients. In the tenth chapter which deals with the action and behavior of this political group, we read that

a dissension rose again among *the Jews* . . . and many of them said: He hath a devil and is mad . . . In Solomon's Porch *the Jews* therefore came to him and said to him . . . If thou be the Christ tell us plainly . . . *The Jews* then took

up stones to stone him . . . *The Jews* answered him—For a
good work we stone thee not, but for blasphemy.

John was more careful in his choice of words when he
described the details of the crucifixion. He laid special emphasis on the fact that Christ was crucified, not by the Jews,
but by Roman soldiers. "The soldiers therefore, when they
had crucified him took his garments . . . and also his coat
. . . they said to one another: Let us not cut it, but let us
cast lots for it . . . and the soldiers indeed did these things"
(XIX: 23, 24). Nevertheless, in John's story of the apprehension, trial and death of Christ, responsibility is laid, as much
as inference can lay it, on the whole Jewish people; a prominence is given to the action of "the Jews" which the events as
recorded by the other evangelists do not justify.[17]

Père Lagrange suggested that John made use of the phrase
"the Jews," as a literary device to save constant repetition of
the words "High Priests and Pharisees." [18] It is a pity that this
interpretation of John's meaning did not occur to any of
the early Fathers. When Origen wrote at the beginning of
the fourth century that "the Jews . . . nailed Christ to the
cross," [19] he also may have meant something different from
what he said—but for many centuries his words were taken as
literally true by all Christendom. And consequently, as an
English historian in our own time has admitted, "The crime of
a handful of priests and elders in Jerusalem was visited by the
Christian Churches upon the whole Jewish race." [20]

This tradition has been handed on without much respect
for the actual facts as related in the Gospels. Thus, in the
thirteenth century, a pious monk, Jacques de Vitry, went to
the Holy Land, visited the site of Calvary and sat in meditation, as he recorded in his Chronicle, "on the very spot where
*the Jews* divided the garments of Christ, and for his tunic cast
lots." [21] When, however, mediaeval writers had to report anything which they feared might arouse Christian sympathy for
the Children of Israel they called them, in such a context, not

"Jews" but "Hebrews." Jacques de Vitry, for instance, described how Christ was welcomed on his entry into Jerusalem by "the Hebrews"; this terminology is still used in the Church's liturgy on Palm Sunday: *Plebs Hebraea cum palmis obviam venit.* The mediaeval mystics, in whose writings religious sentiment was exhibited in its most popular form, show how hatred had become the constant companion of devotion. Juliana of Norwich, an English anchoress whose *Sixteen Revelations of Divine Love* (1373) has been described by Dean Inge as "one of the most precious gems of mediaeval sacred literature," excluded from her programme of love only one section of humanity:

> For though the Revelation was made of goodness in which was made little mention of evil, yet I was not drawn thereby from any point of Faith that Holy Church teacheth me to believe. . . . I saw not so properly specified the Jews that did Him to death. Notwithstanding I knew in my Faith that they were accursed and condemned without end, saving those that were converted by grace.[22]

These words read as if they had been added by Juliana at the suggestion of her confessor, or some religious censor who had been shocked by finding that the *Revelations of Divine Love* did not refer to the part which, according to popular mediaeval belief, had been played by Jews personally in the crucifixion of Christ.

This omission was atoned for by Margery Kempe, a slightly later visionary who, in her description of the Passion, which she imagined she had actually witnessed, followed the common conviction that Jews had nailed Christ to the cross. "Sche beheld how the cruel Jewys leydyn his precyows body to the Crosse and sithyn tokyn a long nayle . . . and wyth gret vilnes and cruelnes thei dreuyn it thorw hys hande."[23] Pictures of Jews hammering in the nails helped to encourage both hatred and piety. A writer at the beginning of the six-

teenth century mentions "a Church where there was placed a
Jew, of wood, before the Saviour, grasping a hammer." [24]

Pious ingenuity reached a new peak in Spain where, in the
first quarter of the eighteenth century, two hundred years
after all the Jews had been expelled, hatred continued to
flourish alongside Christian faith and Christian superstition.
A collection of the fables popular in the Middle Ages, printed
in 1728, entitled *Centinela Contra Judios*, revived the belief
that certain Jews, who were "born with worms in their
mouth . . . were descended from a Jewess who ordered the
locksmith who made the nails to crucify Christ to make the
points blunt so that the pain of crucifixion would be greater."
In the seventeenth century a zealous Catholic who was trying
to convert Spinoza asked him to remember "the terrible and
unspeakably severe punishments by which the Jews were reduced to the last stages of misery and calamity because they
were the authors of Christ's crucifixion."

In order to fortify these traditions, Christian commentators
tended increasingly to ignore the obvious meaning of the
Gospel texts and sometimes substituted the phrase "the Jews"
where John himself had written "the High Priests and the
Pharisees." Dom Prosper Guéranger, Abbot of Solesmes,
seems to have had access to some hitherto unknown source of
information about the story of Martha, Mary Magdalene and
Lazarus, originally told in John's Gospel. He wrote that
"Mary Magdalene knew that the Jews were plotting the death
of Jesus—the Holy Ghost inspired her." [25] This account of
what happened does not agree with the text of John's Gospel
which states that the death of Christ has been plotted, not by
the Jews, but by the "High Priests and the Pharisees."
(John XI: 47.)

In Russia popular Christianity produced a pattern of hate
similar to that of Western Europe. When the Czarina Elizabeth (1741–1761) was asked to admit Jews into the country
for economic reasons, she replied: "I do not wish to obtain

any benefits from the enemies of Christ." More than a hundred years later, in 1890, when Alexander III was shown the draft of an official report recommending some relaxation of the oppression from which the Jews of his empire were suffering, he noted in the margin: "But we must not forget that the Jews crucified Christ." The pious Russians were not allowed to forget: "Representatives of the court clergy publicly preached that a Christian ought not to cultivate friendly relations with a Jew, since it was the command of the Gospel 'to hate the murderers of the Saviour.' " [26]

At the beginning of the present century, Charles Maurras, founder and leader of L'Action Française, thought that the Gospels were not sufficiently anti-Semitic. He preferred to follow the mediaeval tradition. While still professing to be a Catholic, he was prepared to reject the testimony of all the evangelists. "I would not abandon," he wrote, "the learned procession of Councils, Popes and all the modern elite of great men, to put my trust in the gospels of four obscure Jews." [27]

From the earliest times to the present day, readers of the Fourth Gospel, with rare exceptions, have taken the phrase "the Jews" in its literal sense without any shading of meaning. Consequently the whole literature of Christendom has contributed throughout the centuries to consolidate a tradition not sanctioned by the text of the Synoptic Gospels—one that has brought immeasurable suffering upon countless numbers of innocent human beings: the tradition that "the Jewish nation condemned Christ to be crucified." [28] Joseph Klausner writes:

> The Jews, *as a nation*, were far less guilty of the death of Jesus than the Greeks, as a nation, were guilty of the death of Socrates; but who now would think of avenging the blood of Socrates the Greek upon his countrymen, the present Greek race? Yet these nineteen hundred years past, the world has gone on avenging the blood of Jesus the Jew upon his countrymen, the Jews, who have already paid the penalty, and still go on paying the penalty, in rivers and torrents of blood. [29]

The extent of Jewish responsibility for the apprehension, trial and death of Christ was defined by the highest authority of the Christian Church, St. Peter, whose judgment corrects the bias shown, a generation later, in the Fourth Gospel. The first papal pronouncement on this question was addressed by St. Peter to "Ye men of Israel," a gathering which had assembled in "the Porch which is called Solomon's"; it was addressed to those men only, in that place, and at that time. St. Peter did not acquit these men of guilt; he knew that they had taken some active part in the plot and at the trial; they were, he told them, accessories to the crime. But the final words he used have often been ignored: "And now, brethren, I know you did it through ignorance; as did also your rulers."

Ignorance, defined by Maimonides as "the want of knowledge respecting things the knowledge of which can be obtained," [30] is acceptable as an excuse only when it is not culpable. Abelard, in the twelfth century, may have extended too widely the proposition that where there is ignorance there can be no sin, when he said that the rulers of Israel acted "out of zeal for their law," and should therefore be absolved from all guilt. Christian tradition, especially in the early centuries, practically ignored St. Peter's statement that the "rulers" acted through ignorance. St. John Chrysostom, indeed, flatly contradicted St. Peter when he wrote that "the Jews . . . erred not ignorantly but with full knowledge." [31] Whatever degree of guilt the "rulers" may have incurred, there is surely no justification for excluding them from the benefit of the petition and the judgment of Christ—"Father, forgive them for they know not what they do" (Luke XXIII:34). In the Gospel text these words refer quite clearly to the Roman soldiers, and not to the Jews.

The belief current in the Middle Ages which Abelard attacked and St. Bernard defended was that "the Jews" were all guilty; that they had acted with deliberate malice; that their guilt was shared by the whole Jewish people, for all time, and that they, and their children's children to the last generation, were condemned to live in slavery as the servants of Christian princes. That was not the doctrine of St. Peter. If Christians had always remembered his words, the history of the Jews in their long exile would perhaps have been very different, and the civilization of the West might not have witnessed the degradation of humanity which was achieved by the Germans in their death camps and gas chambers.

In spite of St. Peter's judgment the popular Christian doctrine has always been that anyone, whether pagan or Christian, who has at any time persecuted, tortured or massacred Jews has acted as an instrument of Divine wrath. A chronicler, writing in the early years of the thirteenth century, admired the patience of God, who "after the Jews had crucified Our Lord, waited for forty-eight years before chastising them." [32] According to Fleury, who wrote, in the first quarter of the eighteenth century, an enormous and still useful ecclesiastical history, God began to take reprisals against the Jews in the year 38 of the Christian era. In that year, anti-Jewish riots broke out in Alexandria. The rioters were secretly encouraged by Flaccus, the Roman commissioner in Egypt, who took no effective measures to prevent the mob from burning down synagogues, breaking into Jewish shops, and scattering the merchandise into the streets of the city. Flaccus showed his "neutrality" by attempting to disarm, not the rioters, but their victims. "He had searches made in the houses of the Jews on the pretext of disarming the nation, and several women were taken away and tormented when they refused to eat swine's flesh." A great number of Jews were murdered, and their bodies dragged through the streets. "In this manner," wrote Fleury in 1732, "divine vengeance began to be manifested against the Jews." [33]

The sacking of Jerusalem and the destruction of the Temple, in the year 70, when more than a million people were massacred with a brutality to which the world has once again become accustomed, were regarded by many pious Christians as part of God's plan of revenge. "The Jews," wrote Sulpicius Severus, "were thus punished and exiled throughout the whole world, for no other account than for the impious hands they laid upon Christ." [34] This interpretation of the event has been repeated for centuries. Bossuet was one of the worst offenders against common sense and historical accuracy. In many of his sermons and in his *Discours sur l'Histoire universelle,* he publicized the sanguinary details of what he called "Divine vengeance" on the accursed race. [35] And in history books written for the instruction of youth, in 1947, the same thesis of hate is repeated:

> The punishment of the deicide Jews (God-killers) was not long delayed. Thirty-six years after the Savior's death, the Roman Emperor Titus captured Jerusalem and utterly destroyed the Jewish Temple. The Jews, dispersed throughout the world, have never been able to become once more a nation. They have wandered about, regarded as an accursed race, as an object of contempt to other peoples. [36]

There are therefore still some people who believe that the Jews were cursed out of Palestine because they had behaved in a manner displeasing to God. If nations were liable to be dispossessed for such a reason, very few of them would enjoy security of tenure. "The Curse," as J.–P. Sartre has recently pointed out, was "geographical."

Whether or not the events of the year 70 were due to the vengeance of God, what really happened has often been misrepresented. "The Jews" were not driven out of Palestine after the sack of Jerusalem. Yet mediaeval Christendom believed, and many Christian writers today continue to repeat, that they were dispersed at that time. "Titus destroyed the Temple of Herod," writes H. V. Morton, "and scattered the race to the four corners of the world." [37] Having paid this tribute to the sentimental tradition, he refers, a few pages further on, to the revolt of the Jews in Judaea, more than a generation later, which the Romans suppressed with their usual ruthless efficiency: "Julius Severus began a merciless war in which . . . 580,000 persons were slain." [38] Assuming that the Romans slaughtered one-quarter of the population, which is a very generous estimate, about two million Jews must have been living in Palestine fifty years after the sack of the Temple. Titus, therefore, did not "scatter the race to the four corners of the world."

After the destruction of the Temple, the Jewish people were still allowed full rights of domicile in Palestine, with the exception of Jerusalem, and, during the first two or three centuries of the Christian era they lived almost exclusively by working on the land.[39] They had, however, been deprived of their national status: they lost all prospect of recovering it after the political victory of Christianity. Under Christian-Roman rule they had hardly any rights. They were prohibited from serving in the army, and thus, as St. Jerome noted, "they lost their manly bearing." In the fourth and fifth centuries they were directed by the laws of the Christian-Roman Empire into the most degrading occupations and reduced practically to slavery, in order to destroy among them any hope of regaining their social and political freedom.

As a result of such legislation and of pulpit propaganda, the word "Jew," in the second half of the fifth century, was already in common use as an expression of contempt.[40] In the collection of letters and decrees known as the *Codex Theodosianus*, the word was officially given for the first time the opprobrious significance it retained throughout Christendom for more than a thousand years: "Even their name is horrible and hideous." [41] "The very name of Jew," said an English writer at the end of the eighteenth century, "has long been associated in the mind with the idea of everything base, false, despicable, and unprincipled." [42] "All over the world," wrote Bishop Newton in 1765, "the Jews are in all respects treated as if they were of a different species." [43]

The men who planned this humiliation and degradation of the Jewish people were convinced that they were carrying out the will of God. Ecclesiastical historians attributed the sufferings of the Jews, for which the Christians themselves were often responsible, to a divine plan of vengeance. Eusebius, in the first paragraph of his *Church History*, declared that his intention was "to recount the misfortunes which immediately came upon the whole Jewish nation in consequence of their plots against our Savior." [44] Sozomen, a generation later, began his *History* by expressing astonishment at the obstinate refusal of the Jews to accept Christianity. "My mind has often been exercised in inquiring how it is that other men are very ready to believe in God the Word, while the Jews are so incredulous." [45]

They were, indeed, difficult to convince. They refused to be impressed by a whole series of astonishing events which the Christians, apparently, expected everyone to accept as evidence of the truth of Christian doctrine. An example of this Jewish obstinacy is given by the ecclesiastical historian, Socrates, who recorded that when the Jews were attempting to rebuild the Temple at Jerusalem, in the reign of the Emperor Julian, "luminous impressions of a cross appeared imprinted on their garments, which at daybreak they in vain attempted to rub or wash out." [46] People who refused to be convinced by the story of such a remarkable manifestation were clearly unfit to live in a Christian society. Some of the faithful thought that such obstinacy should be punished by death, and that to kill Jews was pleasing to God.

More in conformity with modern usage was the excuse, when killings on a large scale had taken place, that the Jews were the aggressors and that the Christians had massacred them in self-defense. Where the Jews were locally strong enough, they may sometimes have been the first to start a riot. But the story of their expulsion from Alexandria, by St. Cyril, would probably be less edifying, from a Christian point of view, if some Jewish account of the incident had survived. Many of the charges brought against them in the early centuries are based on reports written by their enemies, and it is not easy now to draw the line between history and propaganda. Socrates accused the Jews of tying a Christian boy to a cross, at a place called Inmestar, and then scourging him to death. "The Jewish inhabitants of the place," he explained, "paid the penalty of the wickedness they had committed in their pious sport." [47] The story may have been true, but it may have been invented by some one, and repeated by Socrates, to account for a massacre.

To justify the persecution of Jews, two excuses, therefore, were available to Christians: either the Christians were acting in self-defense, or they were carrying out the will of God. The teaching of the early Fathers made the second excuse plausible. There was no direct incitement to violence. Athanasius did not tell the people to go out and beat up Jews. But he told them that "the Jews were no longer the people of God, but rulers of Sodom and Gomorrah"; [48] and he asked the ominous question: "What is left unfulfilled, that they should now be allowed to disbelieve with impunity?" [49]

When St. Ambrose told his congregations that the Jewish synagogue was "a house of impiety, a receptacle of folly, which God himself has condemned," no one was surprised when the people went off and set fire to one. St. Ambrose accepted responsibility for the outrage. "I declare that I set fire to the synagogue, or at least that I ordered those who did it, that there might not be a place where Christ was denied. If it be objected to me that I did not set the synagogue on fire here, I answer it began to be burnt by the judgment of God." [50] He told the Emperor that people who burnt a synagogue ought not to be punished, such action being a just reprisal because Jews, in the reign of the Emperor Julian, had burnt down Christian churches. In any case, he added, since the synagogues contained nothing of any value, "what could the

Jews lose by the fire?" When they complained to the
Emperor, he was indignant at their impertinence. They had
no place in a court of law, he declared, because nothing they
said could ever be believed. "Into what calumnies will they
not break out, who, by false witness, calumniated even Christ!"

The Emperor, however, who did not approve of fire-raising
propaganda, endeavored to protect the synagogues from the
fury of the mob. He received a letter, from an unexpected
quarter, asking him to revoke the orders he had given for
punishing the offenders, a letter dispatched from the top of a
pillar by St. Simeon Stylites. This ascetic, who achieved distinction by living for thirty-six years on top of a pillar fifty
feet high, had given up, as G. F. Abbott remarked, "all worldly
luxuries except Jew-hatred." [51] He is not the only saint who
was unable to renounce the consolations of anti-Semitism.

In the fourth century the natural goodness of men, and even
saintliness, did not always operate for the benefit of Jews.
St. Gregory of Nyssa, with the eloquence for which he was
famous, composed against them a comprehensive indictment:

> Slayers of the Lord, murderers of the prophets, adversaries
> of God, haters of God, men who show contempt for the law,
> foes of grace, enemies of their father's faith, advocates of the
> devil, brood of vipers, slanderers, scoffers, men whose minds
> are in darkness, leaven of the Pharisees, assembly of demons,
> sinners, wicked men, stoners, and haters of righteousness.[52]

Such exaggeration may have been an offense against charity,
but it is not so harmful to the soul as the modern hypocrisy
which pretends that the early Christian Fathers were invariably
models of proper Christian behavior. "Our duty," wrote
Basnage in the seventeenth century, "is to excuse the Fathers
in their Extravagance, instead of justifying them, lest such
forcible Examples should authorize Modern Divines, and confirm the Hatred and Revenge of writers." [53]

St. John Chrysostom, the Golden-Mouthed, one of the
greatest of the Church Fathers, spent his life, in and out of

the pulpit, trying to reform the world. Christian writers, of varying shades of belief, have agreed in admiring his fervent love for all mankind, in spite of the fact that he was undoubtedly a socialist. "Chrysostom," said a Protestant divine, "was one of the most eloquent of the preachers who, ever since apostolic times, have brought to men the Divine tidings of truth and love." [54] "A bright cheerful gentle soul," wrote Cardinal Newman, "a sensitive heart, a temperament open to emotion and impulse; and all this elevated, refined, transformed by the touch of heaven,—such was St. John Chrysostom." [55]

Yet in this kindly gentle soul of the preacher who brought to men the tidings of truth and love, was hidden a hard core of hatred. "It must be admitted," wrote an honest French hagiographer, "that, in his homilies against the Jews, he allowed himself to be unduly carried away by an occasional access of passion." [56]

A great deal more than this must be admitted.

The violence of the language used by St. John Chrysostom in his homilies against the Jews has never been exceeded by any preacher whose sermons have been recorded. Allowances must, no doubt, be made for the custom of the times, for passionate zeal, and for the fear that some tender shoots of Christian faith might be chilled by too much contact with Jews. But no amount of allowance can alter the fact that these homilies filled the minds of Christian congregations with a hatred which was transmitted to their children, and to their children's children, for many generations. These homilies, moreover, were used for centuries, in schools and in seminaries where priests were taught to preach, with St. John Chrysostom as their model—where priests were taught to hate, with St. John Chrysostom as their model.

There was no "touch of heaven" in the language used by St. John Chrysostom when he was preaching about Jewish synagogues. "The synagogue," he said, "is worse than a brothel . . . it is the den of scoundrels and the repair of wild

beasts . . . the temple of demons devoted to idolatrous cults
. . . the refuge of brigands and debauchees, and the cavern
of devils."

The synagogue, he told his congregations in another sermon,
was "a criminal assembly of Jews . . . a place of meeting for
the assassins of Christ . . . a house worse than a drinking
shop . . . a den of thieves; a house of ill fame, a dwelling of
iniquity, the refuge of devils, a gulf and abyss of perdition."
And he concluded, exhausted at length by his eloquence:
"Whatever name even more horrible could be found, will
never be worse than the synagogue deserves."

These sermons have not been forgotten; nor has contempt
for Judaism diminished among the Christian congregations
since they were first preached more than fifteen hundred years
ago: "The Synagogue is nigh to a curse. Obstinate in her
error, she refuses to see or to hear; she has deliberately per-
verted her judgment: she has extinguished within herself the
light of the Holy Spirit; she will go deeper and deeper into evil,
and at length fall into the abyss." [57] St. John Chrysostom was
right in suggesting that future generations would think of even
more horrible insults. "Sympathy for the Jews," wrote Léon
Bloy, "is a sign of turpitude. . . . It is impossible to earn the
esteem of a dog if one does not feel an instinctive disgust for
the Synagogue."

In reply to some Christians who had maintained that Jewish
synagogues might be entitled to respect because in them were
kept the writings of Moses and the prophets, St. John Chrysostom answered: Not at all! This was a reason for hating them
more, because they use these books, but willfully misunderstand their meaning. "As for me, I hate the synagogue. . . .
I hate the Jews for the same reason."

It is not difficult to imagine the effect such sermons must
have had upon congregations of excitable Orientals. Not only
every synagogue, Chrysostom told them, but every Jew, was a
temple of the devil. "I would say the same things about their

souls." And he said a great deal more. It was unfit, he proclaimed, for Christians to associate with a people who had fallen into a condition lower than the vilest animals. "Debauchery and drunkenness had brought them to the level of the lusty goat and the pig. They know only one thing, to satisfy their stomachs, to get drunk, to kill and beat each other up like stage villains and coachmen."

The clear implication in all this rhetoric is, not that some Jews were living on the level of goats and pigs, but that *all* Jews lived thus because they were Jews. A variation of this theory has always been, and still is, one of the predominant principles of Judaeophobia, and, with a variety of applications, is still accepted, often subconsciously, by many people at the present time.

A typical example of this common prejudice, which is most pernicious when it is unconscious, occurs in a life of St. John Chrysostom, written in 1872 by an English clergyman, W. R. W. Stephens. "Allowing for some exaggeration in the preacher," he said, "the invectives of St. Chrysostom must be permitted to prove that the Jewish residents in Antioch were of a low and vicious order." [58] No doubt most of them were; and so were most of the Christians. But in the mind of St. John Chrysostom, and in the mind of the Rev. Mr. Stephens, the Jews of Antioch lived like goats and pigs because they were Jews; as for the Christians, that was a very different story.

"The mass of the so-called Christian population," explained the Rev. Mr. Stephens, "was largely infected by the dominant vices—inordinate luxury, sensuality, selfish avarice, and display." It would be startling to read in an English newspaper that "the *so-called* Jewish population of London, or Paris, largely infected by the dominant vices of luxury, sensuality and avarice, were dealing extensively in the black market." A Jew never becomes "so-called" when he does anything wrong. If he behaves well, people say that he behaves like a Christian. In the twelfth century, when some Christians behaved badly, St. Bernard of Clairvaux did not describe them as "so-called," he simply said that they behaved like Jews. The wickedness of Jews consists, not in their conduct, but in their Jewishness. This was the doctrine of St. John Chrysostom.

The Jews, he told his congregations, are men possessed by an evil spirit, they are habitual murderers and destroyers. "We should not even salute them, or have the slightest converse with them." He employed in the pulpit every word of abuse that he could think of. He called them "lustful, rapacious, greedy, perfidious robbers." He was the first Christian preacher to apply the word "deicide" to the Jewish nation. The fervor of his hate has perhaps never been surpassed, even in modern times. "The Jews have assassinated the Son of God! How dare you take part in their festivals? . . . you dare to associate with this nation of assassins and hangmen! . . . O Jewish people! A man crucified by your hands has been stronger than you and has destroyed you and scattered you . . ."

All Jews were guilty, they had been punished by God, and the punishment would endure for all time. They were condemned by God, said Chrysostom, to a real hell on earth, condemned to a misery which would endure as long as the world lasted. After describing the misfortunes from which they had suffered under Roman tyranny, planned by a vindictive God, he pointed triumphantly to their present condition. "See how Judaea is a desert, and how all is desolation and ruin in that nation!" He foretold, moreover, that the present calamities would have no end. "Your situation, O Jewish people, becomes more and more disastrous, and one cannot see showing on your foreheads the slightest ray of hope." [59]

Such logic would justify the German race murderers. St. John Chrysostom could have preached a powerful sermon beside the mass grave at Dubno. He could have explained that a revengeful God had chastised the little Jewish boy who had tried to keep back his tears so that the Germans would not see that he was afraid; and the little baby, and the Jewish family, who all went down into the pit. He did, indeed, provide a suitable text for such a sermon in his "Sixth Homily Against the Jews":

> But it was men, says the Jew, who brought these misfortunes upon us, not God. On the contrary it was in fact God who brought them about. If you attribute them to men, reflect again that, even supposing men had dared, they would not have had the power to accomplish them, unless it had been God's will.

Another passage from the same sermon would have been useful to the defense at Nuremberg: "So *whenever* the Jew tells you: It was men who made war on us, it was men who plotted against us, say to him: Men would certainly not have made war unless God had permitted them."

Chrysostom, said Duchesne, "was one of those unyielding Saints in whose eyes principles are made to be put into practice." [60] Immediately after his arrival at Constantinople in 398, he brought his influence to bear on the Emperor, who had granted certain privileges to the Jews, so that all the laws in their favor were suspended. A few years later, when he was driven out of the city, legislation favorable to the Jews was restored.[61] He hated them; and he did his best to make the whole world hate them too. But even this was not enough. You are, he told them, a people whom God has deprived of their inheritance. "Why then did he rob you? Is it not obvious that it was because he hated you, and rejected you once for all?" [62]

When the usual allowances have been made for the manners of the time, pious zeal, oriental imagery, and for any context, setting, or background which might be urged in mitigation, these are words difficult to justify. This condemnation of the people of Israel, in the name of God, was not forgotten. It helped to strengthen the tradition of hate handed on through the Dark Ages and welcomed by mediaeval Christendom, a tradition which has disfigured the whole history of Western Europe.

For many centuries the Jews listened to the echo of those three words of St. John Chrysostom, the Golden-Mouthed: "God hates you."

*It is either impossible, or a task of no
mean difficulty, to alter by words what
has been of old taken into men's very
dispositions.*

GUILLAUME DE VAIR (1556–1621)

# 2

............................................

# Thy Brother's Blood

DURING THE DARK AGES, from the sixth to the tenth century,
the Jews in Western Europe lived in comparative peace, for
they were not yet subject to unintermittent and organized
oppression, although the doctrine which denied them the same
rights as other human beings was already generally accepted
throughout Christendom. The continued existence of these
people was supposed to be due to the inexplicable mercy of
God who permitted them to survive because of their value as
witnesses to the Christian interpretation of the messianic
prophecies. Special stress was laid on the text of St. Paul's
Epistle to the Galatians: "Cast out the bondwoman and her
son; for the son of the bondwoman shall not be heir with the
son of the freewoman." In order, therefore, that the Scripture
should be fulfilled, the Jews had to live as outcasts.

This tradition of anti-Jewish hostility, handed on from the
early Church Fathers to the New Europe after the decline of
Roman power, could not have survived without ecclesiastical
encouragement. Charlemagne appreciated from a practical
point of view the economic value of the industrious Jews, and
his son Louis looked after their interests for the same reason.
He appointed a special official (*Magister Judaeorum*) to protect them from the intolerance of some of the clergy. But
St. Agobard, Archbishop of Lyons, wrote several letters to

Louis on the subject of Jewish "insolence" (*De Insolentia Judaeorum*, A.D. 826–828), protesting against this appointment. Whenever ecclesiastics, at any period of history, wrote about the "insolence" of Jews, it is safe to assume that the civil powers were treating them as human beings. Although the archbishop told the emperor in one of these letters that in the eyes of God the Jews ranked lower than the inhabitants of Sodom and Gomorrah, a modern French writer maintains that, far from attacking the Jews, he was merely trying to defend the Christians whom he advised to treat them "with prudence and humanity." [1] St. Agobard used the words "prudence and humanity" with a special ecclesiastical meaning, as he explained in a fierce letter to the Bishop of Narbonne, reprimanding him for associating with Jews. He borrowed most of his invective from Deuteronomy:

> Knowing therefore, Venerable Father, that "as many as are of the works of the law are under a curse," and consigned, as to a garment, to a curse which entered into their very bowels, like water, and into their bones like oil: cursed also in the cities, and cursed in the fields: cursed in their going in, and cursed in their going out: cursed the fruit of their wombs and of their lands and of their flocks; cursed their cellars, their granaries, their warehouses, their food, and the very remnants of their food: and that none of them may escape that curse, so monstrous and so horrible, except through Him who for us is a curse. [2]

"Let us deplore," said Basnage, who quoted this great malediction, "the weakness of the greatest of men. What Choler possesses the souls of Holy Bishops!" What had annoyed the holy bishop was the fact, which his letter reveals, that the Jews were living prosperously, and not like outcasts, both in the cities and in the countryside, where they cultivated the soil, and owned flocks, granaries, cellars for the wine they made, and warehouses. They were not occupied in lending money or in selling old clothes; these were trades to which they were driven many centuries later.

In an endeavor to discover some traces of toleration in the Middle Ages, a French historian has recently pointed out that, if the Jews had not been tolerated, not one of them would have survived. The civil and ecclesiastical powers, he says, could easily have exterminated these unbelievers, who were few in number and unable to defend themselves. "Their complete extermination would have been facilitated by the fact that everywhere all classes would have taken part in the enterprise with enthusiasm." [3]

Of no period in the Middle Ages would it be true to say that everywhere all classes were eager to exterminate the Jews. The people who did in fact express such a desire, or who did make the attempt, were not people born with an instinctive hatred in their blood; nor were the Jewish people, anywhere, such contemptible and loathsome creatures that no one could help hating them. Hatred was the product of a clerical propaganda which was not everywhere equally effective. In Spain, no social class except the clergy showed any inclination to attack the Jews, who, owing to their intelligence and their industry, were contributing to the prosperity of the country. The Spaniards in those days were naturally a tolerant people and not easy to infect with race-hatred.

But Jewish prosperity anywhere was regarded by the Papacy as contrary to Holy Writ and a menace to Christendom. Jewish culture and learning threatened to cross the Pyrenees. Pope Gregory VII (Hildebrand) did his best to avert the danger. He wrote to Alphonso VI of Castille, in 1081:

> We admonish your Highness that you must cease to suffer the Jews to rule over Christians and exercise authority over them. For to allow Christians to be subordinate to Jews, and to be subject to their judgment, is the same as to oppress God's Church and to exalt the synagogue of Satan. To wish to please the enemies of Christ means to treat Christ himself with contumely. [4]

Hildebrand's admonition produced very little effect. Although the efforts of the clergy to stir up hatred led to occasional pogroms, the Jews, during the greater part of the Middle Ages, lived more happily in Spain than anywhere else in Europe. This state of affairs was usually, but not invariably, watched by the Papacy with disapproval. "I perceived the tremendous greatness of those far off times," wrote Léon Bloy, "when the Papacy sheltered the Jews from the fury of the whole world." What that inconsistent and often ill-informed enemy of injustice perceived, was, however, only one part of the story. The Papacy itself was often responsible for this "fury of the whole world" from which the Jews fled for shelter. When the people of those great far-off times, inflamed by pulpit preaching and papal letters, went beyond the prescribed limits of oppression and began to kill Jews, then, and only then, did the Papacy endeavor to provide the victims with some sort of protection from the storm. "General prohibitions of maltreatment availed little, when prelate and priest were busy inflaming popular aversion, and Popes were found to threaten any prince hardy enough to interfere and protect the unfortunate race." [5]

The machinery of propaganda was entirely in the hands of the Church officials—preaching, chronicles, mystery plays, and even ecclesiastical ceremonies were the principal agencies available for the dissemination of hate. Preachers dwelt with a morbid and sometimes sadistic realism upon the physical sufferings of Christ, for which they blamed all Jews of the time and all their descendants. For many centuries the Bishops of Béziers preached a series of sermons during Holy Week, urging their congregations to take vengeance on the Jews who lived in the district; stoning them became a regular part of the Holy Week ceremonial. At Toulouse, it was the annual custom at Easter time to drag a Jew into the Church of St. Stephen and slap him on the face before the altar. This ceremony was sometimes carried out with excessive vigor. On one

occasion, recounts a monkish chronicler (without, however,
expressing any disapproval), a distinguished nobleman who
was taking the part of chief celebrant "knocked out the eyes
and the brains of the perfidious one, who fell dead on the
spot . . . his brethren from the synagogue took the body out
of the Church and buried it." [6]

The most trivial pretext was often enough to start a massacre. In 1021, a slight earthquake, accompanied by a high
wind, disturbed at Rome the celebration of Easter. The Jews
were accused of having produced both the earthquake and the
storm by means of their magical practices. After some of them
had been put to the sword, "the fury of the wind was ap-
peased." [7] Ten years earlier, when the Church of the Holy
Sepulchre in Jerusalem was destroyed by the Khalif, no one
thought it unreasonable to blame Jews at Orléans, and a large
number of them were slaughtered. A few managed to escape
with their lives, thankfully records the chronicler, "because
it is necessary that some should remain alive to provide a constant proof of their crime, to bear witness to the blood of
Christ." [8]

The Dark Ages of Jewish history in Western Europe date
from the First Crusade (1096), which began and ended with a
massacre. "The men who took the cross," wrote Acton, "after
receiving communion, heartily devoted the day to the extermination of the Jews." They killed about ten thousand of
them. When Godfrey of Bouillon, in the summer of 1099,
succeeded after a heroic assault in capturing Jerusalem, he
spent the first week slaughtering the inhabitants. The Jews
were shut up in their synagogue, which was then set on fire.
"If you want to know what has been done with the enemy
found in Jerusalem," wrote Godfrey to the Pope, "learn that
in the Porch and in the Temple of Solomon, our people had
the vile blood of the Saracens up to the knees of their horses."
And then, said Michelet, sweeping aside the glamor and the
piety, "and then, when they thought the Saviour had been

sufficiently revenged, that is to say, when there was hardly anyone left alive in the town, they went with tears to worship at the Holy Sepulchre."

The preaching of the First Crusade seems, however, to have had very little effect in England, where Jews continued to live on good terms with their neighbors, perhaps owing to the influence of Anselm, Archbishop of Canterbury, a saint whose love for humanity did not exclude the children of Israel.

There is one story told at that time, of a kind rare in the annals of the Middle Ages, about the friendship of an English abbot with a Jewish rabbi. Gilbert Crispin, Abbot of Westminster, was educated at the monastery of Bec, in Normandy, where St. Anselm was one of his teachers. He entered the novitiate in 1077, and about twelve years later was called by Lanfranc to Westminster. He died in 1121 and was buried in the Abbey, where a stone slab with his effigy is still preserved.[9] Some details of his meetings with a Jewish rabbi are given in an account he sent to Anselm of a public religious discussion which took place between them. Gilbert had made the acquaintance, he said, of "a certain Jew," a man of culture and learning, who often visited him at the Abbey to discuss business, and most of the time talked about religion. They decided to hold a conference to which friends on both sides were invited. The Abbot wrote a report of the discussion that took place, and sent it to Anselm along with a covering letter:

> I sent you a little work to be submitted to your fatherly prudence. I wrote it recently, putting to paper what a Jew said when formerly disputing with me against our faith in defence of his own law, and what I replied in favour of the faith against his objections. I know not where he was born, but he was educated at Mainz; he was well versed even in our law and literature, and had a mind practised in the Scriptures and in disputes against us. He often used to come to me as a friend, both for business and to see me, since in certain things

I was very necessary to him, and as often as we came together we would soon get talking in a friendly spirit about the Scriptures and our faith. Now on a certain day God granted both him and me greater leisure than usual, and soon we began questioning as usual. And as his objections were consequent and logical, and as he explained with equal consequence his former objections, while our reply met his objections foot by foot, and by his own confessions seemed to be equally supported by the testimony of the Scriptures, some of the bystanders requested me to preserve our disputes as likely to be of use to others in the future. . . .

Gilbert was perhaps a little disappointed by the results of the conference. "Poor as my work is," he wrote, "one of the Jews in London, the mercy of God helping, was converted to the Christian faith at Westminster and, becoming a monk, has remained with us." A monastery was the only available refuge for converted Jews. According to the law of the land they forfeited all their possessions to the king when they became Christians, and even the waters of baptism did not ensure them a welcome into Christian society. In the correspondence of St. Anselm, there is a reference to a second Jew, named Robert, who was converted about this time, presumably as a result of the abbot's conference, and had been treated unkindly by his new Christian friends. St. Anselm wrote to Arnulf, Prior of Canterbury, begging him to look after the convert and his family:

Let no poverty, or other accident which we can prevent, cause him to regret having left his parents and their law, for Christ's sake. . . . Do not let him and his little family suffer from any harsh want, but let him rejoice that he has passed from perfidy to the true faith, and prove by our piety that our faith is nearer to God than the Jewish. . . . For his misery, both in victual and clothing, touches my heart. Release my heart from this wound, if you love me. . . .

In the story told by Gilbert Crispin, and in the letters of St. Anselm, there is a note of kindliness and goodwill towards

Jews which is seldom found in the writings of either abbots or saints during the twelfth and thirteenth centuries, anywhere in Europe. St. Bernard of Clairvaux has been described by historians generally as the great friend and protector of Jews in the Rhineland when, about forty years after the death of St. Anselm, they were in danger of extermination by zealous crusaders. Yet in his letters and sermons there is little trace of sympathy for the sufferings of these persecuted people, and not a single word that suggests the possibility of friendly personal relations with any of them.

One of the most notable victims of the German pogroms was a German-born rabbi who had lived in England, probably while Gilbert Crispin was still alive, and, in his old age, had returned to Germany to help his people. In the *Martyrology* of Ephraim of Bonn it is recorded that in 1146, a certain Simeon Ha-Hasid was returning from England, where he had lived for many years. On his way to his native town of Treves, Simeon was murdered near Cologne by the crusaders, at the instigation of Ralph, a Cistercian monk, who was preaching the crusade in that city. Some details of the outrage were given by Rabbi Joseph Ha Cohen, physician and historian, who wrote in the sixteenth century a chronicle of Jewish suffering entitled *Emek Ha-Bakha* ("The Valley of Weeping") based on Ephraim of Bonn's account:

> And it came to pass, in the month of Elul, when the priest Rudolf (may God pursue and drive him out) came unto Cologne, that Rabbi Simeon went out from the city, to return unto his city of Treves; for there was his dwelling. And vain fellows met him, of them which loiter about; and they pressed him to be defiled by water; but he harkened to them not. And there came a Gentile of fierce countenance, who regarded not the person of an old man, and he cut his head from off him, and placed it upon a corner of the roof; and his carcase was like dung upon the face of the field that none gathereth. And when the Jews heard it they were grieved; they trembled greatly and bitterly at that time. . . . And

the people wept very sore. And the heads of the congregation went forth and spake unto the principal man of the city; and he gave them back the head of the righteous and his corpse; and they buried him in their own sepulchre.[10]

The massacre of Jews at Cologne, and many other German cities, in the summer of 1146, was organized by Rudolph, or Ralph, a Cistercian who left his monastery at Clairvaux, apparently without authority, in order to enlist recruits in Germany for the rescue of the Holy Land. He told the Germans it was their duty first to kill the enemies of Christ in their own country. Nothing is known about the personal history of this enterprising monk. His activities were brought to an end, although the pogroms were only partly checked, by the intervention of St. Bernard. The story was told by contemporary chroniclers with the usual emphasis on edification. Historians generally have followed their example.

When Bernard, Abbot of Clairvaux, was commissioned by Pope Eugenius III in 1145 to preach the Second Crusade, he opened his recruiting campaign at Vézelay, in Burgundy, where the vigor of his word inspired immense crowds to take the cross. Although he was asked to lead them to the Holy Land, he declined on account of ill health. He could find no one capable of taking his place. The expedition ended in disaster, for which he was unjustly blamed. But he ought, perhaps, to have gone with them. A man who had founded a hundred and sixty monasteries must have been a good organizer, if not necessarily a leader of men. Even if they had had to carry him part of the way on a stretcher, his sanctity, his magnetic personality and the fear of his word might have imposed on the armies, and on their leaders, some sort of order and discipline. The success of the enterprise was imperiled, even before it started, by Ralph, the monk in the Rhineland, who diverted public attention from the infidels in Palestine to the Jews at home.

A monk does not leave his monastery without the approval,

or at least without the knowledge, of his abbot. In a letter to the Archbishop of Mainz, who had written to complain about Ralph, St. Bernard denied that he had given him authority to preach. A contributor to the *Cambridge Mediaeval History*, disregarding the texts, refused to believe that the monk had gone off on such a mission without the sanction of his superior: "St. Bernard's emissary, a monk of Clairvaux, damaged the cause by raising the cry against the Jews, instead of against the Turkish infidel." [11] There is nothing in the texts which justifies the description of Ralph as an "emissary" of St. Bernard's. The monk probably left the monastery in the company of some preacher, thus "having no authority" himself, and then proceeded to act independently.

Many ecclesiastical historians have treated the whole affair as if it had been merely an unfortunate incident, due to the ignorant fanaticism of a single individual, and not, as in fact it was, characteristic and inevitable in the world of the twelfth century. "An ignorant monk," wrote Neander, "Rudolph by name, had stepped forward as a preacher of the Crusade." [12] There is no evidence that Ralph was ignorant, and, if he was, that would have been the fault of his abbot. The suggestion that monks who were not ignorant might have refused to take part in such a campaign would be absurd. Ralph had a great deal of support from monks, and from the local clergy. On his way to Germany he picked up in Belgium the Abbot of Lobbes, who acted as his interpreter. Perhaps Neander meant that Ralph was ignorant because he did not know any German; but St. Bernard did not know any either. The story of Ralph's independent crusade is obviously incomplete. There were probably some unedifying details about the initial stages of his adventure which contemporary chroniclers did not know about, or may have successfully suppressed.

St. Bernard had gained many recruits by announcing that the killing of an infidel would merit a place in heaven. But Ralph told his congregations that these infidels, violent men, and well armed, were a long way off, and that it was much safer, and equally meritorious, to kill unarmed Jews at home. This doctrine was readily accepted by the populace, whose minds for generations had been prepared for such ideas by ecclesiastical propaganda. The massacre began, without regard to age or sex, at Spires, Cologne, Mainz, and many other cities in Germany. When news of these outrages reached Bernard, he wrote, after some delay—occupied no doubt in verifying the facts—two letters, one to the Archbishop of Mainz, and another, in the form of an encyclical, to "The lords and very dear Fathers, the Archbishops and Bishops, with the whole clergy and the faithful people of Eastern Europe and Bavaria."

These bishops had been unable to stop the slaughter, and there is no evidence of their having made any strenuous efforts to do so. St. Bernard had to visit Germany himself. He made a tour of the Rhineland, where he was received with hostile demonstrations on the part of the mob. He was able, however, to prevent them from carrying out their plan for the extermination of Jewry. The Jews never forgot that service. "If the mercy of God had not sent that priest," wrote Rabbi Joseph in the sixteenth century, "not a single Jew would have escaped with his life."

St. Bernard's efforts were not entirely successful. In February, 1147, after his departure from Germany, the Crusaders attacked the Jews at Wurzburg, slaughtered about twenty of them and treated many more with outrageous cruelty. Similar scenes of terrorism took place about the same time in France. "At no great distance from the monastery of Clairvaux, under the eyes of Abbot Bernard, the savage bands of the crusaders continued undismayed to carry on their bloody work." [13] These ruffians could not be effectively intimidated by writing letters or by preaching sermons. They needed something more drastic. Ralph was reprimanded by St. Bernard and sent back to his monastery—whereas he should have been tried and hanged. St. Bernard's intervention, however, undoubtedly saved the lives of many hundreds of Jews. His sermons could not have had much effect on the mob, for he did not speak their language. But he was able to make the German bishops understand that it was their duty to put an end to atrocities for which they were partly responsible.

In writing his encyclical letter, St. Bernard was faced with a dilemma. He knew that the German pogroms would imperil the success of his crusade, yet he was apparently afraid of saying anything which might have a detrimental effect on recruiting or would create the impression that Jews should be treated like ordinary human beings. Four-fifths of the letter consists of a recruiting appeal. Bernard does not refer directly to the outrages which had been reported from the Rhineland. He had, no doubt, sound political reasons for writing about murder with such restraint. He begins by advising the Bavarians to give up their senseless habit of fighting among themselves, and telling them to enlist in the army of God. He writes, perhaps with a note of sarcasm which few of his readers would have noticed:

> Now O brave knight, now O warlike Hero, you have a battle you may fight without danger: when it is glory to conquer and gain to die. If you are a prudent merchant, if you are a desirer of the world; I show you some great bargains, see you lose them not. Take the sign of the cross, and you shall gain pardon for every sin that you confess with a contrite heart.

He approaches the subject of murder with diplomacy. "We have heard and rejoiced that the zeal of God abounds in you, but it behoves no mind to be wanting in wisdom." It was a mistake to kill Jews, he explained, because their existence helped to fortify Christian Faith:

> Consult the pages of Holy Writ. I know what is written in the Psalms as prophecy about the Jews: *God hath shown me*, saith the Church, *thou shalt not slay my enemies, neither shall my people ever be forgotten.* They are living signs to us,

representing the Lord's Passion. For this reason they are dispersed to all regions, that they may pay the penalty of so great a crime, that they may be the witnesses of our redemption.[14]

St. Bernard's denunciation of murder with an argument based on religious rather than on moral grounds was perhaps the best line to take with fanatics who had been told that the killing of Jews was a religious duty. On the main issue of the moral law he spoke frankly and fearlessly to the mob: "You should not slay the Jews, you should not persecute them, or even put them to flight." These admonitions were backed up with quotations from Holy Writ, but not, as might have been expected, with any text from the fourth chapter of Genesis where it is written: "And the Lord said to Cain. . . . What hast thou done? The voice of thy brother's blood crieth to me from the earth." That was a text which St. Bernard quoted only when Christians were murdered. He modified his recommendations not to persecute Jews or drive them away (recommendations which were opposed to mediaeval opinion and practice), by explaining that the Jews ought not to be persecuted too much; if they were treated too harshly, it would be difficult to convert them. "If the Jews are altogether ground down, how shall, in the end, their salvation and conversion prosper?" Such concessions to the temper of the age were, no doubt, a diplomatic necessity. St. Bernard defended the Jews from a sense of duty, but without much enthusiasm. His encyclical letter does not contain any expression of commiseration with their sufferings; yet he appeals on their behalf to principles of justice and humanity. He acquits them of the charge of unduly harsh usurious practices, which was on this occasion, as always, one of the popular pretexts for attacking them.

"I do not enlarge," he writes, "on the lamentable fact that where there are no Jews, there Christian men judaize even worse than they do in extorting usury." [15] He also insists that

Jews should be spared because they are unable to defend themselves, and because their lives are, in a sense, specially sacred. "It is, too, a mark of Christian piety both to wage war on the proud and to spare the humble, especially those of whom was Christ according to the flesh."

His letter ends with some words of consolation for recruits who were now forbidden to exercise their swordsmanship upon defenseless civilians. "But you may demand from them . . . that all who take up the cross, shall be freed by them from all exactions of usury." The Crusaders, therefore, could now make the Jews pay for their expenses to the Holy Land. The announcement that anyone who took the cross was thereby freed from debts, whether owed to Christian or Jew, naturally led to the enrollment of a large number of adventurers who were in financial difficulties. It would be easy to recruit a mob on such terms anywhere in the world at the present day. St. Bernard, characteristically, blamed God for the fact that the crusading armies included some of the riffraff of Europe: "What opportunity of salvation has not God tried and sought out when the Almighty deigns to summon to his services murderers, robbers, adulterers, perjurers and those guilty of other crimes." No one in Europe had reason to regret the departure of the Crusaders. "The most joyful and salutary result to be perceived," wrote St. Bernard, "is that in such a multitude of men who flock to the East, there are few besides scoundrels, vagabonds, thieves, murderers, perjurers, and adulterers, from whose emigration a double good is observed to flow, a twofold joy. Indeed they give as much delight to those whom they leave as to those whom they go to assist." [16] A contemporary chronicler, Otto, Bishop of Freisingen, made similar comments on the recruitment of the crusading army: "By a conversion which could only be the work of God, thieves and brigands repented of their conduct, and swore to shed their blood for Jesus Christ."

No obligation was imposed on any of these recruits, whether

brigands or not, to set out for the Holy Land on any specified
date and, moreover, Crusaders could always obtain remission
of their vows by a money payment or by persuading someone
else to take their place. Many of them, having obtained relief
from their debts, preferred to remain at home, where, as the
courts of justice did not dare, without permission from the
Pope, to arrest criminals who had taken the cross, they found
safe opportunities for loot and murder.

The Pope sent an official to England to absolve Crusaders
from their vow of pilgrimage "after the receipt of money,"
a proceeding which made people wonder, wrote Matthew
Paris, "at the insatiable cupidity of the Roman court." [17]

A crusade offered many opportunities to neutrals and non-
combatants for making money. But Jews were not the only
war profiteers. Many enterprising Christians during the Third
Crusade got into trouble for trading with the enemy and incurred the righteous indignation of the Fourth Lateran
Council:

> Particularly we excommunicate and anathematize those
> false and impious Christians, who, against Christ himself and
> the Christian people, convey to the Saracens arms, iron and
> wood for galleys. Also we decree those who sell to them
> galleys or ships, and those who act as pilots on the piratical
> ships of the Saracens, or give to them any aid or counsel in
> machines or in any other things, to the damage of the Holy
> Land, to be punished by deprivation of their property and to
> become the servants of those taking them.

This decree was published in all the Mediterranean seaports.
Christians were forbidden, for four years, "to send across
their ships, or go across to the lands of the Saracens who dwell
in eastern parts . . . so that the great aid which is accustomed
to issue forth from this to the aforesaid Saracens may be taken
away from them." [18]

The idea of making the Jews pay for the expenses of the
Crusade was encouraged by Peter the Venerable, who wrote

from his comfortable monastery at Cluny: "Why should not the Jews contribute more than anyone else to the expenses of the holy war? Robbers they are; this is the very occasion for compelling them to disgorge. Sacrilegious blasphemers, this is the way in which to punish their impiety!"

(Almost exactly eight hundred years later, Lieutenant General Sir Evelyn Barker, G.O.C. Palestine, had the same idea, which he expressed to his officers in the same sort of language. In a circular letter, dated July 26, 1946, he told them that he intended to punish the Jews "in a way the race dislikes as much as any, by striking at their pockets and showing our contempt for them.")

St. Bernard begins his letter to the Archbishop of Mainz by suggesting, at least to the modern reader, that the subject it deals with is not of supreme importance. He has got other and more urgent matters to attend to. "My reply," he says, "must be brief, on account of the multiplicity of business with which I am burdened." The archbishop's complaint about the activities of Ralph had probably not been, primarily, concerned with his campaign of murder, for St. Bernard continues: "Who am I . . . that an Archbishop should refer to me a contempt for his authority and an injury to his metropolitan See?" Obviously the archbishop had complained to Bernard that this monk of Clairvaux was conducting a mission on the Rhine, claiming to have been sent there by his abbot.

St. Bernard's unequivocal denial of this claim makes it clear that the archbishop's complaint was not justified by the facts. "That man of whom you speak in your letters is sent neither by man, nor as man, nor for man, nor yet by God." [19] St. Bernard, moreover, accused him of being "a sacrilegious deceiver filled with the spirit of falsehood." It is probable therefore that, having invented some plausible story, the monk had left his monastery with the abbot's permission, perhaps without any clear idea of what he intended to do; then, when he arrived in the Rhineland, he met some of the local anti-Semites and took advantage of the opportunity to satisfy his longing for notoriety.

St. Bernard does not refer to the monk in terms which are generally applied to a murderer. He calls him "a man without feeling or modesty." He even suggests that he is to be blamed for his want of tact. "His foolishness has been placed, as it were, upon a candlestick, so that it may appear plainly to all." Three charges are mentioned in chronological order: "There are three things in him most worthy of blame: his usurpation of the right to preach, his contempt of the authority of the bishop, and finally his incitement to murder." St. Bernard then quoted a number of passages from Holy Writ, including Matthew XXVI:52: "He who takes the sword shall perish by the sword"—a text which might be read as a warning for the archbishop to pass on to the guilty monk. But the warning is weakened by the argument that it is better to convert Jews than to go on killing them. "Does not the Church triumph a hundred times better over the Jews in convincing them every day of their error and in converting them to the faith, than if it were to exterminate them once for all by the edge of the sword?"

Various texts from the Psalms are also utilized, such as "See thou slay them not" (LIX:12), and, perhaps less relevant in a murder charge, "The Lord doth build up Jerusalem and will gather together the dispersed of Israel" (CXLVII:2). St. Bernard points out that, if all the Jews were killed, these prophecies will be rendered void of meaning.

The main offense committed by Ralph in the eyes of St. Bernard—or at any rate in the text of his letter—is that the monk's preaching involved a form of heresy:

> Are you not the man who will make the prophets liars, and will render empty all the treasures and the piety and the mercy of Jesus Christ? Your doctrine is not yours, but that of your father who sent you. It is not surprising if you are

as your master; for he was a murderer from the beginning, a liar and a father of falsehood.

This denunciation of murder, wrapped up in a biblical text, may have impressed the mediaeval reader, but it would not be accepted at the present time as an adequate censure of a monk who was responsible for the massacre of hundreds of helpless men, women and children. St. Bernard's final summing up is severe, but it contains no mention of murder or of incitement to murder and merely stresses the iniquity of failing to observe monastic discipline, and of trying to prevent Scripture from being fulfilled: "O fearful knowledge, O infernal wisdom, contrary to the prophets, hostile to the Apostles, subversive of piety and grace. O unclean heresy, sacrilegious deceiver, filled with the spirit of falsehood, which hath conceived sorrow, and brought forth ungodliness. I would wish, but fear, to say more."

The letter ends, as it began, by giving the impression that, in the opinion of the writer, the whole affair was of little importance, and that an insubordinate monk had been merely indiscreet: "To sum up briefly all that I think upon these matters: the man is great in his own eyes, full of the spirit of arrogance. His words and his actions reveal that he is striving to make a name for himself among the great of the earth, but he has not the means to succeed in his object. Farewell."

It is not easy to understand why St. Bernard was "afraid to say more"; perhaps he did not want to be accused of interfering with the jurisdiction of the Archbishop of Mainz in whose territory the offense had been committed. Ralph was a scoundrel who, in 1946, would have been placed in the dock alongside many Germans who have so recently followed his example: Germans without feeling or modesty; Germans who "set their foolishness upon a candlestick"; Germans whose "infernal wisdom was subversive of piety and grace." St. Bernard would have said a great deal more if Christians instead of Jews had been the victims of a massacre. He did not say

enough, even before the event; he did not say a single word in
condemnation of that hatred of the Jewish people preached at
the time most vigorously by his friend Peter the Venerable,
Abbot of Cluny, whose language could not fail to arouse the
passions of the mob.

The moderation of St. Bernard's protest against the slaughter
of Jews in the Rhineland should be compared with the indignation he had expressed, some twelve years earlier, at the murder
of Master Thomas, Prior of St. Victor, who had been assassinated at the instigation of Theobald Notier, Archdeacon of
Paris. Notier had exceeded his archidiaconal functions by
ordering his two nephews to murder the prior. When he fled
to Rome for protection, St. Bernard wrote to the Pope. He
did not refer to Notier as a man without feeling or modesty,
who had placed his foolishness upon a candlestick. "This
wild beast," he said, "has fled to you for shelter." St. Bernard
did not quote any verses from the Psalms. He found in the
fourth chapter of Genesis a text suitable for Notier: "Do you
dare with jaws foaming and mouth yet marked with the
blood of the son you have just slain, to flee to the breast of
the mother, and appear before the eyes of the father? Does
not the voice of your brother's blood cry out against you from
the ground?" And even in his anger at this priestly assassin
who had made the mistake of killing a Christian instead of a
Jew, St. Bernard did not miss the occasion to introduce into
his indictment an irrelevant reference to the Jewish people:
"If Theobald," he said, "will venture to reply: It was not I
who actually slew him, Bernard will answer: No, not directly,
but it was your friend who did, and for your sake. . . . If you
are to be excused, then the Jews ought not to be held guilty
of the death of Christ, inasmuch as they were wary enough to
withhold their hands from it."

The monk who had incited a German mob to murder, not
only the old Rabbi Simeon, but hundreds of Jewish men,
women and children, was told that he lacked feeling and

modesty and sent back in disgrace to his monastery. But an archdeacon, who had been accessory to the murder of one Christian, could not get off so easily. St. Bernard begged the Pope to inflict upon the criminal such a sentence, that "another generation may hear, not only how audacious was the crime, but also how terrible was the punishment." [20]

In the twelfth century, killing Christians was regarded as a more serious offense than killing Jews. This distinction prevailed, not only during the Middle Ages, but for long after. The mediaeval chroniclers, as Gibbon noted, took the slaughter of Jews "very coolly." And even in the eighteenth century many learned writers seem to have regarded such killing as an excess of virtue, a misdirected religious enthusiasm. Fleury, in his *Histoire ecclésiastique*, refers to "the indiscreet zeal of a monk named Rudolf." And Mabillon, in the preface to his edition of St. Bernard's works, wrote that "a certain monk named Ralph, while preaching the crusade . . . excited the Christians to commence by the murder of a number of Jews. St. Bernard repressed his zeal by a letter." [21]

The mediaeval opinion that Jewish lives were of less importance than the lives of Christians had some followers in the present century, even before the advent of Hitler. G. K. Chesterton expressed his approval of the crusading gangsters in a book commissioned by a well-known English newspaper, written during his visit to Palestine in 1920 without, as he admitted, any preliminary study of the subject. "An excellent offer has been made me," he said in a letter to Maurice Baring, "to write a book about Jerusalem. . . . I only want to write semi-historical rhetoric on the spot." [22] He condoned the killing of Jews, during the First Crusade, as "a form of democratic violence," and regretted that the killers could not be canonized:

The canonization of such a crowd might be impossible, and would certainly be resisted in modern opinion, chiefly because they indulged their democratic violence on the way

by killing various usurers, a course which fills modern society
with an anger verging on alarm. A perverse instinct leads me
to weep rather over the many slaughtered peasants, than over
a few slaughtered usurers.[23]

Few critics found anything amiss in this "semi-historical
rhetoric." Georges Goyau indeed took it all quite seriously;
he recommended to his French readers "the pages about the
Crusaders in *The New Jerusalem* of G. K. Chesterton" which
are "seasoned by a certain flavor of paradox, with a penetrating
historical intuition." [24] Although Chesterton thought that the
Crusaders, when they were killed in battle, deserved more
sympathy than the unarmed civilians they murdered in cold
blood, he would probably not have carried his fancy for
paradox so far as to weep more bitterly over the death of
German soldiers in battle than over the death of the Jews they
drove into the gas chambers.

When German Crusaders killed Simeon, the old Rabbi,
they killed him because he was a Jew; the accusation of usury,
as St. Bernard pointed out, was merely the universal excuse for
loot and murder. Jews were not always the only victims of
these brigands. The English Crusaders, who were neither
better nor worse than those of other nations, also sharpened
their swords on the unarmed Jews at home before leaving for
the Holy Land; and when they arrived at Lisbon, in 1190
(Third Crusade), the citizens of that town "were compelled
to arm for the protection of their wives and property." [25]

The preaching of a Cistercian monk, whether he was
ignorant or not, whether he had authority or not, could never
have aroused the fanaticism of a German mob to such a pitch
of fury if their minds had not been previously infected with
hatred. Ralph neither could nor would have done what he did
to the Jewish people, if the way had not been actively prepared
for him by the Church's unfriendly attitude towards the Jews,
and by the anti-Semitic teaching in the schools and in the
monasteries.

St. Bernard's interest in Jews was professional. He seems to have still hoped to convert some of them, and for this reason, more than from any motive of humanity, he intervened to protect them from excessive persecution. A certain amount of "grinding down" was an ecclesiastical necessity. Jews who lived in luxury, or even in comfort sufficient to make them look happy, were a scandal which could not be tolerated. They had to live in misery because their unhappy appearance was supposed to be part of the scriptural evidence for the truth of Christianity. "We see," wrote Peter of Blois, fifty years later, "the Passion of Christ, not only in their books, but in their faces." This was the doctrine taught by St. Bernard at Clairvaux. He preached sermons which had the effect of impressing upon the minds of his monks the conviction that Jews were not even human. Only a few of these sermons have been preserved; they are almost as provocative as the homilies of St. John Chrysostom, the Golden-Mouthed:

> O intelligence coarse, dense, and as it were bovine, which did not recognize God, even in his own works! Perhaps the Jew will complain, as of a deep injury, that I call his intelligence bovine. But let him read what is said by the prophet Isaiah, and he will find that it is even less than bovine. For he says "the ox knoweth his owner, and the ass his master's crib; but Israel doth not know, my people doth not consider." (Isaiah I:3.) You see, O Jew, that I am milder than your own prophet, I have compared you to the brute beasts; but he sets you even below these . . .[26]

St. Bernard, like the rest of his generation, believed that the Jewish people refused to accept the Christian religion, not owing to any fault of Christian dialectic or behavior, but because they had been "blinded" by the act of God. Discussions about the personal responsibility of a man who had been "blinded" had been going on since the time of Pelagius and St. Augustine, and had given currency to a number of subtle distinctions as well as plausible fallacies. But it was surely illogical to blame, as St. Bernard did, a whole community of men, numbering several millions, and all their uncountable descendants, for an event which—whether through blindness or not—a few hundred individuals at most had been originally responsible for. To charge the whole Jewish people, as St. Bernard did, with "a stupidity bestial and more than bestial," and "a blindness as marvelous as it was miserable," lowered Christian dialectic to a primitive level—to the level, in fact, of the Old Testament.

The "bestiality" of the Jews was a favorite topic among pious writers in the Middle Ages. Peter of Blois, who wrote a treatise "Against the Perfidious Jews," using the adjective in its most abusive sense and interlarding his text with quotations from the early Fathers, regarded the Jewish people as brute beasts, incapable of rational argument. He disapproved of Christians holding discussions with a race "stiff-necked and truly bestial." Peter lived for many years in England where he held, at Bath, the office of archdeacon. He was transferred to London owing to a charge which had been brought against him of committing "a shameful crime." [27] In London he was paid such a small salary that he could not live on it, and he wrote to the Pope asking that the value of the benefice might be increased. His financial troubles may have sharpened his pen against the Jews. Perhaps one of the perfidious beasts had refused to lend him any money.

St. Bernard explained, in another of his sermons, to the monks and to the whole world—where for many centuries the power of his word prevailed—that the Jews were a degraded and unproductive people, whom Christ had cursed, as he had cursed the barren fig tree:

> O evil seed . . . whence hast thou these figs crude and coarse? And in truth, what is there in that people which is not crude and coarse, whether we consider their occupations, their inclinations, their understanding, or even their rites with which they worship God. For war was their business, wealth

their whole craving, the letter of the Law the only nurture of their bloated minds, and great herds of cattle, bloodily slaughtered, their form of worship.[28]

Among the monks who listened to this sermon, or to others of the same kind, sat Ralph the realist, who absorbed all this rhetoric and drew from it the conclusion that to kill these people would be pleasing to God. For St. Bernard had said they were murderers: "a race who had not God for their father, but were of the devil, and were murderers as he was a murderer from the beginning." [29] These are the words reported in the Gospel according to St. John (VIII:44) to have been addressed by Christ to a few individual Jews during a discussion in the Temple at Jerusalem. St. Bernard, following the usual custom of Christian commentators, applied them to the whole Jewish people, not only at that time, but for all time to come. In 1941, Julius Streicher adopted the same dialectical device when he recommended "the extermination of that people whose father is the Devil." [30]

While St. Bernard was explaining to his monks at Clairvaux that the Jews were lower than beasts, his friend Peter the Venerable was preaching the same doctrine, with even more vigor, to his monks at the Abbey of Cluny. The abbot is reputed to have been "one of the kindest and most genial natures to be met with in this or any other time . . . the meekest of men, a model of Christian charity." [31] "A man of peace," wrote Abbé Vacandard, "the most peace-loving man of his time. A man of boundless charity." [32] Although his genial nature did not permit him to approve of murder, the Abbot's protest against the crusading practice of slaughtering Jews was not worded with much enthusiasm. His "boundless charity" stopped at the frontiers of Israel. "I do not require you to put to death those accursed beings. . . . God does not wish to annihilate them. . . . They must be made to suffer fearful torments and be preserved for greater ignomiy, for an existence more bitter than death." [33]

Jews could not expect much mercy from anyone who listened to the sermons or read the treatises of the Abbot of Cluny: "You, you Jews, I say, do I address; you, who till this very day, deny the Son of God. How long, poor wretches, will ye not believe the truth? Truly I doubt whether a Jew can be really human." The abbot had, in fact, no doubt about it, for he continued: "I lead out from its den a monstrous animal, and show it as a laughing stock in the amphitheatre of the world, in the sight of all the people. I bring thee forward, thou Jew, thou brute beast, in the sight of all men." [34]

It would be mere humbug to pretend that the sermons of Peter the Venerable, or the homilies of St. Bernard, could have had much restraining effect on the misdirected enthusiasm of the Crusaders. The doctrine that Jews were brute beasts led, indeed, to practical results. "When the Council of Paris, in 1212, forbade, under pain of excommunication, Christian midwives to attend a Jewess in labor, it shows that the Jews were authoritatively regarded as less entitled than beasts to human sympathy." [35]

There is a curious reference to St. Bernard's view that Jews should be ranked lower than animals, in a well-known standard history of France, published in 1901 by Lavisse. "That soul [of St. Bernard] was not without curious paradoxes. A gentleness, an unction, a goodness, extended unto animals, unto Jews (which is characteristic of the Middle Ages), along with an impetuous will . . ." [36] This sentence seems to mean that it was characteristic of the souls of holy men in the Middle Ages to love, not only human beings, but also animals and Jews, with a slight preference in favor of animals. The idea that anyone could love Jews better than animals, or, indeed, could love them at all, was incomprehensible to Léon Bloy. "Strictly speaking, I know quite well," he wrote, in a book which he regarded as his finest work, "that the Israelites can be called 'our brethren'—on the same grounds, I fear, as plants or animals. . . . But to love them as such is a

proposition at which nature revolts. It is a miraculous excess
of the most sublime sanctity, or the illusion of an unreal
religiosity." [37]

The Jews were not the only people in the twelfth century
whose eyes were covered with a veil. St. Bernard's indifference to life and literature outside his own ecclesiastical
circle was no greater than that of most clerics of his time. Yet
it is difficult to believe that he knew nothing of the high
standard of culture reached by the Jews in Spain, where they
were still allowed to live more or less on the same terms as
other human beings. But St. Bernard must have heard of
Gabirol (1021–1070), whose fame was universal—although
he probably did not know that Gabirol was a Jew: [38]

> Great Gabirol, true and loyal,
> God-devoted minnesinger,
> Pious nightingale who sang not
> To a rose, but to God—
> Tender nightingale who sweetly
> Sang his love song in the dimness,
> In the darkness of the Gothic,
> Of the mediaeval night! [39]

The monks of Clairvaux and Cluny would have been surprised
to hear that the chief inclinations of this Jewish poet and
philosopher (known to the Christian Middle Ages as Avicebron) were devoted to the pursuit, not of gain, but of wisdom:

> How shall I forsake wisdom?
> I have made a covenant with her.
> She is my mother, I her dearest child;
> She hath clasped her jewel about my neck.
> Shall I cast aside the glorious ornament?
> While life is mine, my spirit shall aspire
> Unto her heavenly heights.
> I will not rest until I find her source. [40]

St. Bernard had probably never heard the name of his own
contemporary, Jehuda Halevi. In the twelfth century, few
scholars in France knew Hebrew, and the monks at Clairvaux

were not allowed to learn that language from Jews. There
was hardly anyone else who could have taught them, except
Abelard, who knew a little, and Héloïse, who is said to have
read Hebrew as easily as Latin. Cistercian monks, moreover,
were forbidden to read or write poetry. St. Bernard did indeed grant himself a dispensation and wrote a few hymns; but
they have no literary value.[41]

Halevi was born at Toledo in 1086, at a time when it was
possible for Jews to live there in peace. He practised medicine
for many years in his native city, and, at the age of fifty, took
ship for the land of Israel; no more noble spirit has ever made
that pilgrimage. All that needs to be known of his life, his
love of God, his unshaken confidence in the justice of God,
is expressed in his poetry with a grandeur and a simplicity
which hitherto had been achieved only by the Psalmist. His
"Ode to Zion" was incorporated into the Jewish liturgy and
has been read in the synagogues for centuries:

> Zion! wilt thou not ask if peace be with thy captives
> That seek thy peace—that are the remnant of thy flocks?
> From West and East, from North and South—the greeting
> "Peace," from far and near, take thou from every side;
> And greeting from the captive of desire, giving his tears
>   like dew
> Of Hermon, and longing to let them fall upon thine hills . . .

Halevi is not merely a melancholy recorder of sorrow, be-
moaning with tears and lamentations the unhappy fate of
Israel. He is the prophet who spoke for all his people words
which they remembered in the darkest moment of their recent
sufferings, words which were still remembered in the camps of
Europe where a remnant was detained, homeless, stateless, on
the eve of the day of fulfillment:

> Zion! perfect in beauty! love and grace thou didst bind
>   onto thee
> Of olden time; and still the souls of thy companions are
>   bound up with thee.

It is they that rejoice at thy well being, that are in pain
Over thy desolation, and that weep over thy ruin—
They that, from the pit of the captive, pant toward thee,
    worshipping,
Every one from his own place, toward thy gates;
The flocks of thy multitude, which were exiled and scattered
From mount to hill, but have not forgotten thy fold. . . .

Jews who endured a tortured life during the long years of
Nazi tyranny, and who finally escaped from "the pit of the
captive," were sustained, not as some of their enemies now
profess to believe, by the prospect of being some day released
and allowed to go to America and make money, but by the
hope and the faith, and the love of Zion, which they shared
with Jehuda Halevi:

They ask the way to Zion—they pray toward her—
The children exiled from her border, but which have not
    stript themselves of their adornment.
The beautiful adornment for which they were praised, for
    this they are slain and defiled—
The treasures they inherited at Horeb, whereby they are
    justified and proud;
Slaves bear rule over them, but they will never cease to call
    Thee
Until Thou turn our captivity and comfort our waste places.

A Jewish immigration officer, after a visit to the internment
camps of Europe, stated on January 20, 1947, at Givat
Brenner, in Israel, that "a majority of the survivors were religious Jews, and/or Zionists. One of them said: 'I have lived
for three years on the pickings from refuse bins, and the only
thing that kept me alive was my hope of Zionism.'" Men
and women, branded with the German prison mark when
"freed" at last by the Allied armies, but still kept for years
behind barbed wire, did not require, as an English weekly
journal has suggested, "Zionist propaganda" to build up among
them "emotional reasons" for wanting to go to Palestine.[42]
They were inspired by a "propaganda" which has been con-

tinuous among the Jews of the Diaspora for many centuries.
Halevi left his prosperous medical practice in Toledo, "for
emotional reasons." According to tradition, shortly after his
arrival in Israel he was killed by an Arabian horseman; as he
died, within sight of the ruins of Jerusalem, he repeated the
last verse of his "Ode to Zion":

> Happy is he that waiteth, that cometh nigh and seeth the
>   rising
> Of thy light, when on him thy dawn shall break—
> That he may see the welfare of thy chosen, and rejoice
> In thy rejoicing, when thou turnest back unto thine olden
>   youth.

The inclinations of this "perfidious" Jew were not all devoted to the pursuit of gain, and his poetry contains many
ideas which St. Bernard would not have described as crude
or coarse:

> O Lord, before Thee is my whole desire—
> Yea, though I cannot bring it to my lips.
> Thy favor I would ask a moment, and then die.
> Ah! would that mine entreaty might be granted,
> That I might render up the remnant of my spirit to Thine
>   hand.
> Then should I sleep and sweet my sleep would be.
> When far from Thee, I die, while yet in life;
> But if I cling to Thee I live though I should die. . . .

This monstrous animal, this Jew, this brute beast, led from its
den and showed as a laughing stock in the amphitheater of the
whole world, was able, in his poems, to rise a little higher than
the animals; nor did the letter of the Law provide, as St.
Bernard had said, "the only nurture of his bloated mind":

> To meet the fountain of the life of truth I run,
> For I weary of a life of vanity and emptiness.
> To see the face of my King is mine only aim;
> I will fear none but Him, nor set up any other to be feared.

Would that it were mine to see Him in a dream!
I would sleep an everlasting sleep and never wake.
Would I might behold His face within my heart!
Mine eyes would never ask to look beyond.

The Jewish poets of the Middle Ages have been kept out of
the record of European culture, partly by mediaeval ignorance
of Hebrew, but chiefly by the modern tradition which refused
to recognize, or give publicity, to any Jewish success except
in the trade of moneylending. "Outside Christianity," wrote
the French literary critic, Barbey d'Aurevilly, "there is no
vigorous and profound poetry." [43] Judaism, according to a
French contributor to the *Catholic Encyclopedia*, "remained
the barren fig tree which Jesus condemned during his mortal
life." [44]

"In cursing the fig tree," writes another French commenta-
tor, about thirty years later, Jesus was condemning "the inveterate sterility of Israel." [45] Nearly all modern Christian
exegetes, both Catholic and Protestant, following the Fathers
of the Church, agree in explaining that the barren fig tree
represents Israel. [46] Lagrange, however, while regarding this
interpretation as admissible, pointed out that it is not supported by a single word of the text itself. Many Christian
commentators still continue to read into the words of. Christ
a meaning which is derived from their own contempt for
the Jewish people. "The malediction of the fig tree," wrote
the Rev. Dr. Richard Downey, "is obviously symbolical of the
fate of Judaism . . . with its extravagant programme and
barren achievement." [47]

It would be interesting to know exactly what all these
writers mean—especially Father Denis Buzy—by "the inveterate sterility of Israel." [48] Were not the people of Israel
spiritually the most productive of all the nations of the world,
before the Christian era? And after? During long centuries they were constantly humiliated by ecclesiastical legislation designed with that purpose; they suffered everywhere

from intermittent terrorism; they were uprooted and expelled —homeless and destitute—from one country after another; and finally they were almost exterminated by the inhabitants of a country which an English general, in 1948, described as "Christian and civilized." After all that, to reproach such a people with "inveterate sterility," ignoring their high achievement in religion, in philosophy, and in science—to repeat that reproach in 1948 is surely adding insult to immeasurable injury.

A naïve contempt for the unproductive race was expressed, in the manner of St. Bernard, by the Rev. W. B. Morris, of the English Oratory, a disciple of Newman, a gentle priest who assuredly did not realize that he was a carrier of the anti-Semitic germ: "While spiritually the Jews are the most sterile and unprogressive of nations, they are a portent and a terror to the world in that struggle for its visible treasures in which their success has been so prodigious, that, in the minds of most men, it obscures every other natural characteristic." [49] A distinguished English Dominican, the late Father Bede Jarrett, likewise accepted the view, which Hilaire Belloc had popularized among English Catholics, that Jews were more interested in money than in anything else, and more interested in the pursuit of gain than Christians ever were. "I must admit," wrote this Dominican Friar, in a Jesuit periodical, "that it came to me rather as a shock, a bewilderment to find that Judaism could still be considered a religion at all. One had got to think about it almost entirely in terms of finance, or of politics, or of art, or perhaps of a wise sanitary code, but hardly a religion." [50] About twenty years after these words were written, this "wise sanitary code" brought consolation to trainloads of victims, packed tightly into closed cattle trucks, who, as they journeyed through a Christian land to the death chambers of Auschwitz, sang the songs of Israel, chanted the Hebrew prayers of faith and trust in God—the same prayers which Father Bede Jarrett had the duty, as a Catholic priest, to read every day in his breviary. One of the few who survived writes:

> I cannot refrain from recalling a memory of those hours of anguish: the memory of a poor woman, a Jewess, threatened with deportation, who was consoling her frightened child, her little son Emmanuel, seven years old, with words which I do not hesitate to describe as sublime: "That will do, Emmanuel; you must not cry. God is with us. He was with us when we came to this place. He will be with us if we have to go. He will be in the train which takes us away. He will be with us always, everywhere." A Jewess, a simple Jewess, as Jesus was "a simple Jew," but the ashes of millions of Jewish martyrs are not yet cool when already the pious tradition of insults and reckless accusations has been revived.[51]

In spite of Torquemada; in spite of fire and torture, and the gentler roads to destitution and death, opened by economic sanctions and exile; in spite of crowds of desperate people baptized by terror—Judaism as a religion has survived. And it is perhaps not surprising that a learned Dominican, who knew the history of his own Order, was shocked and bewildered to discover that it had not been completely destroyed.

"The world," said Achad Ha-Am, "has annexed our God, and then reproaches us for having lost Him."

The existence of a Jewish mediaeval literature was unknown in the first quarter of the present century, not only to Dominican Friars, but to men of a different and, perhaps, more modern culture. "It cannot be denied," wrote George Moore, "that there was neither art nor literature in Europe in the Middle Ages from the sixth, shall we say, to the twelfth century." [52] Shall we not say, rather, that the ancient tradition of contempt was still so effective that educated Christians, even when they had abandoned belief in Christianity, were unable to perceive the existence of a Jew unless he was a moneylender? This tradition has been built up, not only by exaggerating the vices, but by consistently ignoring the virtues and the achievements, of the Jewish people. Consequently, from the twelfth, shall

we say, to the end of the nineteenth century, Jewish literature
was seldom mentioned in the schools of Christendom. Erasmus, at the beginning of the sixteenth century, could not shake
off this habit of thought. He agreed with St. Bernard's comparison of the Jews to a barren fig tree. He had, indeed, "begun to look at Hebrew," but "frightened at the strangeness of
the idiom," he gave it up. He evidently thought that learning
Hebrew was a waste of time, because the Jews had never produced, since the Old Testament, anything worth reading. He
wrote to a friend, in 1518,

> I should wish that you were more inclined to Greek than
> to those Hebrew studies of yours, though I find no fault
> with them. But I see that nation filled with the coldest fables
> and producing nothing but smoke, Talmud, Cabala, Tetra-
> grammaton, Portae Lucis—empty names. I had rather see
> Christ infected by Scotus than by that rubbish.[53]

Ignorance of Jewish achievements in the realm of literature
is sometimes found among men of letters at the present day.
Jérôme and Jean Tharaud, who were both educated at the
Lycée Louis-le-Grand, in Paris, at the end of the nineteenth
century, were surprised that Jews, who had been through so
much tribulation, had never written any good poetry. "Israel
has suffered, but has not written the poem of her unhappy
fate." [54] The schools of Paris at the end of the nineteenth century had evidently not extended the syllabus of literary instruction since Heinrich Heine explained, in verse to his wife,
the cause of her ignorance:

> Dearest child, I answered gravely,
> This sweet ignorance of yours
> Only shows how very faulty
> Is the education given
>
> In the boarding schools of Paris
> Where the maidens—future mothers
> Of a great and free-born people—
> Are supposed to be instructed.

If one asks the name most famous
In the glorious golden age,
Of the Jewish school of poets,
The Arabian Old-Spanish—

For the starry trio asks them,
For Jehuda ben Halevi,
For great Solomon Gabirol
Or for Moses Ibn Esra—

For such names if one should ask them
Then they know not what to answer,
And the children stare dumbfounded,
Puzzled stare with wondering eyes.

I advise you strongly, dearest,
To retrieve those past omissions
And to learn the Hebrew language.
Leave your theaters and concerts

And devote some years to study.
You will then with ease be able
In the ancient texts to read them—
Ibn Esra and Gabirol,

And of course the great Halevi—
The triumvirate poetic,
Who of old the sweetest music
Drew from out the harp of David. . . .

Amidst the clamor of the twelfth century, music from the harp of David was heard by one man—Peter Abelard, who, although he was never canonized, has won, in company with the great Héloïse, the sympathy and the love of posterity. His liberal ideas threatened at one time to obtain a hearing and his defeat was due chiefly to the energy of St. Bernard, who, when Abelard appealed to Rome, obtained from the Pope a condemnation of his writings before the case had been tried by the Roman tribunal. The obvious illegality of this verdict did not escape the tactful censure of Vacandard: "The hasty action of Innocent II came near to compromising the reputation of mature wisdom which belongs to all the decisions of the Holy See." [55]

Abelard was the only leader in the Middle Ages who ventured to attack, openly, the anti-Jewish tradition of Christendom. He attacked the tradition at its root. He said that the Jewish people were not responsible for the death of Christ. He horrified many of his contemporaries, especially the monks of Clairvaux and Cluny, by asserting that if the judges who condemned Christ had believed in his guilt, they would have sinned grievously by acquitting him.

It was, and is, easy for theologians to pick holes in Abelard's teaching. He himself admitted, without pressure, that he had sometimes expressed his opinions too carelessly; but he always declared his readiness to submit, and did in fact submit, his doctrines to the judgment of the Catholic Church. St. Bernard, however, hardly ever mentioned his name without adding some unkind word. The contrast between the two men, expressed concisely and frankly by the Benedictine authors of the *Literary History of France*, has not often been quoted by modern hagiographers:

> Abelard was led astray by his tender heart and his inquisitive mind; his adversary was protected against both kinds of seduction; against the first by a life of austerity, and against the second by a determined adherence to ideas which were commonly accepted, by an invincible horror for every new opinion, and even for investigations which could lead to any innovation.[56]

The fate of the Jews in Europe, from the twelfth to the sixteenth century, was determined, not by tender hearts or inquisitive minds, but by the hard policy of St. John Chrysostom and St. Bernard. At the beginning of the thirteenth century, this policy received the sanction of the Church at the Fourth Lateran Council.

*I hate them with perfect hatred:*
*I count them mine enemies.*

PSALM CXXXIX:22

# 3

· · · · · · · · · · · · · · · · · · · · · · · · · · · · · · · · · · · · · · · · · · · · · · · ·

# Wanderers Upon the Earth

THE POPES OF THE MIDDLE AGES often intervened, not always effectively, to defend Jews against personal violence, but seldom wrote a line to condemn the ill-will which made such violence inevitable. A single papal letter recommending that the faithful observe the chief commandment of the Law—"Thou shalt love thy neighbor"—would have been more appropriate than lists of prohibitions and restrictions.

Shortly after the accession of Innocent the Third to the papal throne, in the last year of the twelfth century, the Jews of France applied to him for help. Certain Crusaders had begun to celebrate their impending—but often postponed—departure for the Holy Land by massacring unbelievers in their own neighborhood. The Pope replied with an edict known as the *Constitutio pro Judaeis*, "the most memorable charter of liberties for Jews," [1] which had first been issued by Pope Calixtus II, in 1120. By issuing this edict, wrote a modern historian of the Papacy, "Innocent took even the persecuted Jews under his special protection." [2] This indeed was the general opinion of writers in the nineteenth century, including those who were critical of the Catholic Church. "It is no more than justice to Innocent's memory," wrote one such opponent, "to state that he was tolerant towards the Jews, even claiming a sort of respect for them, as living witnesses of Christianity." [3]

It is, of course, incorrect to say that Innocent III, or any other Pope in the Middle Ages, was "tolerant towards the

Jews," if the word "toleration" is used in its proper meaning. Judaism was never regarded by the Papacy as an evil thing, like heresy, which ought to be eradicated, but which might sometimes have to be tolerated on account of the greater evil involved by an attempt at its destruction. Heretics were tolerated only when it was found impracticable to exterminate them. But Jews were on a different footing. The Church, conscious that Christianity is founded on Judaism, recognized their right to live and to practice their religion without interference. Jew and Christian belonged to the same family; both were sons of Abraham. The *Constitutio pro Judaeis* was not, therefore, a measure of toleration, but a recognition of Jewish rights, the most important of which was their right to live. This right, however, was conditioned by the stipulation, which the Fathers of the early Church had often emphasized, that they were to live in a state of misery and degradation. The sons of the bondwoman must be kept in subjection to the sons of the freewoman. The word "protection" can be applied to any action taken by Innocent III on behalf of the Jews, only with a restricted meaning; and the phrase "special protection" used by Dr. Horace K. Mann seems to have no meaning at all.

Innocent undertook the duty of protecting them without much appearance of enthusiasm. An unrestricted denunciation of murderers, and some expression of sympathy for their victims, would have been more suitable to the times than a re-edition of the cautious pronouncement of Pope Calixtus, which begins with the recommendation, surprising to the modern reader, that Jews may be persecuted, provided they are not persecuted too much. "Although the Jewish perfidy is in every way worthy of condemnation, nevertheless, because through them the truth of our own faith is proved, they are not to be severely oppressed by the faithful" (*non sunt a fidelibus graviter opprimendi*). "They are not to be severely oppressed"—the history of succeeding centuries shows how this sentence was interpreted by zealots who thought no oppression too severe for the "enemies of Christ," and by thugs who were chiefly interested in acquiring Jewish property without paying for it.

The Pope's prohibition against killing Jews reads as if it were based, not primarily on their natural rights as human beings, but on motives of ecclesiastical expediency:

> Thus the prophet says "thou shalt not kill them lest at any time they forget thy law," or more clearly stated, "thou shalt not destroy the Jews completely so that the Christians should never by any chance be able to forget Thy Law, which, though they themselves fail to understand it, they display in their book to those who do understand . . ."[4]

The suggestion that it was wrong to destroy people "completely" might have been read as a restriction of their right to live. This right is, of course, one which no Pope, no Catholic theologian, has ever denied to the Jews—a right which no ruler in Christendom ever denied to them until the advent of Adolf Hitler.

Innocent prescribed a line of conduct for the faithful which contained the following prohibitions:

(1) No Christian shall use violence to force the Jews to be baptized.
(2) No Christian shall presume to wound them or kill them, or rob them of their money.
(3) No one shall disturb them in any way by sticks or stones while they celebrate their festivals.
(4) No one shall presume to desecrate their cemeteries, or to exhume bodies there buried with the object of extorting money.

To this charter of liberties a proviso was added that it was to apply only to "those Jews who have not presumed to plot against the Christian faith." This would be useful to Crusaders and others who maintained that "the Jews" were perpetually engaged in a conspiracy against Christianity. Moreover, the ghoulish practice of digging up dead bodies and selling them might go on without interruption, as in fact it did. For the bandits who robbed or murdered Jews, or dug up Jewish corpses, could say their victims were blasphemers or conspirators. Yet these four freedoms gave the Jews a charter which, had it been respected, would have enabled them to live in no greater condition of insecurity than their fellow citizens. But the spirit of the times would not allow such a privilege—in conformity with the Papal principle that, since they had been condemned by God to perpetual servitude, they must be compelled to live more miserably than Christians.

The prohibition of forcible baptism, if it had been effective, would have relieved the Jews of a menace which to many of them was more terrifying than death. Theologians generally admitted, even before St. Thomas Aquinas had said it, that "belief cannot be forced because belief is an affair of the will." Yet, in practice, this obvious truth was often ignored by powerful proselytizers. King Chilperic, in the sixth century, imprisoned an obstinate Jew named Priscus, in order, as Gregory of Tours quaintly remarked, "to make him believe in spite of himself." For many centuries, the principle, accepted in theory, that force must not be used did not give much protection to the protesting victim of an over-zealous Christian.

Theologians argued, and sometimes disagreed, as to whether Jewish infants could be lawfully baptized without their parents' consent. Duns Scotus held that they could, but only with the consent of some public authority acting *in loco parentis*. The final decision was that such baptisms, although illicit, were always valid; the children therefore were regarded as Christians, and subject to ecclesiastical discipline. And so it sometimes happened that infants who had been kidnapped and taken away to be baptized were not allowed to return to their mothers.

The doctrine that souls could not be saved from eternal

torments, except by baptism, had been specifically applied to
Jews by St. Fulgentius in the sixth century: "Hold most firmly
and doubt not," wrote that eminent Father of the Church,
"that not only all pagans, but also all Jews . . . who depart
this life outside the Catholic Church are about to go into
eternal fire, prepared for the Devil and his angels." [5]

Baptism imposed upon adults by force was never regarded
as valid. The Church did not approve either the crude procedure employed by Chilperic, who used to carry Jews off
to the font himself and hold their heads down in the water
while a priest performed the ceremony, or the even more drastic action of Charlemagne, who, after defeating the Saxons in
785, issued a decree ordering that all prisoners of war who
refused to accept baptism were to be executed.[6] Economic
pressure of almost any kind was, however, generally presumed
to be permissible. Although Gregory the Great reprimanded
the Bishops of Arles and Marseilles for baptizing Jews by
force, he allowed special privileges to his own agricultural
tenants on the Papal estates in Sicily, provided they accepted
the sacrament. If they did not thus become genuine Christians, he said, their children would be validly baptized and
brought up in the Christian faith.[7] In the first decade of the
eleventh century the Bishop of Limoges offered the Jews in
his town the alternatives of exile or baptism. Three or four of
them yielded, but the rest "made all speed to seek refuge in
other cities, with their wives and children. Some of them
cut their throats rather than submit to baptism." [8]

Innocent III was apparently reluctant to renounce the ad-
vantages of the right to use some form of pressure. He explained that there are kinds and degrees of violence, some of
which were permissible. "Those who are immersed, even
though reluctantly, do belong to ecclesiastical jurisdiction, at
least by reason of the sacrament, and might therefore be
reasonably compelled to observe the rules of the Christian
faith." This ruling would cover the case of a Jew who, as

a result of economic pressure, had declared himself willing to receive baptism and had afterwards repented. Yet the Pope stated clearly that force must not be used. "It is, to be sure, contrary to the Christian faith that anyone who is unwilling and wholly opposed to it should be compelled to adopt and observe Christianity." [9] He recognized, however, distinctions between "kinds of unwilling ones and kinds of compelled ones"; and his definition of "force" was somewhat narrow. Torture was evidently not supposed to be a form of compulsion, for the Pope maintained that "anyone who is drawn to Christianity by violence, through fear and through torture, and receives the sacrament . . . may be forced to observe the Christian faith, as one who expressed a conditional willingness, though, absolutely speaking, he was unwilling."

In the Middle Ages fear often meant fear of torture, which it is difficult for the modern mind to disassociate from the idea of "absolute coercion." Pope Nicholas III, in 1278, decided that those "who through fear, though not absolutely coerced, had received baptism, and had returned to their Jewish blindness, should be handed over to the secular power." It was then the duty of the secular power to burn them alive. The same ruling was applied to those who, through fear, had allowed their children to be baptized. Ten years later, Nicholas IV decreed that Jews who had received baptism to avoid persecution must be treated, if they relapsed, as heretics. At no period during the Middle Ages were the Jews effectively protected by papal decrees from the danger of compulsory baptism.

The theory that threats of exile and confiscation of property were not forms of compulsion, was still maintained by some theologians at the end of the seventeenth century. Such measures were said to be merely "a holy severity," and were described as "persuasions rather than violence or constraint. Whatever is done to avoid them is still voluntary and free." [10] When a man was told that, if he did not accept baptism, his children and his property would be taken from him and he would be driven into exile, he had not really—so some people believed—been subjected to any compulsion. This zeal for converting Jews, either singly or in groups, by hook or by crook, by force or by threats, reached the peak of enthusiasm in Spain during the fifteenth century. St. Vincent Ferrer and other preachers sent thousands of panic-stricken people to the font where a priest mechanically turned them into Christians. Theologians may have decided that these mass-produced Christians had been validly baptized, but no one will readily deny that the policy of using force, or the slightest threat of force, is contrary, not only to common sense, but to the decrees of the Second Council of Nicaea. The bishops and doctors of the Church, assembled at this Council in the year 787, had declared, in effect, not only that Jews must not be chased into the Church, but that they were not to be received, even if they presented themselves of their own free will, without careful examination of their motives. "But if any one of them, out of a sincere heart and in faith, is converted and makes profession with his whole heart . . . , such a one is to be received and baptized." [11]

Although the Popes in the Middle Ages safeguarded the principle that people should not be baptized against their will, they were not able to eradicate the practice. The simple faith of the Crusader was not disturbed by distinctions between degrees of compulsion and degrees of unwillingness. If a Jew had money, he was offered baptism; when he refused, he was knocked on the head. Thus at one stroke the Crusader attained, not only a useful addition to his material comfort in this world, but an assurance of salvation for his soul in the next. If, as sometimes happened, the victim, under threat of torture or instant death, accepted the proposal, he was carefully watched and, at the first signs of any lack of enthusiasm in the practice of his new faith, he would be accused of apostasy; he would then lose his property, and probably his life.

During the twelfth century many of the Jews in France had attained a comfortable prosperity; but their social position, their property, and even their lives, were constantly threatened by the jealousy or the fanaticism of some Christian neighbor. Conversion of souls and confiscation of property were often the associated objectives of proselytism and persecution. In the spring of 1182, the King of France, Philip Augustus, then a youth of seventeen, was persuaded to drive the accursed race out of the country. "He hated the Jews," says a contemporary chronicler, "and had heard many accusations against them, of blaspheming the name of Jesus Christ." These accusations were used as an excuse for pillage:

> This Prince, assuming Airs of Devotion, banished the Jews out of his Kingdom, confiscated their Estates, and only permitted them to sell their Moveables, and to carry away their Money, which was reducing 'em to the last Extremity; since People, taking advantage of this Circumstance, refused to purchase, or to pay. Historians even complain that they robbed the Fugitives of their Money, and brought them to such great Straits, that a great many had much ado to bear it. Some lost their Lives, as Jacob of Orleans, who was knocked on the Head in the City that gave him his Birth and his Name.[12]

This dispersion of a large number of industrious citizens led to a dislocation of business and a slump in trade. Philip Augustus, therefore, in 1198 decided for economic reasons to ask them to return—an act of statesmanship which did not meet with the approval of Innocent III. A wealthy Jew was a danger, although useful to princes and prelates in need of money; but a pious Jew who lived happily with his family was a scandal to Christendom. Neither the comfort provided by wealth, nor the happiness of peaceful family life, could be allowed to slaves who had been condemned by God to per-

petual misery. The Pope never showed much sign of sympathy for their sufferings. He wrote, not to save them from
severe oppression, but to reprimand princes who treated them
too kindly. Innocent never "took the Jews under his special
protection." He took special care to make sure that they were
not protected too much by anyone else. If preachers had let
them alone, they would have been able to live on good terms
with their neighbors. The best proof that they behaved as
good citizens, and were seldom guilty of grave offenses
against such law and order as there was, is the fact that the
charges made against them in the papal documents were
usually of a comparatively trivial nature. In the year 1205,
Innocent wrote two important letters about them, one to the
King of France and the other to the Archbishop of Sens and
the Bishop of Paris (July 15). The indictment contained in
these two letters, drawn up by a Pope who was the greatest
jurist of the Middle Ages, deserves more attention than it has
usually been given by historians.

The letter addressed to the French hierarchy begins with a
long preamble which reaffirms the principle laid down by
former Popes, and by Innocent himself, in the *Constitutio pro
Judaeis,* that the Jews are condemned to perpetual slavery "because they crucified the Lord," and are allowed to live only by
the gracious permission of Christian piety. The Pope pointed
out that they showed no sign of appreciating such generosity;
on the contrary: "While they are mercifully admitted into
our intimacy, they threaten us with that retribution which
they are accustomed to give to their hosts, in accordance with
the common proverb 'like the mouse in a pocket, like the snake
round one's loins, like the fire in one's bosom.'" His chief
complaint about Jewish misbehavior—the one, at least, to
which most space is given in this and in other letters—does not
seem, at the present day, sufficiently important to justify a
public reprimand. He objected to the employment of Christian female servants by Jews. He had been told that Christian

nurses in Jewish households were sometimes compelled at Easter "to pour their milk into latrines for three days before they again gave suck to the children." In addition to this curious practice, "the Jews also perform other detestable and unheard of things against the Catholic Faith." The mediaeval reader would of course assume that they had been up to some other new unmentionable wickedness. The letter concludes with a command, which the archbishop was to pass on to the king, ordering that measures be taken to make sure that they should not dare "to raise their neck bowed under the yoke of perpetual slavery"; and insisting, with more references to mice, serpents and fire in the bosom, that they must be prevented from employing Christian nurses "or any other kind of Christian servants." If they did not obey this order, they were to be subject to a trade boycott. "We give you our authority to forbid any Christian in the district, under pain of excommunication, to enter into any commercial relations with them."

There may have been some foundation of fact behind the story of the nurses pouring their milk into latrines. It is hardly credible, however, that any Jew, even in the Middle Ages, when superstition was not confined to Christians, would have implicitly expressed his belief in the doctrine of transubstantiation by compelling a Christian nurse to refrain from suckling his child after she had received Holy Communion. People at the time would no doubt have replied that such a prohibition provided one more proof that the Jews were secretly convinced of the truth of Christian doctrine and refused to enter the Church out of culpable obstinacy. There is, however, another explanation of the story which is, perhaps, less improbable.

The date of Easter corresponded approximately to the period of the Jewish *Pesach* when Jews were obliged by their law to eat unleavened bread. If a Christian nurse insisted upon eating ordinary bread at that time, her employer might have been superstitious enough to believe that her blood and her milk would be defiled, and he would therefore object to her suckling his child during *Pesach*. Such an objection could easily lead to a domestic quarrel. The mistress of the house would tell the nurse that if she refused to eat unleavened bread she would have to give up, for a few days, suckling the child. The nurse would then leave the house or be dismissed, and would spread a story creditable to herself, which would put the blame for her dismissal upon her mistress.

A more rational reason for prohibiting the employment of Christian nurses in a Jewish household, the possibility that the Christian woman might lose her faith, or her virtue, or both, was not given too much prominence. The object of the Pope's letter was to discredit the Jews, and a reference to the conversion or the seduction of a Christian nurse by her Jewish employer would bring equal discredit on both parties. But the story of Christian women compelled to pour their milk into latrines provided an excellent picture for a propaganda which was designed to represent the Jew as a creature outside the pale of humanity, constantly committing, in secret, crimes so horrible that they could not even be mentioned.[13]

The second letter (January 16, 1205) to the King of France, worded with more severity than the one addressed to the French hierarchy, contained additional and more serious accusations: the Jews were charged with habitually committing blasphemy, usury and murder. They had now begun to come back to France again and apparently the king was allowing them too much liberty. The Pope therefore administered a suitable reproof. He told Philip that princes "are exceedingly offensive in the sight of the Divine Majesty who prefer the sons of the crucifiers, against whom to this day the blood cries to the Father's ears, to the heirs of the crucified Christ, and who prefer the Jewish slavery to the freedom of those whom the Son freed, as though the son of a servant could and ought to be an heir along with the son of the freewoman." These observations were, however, completely irrelevant to the economic situation in France, where "the sons of the crucifiers," owing to their business ability, had proved to be indispensable. They were, moreover, competing with Christian traders and, what was even worse, depriving clerics of their monopoly in the management of business, in the supervision of estates and in all positions of trust where ability to read and write was essential.

The Pope then continued, at great length, to tell the story of "Jewish insolence." First he accused them of usury, using the word in the sense afterwards defined by the Council of Béziers (1246): "Taking anything above the principal." Both Christians and Jews were equally guilty of this practice. The Church was still fighting the battle against usury; but defeat was already in sight.

The Pope wrote:

> Know then that the news has reached us to the effect that in the French kingdom the Jews have become so insolent that by means of their vicious usury, through which they extort not only usury, but usury upon usury [compound interest], they appropriate ecclesiastical goods and Christian possessions. Thus seems to be fulfilled among the Christians that which the prophet bewailed in the case of Jews, saying, "our heritage has been turned over to strangers, our house to outsiders."

This, however, is only one side of the story. The King of France—like the Pope himself—could not conduct his affairs without capital; and no one, whether Jew or Gentile, would hand over capital free of charge. When Jews were being driven out of every occupation except the trade in money, were deprived of the rights of citizenship and repeatedly described in public documents as outcasts, it is not surprising that some of them were always on the lookout for an opportunity to squeeze the superior beings who condescended to borrow money from them. And, moreover, as Arthur J. Balfour pointed out, "If you oblige many men to be money-

lenders, some will assuredly be usurers." [14] In the Middle Ages
the sin of usury was generally first heard of when a debt had
to be paid and the debtor had no means of fulfilling, or wished
to avoid, his obligation. Nothing was said about usury when
a transaction went through smoothly, when a church or a
monastery was built with money lent by a Jew, or by a Christian, on interest, and the investment had proved sufficiently
profitable to enable the loan to be repaid. The Pope had no
reason to complain more about the usurious practices of
French Jews than about those of French Christians, for whose
souls he might be held responsible.

Blasphemy was an offense, difficult to define, which in the
Middle Ages was sometimes punished with death; it often provided a convenient pretext for depriving Jews of papal protection and for robbing them of their property. Innocent's
notions of what constituted blasphemy were wide enough to
include almost any statement which a Jew might make about
the Christian religion. He complained to the king.

> They blaspheme against God's name, and publicly insult
> Christians, by saying that they [the Christians] believe in a
> peasant . . . but we do not admit that He was a peasant
> either in manners or in race. Forsooth they themselves can-
> not deny that physically He was descended from priestly
> and royal stock, and that His manners were distinguished
> and proper.

Innocent had obviously some difficulty in building up his
case. His charges of usury, blasphemy, and employing Christian nursemaids were not likely to make much impression on
the French king. He concludes his indictment, however, with
an accusation which could not fail to arouse throughout Christendom, among those who respected a papal pronouncement,
fear and hatred of the outlawed people. He accused them of
habitually murdering Christians whenever they got a chance
to do so without any risk of discovery. The Pope had been
told a story, which may have been true, about "a certain poor

scholar who had been found murdered in a Jewish latrine," and he assured the King of France, and the whole of Christendom, that this was the sort of crime which "the Jews" were in the habit of committing. The Jews, he declared, "take advantage of every opportunity to kill in secret their Christian hosts." [15] When every allowance has been made for pious zeal and for the manners of the age, this is a papal pronouncement which it would be difficult to justify. And it is even more difficult to explain why Innocent told the King of France that if he succeeded in preventing Jews from employing Christian nursemaids, he would be granted a plenary indulgence. He assured the king that, if he would "restrain the Jews from their presumptions in these and similar matters . . . we join thereto a remission of sins."

The behavior of Jews often gave the Pope grounds for complaints which were not unreasonable. In his letter to the Count of Nevers, January 17, 1208, he protested, in the exaggerated style which was the common form of the age, against certain Jewish practices which were giving the Church a lot of trouble. The civil powers, "certain princes," found it difficult to conduct their affairs without employing capital and, unable to borrow money owing to the ecclesiastical prohibition, they had appointed certain Jews as their agents. When these agents foreclosed and took away "castles and villas," they refused to pay the Church tithe; thus the civil powers were able to evade payment of ecclesiastical rates and taxes. In spite of such provocation, the Pope did not recommend that the offenders should be killed, but he hinted that they ought to be asked to resume their wanderings. "The Jews, against whom the blood of Jesus Christ calls out, although they ought not to be killed, lest the Christian people forget the Divine Law, yet as wanderers ought they to remain upon the earth, until their countenance be filled with shame." This was rather hard on people who had done, at the moment, nothing worse than to assist in the circumvention of ecclesiastical regu-

lations for the payment of the tithe. "The harps of the
Church," the Pope declared, "were hung on willows," because the priests were deprived of their revenues.

During the first few years of his pontificate, Innocent still
hoped that many Jews would be converted to the Christian
faith, and his failure to achieve any notable results may have
aroused his temper against those who could be neither persuaded nor compelled to come into the fold. In the confusion
of conflicting political, economic and ecclesiastical business,
he never failed to show a paternal interest in the welfare of
Jewish converts. The harvest was not great. In spite of
compulsory attendance at sermons, baptism enforced by varying degrees of compulsion, economic pressure and even threats
of torture and death, very few Jews consented to abandon
their old religion. Those who yielded, whether from genuine
conviction or not, found themselves in a difficult situation,
with no friends, no means of livelihood and very often without
adequate food and clothing. They were so few in number that
no organization existed for looking after them. They became
a burden on the local bishop who was sometimes unsympathetic. So deeply had mistrust been ingrained in Christian
minds that, even after the converts had been cleansed in the
saving water, they were still regarded by many Christians
with suspicion or contempt. But Innocent did his best to
help them. His correspondence contains three references to
converts, one in England and two in France. He wrote
several letters to the Bishop of Autun, severely reprimanding
him for refusing to help a converted Jew and his daughter
who were continually appealing to Rome for money.

He wrote in the same year (December 5, 1199) to a con-
vent at Leicester, on behalf of a man "who rather than to
wallow in the mire of wealth had received the baptismal sacrament at the persuasion of a certain nobleman," and was now
completely destitute. In a letter to Peter of Corbeil, Archbishop of Sens, Innocent tells a more detailed, unfortunately

incomplete, but still extremely interesting story about the third case of a Jewish conversion he had to deal with (June 10, 1213). A French Jew named Isaac, who had gone to Rome with his whole family, had there become converted to the Catholic faith, not indeed by the persuasive arguments of Roman ecclesiastics or by the edifying spectacle of the Roman Court. A special miracle was required, and an account of it is given by the Pope on the authority of the man himself. "We have caused to be added to this document also that which we have heard from him, the substance and the sequence of his story, for it is pleasant to relate the wonders of God":

> Recently a certain Christian woman was living in the home of this man's father and, by Jewish seductions, she was estranged from the Catholic Faith, so that she constantly asserted, while she was under the shadow of the Jewish error, that Christ could not profit or injure her, and that bread taken from any ordinary table is as efficacious as the host of Christ which is taken at the altar. Fearing the punishment she would incur if she were publicly to deny the Christian Faith, she pressed on to the Church along with the other Christians on the Feast of the Resurrection, then at hand, and she received the eucharist, and hid it in her mouth.

The woman then brought the host back to the Jewish house and gave it to the father of Isaac.

So far the story follows the usual tradition. Readers familiar with such stories would naturally expect the host to bleed, and the whole Isaac family to fall on their knees and acknowledge the miracle. But the sequence was not so simple, and indeed is more improbable than most mediaeval tales of this kind.

> [As Isaac was about to put the host] into a certain empty box which he had in the closet, he was called to his door and, fearing lest someone by chance should come into his house, he, unwittingly and on account of his haste, placed it in another box, in which were seven Parisian livres. He

then opened the door to the one who was knocking. When,
hurrying from the door, he returned to the closet and did
not find it [the wafer] in the empty box in which he believed he had placed the said host, he looked into the other
in which he kept the money, and saw it full—not with coins,
but with wafers. Astonished and trembling, he called together his friends and, after telling them the above story as
it happened, he began in their presence to turn over the
wafers with a straw, in order to see the one that had been
somewhat moist when given to him, that he might separate
it from the others, hoping that, after this one had been removed, the coins would turn back to their original nature.
When he was unable to distinguish this one from the others,
the people standing about perceived the greatness of the
divine miracle and decided to become converted to Christianity.

It is interesting to speculate about what really happened during that Easter week in the Isaac household. The ingenious
convert may have invented the whole story; but this is most
unlikely. Among many possible reconstructions of the "crime"
which agree with the available data, the following seems to be
the most probable:

The woman who had become a Jew, wanting to keep her
decision secret, would go to church at Eastertide in order to
prevent local gossip. The neighbors would be furious with her
for associating with Jews. When she was seen returning from
the church, someone spread the rumor that she had stolen a
host and given it to her friends for their magic rites. The
credulous neighbors, jealous perhaps of Isaac's prosperity,
eagerly believed the story, and the arrest of the woman was
imminent. She went to Isaac and told him of her danger. He
knew better than the woman what the consequences of such
an accusation would be. Mere denial would be useless, and
the household might at any moment be massacred by an infuriated mob. So the family sat down to debate how they
could save the woman, and themselves. She, realizing now
her own danger and the peril in which she had innocently in-

volved the Jewish community, may have exclaimed in despair: "Nothing but a miracle can save us." Isaac thereupon replied: "You are right indeed, we must provide a miracle." He then suggested that, as it would be useless to deny the accusation of sacrilege, the best thing to do would be to confuse the issue and forestall the impending trouble by making up a startling story. A man so resourceful as Isaac would have no difficulty in obtaining unconsecrated wafers; they were put into the box in place of the coins; and the rest was easy. He called in the neighbors and showed them how God had punished his Jewish usury by changing his money into wafers.

But the situation of Isaac and his family was still precarious. The woman was safe; and now they were all Christians. The originality and extravagance of his tale would make it at first readily acceptable. But people might soon begin to get suspicious. The Pope was not quite sure whether or not the story was true; something unusual had no doubt happened in the Jewish household, but the affair had brought credit to the city and court of Rome where the conversion of a Jew was almost as rare as a miracle. Isaac and his family must have felt very uncomfortable. They had all been carefully instructed in the Christian faith, and were, no doubt, being carefully watched for any signs of faltering in its practice. They must have been relieved—they had probably asked—to be sent back to France. The Pope, who was paying all their expenses, was glad to get rid of them. He had soon discovered that "a new plant of this kind" had to be strengthened "not alone by the dew of doctrine, but also nourished by temporal benefits," and he told the archbishop to make sure that the converts were "provided with the necessities of life . . . and so not be forced on this account to bother anew the Apostolic Throne." So back they all went to Sens; and the Pope had to pay their passage. What kind of story Isaac told the bewildered archbishop is another interesting speculation. Innocent must have been a little suspicious, for he ends his letter to the archbishop with a hint that he was not quite sure of what had really happened. "After you have found out more of the truth about the above mentioned miracle, write faithfully of it to us."

Because the Jewish people refused to accept Christianity, Innocent regarded them as enemies, not only of religion, but of the social order he was trying to establish. "He was convinced that the Papacy alone could guarantee a richer ethical and religious life to the world, and that it must therefore govern men's lives by means of an organized divine society, the Church." [16] He would have liked to destroy this small group of people so immovably hostile to the ideal of an united world under the spiritual supremacy of the Papacy. But since God, in his incomprehensible mercy, had decreed that this people were not to be completely destroyed, the Pope decided that it was his duty to weaken their power as much as possible. Trade boycott, social ostracism, expulsion from all offices of authority and trust, were the chief economic weapons he was able to use effectively against them. He was determined to disgrace them in the eyes of the world, to make them an object of universal contempt and universal hatred— "to fill their countenance with shame." This policy of degradation was not prompted by any common passion; it was a policy of defense—defense of the Christian world, so difficult to keep united, against a people who refused to enter the Christian commonwealth, and by their refusal seemed to endanger its security.

The Pope's plan was approved in 1215 by the Fourth Lateran Council, over which he presided. Four sessions were devoted to consideration of the Jewish problem. The delegates, over a thousand in number, began with the difficult economic question of usury, and decided, no doubt after much heated discussion, to censure the abuse rather than the practice of moneylending. The Jews were forbidden to extort "heavy and immoderate usury"—a prohibition which applied also to the Christians, although to them the wording of the decree was more lenient. The "princes" were advised "not to be aroused against the Christians because of this, but to try rather to keep the Jews from this practice."

The attitude of the Council was consistently hostile to the Jews. The following three sessions produced a number of humiliating and restrictive orders. Jews were forbidden to walk in public on certain days, especially at Easter. They were not allowed to wear their best clothes on Sundays. Those who "presumptuously blasphemed" (a dangerously comprehensive charge) "were to be duly restrained by the secular rulers." They were to be turned out of all public offices, and the money they had earned in such employment had to be handed over to Christians. The decrees were deliberately worded in order to inflame public opinion. Jews were to be "disgraced" and removed "from offices they had shamefully assumed."

Of all the devices adopted by the Fourth Lateran Council to drive them out of social life and to degrade them in the eyes of the Christian world, none was so effective as the order that they must wear on their clothing a distinctive badge, like lepers or prostitutes. "It is evident," as a French historian has cautiously written, "that the wearing of this badge was not intended to encourage Catholics to seek their company." [17] Jews did not submit to this indignity without a struggle, and for a time it was not everywhere successfully enforced. But the fact that such an order had been issued by an Ecumenical Council was enough to impress upon the public mind the conviction that the Jews were a race of outcasts, branded with the mark of Cain.

The Fourth Lateran Council settled the destiny of the Jewish people for many centuries; they continued to wander over the face of the earth, without rights, except by gracious concession, without a home, and without security; treated at all times, in years of peace and in years of persecution, as if they were beings of an inferior species.

*What, bring you Scripture to confirm your*
    *wrongs?*
*Preach me not out of my possessions.*
*Some Jews are wicked, as all Christians are,*
*But say the tribe that I descended of*
*Were all in general cast away for sin,*
*Shall I be tried for their transgressions?*

CHRISTOPHER MARLOWE,
*The Jew of Malta*

# 4

. . . . . . . . . . . . . . . . . . . . . . . . . . . . . . . . . .

# The Badge of Shame

PRINCES AND PRELATES might perhaps be excused for having paid little attention to papal letters commanding them to refrain from maltreating Jews who were almost invariably described in those same letters as "perfidious, obstinate, ungrateful and insolent" people.

The adjective "perfidious" has been attached to the word "Jew" as a permanent title of ignominy. In the official liturgy of the Church, the faithful were exhorted for hundreds of years (up to 1948) to pray on Good Friday for "the perfidious Jews": *Oremus et pro perfidis Judaeis*. It is true that the word *perfidia* at the time when it was first introduced into the liturgy, meant, in the mind of the Church, "lacking in faith," and that the most nearly correct English equivalent would be "unbelieving." But the word has been used and understood with an offensive meaning, by the clergy and by their congregations for hundreds of years. At the end of the thirteenth century, Christians were sometimes recommended not to pray for the Jews too fervently.[1] It is not surprising, therefore, that the laity refused to kneel when the prayer was recited in the churches, a prayer which, up to 1948, was still said standing.

"When praying for the perfidious Jews," explained the R. P. Constant, O.P., "the faithful do not kneel, as they do for other prayers, because of the perfidious and derisory genuflections with which they [the Jews] insulted the Savior." [2] Père Constant affirmed, moreover, that "the Church always starts from the premise, which she regards as certain, that the Jew, merely as a Jew, is predisposed to treachery," and it is for this reason, he pointed out, that "at the most solemn moment of her liturgy . . . she does not think it possible to implore mercy for the Jews without adding to their name that epithet which justice requires: *Oremus et pro perfidis Judaeis.*" [3]

The use of the word *perfidia* in the liturgy of the Church, its mistranslation with an abusive meaning, could not fail to perpetuate pious hatred in stupid minds. Not only is the word mistranslated, but it has been explained, in an approved book of instruction on the ceremonies of Holy Week, to have a meaning which is contradicted by one of the fundamental facts recorded in the Gospels, the fact that Christ was crucified by Roman soldiers. Dom Prosper Guéranger, in *L'Année liturgique*, began his commentary on the Good Friday prayer with the following words: "The Church has no hesitation in offering up a prayer for the descendants of the executioners of Jesus." [4] And so, in spite of the testimony of St. John the Evangelist, who wrote that the Roman soldiers "did indeed do these things," the faithful continued until 1948 to pray—reluctantly, and refusing to kneel—not for the Italians, but for the perfidious Jews: *Oremus et pro perfidis Judaeis.* [5]

Jews were accused of obstinacy because they refused to be convinced by Christian arguments and were not impressed by mediaeval miracles. They were also told, on the other hand, that God had blinded their eyes and hardened their hearts—operations which should surely have absolved them from any responsibility for failing to respond properly to attempts at their conversion. Some of them may have remembered how, in former times, Christians also had been accused of obstinacy.

"If the Christians persevered in their faith," wrote Pliny to the Roman Emperor, "I order them to be executed; for I did not doubt but that this inflexible obstinacy deserved to be punished." When Innocent II went to Paris, in the year 1135, the Jewish community ventured to present him with a Scroll of the Law (*Torah*) wrapped in a silken veil. The Pope showed much interest in them, and looked at them benevolently; he thanked them, and said that "he hoped God would remove the veil from their hearts." [6] The reaction of the rabbis to this papal greeting has not been recorded. A line from Paul Claudel would have supplied them with an answer in words which were no doubt deep in their hearts: "Mais vous autres qui voyez, qu'est-ce que vous faites donc de la lumière?"

Insolence and ingratitude are defects which were often ascribed by the Romans to their slaves and, in modern times, by the idle rich to their discharged domestic servants. The Jews were told that they were ungrateful, because they did not appreciate the favor of being allowed to live; and they were accused of "insolence" when they did not humbly accept the situation of inferiority to which they were condemned by the Church.

From the wording of some papal decrees and Church councils, it might almost seem as if it had been the object of the Church to foster among the faithful feelings of contempt, and even hatred, for the whole Jewish people. In these documents the Jews are nearly always described as perverse, obstinate and wicked, condemned by God to a life of misery; and ecclesiastical authority sometimes suggested that it was the duty of Christian princes to see that God's sentence was duly carried out. The English bishops at Oxford, in 1222, issued an injunction forbidding Christians, under pain of excommunication, to sell any provisions to the Jews; but the king refused to sanction such a barbarous proposal. Local councils did, however, try to protect them from personal violence. "We emphatically prohibit," said the bishops at Tours, in 1236, "any

Crusader, or other Christian, to dare to kill Jews, or to flog them, or to invade their property, or carry it off, or bring any other kind of injury upon them."

To carry out God's sentence, to make sure that they lived in misery, was, apparently, not enough; some ecclesiastics taught that it was the duty of a good Christian to hate them. Nothing can be more definite than the recommendation of Peter the Venerable, Abbot of Cluny, who told the faithful that it was their duty to hate the Jews, but not to kill them: *Execrandi et odio habendi sunt Judaei, non ut occidantur admoneo.* St. Thomas Aquinas, whose opinion carried more weight than that of the exuberant abbot, affirmed, however, that they "are not to be excluded from divine and natural rights." Yet this concession does not appear to have included the right to be treated as "neighbors"; for Aquinas agreed with the view current at the time, that they must be compelled to live in perpetual servitude, and that Christians were entitled to make use of their property—with the reservation that this use must be moderate, so that they might be permitted to keep what was required for their subsistence.

In the view of the mediaeval age, Jews were allowed a status not much higher than that enjoyed by domestic animals at the present day. They were to be kept in proper subjection, and to achieve this end a moderate amount of severity was permissible; they had, moreover, one privilege not shared by animals; no one had a right to kill them. They ought to be enslaved, but they must not be killed. The principle was clearly expressed by Robert Grosseteste, Bishop of Lincoln (1235–53): "As murderers of the Lord, as still blaspheming Christ, and mocking his Passion, they were to be in captivity to the princes of the earth. As they have the brand of Cain, and are condemned to wander over the face of the earth, so were they to have the privilege of Cain, that no one was to kill them." "The privilege of Cain" did not always protect them from zealots who wanted their money. Innocent III had decreed that those who "blasphemed" were not to get any benefit from the *Constitutio pro Judaeis* No record of murderers and their motives was kept in the Middle Ages, but it is safe to assume that blasphemy was an offense most frequently charged against people who had property worth confiscating.

Although the *Constitutio pro Judaeis* afforded very little protection to the Jewish people, the Papacy was the only court in Europe to which they could apply for help when their condition became desperate, and the fact that they applied so often suggests that their appeals were sometimes successful.

When the subjects of St. Louis began to kill Jews, Gregory the Ninth wrote letters of protest to the king and to the French hierarchy. Crusaders were testing their swords in the usual way before setting out to fight the battles of the Lord in the Holy Land. The survivors appealed to the Pope. Gregory was shocked at the terrible news. The Crusaders had gone far beyond the limits of oppression which had been set by Innocent the Third. They were attempting "to wipe out the Jews almost completely off the face of the earth. In an unheard of and unprecedented outburst of cruelty, they have slaughtered, in this mad hostility, two thousand five hundred of them—old and young, as well as pregnant women. Some were mortally wounded, and others trampled like mud under the feet of horses." [7] Gregory was not deceived by the pretext of piety used to cover these atrocities. He made it clear to the bishops that this behavior could not be attributed to a religious motive. "After foully and shamefully treating those who remained alive after the massacre, they carried off their goods and consumed them." Among these gangsters there were no doubt many genuine fanatics who really believed that by massacring Jews they were acting in accordance with the mind of the Church. They had been told that these people must be allowed to live because some of them might be eventually converted to Christianity; and they assumed therefore that all who obstinately refused baptism might be religiously and lawfully put to death. Such was the pretext used on this occasion by the French Crusaders. "In order that they may be able to hide such an inhuman crime under the cover of virtue, and in some way justify their unholy cause, they represent themselves as having done the above, and they threaten to do even worse, on the ground that they, the Jews, refuse to be baptized."

The Pope forwarded a copy of his letter to St. Louis, adding a strong recommendation that the offenders should be severely punished for crimes "so unspeakably offensive to God." But when Jews were in trouble, St. Louis was unsympathetic, unless he saw some chance of converting them. He used to serve the Christian poor with food at his own royal table, and he exercised the virtue of humility by washing the feet of Christian lepers. But he told his people that instead of arguing with a Jew, they should stick their swords into his belly right up to the hilt: "And so I say to you," said the king, "that no one, unless he be a very good clerk, should argue with them: but the layman, when he heareth the Christian law reviled, should not defend it but by his sword, wherewith he should pierce the belly of the reviler as far as it will go." The phrase "when he heareth the Christian law reviled (*quand il ouit medire de la loi chretienne*)" would be applied to any statement denying the truth of a Christian doctrine. The real significance of the episode is that St. Louis did not approve of ignorant laymen taking part in religious discussions. His suggestion that knights should silence criticism with the sword is in accordance with the dialectical practice of mediaeval chivalry.

Joinville described at some length the scene which prompted St. Louis to make his well-known recommendation. Two Jewish rabbis had been invited to a monastery to take part in a religious discussion. The arguments they used aroused the anger of a pugnacious knight who proceeded to hit them over the head with a club and drive them from the building. The unfortunate rabbis were not in a position to reply, or they might have quoted against the knight, and against St. Louis, a passage from the works of a contemporary writer, Judah Al Harizi (1165–1225); his *Sefer Tahkemoni* includes a "Discussion between the Sword and the Pen," wherein, after several pages of bragging by the Sword, the Pen has the last word:

> I keep silence; but when I review my armies I send fear into the men of pride.
> My discourses adorn the heads of kings, and my excellent words rejoice the hearts.
> Is it not through me that the earth is founded on righteousness, and no injustice is in my deeds and works?
> Through me the Rock has inscribed the Ten Commandments, and on Mount Horeb gave them to my hosts.
> When the sword arises overwhelmingly, I raise my standard above its head.
> When it comes with pride to join battle with me, I stand erect, and it falls at my feet.

No notice was taken of the Pope's command that the Crusaders were to restore to the Jews all the property that had been stolen. A few years later, in 1253, the king attempted to drive all Jews out of France—a plan prompted by a curious kind of piety. "For it had been hinted to that king by the Saracens," wrote Matthew Paris, "that we have little love or veneration for our Lord Jesus Christ who suffer his murderers to remain amongst us." St. Louis ignored the advice of a few wise councilors who tried in vain to make him understand that the lending of money at interest was an economic necessity without which neither industry nor agriculture could prosper.[8] He was, however, supported in his idealistic campaign against moneylending by many of his subjects who were far from being idealists—by the nobles who wanted to get rid of their liabilities, by traders who were afraid of Jewish competition, and by the Christian usurers. And so it happened, concluded Matthew Paris, "the Caursins eagerly took possession of the places and the offices of the exiled Jews." These Italian money traders had at Cahors a banking institution which they made the center of their financial operations in France, in England, and in Germany. The inhabitants of Cahors also joined in the business, and Dante put them in Hell alongside the sodomists.[9]

Moneylending in the Middle Ages was a complicated business, and the high rates of interest—sometimes 50 to 80 per cent—should not be compared to the rates charged by modern bankers. The rate was fixed by royal edict. Kings and princes took a large share of the profits of Jewish lenders, who were legally the king's personal property, and often confiscated their capital. Owing to the ecclesiastical prohibition, Christian moneylenders ran equally great risks; they had to operate in a black market, and they became notorious for their harsh practices. A mediaeval chronicler, Geoffrey of Paris, admitted that the exiled Jews when compared with their Christian rivals in business, had been pleasant and easy to deal with:

> For Jews were mild and debonair
> Much more in handling such affair
> Than now the Christians are.

A curious mixture of business and religion is recorded in the story of a pious usurer who introduced into the Lord's Prayer an interpolation of his own, in order to obtain relief from Jewish competition: "Forgive us our trespasses, as we forgive them that trespass against us—these accursed Jews have plotted to ruin us by lending to our customers at a lower rate than we do. Dear God, remember that they crucified you, and curse them."[10]

In England, also, people complained when they were left, after 1290, at the mercy of the rapacious Christian moneylenders. "They are worse than the Jews," wrote Thomas Wilson, "for go whither you will throughout Christendom, and deal

with them [the Jews], and you shall have for ten under the
hundred, yea sometimes for six at their hands, whereas English
usurers exceed all God's mercy, and will take they care not
how much." [11]  Bishop Grosseteste, who was no friend of the
Jews, on his death bed warned the faithful "to shun the Christian usurers because they were all without mercy, and to resort
to Jewish ones instead." [12]

The comprehensive charge of unconscionable usury often
brought against the Jews of the Middle Ages, and sometimes
against the Christians, is based on ignorance of the economic
world in which they lived. In the business of moneylending
the State acted as the profiteering partner. The rate of interest
was fixed by government decree, but the rate of taxation on
moneylending profits was arbitrary, and it might—and often
did—amount to confiscation of both interest and capital.
"There is not a Banker in London, or an underwriter at
Lloyds," wrote Thomas Witherby in 1804, "who would be
content to run such risks as the Jews did, at a less premium." [13]

The popular belief that moneylending in the Middle Ages
was a business conducted only by Jewish profiteers who
prospered by plundering honest hardworking Christians is one
of the favorite doctrines of modern anti-Semitic literature.
At no period in mediaeval history did they have a monopoly,
for any length of time, in the traffic in money. "The part
played by the Jews in the credit system of the Middle Ages,"
wrote H. Pirenne, "has certainly been exaggerated, and, compared with the efflorescence and ubiquity of Italian credit,
appears a very small affair." [14]  At the end of the thirteenth
century the money markets of Europe were controlled by
Christian merchants. The testimony of Matthew Paris shows
that Christian usurers in England were as rapacious as any Jew
had ever been:

> In these days [1235] the abominable plague of Caursins
> raged so fiercely that there was scarcely any man in all Eng-
> land, especially among the prelates, who was not entangled

in their nets. The King himself also was in debt to them for an incalculable amount. They circumvented the indigent in their necessities, cloaking their usury under the pretence of trade. . . . That same year, Roger, Bishop of London, a learned and reliable man, when he saw how these Caursins practised their usury, publicly and unabashed, and led a most unclean life, and harried religious folk with divers injustices, cunningly amassing money, and compelling many folk under their yoke, he was moved to wrath.

But the anathemas of the Bishop were treated by the Caursins "with mockery, derision, and threats"; they appealed, successfully, to the Court of Rome, and the Bishop "was cited to Rome for the injury done to the Pope's merchants."

Matthew Paris also recorded the complaint of Bishop Grosseteste about papal support of Christian usurers who were driving the Jews out of business. "Now the Lord Pope's merchants or moneychangers practise their usury publicly in London, to the disgust of the Jews. They plot divers and grievous machination against men of Holy Church, and especially Religious, compelling men under pressure of penury, to lie and append their signature to false deeds." All sorts of dishonest devices were adopted to avoid a formal indictment of usury. Thus, if a borrower wished for a loan of one hundred marks, he was compelled to sign a bond for one hundred pounds, and even if he wished to repay the money after a short interval, the lender still insisted upon being paid, not a hundred marks, but a hundred pounds. "This is worse," says the chronicler, "than the Jew's conditions; for the Jew will still receive the principal courteously whensoever thou shalt return it, with only such interest as is proportionate to the time for which thou hast it in hand."

The Italians dominated English finance in a comparatively short time because they were able to combine moneylending with commerce. They did not suffer from restrictions which confined their activities to traffic in money alone. They came to England, moreover, with the prestige of agents for the

Papacy, and were charged with the collection of Peter's
Pence and other taxes due to the Holy See. From these sources
they could command a considerable amount of ready money.
In 1228, several Florentine families were settled in London as
bankers to Henry III, and twenty years later had become
wealthy enough to arouse the jealousy of the English. "These
transalpine usurers," wrote Matthew Paris, "were so multi-
plied, and became so rich, that they built noble palaces for
themselves at London, and determined to take up a permanent
abode there, like the native-born citizens."

The prelates dared not complain too much, because the
Caursins were agents of the Pope's; nor did the citizens venture
to express their discontent, because "these men were protected
by the favor of certain nobles whose money," as was reported,
"they put out to amass interest after the fashion of the
Roman Court." Some of them, however, were brought to
trial, charged "with polluting the Kingdom of England with
their base trade of usury," and committed to prison. These
proceedings were watched by the Jews with much rejoicing,
because, as Matthew Paris said, "they now had participators
in their state of slavery." But the Italians, after payment of a
large sum of money, were released, and were able to continue
their traffic undisturbed.

Now that the services of the Jews were no longer essential
to the business of the country, they were no longer afforded
even a pretense of protection. Hounded on all sides by both
church and state, the Jewish community in England during the
second half of the thirteenth century was gradually reduced
to such a condition of impoverishment that at times even
Christian hearts were moved to sympathy with their sufferings.
Matthew Paris, who like most of his contemporaries believed
that it was the will of God that these people should live in a
perpetual state of miserable slavery, showed some sign of pity
for their fate. Entries from his *Chronicle* for the years 1252–
1256 show that the king was determined to make it impossible

for them to live in England, and at the same time unwilling to allow them to leave the country; his policy was the policy of Hitler in 1935.

In 1252:

> The King extorted from the Jews whatever visible property those wretched people possessed, not only, as it were, skinning them merely, but also plucking out their entrails. Thus this dropsical thirster after gold cheated Christians as well as Jews out of their money, food, jewels, with such greediness that it seemed as if a new Crassus had arisen from the dead.

The Jews were now so poor that the King began to squeeze the Christian citizens of London, and to treat them "as if they were of the lowest order of slaves; indeed they seemed to be considered in the same light as, or perhaps of a little less consequence than that servile race, the Jews."

In 1254: "The King vented his fury against the wretched rabble of Jews to such a degree that they hated their lives." In reply to a further demand for a large sum of money to be paid "under penalty of imprisonment and ignominious death," they replied by asking permission to leave the country. "How can the King," they said "love us or spare us who destroys his natural English subjects? He has Papal merchants who amass endless heaps of money. Let the King depend on them . . . they it is who have destroyed and impoverished us." But the request was refused because the Jews had nowhere to go. "Whither could you fly, wretched beings? The French King hates you and persecutes you, and has condemned you to perpetual banishment." "And thus," concludes Matthew, "the small remnant of their small substance, which if left would only afford them a meagre subsistence, was extorted from them by force."

But the King, whose policy of economic extermination was backed up by the local clergy, gave a last turn to the screw in the following year. In 1255: "When Lent drew near the

King with great urgency demanded from the oft impoverished Jews the immediate payment of eight thousand marks, on pain of being hung in case of non-payment." They again asked to be allowed to leave the country: "No hope remains to us of breathing freely, the Pope's usurers have supplanted us: therefore permit us to depart and we will seek another abode somewhere or other." They had no hope of being allowed to return to their own country. The gates of Palestine were more effectively closed to them in the thirteenth century, and for long after, than they were during Hitler's reign of terror and after, until the termination of the British mandate. A few did, in fact, succeed from time to time in getting back, but they were always regarded as "illegal immigrants."

In England they were literally the king's chattels; they were not allowed to move anywhere without his permission. Now they had been squeezed almost to the last drop. The king, therefore, sold them to his brother, Earl Richard, in order that "he might disembowel those whom the King had skinned." The earl could get nothing more out of them. He spared them, says Matthew Paris, "out of consideration for the diminution of their power, and their ignominious poverty." A generation later, in 1290, when Edward I expelled them all from England, they had long been reduced to a condition of almost complete destitution.

Italians, citizens of Rome or Florence, who came to England in the thirteenth century to seek their fortunes, were not given an encouraging welcome by the people, although they were befriended by the kings who were always in need of money. They were hated by the English churchmen, but they were not blamed for the guilt of their ancestors, the Roman soldiers who had nailed Christ to the cross. The extortionate practices of Italian usurers were naturally associated in the minds of the people, and of some of the clergy, with the increasing financial exactions of the Papacy. It is not improbable that Italian usury may have sown the seed of that hostility of the English

Church to Italian ecclesiastical authority which finally led to the breach with Rome. Before the end of the century, the Italian financiers were firmly established in England. The Frescobaldi, a powerful Florentine family of merchants and moneylenders, had a branch of their business in London, and lent large sums of money to Edward I.

This achievement was not accomplished without a considerable effort. How these Italians set about their "conquest" of England is told by a member of the firm, Giovanni Frescobaldi, who summarized his business experience, for the benefit of his fellow countrymen, in a sonnet:

Advice to those passing into England:
Clothe yourself in dingy colors, be humble,
Stupid in appearance, subtle in fact;
May evil come to the Englishman if he molest you.
Fly from trouble and warlike people;
Spend freely, and do not appear mean;
Pay on the appointed date, be courteous in collecting debts,
Showing that necessity compels you.
Do not ask unnecessary questions;
Buy whenever you see it is profitable;
Keep clear of men from the Court.
Observe who is in power.
You will be well advised to unite with your fellow-country-
   men
And see your door is well bolted early.[15]

If this sonnet had been written by a Jew it might have been given a more prominent place in English historical textbooks, with appropriate remarks about Jewish skill and duplicity in money matters, and with perhaps a note about the habit which Jews have of conspiring together to defraud the simple-minded Englishman. Most writers who condemn Jews for their sordid interest in money, have, as a rule, very little to say about the Italian moneylenders, whose business one student of mediaeval finance has described as an inspiring and ennobling vocation: "The energy, skill, and enterprise," he wrote, "which made the Italians the bankers of Europe, were only another phase of the vigorous life which brought forth the chastened passion of *La Vita Nuova*, and the fierce denunciations and sombre imaginings of the *Inferno*." [16]

The notion that Jews have a special aptitude for the non-productive traffic of moneylending, and that they are by nature more rapacious than men of other cultures, derives from a prejudice which has been strengthened in England, not only by the bias of individual historians, but by the unkind commentary of English literature, from Shakespeare to Dickens. The people of Israel, who were tillers of the soil when England was a land of swamps and forests, appeared to Goldwin Smith as a contemptible rabble who, behind the noble scene of Christian valor and high purpose, "were patiently plying their tribal trade of finance." [17]

Jews in the Middle Ages often got the better of their neighbors by methods which were usurious or dishonest, but there is no record of their obtaining money from Christians by resorting to physical violence and torture. In the original legend from which Shakespeare took the story of Shylock, the villain of the piece who insisted on his pound of flesh was not a Jew, but a Christian. People who lent money, even at usurious rates, were surely better citizens than men who enriched themselves by torturing their victims until they surrendered all their wealth. This easy method of making money, authorized, and indeed employed sometimes, by civil and even by ecclesiastical authorities, become popular for many centuries. "It was always by threats and by torture," writes Mario Esposito, "that confessions were obtained to justify the persecution and spoliation of the Jews." [18]

Gregory was moved to another protest by the shocking accounts he had received about the brutality of some French Christians who, taking advantage of the king's religious aversion to the Jews, were extracting money from them by torture. In a letter to the archbishops and bishops of France (April 6,

1233), he used the word *perfidia* in its original meaning—"lacking in faith"—and he suggested that this lack of faith should not be regarded as a complete barrier to social contacts. He laid down the moral law against murder in words which his correspondents could not fail to understand:

> Although the perfidy of the Jews is to be condemned, nevertheless their relation with Christians is useful and, in a way, necessary; for they bear the image of our Savior and were created by the Creator of all mankind. They are therefore not to be destroyed, God forbid, by His own creatures, especially by believers in Christ . . . for their fathers were made friends of God, and also their remnant shall be saved . . .

Some Frenchmen thought that since the Jews had been sentenced by God, a sentence confirmed by many papal decrees, to live in misery, there could be no harm in reducing them to penury by extracting from them money by torture. The Pope, of course, did not approve of this reasoning. He had been informed that "Certain Christians of the French kingdom . . . persecute and afflict the Jews . . . torture them by intolerable tortures of the body . . . certain ones of these Lords rage among the Jews with such cruelty . . . they tear their finger nails and extract their teeth, and inflict upon them other kinds of inhuman torments." [19] Gregory patiently explained that these practices were wicked. He concluded by giving the bishops a piece of sensible advice: "Such kindness must be shown to Jews by Christians, as we hope might be shown to Christians who live in pagan lands." This type of exhortation seldom produced any result.

The Popes, as a rule, took no vigorous prophylactic measures to forestall persecution. The mildness of papal letters prohibiting ill-treatment of Jews should be compared with the vigor of their language when complaining about Jewish misdemeanors. Gregory's protest against the Christian practice of tearing the finger nails and extracting the teeth of Jews ends with a recommendation that the bishops are to "warn all faithful Christians, and induce them, not to harm the Jews in their persons, not to dare to rob them of their property, nor for the sake of plunder to drive them from their lands." On the same day, April 6, 1233, the Pope wrote to the same archbishops and bishops, complaining that the Jews were guilty of their usual enormities, engaging Christian nurses, and so on. But he did not suggest that his correspondents should "induce" the Jews to behave properly. The Pope commanded, in vigorous language that "these excesses must be completely suppressed; and in order they [the Jews] should not again dare to straighten their neck bent under the yoke of slavery . . . you may call in for this purpose the secular arm."

Gregory continued to warn the faithful, that, although Jews were not to be tortured or grievously ill-treated, they must be compelled to live in a state of misery so that they might be witnesses to the true faith. He reaffirmed this principle in a letter written a month later, on May 18, to the Archbishop of Compostella. The Jews in Spain were living at this time in comparative security and, what was worse, in comfort, a state of affairs which could not be tolerated. Jews who lived in comfort had no propaganda value. "Since their own sin consigned them to eternal slavery," the Pope begins, "the Jews ought to acknowledge as just the misery of their condition, and ought to live without troubling those who accept and tolerate them out of kindness alone." In Spain, he continues, "they have become so insolent, that they are not afraid to commit excesses which it would be not only improper but even inhuman for the faithful of Christ to tolerate." The reader might expect to hear that they had been guilty of tearing off the nails and extracting the teeth of Christians. But the "excesses" of which the Pope complains were hardly of so barbarous a character. The Jews refused to wear the badge of shame; they had the impertinence to occupy public offices; and they even went to the length of employing Christian nurses for their children. They also, the Pope adds, almost as an afterthought, "extort usury and do other unspeakable things against the Catholic faith."

The style of these letters suggests that they were routine documents which were sent out from time to time by a papal secretary whenever the Pope thought that the state of Christendom called for a more strict supervision of the perfidious race. The repetitions of warnings against the employment of Christian nurses may perhaps be due to some particular scandal or scandals, which once they had found a place in a papal letter would be constantly referred to as if they had happened quite recently. The story of the milk poured into latrines was brought up against "the Jews" by Gregory XIII in the last quarter of the sixteenth century. It is worth noting that, although this curious accusation was so often repeated, no reference was ever given to the time when, or to the place where, the offense was committed. Nor was any individual named as an offender.

Gregory had good reasons for not putting usury into the forefront of Jewish offenses; he knew that the Jews no longer monopolized the forbidden traffic, and he himself sometimes borrowed money from them.[20] Everybody knew how to get round the ecclesiastical laws. The Church was fighting a battle which had been fought long ago, in the same way, and lost for the same reasons, by the Synagogue. In spite of the efforts made by the rabbis to compel their people to obey the Mosaic Law against taking interest on loans, Hebrew jurists, as appears plainly in the Talmud, had found legal ways of getting round it.[21]

The Pope continued to write to Christian princes warning them against the iniquity of allowing the Jews in their dominions to lead normal lives. In a repetition of the letter sent to the King of France, he exhorted the King of Castille to repress their "insolence," so that "they shall not dare to straighten their necks bent under the Christian yoke of perpetual slavery . . . so that the perfidious Jews shall never in the future grow insolent, but that in servile fear they shall ever publicly suffer the shame of their sin." He wrote at the same time to the archbishops and bishops of Germany, complaining that the Jews were not living in that state of complete misery to which they had been condemned by God. Some of them had been allowed to take part in the administrative life of the country; they refused to wear the badge, and some even had Christian slaves. They were behaving with their usual insolence: "Ungrateful for favors and forgetful of benefits, they return insult for kindness and a reward of impious contempt for goodness, they, who out of mercy only, are admitted into intimacy with us and who ought to know the yoke of perpetual enslavement because of their guilt." Moreover, good relations between Jews and Christians in Germany had sometimes led to religious complications. "Some Christians," the Pope complains, "had, of their own free will, turned Jew." He ends his letter with a prohibition against holding disputations with Jews about religion, "lest the simple-minded slide into a snare of error." [22]

This fear of the possible consequences of religious discussion between Christians and Jews was one of the principal reasons why the Popes tried to keep them apart. In general culture and in knowledge of the Bible, the average Jew in the Middle Ages was far superior to the average Christian who, as a rule, was not even well instructed in his own religion. To isolate the Jews, to keep them away as much as possible from all social contact with the Christian world, was supposed to be a measure necessary for the safety of Christian souls. This was why the Council of Paris, in 1223, forbade Christians to serve in Jewish households: "Lest through the superficial plausibility of their law, which they wickedly pretend to explain, they may lead into the pit of disbelief the Christian servants who dwell with them."

When Jews began to emigrate in considerable numbers to

Eastern Europe, in order to escape the attentions of Crusaders and the oppressive legislation of the Church, they found shelter, and for a short time peace, in Poland. But there was no escape from the shadow of the Fourth Lateran Council. Although the civil powers in Poland were prepared, for economic considerations, to accord these immigrants elementary rights of citizenship, the ecclesiastical authorities were determined to exclude them, like lepers, from all contact with Christian society. In 1266, the Council of Breslau decreed that they were not to be allowed to live side by side with Christians, on the pretext that the Christian population "might fall an easy prey to the influence of the superstitious and evil habits of the Jews living amongst them." [23] The council, moreover, applied to them all the restrictions and impositions which Innocent III had devised for their degradation. The Council of Vienna, in 1267, confirmed this policy, thus urging still further "that most dangerous plan of persecution, the total separation of the Jews from the society, and consequently from the sympathy of their fellow-men." [24] The decrees of the Fourth Lateran Council led logically and inevitably to complete segregation in the ghetto.

In 1239, a new pretext was discovered to inflame public opinion against the Jews and to widen the breach between them and their Christian neighbors. A converted Jew, Nicholas Donin, drew up and sent to Gregory a formal accusation against the Talmud, a collection of religious maxims and laws more than a thousand years old. Heine described it as "the Catholicism of the Jews—a Gothic cathedral, which, although overloaded with childlike and grotesque ornament, yet amazes with its heaven-soaring giant splendor." The Pope seems to have known very little about it, and indeed, judging from the tone of his letter on the subject, he had only just heard of its existence. He wrote to the French bishops warning them that the Jews "were now following a new book, called the Talmud, which is full of blasphemy, abusive and unspeakable." And he commanded that all Jewish books should be handed over for examination to "our dear sons the Dominican and Franciscan friars." Similar orders were sent to England, Spain and Portugal, but no one took any action except the King of France. Twenty-four cartloads of Hebrew books were burnt.[25] This was the beginning of a war on Jewish literature which continued for many centuries. The Dominicans led a final and unsuccessful assault in the sixteenth century, in collaboration with an almost illiterate Jewish convert, Johann Pfefferkorn, who, in the opinion of Erasmus, did not achieve any spiritual benefit from changing his religion: "*Ex scelerato Iudaeo, sceleratissimus Christianus.*"

Although the friars were not able to destroy the Talmud, they succeeded in creating a prejudice against it which is still active. The misrepresentations of its texts and teaching, first circulated in the thirteenth century, have endured until the present day, and may still sometimes be found in historical textbooks used in seminaries and schools. Modern Catholic censorship, which watches over faith and morals, does not, unfortunately, often take any cognizance of lies, however blatant and absurd, which affect the reputation or the welfare of people who do not belong to the Church. "The Talmud," R. F. Rohrbacher was allowed to write in the middle of the nineteenth century, "not only permits the Jew, but recommends, nay commands him to cheat and to kill a Christian whenever he can get the opportunity. *This is a fact beyond doubt,* which deserves the attention of nations and kings." [26] A French student of thirteenth-century history maintained, in 1880, that the attempt to destroy the Talmud was a measure of self-defense. "The Church was guilty only of trying to defend herself, and the Jews were properly reminded that, although the Christians tolerated their presence, they would not submit to their insolence." [27]

Papal decrees of the thirteenth century clearly indicate the

Church's determination to isolate the Jewish community, intellectually and socially, from all contact with the Christian world. The attack on the Talmud was part of the plan, not only to isolate them, but to disintegrate and degrade them. It provided a pretext for interfering in their private life and in the practice of their religion. This policy of petty persecution and oppression (*non graviter*), would, it was hoped, "soften up" Jewish resistance to conversion; if the life of a Jew was made too uncomfortable, he would, in course of time, decide to accept Christianity.

Jews were protected from personal violence, not by their divine and natural rights as human beings, but by theological arguments and distinctions which afforded them little security in a cruel and credulous world. Their exclusion from the common law of humanity was, indeed, explicitly affirmed in 1268, by the Jewry-law of Brünn, where it was written: "The Jews are deprived of their natural rights and condemned to eternal misery for their sins." Yet they could not have been admitted without difficulty into the mediaeval pattern of society, even if the Papacy had been willing to make the attempt. "The feudal authorities drove them from the land, and the burghers from trade and handicrafts. Thus the normal incorporation of the Jew within the community was made impossible." [28] Into the Christian community of the Middle Ages there was no admission except through baptism, a sacrament deemed necessary for salvation in this world as well as in the next. For if a man was not baptized, he was not accepted in society as a complete human being; he was excluded from the brotherhood of man. The second great commandment of the Jewish Law, which Christ had taught to his disciples—"Thou shalt love thy neighbor as thyself"—did not, therefore, apply to Jews. They were not regarded as neighbors. On the contrary—they were hated, said a medieval versifier, both by God and man:

Many hate them, and I hate them too;
God hates them, just as I do;
And by the whole world they must be hated.[29]

Within a single generation the plan of Innocent III had been successfully carried out. The Jews were excluded from all social life, and they lived as outcasts in the misery to which they were supposed to have been condemned by God. "However unhappy they are," wrote Matthew Paris, "no one finds them worthy of pity." [30] This was the tragedy of the Jewish people, deplored nearly a thousand years ago by Jehuda Halevi, one of the greatest religious poets of the Middle Ages, or indeed of all times:

The banner of brotherhood is removed from me
And the foot of pride is yoke and band upon me;
And I am chastened with cruel castigation,
Exiled and prisoned, vexed and thrust away;
Without marshal or chief, without king or prince,
While the foe turneth towards me, and my Rock turneth
    away.

In the unity of a Catholic society the Jews could be given no place; yet, by excluding them from all social contact with Christians, the Church may have lost in the long run far more than she has ever gained. The policy of degradation, recommended by Innocent III and adopted by the Fourth Lateran Council, could not be effectively carried out, as in fact it was, without lowering the level of Christian morality. Although Gregory IX endeavored to protect the Jews from personal outrage, his public pronouncements did little to discourage in Christian minds a disposition to regard them with contempt, and with that hatred which was destined to have so terrible a history.

FRIAR BARNADINE.   . . . *then go with me, and help me to ex-*
                   *claim against the Jew.*
FRIAR JACOMO.      *Why, what hath he done?*
FRIAR BARNADINE.   *A thing that makes me tremble to unfold.*
FRIAR JACOMO.      *What, has he crucified a child?*

CHRISTOPHER MARLOWE, *The Jew of Malta*

# 5

................................

# The Murderous Lie

AT THE BEGINNING OF HIS PONTIFICATE, Innocent IV treated
the Jews with the contempt his predecessor had shown. He
referred to them as slaves, insolent and perfidious, who refused
to accept meekly the condition of servitude to which God had
condemned them for their sins. In his letter to the King of
France, May 9th, 1244, he complained that, in addition to their
unseemly arrogance, they had been guilty of "unspeakable
crimes":

> The wicked perfidy of the Jews, from whose hearts our
> Redeemer had not removed the veil of blindness . . . ,
> does not heed, as it should, the fact that Christian piety re-
> ceived them and patiently allows them to live among us
> through pity only. Instead, their perfidy commits such
> enormities as are stupefying to those who hear of them,
> and horrible to those who tell them.

All this is merely a repetition, in the exaggerated style of the
period, of the complaints previously made by Gregory IX.
"The unspeakable crimes" are not precisely defined; they were
apparently so dreadful that they could not be revealed in detail lest they sully the pure minds of the faithful. And this
indeed may have been the real reason for making such a mystery of the chief accusation to which the Pope's letter refers.
The Jews were still employing Christian nurses for their chil-

dren and were committing with these nurses "many shameful actions." There may have been scandalous goings on in some Jewish households—"enormities" between a Jewish man and a Christian woman of a kind in which the guilt cannot often be justly restricted to one of the parties concerned. They were also accused of neglecting the truths of their own religion by "despising the law of Moses and following some tradition of their elders." This charge followed from the action of some Jewish sectarians, who claimed that the teaching of the cabala (tradition) represented orthodox Judaism. Their mystical doctrines included belief in the transmigration of souls. The cabala, according to Graetz, was "a false doctrine which, although new, styled itself a primitive inspiration; although un-Jewish, called itself a genuine teaching of Israel." Papal intervention in these disputes was justified by the foolishness of Solomon of Montpellier, a Jew who had imprudently appealed to the Dominicans for help in combating the doctrine of Maimonides.

The Pope ordered that Jews were to be prevented from committing these enormities. The employment of Christian servants by Jews was to be severely punished. Copies of the Talmud must be confiscated and burned. Jews must be kept in their proper place and compelled to "recognize themselves as slaves of those [the Christians] whom Christ set free, while condemning them [the Jews] to slavery." Bible texts from Genesis (XXI:10) through St. Paul (Galatians IV:30,[1]) which often recur in papal bulls during the Middle Ages to justify social and economic discrimination against the Jewish people, were accepted by the clergy and the faithful, and no doubt by the staff of the papal secretariat, as a sufficient proof that they were indeed a race of outcasts.

In 1245, the Pope was forced to leave Rome, as a result of his political conflict with the emperor, and take up his residence at Lyons. From that date, his attitude towards the French Jews became not only less hostile, but even friendly.

Some people at the time, and since, concluded that he had been bribed. This judgment, which is not based on any evidence, seems to depend on the assumption that no one could be favorably impressed by meeting Jews and therefore, when anyone tried to be fair to them, bribery is the most likely explanation. Innocent was not the only friend they had at the papal court. "The Jews," wrote Father Mortier, a Dominican historian, "bought with gold the conscience of an archbishop. . . . In place of arguments they had a power superior to the most rigorous logical distinctions: gold. They distributed it in handfuls."[2] The price paid for the archbishop's conscience is unfortunately not mentioned. No proof is provided by Father Mortier that such transactions as he refers to ever took place, but, if they did, then surely the sale of an archiepiscopal conscience is more discreditable to the seller than to the purchaser.

On August 12, 1247, the Pope wrote to the King of France (St. Louis) a letter about the Talmud which was very different in tone from the one he had written two years earlier from Rome. "We do not want," he said, "to deprive the Jews of their books, if as a result, we should be depriving them of their Law," and he ordered Éudes de Châteauroux, the papal legate, to examine these books and report on them. The legate disapproved of the Pope's moderation; he even hinted that Innocent had been suborned. He wrote:

> Lest anyone be fooled in this affair by shrewdness and falsehoods of the Jews, let your Holiness know that at the time of the Holy Pope Gregory, a certain convert by the name of Nicholas [Donin] related to the said Pope that the Jews, not satisfied with the ancient Law which God had transmitted in writing through Moses, and even completely ignoring it, assert that a different Law, which is called Talmud . . . had been given by God.

The legate pointed out that "it would be disgraceful and a cause of shame for the Apostolic Throne if the books so

solemnly and so justly burned in the presence of all the scholars and of the clergy and of the population of Paris, were to
be given back to the masters of the Jews at the order of the
Pope, for such tolerance would seem to mean approval."
After this indignant preamble, the legate quoted all sorts of
theological and ecclesiastical "authority," and finally consented
to examine the books he had already decided to condemn: "I
have asked the Jewish masters to show me the Talmud, and
all their other books; and they have exhibited to me five most
vile volumes which I shall have carefully examined in accordance with your command."

In all his attempts to protect the Jews, Innocent was
thwarted by his officials. It is not surprising that his struggle
against bigotry and stupidity was seldom successful. His first
letter to the French king, about "stupefying enormities" such
as the employment of Christian nurses and the reading of the
Talmud, was perhaps not meant to be taken too seriously; it
may have been composed by a member of the papal secretariat
who had been trained by Gregory IX. The Pope's other
letters, written on more serious topics, are free from such
ridiculous exaggeration. Phrases such as "insolent perfidy,"
"veil of blindness," "condemned to slavery" and so on,
had become as formal, and perhaps as meaningless, as the
corresponding complimentary terms used by the Pope to
"Our venerable brother the Bishop," or to "Our dear son
the King."

The letters written by Innocent IV from Lyons to the King
of Navarre about his Jewish subjects are remarkable documents
of which historians have taken very little notice, although a
French scholar, F. Bourquelot, observed in 1865 that the bulls
of Innocent IV "were inspired by a sentiment of justice and
tolerance remarkable at any time but especially so in the
thirteenth century." These letters contain no expressions of
contempt, no reference to ungrateful slaves, no hint that Jews
may be oppressed provided they are not oppressed too much.

On the contrary, the Pope suggests that merely to refrain from oppression is not enough:

> It is fitting that the Christian faith afford the Jews protection due to them against their persecutors. . . . Know therefore what we have heard from certain Jews of the Kingdom of Navarre who have praised your Royal Highness. They said that you showed yourself kind and benign, and that you treat them humanely, and mercifully take care of them, and cause them to be taken care of by others. All this redounds to your honor and glory.

The Pope implicitly condemns the old tradition of hate, with the word of his supreme spiritual authority, and with a note of tenderness in his words which is seldom noticeable in the letters of Innocent III and Gregory IX: "Wherefore in the name of the reverence due to the Apostolic Throne, and to ourselves, we ask and urgently warn your Royal Serenity to guard them, their children and their property, as you have by your favor guarded them until now."

Innocent had been informed that the ruling of his predecessors against forcible baptism had not always been obeyed, and he begged the king to do all in his power "to prevent any violence being committed against Jews in the matter of baptizing their children, for this should be a voluntary offering, not a forced one." He also urged the king to defend Jews from Christian avarice. These letters will surprise readers who have been brought up on history books where Jews never appear except as greedy usurers who ruined all the countries where they were graciously allowed to live. But the Pope, who had made his own inquiries, knew what was going on, and had been going on for a long time, all over Christendom. The procedure, practised by Christian gangsters, which would now be termed "a racket," was facilitated by the anomalous state of the ecclesiastical laws about moneylending. In the middle of the thirteenth century, the Church's prohibition against loans at interest was seldom observed by anybody. But it drove people who wanted capital into a black market, where money could be got, not only from Jews, but also—although usually at a higher rate—from Christians. The rate of interest was always high, judged by modern practice, but so was the risk; and the productive value of capital was probably greater than at the present time.

The racketeers condemned by the Pope were not interested in the productive capacity of money, or in the rates charged for its use. They used to borrow money from a Jew, and when the loan fell due they appealed to the civil or to the ecclesiastical authorities on the grounds that the transaction was illegal and the rate charged unduly exorbitant. If the appeal failed, they would then circulate "smear stories," organize riots and perhaps stage a ritual-murder accusation. If the mob responded, the gangsters would get rid of their creditor by knocking him on the head and join in the general looting. No doubt the threat of such proceedings was often enough to persuade the creditor to modify or give up his claim. Racketeering is an art as old as history. The Pope was determined to stop such practices, not merely because of the injustice, although that was his chief motive, but because he knew that these disorders were harmful to trade by increasing the risk, and therefore the price, of capital. In July of the same year (July 6, 1247), he wrote again, insisting that Christians must be compelled to pay their just debts: "Although the said Jews make honest loans of their money to these Christians, the latter, in order to drain from them all their wealth . . . refuse to repay their money to them."

Innocent realized more clearly than most of his contemporaries the economic importance of law and order, and the essential function of capital in the development of commerce and agriculture. He was not deceived by attempts to hide organized banditry under the cloak of religion. A story had just been reported to him about outrages inflicted upon the Jews of France: On March 26, 1247, a little girl, two years old, named Mailla, had disappeared from the town of Valréas (Vaucluse), in Dauphiné; next day her body was found in a ditch near the town. A rumor spread that the child had been kidnapped and murdered by the Jews, and her blood used for their religious ceremonies. Three Jews were arrested and tortured until they confessed. Many others in the district were rounded up, tortured and put to death. On May 28, Innocent sent two indignant protests to the Archbishop of Vienne. He condemned in vigorous language "the cruelty of Christians who, covetous of their possessions, thirsting for their blood, despoil, torture and kill all Jews without legal judgment." Not only had these unhappy people been tortured, condemned without trial and burned at the stake, but "their children were forced to be baptized against their wishes."

The Pope, unlike his predecessor Gregory IX, did not waste time by asking the archbishop "to induce" the faithful not to maltreat the Jews. He commanded that "the prelates, nobles, rectors . . . and other disturbers of the peace be restrained by means of ecclesiastical punishment." In a second letter, written on the same day, Innocent gave a horrifying account of what had happened, taken from "a petition of the Jews of the entire province of Vienne, read in our presence." Here the Pope refers, as he did shortly after in his correspondence with the King of Navarre, to information received from a deputation of Jews. It is possible that some sort of committee of inquiry had been set up at the papal court to study the Jewish problem, to sift evidence, listen to complaints and suggest remedies.

The Jews of Vienne had been treated with an inhumanity unsurpassed by anything that has happened in their history, before or since, until the rule of Hitler. A nobleman, Draconet de Montauban, a Crusader who had gone with St. Louis to the Holy Land, is named by the Pope as chief leader of the Christian brigands. From such stock the nobility of France today are sometimes proud to claim descent. The Pope wrote on May 18, 1247:

> The noble Draconet despoiled the Jews of all their goods and cast them into a fearful prison, and without admitting the legitimate protestation and defense of their innocence, he cut some of them in two, others he burnt at the stake, of others he castrated the men and tore the breasts off the women. He afflicted them with divers other kinds of tortures, until, as it is said, they confessed with their mouth what their conscience did not dictate, choosing to be killed in one moment of agony rather than to live and be afflicted with torments and tortures . . .

The noble Draconet was not assisted in his operations by the bishop, although it is probable that some of the clergy were present in the great hall of the castle where the "trial" took place. The churchmen refrained from the shedding of blood; but they shared in the spoils of battle; they took all the Jews that were left into what is now called "protective custody." "As if to add affliction to the afflicted," the Pope continued, "our venerable brother the Bishop of Saint-Paul-Trois-Châteaux, the Constable of Valentinois, and several other nobles and potentates of the same province, taking advantage of an excuse of this kind, threw into prison whatever Jews dwelt in their lands and dominions, after having robbed these Jews of all their property." Innocent ordered "his venerable brother the Bishop of Saint-Paul-Trois-Châteaux" and the other scoundrels to restore the stolen property and render satisfaction to the owners. He had no jurisdiction over Draconet and his gangsters, and they seem to have got off with a reprimand. It is clear that greed was the real motive which had inspired the nobility and gentry at Valréas.[2a]

The Archbishop of Vienne took no action. He refused to restore Jewish property or to allow the Jews to live in peace, and five years later, when they were completely ruined and nothing more could be squeezed out of them, with the Pope's consent, he drove them all out of his province. He explained to Innocent that, owing to the presence of Jews in his district, the "souls of Christians were threatened with serious danger." Although it is difficult to imagine how some of these souls could have become any blacker than they were, by personal intercourse even with the devil, the Pope acceded to the archbishop's request, and thus the unfortunate Jews were compelled once more to resume their wandering over the face of the earth.

In Germany, the ritual-murder legend was the chief, but not the only, excuse for a series of riots all over the country which threatened the Jews with complete extermination. They appealed for protection to the Holy See. In his reply, addressed to the archbishops and bishops of Germany (July 5, 1247), Innocent repeated the familiar story of cruelty and rapacity. "The Jews in Germany," he said, "are oppressed by denial of food, by imprisonment, and by many injuries and oppressions, and by inflicting on them many kinds of punishments, and by condemning enormous numbers of them to a most shameful death, so that they are living in a worse condition than did their ancestors under Pharaoh in Egypt." He recommended the bishops "to show themselves favorably disposed and kindly towards the Jews, and not to permit them to be molested any further." Advice of this kind, addressed to German princes and prelates, was a waste of papal parchment.

But Innocent struck at the root of all the trouble when he issued his remarkable decree commanding the faithful to refrain from using the blood-legend as an excuse for torturing, robbing, and murdering defenseless people: "Among the thunders of terrible excommunications, the strong winds of ambition, it was something," wrote Milman, "to hear the still small voice of humanity, justice, and charity." The voice was heard, but it was not obeyed, although the Pope's command was pronounced in plain straightforward language which no one could pretend to misunderstand: "Nor shall anyone accuse them of using human blood in their religious rites . . . , since at Fulda, and in several other places, many Jews were killed on such a pretext. We strictly forbid the recurrence of such a thing." [3]

The incident at Fulda had taken place about ten years earlier, in 1236, when "thirty-four Jews of both sexes were put to the sword by Crusaders because two Jews had, on Holy Christmas Day, cruelly killed the five sons of a miller." The Jews were accused of collecting the blood of their victims, but no accusation of ritual murder seems to have been made. [4] The Pope knew that at Fulda, at Valréas, at Frankfort, and other places, Christian greed had been the pretext which covered the slaughter. Even when they were dead, Jews were not safe from such rapacity. For in this decree, Innocent repeated the prohibition of his predecessors and condemned "the wickedness and avarice of evil men . . . who presume to desecrate the cemetery of the Jews or, with the object of extorting money, to exhume bodies buried there." This was the traffic in Jewish corpses which Innocent III, fifty years earlier, had ineffectually prohibited. How profits were made from this practice is not explained; probably the Jews had to pay money to get the bodies back and to be allowed to bury them. Although the Popes repeatedly expressed their abhorrence of such conduct, they did not renounce the doctrine which made it excusable in the eyes of the criminals concerned, the doctrine that Jews were outcasts, slaves who were permitted to live only on sufferance. The ghouls who made money by digging up Jewish bodies were no doubt able to satisfy such remnant of conscience as they had retained, with the reflection that Jews did not rank as human beings.

This gruesome story of Christian body snatchers, rifling tombs and holding up corpses to ransom, suggests that the Jews in the Middle Ages had no monopoly of that lust for money which so many historians have assumed to be a specifically Jewish characteristic. [5]

About twenty years later another Pope, Gregory X, had to reprimand his flock for offenses almost as foul as the desecration of cemeteries. Certain Christian fathers, when their children died, used to hide the dead bodies on Jewish premises, and then proceeded to extort money from the Jews by threatening to accuse them of having murdered the children to obtain their blood for the Pascal rites. On October 7, 1272, the Pope wrote:

> It happens that the fathers of certain dead children, or other Christians who are enemies of Jews, hide in secret these dead children and attempt to extort money from Jews. . . . They affirm most falsely that the Jews themselves have stolen these children, and immolate their hearts and blood.

Dean Milman quotes a story about the Emperor Frederick II which must refer to an incident of this kind.

> That most extraordinary man, Frederick the Second, aggravated the suspicions which attached to his Christianity on account of his high-minded resistance to the Papal power, by extending what was deemed unchristian protection over this proscribed race. They brought him intelligence that three Christian children had been found dead, at the time of the Passover, in the house of a Jew. "Let them be buried then," coolly replied the philosophic Emperor.[6]

Gregory X issued the sensible order that, in all cases where an accusation of ritual murder was brought against Jews, the testimony of Christians was not to be accepted unless an equal number of Jewish witnesses against the accused could be produced.

In vain did Innocent threaten with excommunication those who ignored his decrees. No one was excommunicated; the Pope, it was said, had been bribed by the Jews, and the blood legend went on circulating for centuries, spreading throughout Christendom fear, suspicion, prejudice and hatred. By the end of the thirteenth century, it had already produced an appalling record of human suffering.

This accusation of kidnapping little children, killing them, after torture, and using their blood for a religious rite, proved to be the most powerful instrument of hate propaganda that has ever been invented. It served for hundreds of years to keep alive, and from time to time to inflame, popular hatred of the Jews in Western Europe; it survived until the present day, when it provided the most successful of the many poisons used by the Nazis to infect the German people and to incite them to the commission of atrocities of a kind, and on a scale, which might have horrified even the most murderous brutes in the Middle Ages.

The story, concocted by a monk, a converted Jew, named Theobald, was first put into writing by Thomas of Monmouth, an English monk of the Order of St. Benedict, shortly before the preaching of the Second Crusade, in the middle of the twelfth century. A young boy named William had been found dead in a wood outside the town of Norwich. Some months later, Thomas of Monmouth accused the Jews of responsibility for the boy's death. He said they had enticed the boy into a house, tortured him and crucified him. The monk's tale did not at first meet with the approval of his superiors. But it was soon welcomed by many of the ignorant clergy, both regular and secular, who used it as a new excuse for attacking the "enemies of Christ." Moreover the cultus of Blessed William, the first child martyr, proved extremely profitable. Thomas, a man of feeble intelligence, could not have had any idea of the terrible consequences which would follow from his fantastic invention, and it would not be fair to hold him responsible for what happened. The blame must rest with the men, many of them clerics of high rank, who used his story to stir up "that mighty wave of superstitious credulity, unreasoning hate, and insatiable ferocity, which has not yet spent itself, although more than seven centuries have passed since Thomas first took his pen in hand."[7]

The first ritual-murder tragedy in France was staged at

Blois, in 1171. A Christian groom said that he had seen a Jew throw the body of a child into the Loire. No corpse was produced. There was no other evidence that a crime of any sort had been committed. Fifty-one Jews—thirty-four men and seventeen women—were tortured and burnt at the stake. Before the end of the century, the tale had spread all over Christendom. From the pulpits it was told how the Jews were accustomed to celebrate their hatred of Christ by crucifying a little child, once a year, preferably at Easter or thereabouts. To many religious-minded people in the Middle Ages, this seemed quite a logical thing for a Jew to do. The commemoration of the passion and death of Christ is the central feature of Christian ritual, and it did not seem strange to some Christians that a hostile ceremonial, with inverted rites, might be the central feature of Jewish ritual. Even within recent times, a Dominican writer explained that Jewish ritual murder was a kind of inverted mass "celebrated in memory of Christ crucified, to provide, until the end of time, the crime of Calvary with a horrible memorial. . . . The Jew has sanctified, whenever he was able, every anniversary of the deicide, by the immolation of a Christian." [8]

No lie, ancient or modern, has ever had an effect on the social and political history of Europe to compare with the results of the tale first circulated by Thomas of Monmouth. In 1182, when Thomas, if he lived the normal span, might have still been alive, the King of France, Philip Augustus, drove the Jews out of his country because he believed that they were in the habit of kidnapping and crucifying Christian children. The king, wrote Fleury in 1732, following the contemporary chroniclers,

> . . . had a great aversion to the Jews because he had heard from the nobles of his court that the Jews in Paris used to sacrifice a Christian every year, on Holy Thursday. Many of them had been convicted of this crime during his father's reign, and the body of a child named Richard, who had

thus been killed and crucified by the Jews, was venerated in
the Church of St. Innocent. Several miracles had been
worked at his tomb, according to the evidence of Robert,
Abbot of Mont-Saint-Michel. The same author records the
burning of several Jews at Blois in 1171, and mentions also
the murder of children at Norwich in 1144 [William], and
at Gloucester in 1160, and a child named Robert in 1181.[9]

The legend was still vigorous in France at the beginning of
the eighteenth century. Fleury produced an unusual reason
for believing that all these stories were true. "The Jews," he
wrote, "pretend that they are calumnies. But why should
the Christians have made these charges at that particular
time, rather than at any other time, unless there had been
some foundation for them?" This calumny became an instrument of propaganda, useful to kings and churchmen.
When the Jews were driven out of Spain in 1492 by Ferdinand and Isabella, "it was only with the wide publicity
given to an alleged case of human sacrifice that general
anti-Jewish feeling was aroused to support the order of
expulsion." [10]

The bull of Innocent IV did not pass a final judgment on
the question. The Pope did not make a definite pronouncement that all the accusations were false; he did not have before him the evidence to justify such a decision. He wrote
primarily to remind the faithful of the commandment "Thou
shalt not bear false witness against thy neighbor." He himself obviously did not believe that there was any truth at all in
these blood stories, connected, as so many of them were, with
the horrible traffic in dead bodies. Yet his protest against these
abominations had little effect on the passions and prejudices
of the time. In 1255, eight years after the publication of the
papal bull which condemned the blood myth, a successful
operation was carried out against the Jews of Lincoln, who
were accused of immolating a Christian child. The version
of the contemporary chronicler, Matthew Paris, shows how

the story had developed since the days of Thomas of Monmouth:

The Jews of Lincoln stole a boy of eight years of age, whose name was Hugh, and, "having shut him up in a room quite out of the way, where they fed him on milk and other childish nourishment, they sent to almost all the cities of England where the Jews lived, and summoned some of their sect from each city to be present at a sacrifice to take place at Lincoln, for they had, as they stated, a boy hidden for the purpose of being crucified. They appointed a Jew of Lincoln as a judge, to take the place of Pilate. The boy was subject to divers tortures. They beat him till blood flowed and he was quite livid, they crowned him with thorns, derided him, and spat upon him. They crucified him and pierced his heart with a lance. After the boy expired, they took his body down from the cross and disembowled it." Meantime a search was going on for the missing boy, whose body was found in a well. The people who discovered the body were reminded of a similar find, in a wood, which had been made about a hundred years ago at Norwich. "A man of learning, prudent and discreet," John of Lexington, suggested that the boy had been murdered by the Jews. We know from experience, said this man of learning, that "they have not hesitated to attempt such proceedings." A few Jews were immediately arrested, and one of them, "under threat of torture and death," revealed the whole story, on condition his life would be spared. But the poor wretch was "tied to a horse's tail and dragged to the gallows." Ninety-six other Jews were taken to London, where eighteen of them, "the richer and higher order of the Jews of the city of Lincoln . . . were hung up, an offering to the winds."

Matthew Paris hints that Christian moneylenders were the chief promoters of the whole affair; they were certainly the principal beneficiaries. "If the Jews," he concludes, "were perchance pitied by any Christians, they did not excite any

tears of compassion among the Caursins, their rivals." Seventy
of the accused who had been convicted "by a jury of twenty-
five knights" were released as the result of a plea in their
favor presented by the Franciscans. This deed of Franciscan
charity did not meet with popular approval. People said then,
just what they always say, that the friars had been bribed by
the Jews. "The brethren, (as the world reports, if in such a
case the world is to be believed) influenced by bribes, released them from prison and saved them from the death they
had deserved."

The chronicler was, however, not afraid to record his own
conviction that the Franciscans had acted from the highest
motives; "I believe," he said "that for as long as anyone is
breasting the path of life in this world, he is entitled to his
own opinion." Yet he seems to have been impressed by the
evidence against the accused, which rested solely on the "confession" of one man who had been threatened with torture
and death. "But these Jews, I say, were found guilty on their
trial by jury, from the statement made by a Jew who was
hung at Lincoln in the first place."

The boy, promoted by the piety of the faithful to the rank
of martyr, was venerated for many generations as Little
Saint Hugh of Lincoln; a church was dedicated to his memory
and miracles worked at his tomb, which became a famous
resort for pilgrims who came there from all over Christendom
—to pray, to wonder at the miracles, and to refresh their
hatred. A more permanent publicity for the gruesome story
was provided by Chaucer in the *Canterbury Tales*. Christian
literature and Christian religion combined to exploit the most
hideous calumny in human history—and the most successful—
with a place in English literature, in the English literature of
modern times. "I have in the abstract," wrote Charles Lamb,
"no disrespect for the Jews. . . . I should not care to be in
habits of familiar intercourse with any of that nation. I confess that I have not the nerves to enter their synagogues. Old

prejudices cling about me. I cannot shake off the story of Hugh of Lincoln." [11]

Although pilgrims continued for centuries to pay homage, and money, at the shrine of Little Saint Hugh, the whole affair was a tragic farce. There was no evidence, except under torture, that the boy had been killed by anyone.

All over Europe, in every country, in every province, this cultus of little children, with its statues, its miracles, its pilgrimages, provided stimulants for a hate which was driven deep, in the course of centuries, into the Christian mind. Every pilgrim returned to his home to be welcomed, not as a witness to a holy example of sanctity, but as an expert on the inconceivable wickedness of the Jews. Every pilgrim was an apostle of hate. These blood legends were different in one important respect from the hagiographical romances written to glorify the memory of some holy man: their purpose was to vilify the Jews. There is nothing to be found in them about the beauty of the Christian faith or the ideal of sanctity. The cultus of the child martyrs excited, in the minds of the faithful who paid them honor, feelings of hatred and a desire for revenge, rather than of piety and devotion and the fear of God.

Blood accusations became so frequent that it is difficult to make a complete record. The number of human beings who were barbarously put to death without trial on this grotesque charge will never be known. In 1279, some Jews in London, accused of having crucified a Christian child, were torn to pieces by horses. At Eastertime in 1283, a dead child was discovered near Mainz. Ten Jews were killed by the Christian mob. At Munich in 1285, the mob, with a similar pretext, set fire to a synagogue. One hundred and eighty Jews were burned to death. The following year, at Oberwesel, for the same reason, forty Jews were brutally put to death. In the history of hatreds there is nothing comparable to these condemnations, continuing for seven hundred years, on a grotesque charge, of thousands of innocent people against whom there was never any evidence other than confessions extracted by torture.

Although an accused person in the Middle Ages was seldom put to the question unless there was some reasonable presumption of guilt, this proviso did not offer much protection to Jews, who were nearly always presumed guilty of any crime imputed to them against a Christian, or against the security of Christendom. They were supposed to be engaged in a permanent plot to destroy Christianity and, wherever they were grouped together for mutual protection, they were suspected of being occupied in some sort of conspiracy against which the Christians had to act in self-defense. When the evidence against a Jew charged with some individual crime, such as kidnapping a child, was insufficient even for a mediaeval tribunal to convict, the accused would probably be condemned on the general charge of Jewish wickedness. A somewhat similar practice obtained in some countries only a few years ago. During the course of a trial which became notorious, many Frenchmen used to say—and some still say—that no proof was necessary to establish the guilt of the accused; it was enough to know that he was a Jew.

Between 1144 and 1490 many child martyrs were beatified by the Church and venerated by the faithful with the title of "Blessed." Through the intercession of these "Little Saints" miracles were worked; and the cultus continued for centuries —even in the affair of the Holy Niño of La Guardia where there is no satisfactory evidence that the "victim" ever existed.[12] The fact that no body was ever discovered made no difference to the popularity of this martyr but merely stimulated the imagination of the faithful. The parish priest of La Guardia, writing in 1785, said that "it was universally believed that God had completed the parallel between Christ and the Niño, and, on the third day, had carried the body up to heaven."

The non-existent child martyr was avenged on November 16, 1491. Five Jews were arrested by the Inquisition (three of them being *Conversos*), were strangled and then burnt; the other two were torn to pieces with red-hot pincers. The whole affair had been staged by Torquemada in order to strengthen his case for the expulsion of the Jews from Spain. "Although it would be too much to say that this won Ferdinand's consent to the expulsion, it undoubtedly contributed largely to that result." [13]

The story of Blessed Andrew of Rinn (1482) is another legend of the same type. "There was no charge, no trial, and no condemnation." [14] Benedict XIV, in 1754, granted a plenary indulgence to all who visited the Church at Rinn, in the Tyrol, where the relics were honored. The Bull *Beatus Andreas*, Feb. 22, 1755, expresses no doubt about Jewish ritual murder. Yet there is no evidence, acceptable by any court of justice, to prove that any one of all these child martyrs had in fact been killed by the Jews, or by a Jew. "Not a single case," concluded Abbé Vacandard, "has ever been historically established." [15] But people who want to believe in a story do not need evidence. Mere repetition is accepted as a kind of proof.

An exceptionally potent variety of anti-Semitism must have distracted the mind of a Jesuit writer on the staff of *La Civiltà Cattolica*, who, in 1881, wrote a series of articles in which belief in the Jewish practice of ritual murder is expressed with a curious disregard of the elementary principles of historical criticism. "It is morally impossible," he declared, "to admit the existence of a conviction and a tradition so continuous, propagated in so many places and for so many centuries, without some real foundation. . . . Such atrocious Hebrew deeds in the Middle Ages must be partly founded on fact because they excited so much the anger of the people and of the kings." [16] A similar argument was repeated in 1901 in a popular English textbook: "It is difficult to refuse all credit to stories so circumstantial and so frequent." [17]

This is the way a legend grows. When a statement, however fantastic, has been repeated often enough, it becomes "well known" and is then used as corroborative evidence for other similar statements. The process sometimes goes on for generations. A. W. Pugin (1812–1852), better known as an architect and archeologist than as a historian, thought that "there were no reasonable grounds whatever" for disbelieving the story of Little Saint Hugh, because "the Jews are well known to have committed similar atrocities at various periods." A painful death, he concluded, was what they deserved: "It is satisfactory to know that the perpetrators of the horrible barbarity received the punishment of death in a severe form." [18]

The Rev. Urban Butler, in the *Catholic Encyclopedia* (article "Little Saint Hugh of Lincoln"), realized that the time had come to withdraw from a position which had become too difficult to hold; but he did not retire without firing a last shot: "Whether there was any basis of truth," he wrote, "in the accusation against the Jews, there is now no means of ascertaining." This reluctant admission that something had gone wrong with the tradition reads like a ministerial answer to an inconvenient question asked in the House of Commons. Dr. Butler would perhaps have worded his apology less ambiguously if he had been defending Catholics, instead of Jews, against some preposterous calumny.

When the lack of evidence for any single instance of the ritual murder of a Christian child by a Jew—or by the Jews—could no longer be denied, the Church authorities, having locally allowed or promoted the cultus of many such children, was placed in a difficult but not inextricable position. For these child saints had been beatified, not canonized, by a process known to theologians as "equivalent beatification"; this is merely (as understood today) the official recognition by due authority, local or central, of a local cultus initiated without such authority. Belief in the validity of an approved cultus, could not, however, be questioned, nor could the alleged facts upon which the cultus, or its approval, had been based be "temerariously" challenged without incurring ecclesiastical censure.

Some theologians were obviously afraid of facing the absence of facts. Consequently, we find a Jesuit writer in *The Nineteenth Century* informing the Protestant world that the infallibility of the Church in the beatification (as distinguished from the canonization) of saints, is "proximate to the Faith—*proximus Fidei*," and "absolutely certain." Any Catholic denying such belief "commits a grievous sin against the Faith." [19]

It is indeed surprising that such theories should have survived until the twentieth century in spite of the fact that in 1758 the Holy See had officially condemned the cultus of the so-called child martyrs and reaffirmed the falsehood of *all* the ritual-murder accusations. In that year the question was brought to a head because of the revival of persecution in Poland, where ritual-murder trials, since the beginning of the century, had been an almost annual event. The story of the atrocities inflicted on the victims of these trials has been told by S. M. Dubnow. At Saslav, in 1747, "the accused were all sentenced to a monstrous death, possible only among savages. Some of the accused were placed on an iron pale, which slowly cut into their body, and resulted in a slow and torturous death. The others were treated with equal cannibalism; their skins were torn off in strips, their hearts cut out, their hands and feet amputated and nailed to the gallows." In 1753, twenty-four Jews were condemned at Zhytomir. "Eleven were flayed alive, while the others saved themselves from death by accepting baptism." [20] The Jewish communities appealed for protection to the Holy See. In 1758, Cardinal Ganganelli afterwards Pope Clement XIV, presented a report to the Holy Office which exposed the falsehood of the ritual-murder accusation and refused to admit the validity of the cases of all the child martyrs except two, Andrew of Rinn and Simon of Trent. In both these cases of alleged child murder, which are now known to be as fictitious as the rest, the ritual motive was rejected.

The cultus of Simon of Trent (1475) had not been approved until a hundred years after his death. Pope Sixtus IV, under whose pontificate the boy was "martyred," refused to allow him to be honored as a Saint, and subsequent Popes repeated the prohibition. Pope Sixtus V, in 1588, gave way to popular credulity and to popular hatred of the Jews; and the name of Simon of Trent is commemorated in the Roman Martyrology on March 24. His story follows the usual mediaeval pattern:

> According to the statement drawn up at Trent shortly after the tragedy, a Jewish physician decoyed and kidnapped a little Christian child, two and a half years old, in view of the celebration of the Jewish *Pesach*. After crucifying the boy and draining his blood, the officers of the synagogue hid the body for a short time, and eventually threw it into the canal. The crime, however, was brought home to those suspected, who, under torture, admitted their guilt. Horrible punishments were inflicted after conviction, while, on the other hand, a profusion of miracles followed beside the tomb of the infant martyr.[21]

"The truth of such crimes," commented Father Thurston, "was universally credited in the Middle Ages." A report on the proceedings in the case of Simon of Trent was sent to the Pope by Bishop Hinderbach of Trent.

Samuel, the most important man among the Jews who had been arrested, was put to the question several days in succession, at the end of March and the beginning of April, 1475. At the first infliction of the torture, he lost consciousness and had to be carried back to his prison. On the following day, he was stripped naked, bound hand and feet, and hung by a rope, working on a pulley, so that his limbs were nearly torn out of their sockets. He still protested his innocence. The rope was then pulled up, and he was jerked up and down until he fainted. Three days later, the same process was renewed.

He was lifted up "to twice the height of his arms" and dropped with a jerk, several times, and then left to hang for about half an hour. After three days' rest, the torture was again repeated. An iron pan containing burning sulphur was then held under his nostrils. Finally they "tied a piece of wood between his shin bones, whereby the weight became heavier, and the pain greater," jerked him up and down again, and then let him hang for a quarter of an hour. Then the jerking up and down began again, until "his power of resistance was broken." Samuel probably withdrew his confession, for the report states that two months later he was tortured again, "two boiling hot eggs were applied to his armpits," and he agreed "to tell the truth, provided they would promise to have him burned and not put him to any other death." On June 23, he was burned at the stake. All the other Jews were treated in the same manner, even those who had allowed themselves to be baptized. Some, instead of being burned, were broken on the wheel.[22]

The late Father Bede Jarrett, O.P., endeavored to comfort readers and students who might be unduly horrified by reading about such torture with the observation that "in the Middle Ages there was nothing like the same sensitiveness to pain that later ages have developed."[23] There is no warrant whatever for such an assumption; but even if it were true, it does not mitigate in any degree the moral obliquity of any man, whether priest, bishop or Pope, who was responsible for such atrocities. If Christians had been tortured in such a manner by Jews, Father Bede would perhaps have been less ready to assume that the proceedings were not so painful then as they would be now. The evidence of many of the Templars who confessed their guilt under torture, and afterwards recanted, suggests very forcibly that people in the Middle Ages feared and felt pain just as we do. "If I was made to endure such tortures again," said Ponsard de Grisi, "I would deny all that I am saying now. I am ready to suffer torments if they are short; let them cut off my head, or boil me alive for the

honor of the Order, but I cannot endure such long-drawn-out
agony as was inflicted upon me during my two years of
prison." [24]

Those who condone such deeds, or who refer to them, even
indirectly, without condemning them in the strongest terms,
share in the guilt and help to keep alive in men's minds the
wickedness which made such hatred and cruelty possible in
the past and has led to the perpetration, on an enormous scale,
of even worse atrocities within recent years.

Simon was still revered as a saint by many Austrian Catholics at the end of the nineteenth century. Canon Joseph
Deckert, a disseminator of race hatred who was condemned
by the Austrian courts for spreading malicious calumnies,
published, in 1893, a pamphlet on the "Ritual Murder of
Simon of Trent" which was distributed free at the doors of
Vienna churches. Such pamphlets were not inspired by religious motives. A few years earlier, an attempt had been made
to stir up hatred in Austria by reviving belief in the blood
legend. The incident is now of little importance; yet it is part
of the history of that ancient hatred, partly political, partly religious, which has become endemic in many European countries, and can always be wakened into frenzy by unscrupulous
preachers, for a religious or political purpose.

A certain Canon Rohling, leader of a religious group in
Austria, announced that he had discovered some new evidence
which proved the truth of the blood legend. There is nothing
in the story, as told by Canon Vernet (*Dictionnaire d'apologétique*), to suggest that Rohling had been guilty of anything
more serious than an error of scholarly judgment:

A professor in the University of Prague, Canon A.
Rohling, fancied that he had discovered in the Talmud a
text which permits the conclusion that any Jewish child,
not protected by his father's will, might be sacrificed as a
Pascal victim, and since the Jews took victims from among
the youths of their own people, all the more reason there

was for taking non-Jews . . . a book of Rohling's, *Der
Talmudjude*, started a bitter polemic. . . . The chief an-
tagonist was F. Delitzsch . . . in reality the Talmud text
has not the meaning that Rohling gave it.

Readers of this summary must have been grievously misled.
They would naturally believe that the professor had been a
little careless, that he had made the kind of mistake to which all
men are liable when "he fancied he had discovered" something
in the Talmud which justified his accusations. The most important fact was left out by Canon Vernet. Rohling was convicted, not of making a mistake, not of fancying that he had
discovered something, but of *falsifying* the texts. Canon
Vernet must have known, and ought to have told his readers,
that Rohling and his associate Dr. Justus were a pair of rogues
who made money by circulating calumnies about the Jews.
It would not be easy to find a more flagrant case of *suppressio
veri* than this omission in the *Dictionnaire d'apologétique* of
any reference to the notorious Rohling scandal.

The lies published by Rohling, based on fraudulent in-
ventions of his own, masquerading as quotations from the
Talmud, provided the Jew-haters of France and Germany
with useful ammunition. They were able to quote an authority which Catholics would not readily challenge, a man
who was a Catholic priest and professor in a famous university.
But an Austrian rabbi, Dr. Joseph Bloch, publicly denounced
Rohling as "a liar, a calumniator, and a perjurer." The professor sued the rabbi for libel, withdrew the charge at the last
moment, and was condemned by the court to pay all expenses.
Professor Strack of Berlin issued a challenge in the following
words: "I openly accuse Professor and Canon A. Rohling of
perjury and gross fraud. I am prepared to substantiate this
grave accusation before any tribunal." Franz Delitzsch knew
that his adversary in this affair was not a scholar who had made
a mistake, but a perfidious scoundrel who had deliberately
perpetrated a fraud—a scoundrel with sufficient knowledge of

Hebrew to enable him to make such a fraud acceptable to people who had no acquaintance with that language. Delitzsch was indignant not only because the Jewish people had been attacked in so foul a manner by a man who was a Catholic priest, but because a university professor had prostituted his position and besmeared the good name of scholarship. When he wrote the book *Checkmate of the Liars Rohling and Justus*, Delitzsch did not contribute to a "controversy" or take part in a "bitter polemic"; he exposed the villainy of two notorious rascals.

Although the malice of Rohling was exposed by such scholars as deigned to take notice of him, the class of readers for whom he wrote were not in the least perturbed. Many of them seem to have been really convinced that all scholarship which was not violently anti-Jewish had been bought by Jewish gold. There was an interesting and almost exact parallel to the Rohling episode at the beginning of the Christian era. If we substitute for Rohling, Apion the Grammarian, and for Delitzsch, Josephus the Jewish historian, the old story and the new will be recognized as identical in almost every detail.

Apion of Alexandria (died A.D. 45), one of the early fathers of anti-Semitism, knew how to appeal to the credulous imagination of the populace, who were impressed by his vanity and pretensions to learning. His indictment of the Jews was drawn up in a form which has not varied for centuries, and is employed by their enemies at the present day— aspersions on the Jewish race, denial of their loyalty, and crude misrepresentations of their rites and their religious beliefs.

Flavius Josephus, historian and soldier, in his book against Apion, refers to an accusation brought against the Jews, of practices which involved a kind of ritual murder. Apion had published an attack on the Jews full of ridiculous lies.[25] The text is now lost, but it is partly known from the refutation which fortunately Josephus decided to write: "I confess," he says, "I have a doubt upon me about Apion the Grammarian, whether I ought to take the trouble of refuting him or not . . . for the greater part of what he says is very scurrilous; and to speak no more than the plain truth, shows him to be a very unlearned person."

Josephus replied to Apion chiefly because of certain charges he had made which concerned "the sacred purifications, with other legal rites used in the temple." According to the oriental custom, Apion had given publicity to his allegations of criminal practices by means of a short story: A certain Greek was found lying on a bed in a Jewish temple, and, beside him, a table full of dainties. This man, when discovered, said that he had been suddenly seized by foreigners, shut up in the temple and "fattened by the curious provisions set before him." After a while he became suspicious and "inquired of the servants who came to him, and was informed by them, that it was in order to the fulfilling of a law of the Jews . . . that he was thus fed; and that they used to catch a Greek foreigner and fat him thus up every year, and then lead him to a certain wood and kill him, and sacrifice with their accustomed solemnities, and taste of his entrails. . . ." After pointing out to his readers the absurdities of this tale, Josephus concludes that "it was a great shame for a grammarian not to be able to write true history . . . unspeakable mischiefs have been occasioned by such calumnies that are raised upon us. . . ."

Yet in spite of all that Josephus, or any fair-minded man in after years, was able to do, the lies spread by Apion continued to be read and believed by the everlastingly credulous public, and the Jews continued for centuries to suffer in consequence, from "unspeakable mischiefs." Tacitus was not ashamed to repeat these calumnies, although he was probably acquainted with the books of Josephus against Apion. "Among every people," said Isaac D'Israeli, "the Hebrews have found a malignant Apion." [26]

One of the modern links in this long chain of hate was

forged in France at the end of the nineteenth century by the
leader of Jew-baiters in that century, Edouard Drumont.
"The fact of the assassination of Christian children by the
Jews," he wrote, using Rohling as his authority, "is a fact as
evident as the light of day . . . it has been proved beyond
discussion that ritual murder was habitually practised by the
Jews in the Middle Ages." He also assured his readers that
human sacrifices in the forests of West Africa were directed
"according to all probability by men who were Jewish
Semites." [27] Many educated Frenchmen who read this stuff
probably shrugged their shoulders and regarded it as nonsense
of no importance. They were wrong. The significance and
the danger of such writing consist precisely in its ludicrous
absurdity. For there is no limit to human credulity, and the
minds of the majority, the semi-literate and the semi-illiterate,
can often be awakened and impressed only by a fantastic
falsehood.

Drumont's campaign, as the late Mr. Sidney Dark pointed
out, "was almost in every detail the anticipation of Hitler." [28]
The Nazis followed a beaten track. They repeated and magni-
fied the old lies. With an intensive publicity they were able to
infect the minds of the German people. In 1936, seven hundred years after the promulgation in Germany of Pope Innocent's decree condemning the blood lie, a German popular
newspaper, *Der Stürmer*, published illustrations showing Jews
sucking the blood of Christian children. False quotations
from the Talmud, and the blood legend which the Papacy
had endeavored in vain to suppress, became important features
in the propaganda employed to excite a hatred which eventually made murder possible on a scale unknown at any period
of civilized or uncivilized history. The importance of this
blood legend as an agent in the process of German corruption
was recognized by Dr. Cecil Roth, who foretold the consequence with remarkable prevision. He wrote in 1934:

Nazi propaganda in Germany issued periodical warnings to the general population to take special care of their children at Passover time in view of Jewish ritual requirements: and it would not be surprising if semi-official encouragement were to bring about in that country, in the near future, a major tragedy reminiscent of the Middle Ages at their worst.[29]

*Hatred of the Jews has at all times gone hand in hand with love of Jewish money.*

S. M. DUBNOW

6

..............................................

# "Money Was Their God"

ENGLISHMEN WHO LEFT THEIR COUNTRY in the early days of empire-building to seek their fortune in foreign parts were often credited, by their descendants in the nineteenth century, with an altruism they did not always deserve. It might be said, and indeed has been said, that these pioneers invested commerce with a new dignity; that they did not merely love money for its own sake, but were moved by a high instinct and, in fact, builded better than they knew. A historian of the East India Company has told, in noble words, the story of this inspiration:

> The great structure of our Indian Empire has been reared as no human intellect would have designed, and no human hands would have fashioned it. It has been reared for us as for a chosen people, and mighty is the responsibility which a trust so imposed upon us entails. The more we consider all the circumstances of the Rise and Progress of British Power in the East, the more palpable and obstinate appears the scepticism which would attribute so stupendous and mysterious a movement to anything but the special interference of an Almighty Providence for a purpose commensurable with the grandeur of the design.[1]

When Jews first began to leave their pastoral life in Palestine and went out to seek their fortunes in the Roman Empire, generations before the Christian era, they established commercial settlements in every port of the known world, even penetrating to the remote island of Britain; no one, however, has ever suggested that they were conscious of a mighty responsibility, or has praised them for opening up new countries to the ennobling influence of trade. On the contrary, it is often alleged that wherever they went they invariably had a disastrous influence, and brought no profit to anybody except themselves. "Jewry spread over the Roman Empire, and even beyond," said one embittered pessimist, "an immense spider's web."² "At that time," writes a modern French student of Hebrew history, "a new type of Jew appeared, hitherto unknown—the Jew clever at making money out of everything, whose real fatherland is his cash book."³ This "new type" did not, however, introduce into the Roman world any new variations in the worship of money. The cultus of the cash book was already firmly established, not only among the Romans, but also, according to the Emperor Hadrian, among the Egyptians. "Money," he said, "was their god. And this god," he added, "is also worshiped by the Christians, the Jews, and by the whole universe." Thus, in a single short sentence, did the Emperor sum up one aspect of the future history of Western civilization.

Hatred of the Jews on religious grounds, which had provoked the oppressive decrees of the Fourth Lateran Council in 1215, was aggravated during the fourteenth and fifteenth centuries by an increasing fear of their commercial competition in the universal scramble for money which eventually led to the discovery of America. "Abstinence, hard work, and intelligence," as Lord Samuel has recently pointed out, "win success in the competition; they do not win friends among the competitors."⁴ The competitors, therefore, took steps to eliminate their rivals. And the English, with their practical common sense, showed the world how this object could be most effectively achieved. In 1290, all the Jews in England, numbering about fifteen thousand, were ordered to leave the country, legislation having first been passed to ensure that the operation would be carried out in accordance with the requirements of justice. Many families had been settled in England for six or seven generations. They were all turned out at a few months' notice. The exodus was conducted with due observance of law and order. The Jews were permitted to take with them as much personal property as they could carry, and were led to the port of embarkation under military escort. No doubt the English soldiers said that they were "very sorry." Those who were lucky landed somewhere on the coast of an unfriendly Europe. No one cared; no one now knows whether they lived or died. A shipload was landed on the Goodwin Sands by a facetious English sea captain. When the tide began to rise, he sailed away, telling the Jews to pray for help to Moses. "If it could be said with strict precision of language," wrote L. O. Pike in 1873, "that a nation can commit a crime, it would be true that one of the greatest national crimes ever committed, was committed in England when the Jews were expelled through the combined influence of the clergy, the traders, and the Barons." [5]

Thus began in Western Europe the new kind of fear in which the Jewish people have lived from that time to the present day, the fear that at any moment, without warning and without any charge being brought against them, they might be told to pack up their bundles and go into exile; and they knew that they had nowhere to go. Once across the frontier, they were driven like rats from one hiding place to another—like rats, said Léon Daudet, only a few years ago: "the vermin of Europe."

England's example was promptly followed by France. In 1306, Philip the Fair suddenly issued an order that all Jews had to leave the country at a month's notice, under pain of death. The order was relentlessly carried out. One hundred thousand people, some of whose ancestors had settled in France even before the Christian era, were compelled to cross the frontier with nothing but the clothes they wore. Some of them paid the price of safety; they were "converted" to Christianity. Unlike their English brethren, who had been reduced to destitution before they were expatriated, by long years of systematic and, of course, legal oppression, the French Jews were prosperous; some of them were wealthy. Philip had no special grudge against them; he merely wanted their money. "Wagonfuls of Jewish property, gold, silver and precious stones were transported to the King; and less valuable objects were sold at a ridiculously low price." [6]

They were recalled to France a few years later by Louis X on conditions which granted, but did not ensure, security of tenure. There could be no security anywhere in Europe against the combination of fanaticism and greed. The Black Death provided a new excuse for massacre and plunder. In France and in Germany "where the Jews were mortally hated," wrote Petrarch, "they were accused of having made a special journey to India in order to bring back the plague and spread it among the Christians." Thousands of Jews, men, women and children, were burnt alive, having first been tortured in order to make them confess that they had poisoned the wells. The real motive behind these crimes was greed. According to an honest contemporary chronicler: "Their goods were the poison which caused the death of the Jews." [7] Pope Clement VI published a bull vindicating them from responsibility for the plague, and at the same time renewed the papal prohibitions against forcible baptism. But these academic resolutions, passed and published to safeguard a principle, were not accompanied by any change in the papal policy of degradation, were not enforced by sanctions, and had practically no effect whatever on Christian behavior.

When the Jews were finally expelled from France at the end of the fourteenth century, they were unable to find anywhere under French rule a permanent home. Some of them settled in Provence, only to be moved on again a hundred years later by order of Charles VIII. As a result of this pious act of "vengeance," the King was acclaimed as a popular hero, and his hatred of the Jews was lauded, in a contemporary ballad, as a Christian virtue:

> That good King, a second Vespasian,
> He so much hated the Jews and rejected them
> That he is named the King most Christian,
> Who from out of his country thrust the Jews.
> He has cleared them out of his cities,
> Remembering that Jesus his Passion
> Suffered from them; he hates their nation
> And will not grant them place or refuge.[8]

Owing to the peculiar political construction of the Holy Roman Empire, no general and official expulsion of Jews from Germany was possible. They were driven from town after town, and from district after district, by repeated pogroms for which religion provided the pretext; but, as usual, greed was the real motive.

A new method of exciting the mob against Jewry was discovered in the thirteenth century, a system which proved useful when no dead body was available for staging a ritual-murder trial. Jews were accused of stealing the consecrated bread from churches in order to use it for magical purposes. An alternative explanation of the alleged sacrilege was that they were deliberately attempting to take vengeance on the Body of Christ, which they were supposed to believe, as if they were Christians, to be present in the Eucharistic elements. The framework of the story, repeated for centuries all over Europe, everywhere with tragic consequences, and generally accompanied with a "miracle," was nearly always the same. Jews stole or bought a consecrated host, which they then proceeded to stab or mutilate. The host began to bleed. The terrified criminals then revealed what they had done. The evidence for this sequence of events was invariably extracted by torture; the accused were put to an agonizing death, and generally a number of Jews in the district were rounded up and burnt alive; and all their property was confiscated. The proceeds were often devoted to building a church where pilgrims would come for centuries to fortify their faith by contributing to the upkeep of the memorial.

This method of getting rid of Jews and confiscating their money was first put into practice, most appropriately, at Berlin, in 1243, seven hundred years before Hitler improved on the technique. Scores of victims were burned at the stake at a spot outside the city still known as the Judenberg. Similar trials were of frequent occurrence during the following centuries in many parts of Europe. At Paris, in 1290, according to the traditional story, a Jew was accused of stealing a host and handing it over to some of his friends, who first stabbed it and, when the blood began to flow, proceeded to plunge it into boiling water. The host suffered no damage, but the water turned red. After the culprits had been tortured and burned alive, their property was taken over by King Philip the Fair, who used some of it to endow a monastery where a remarkable inscription over the doorway informed passers by, for four hundred years, until 1685: "Under here the Jew boiled the sacred host." This story with even more ridiculous additions, was dramatized, during the fifteenth and sixteenth centuries, in a number of popular mystery plays.[9]

An annual celebration is still held at the Church of Sainte-Gudule, in Brussels, to commemorate the miracle, the murders and the confiscation of Jewish property which took place there in 1370.

The natural impression made on any critical-minded person in the Middle Ages, or at the present day, by the story of the bleeding hosts is that the whole affair was a hoax. A more satisfactory explanation became available in the first quarter of the nineteenth century, when similar phenomena came under scientific observation. The historical side of the problem created by the occasional and hitherto inexplicable appearance of blood on certain foodstuffs was summarized by a contributor to the *Centralblatt für Bakteriologie*, in 1904 (II, Vol. II):

> The frequency with which certain of the red chromo-genic bacteria appear upon foodstuffs has been a matter of observation for centuries. Lucian, in one of his dialogues (second century A.D.), makes Pythagoras give, as reason for forbidding his disciples to eat beans, the fact that white cooked beans, if placed in the moonlight, change into blood. Since the forbidding of beans as food is common to various sects of ancient times—e.g., to the Egyptian priests and to the Zoroastrians, from which latter Pythagoras doubtless obtained the notion—the recognition of this pigmentation appears to be of extreme antiquity. In the year 332 B.C. the so-called blood miracle was of service to Alexander the Great in the conquest of Tyre. The bread of his besieging army was discovered to be reddened when broken; but the priests quieted the terrified soldiery by interpreting the omen to mean that as the "blood" was inside the bread, a bloody fate would fall upon those inside, not outside, the city. (Curtius Rufus, *Hist. Alexandri*, C. 2, Book IV.) The phe-nomenon of the "bleeding host," so often regarded as a miracle in the Middle Ages, was due to a similar cause. The composition of the sacramental bread, rich in starch and poor in acid, was well adapted to the rapid growth of *Schiz-omycetes;* but the popular explanation of the phenomenon was that the host had been stabbed by unbelieving Jews. The number of executions and murders due to this belief was so great that Scheurlen, in alluding to it, remarks that "this saprophyte has destroyed more men than any other pathogenic bacillus."

The more recent news about this bacillus, now rendered harmless by exposure to the light of knowledge, comes from Israel. A scientist writes from the Sieff Institute for Scientific Research, Rehovoth (July, 1948):

> Having once seen the red "bug" growing in a natural state under favorable conditions on starchy foodstuffs, one is not likely to forget it. It really is a horrifying spectacle. Actually I've only seen it thus when I was asked into the

kitchen of a certain restaurant last summer to inspect a
large bowl of potatoes which had gone "bloody"; the thick
dripping film of "blood" was the moist superficial growth
of this harmless red bacterium. The organism is known by
several scientific names, but the two best known are *Serratia marcescens Bizio*, and *Bacterium prodigiosum Ehrenberg*. Bizio in 1819 was the first to publish a description of
the organism and to name it; consequently his name takes
priority. . . . But Ehrenberg's name *Bacillus prodigiosus*, or
the miraculous bacterium, given in 1824, gained more publicity, and admittedly appeals to the imagination as a more
expressive name for an organism with such an historical
record. It is interesting to observe that the younger generation of bacteriologists in Israel refer to the organism as
*Serratia marcescens*, no doubt to be scientifically correct,
but perhaps also to eliminate as far as possible all bitter
thoughts associated with Ehrenberg's name. The organism
is quite common; I have two strains isolated from water and
butter—but normally it grows readily upon moist starchy
foodstuffs containing also a certain amount of protein.

The relation between the growth of *Serratia marcescens*
upon a consecrated host reserved in an ecclesiastical receptacle
and the mediaeval accusation of host desecration is not so logical as it might seem at first sight. The growth of the bacillus
cannot have been a frequent phenomenon, and must have oc-
curred more often upon unconsecrated hosts, which were more
likely to be kept in a damp place. The average mediaeval
priest, if he found the red bacillus on a consecrated host might
readily assume that God had worked a special miracle to
strengthen his own faith in the doctrine of transubstantiation
as officially defined by the Church at the Fourth Lateran
Council in 1215. This assumption would, however, rest upon
an error. For the Catholic doctrine states clearly that while
the "substance" of the consecrated bread changes into the
substance of the body of Christ, the "accidents" of the bread
do not change. Blood forms no part of the accidents of bread.
Therefore, the growth of the red bacillus, or even the ap-

pearance of real blood, upon a consecrated host would have no relevance to the doctrine of transubstantiation. All this would be understood by educated mediaeval ecclesiastics. But the mass of the faithful would not necessarily follow this reasoning. The whole world of believers in the Middle Ages agreed that it was not merely possible, but even probable, that God might produce the appearance of blood upon a host, in order to confirm faith, or confute an unbeliever. From this premise the conclusion would naturally follow, in uncritical minds, that "the miracle" was evidence of divine anger against Jewish obstinacy.

Such a confusion of beliefs is not, however, the complete explanation. The doctrine that Jews had no right to live prosperously provided a rational and religious excuse for depriving them of their property. Whether or not greed was always a predominant motive when criminal charges were framed against them, the result was always the same—the prince and the priest who shared responsibility for burning them at the stake also shared (the former directly, the latter indirectly) in the financial profits of the operation.

When the Jews were driven out of Germany, they were at first welcomed by the civil power in Poland. Casimir the Great (1333–1370) appreciated the benefit his country derived from their industry. But soon after his death they became the victims of commercial jealousy. At the end of the century, the Archbishop of Posen instituted proceedings against them on a charge of having stolen three hosts from a Dominican church. The rabbi of Posen, thirteen elders of the Jewish community, and a Christian woman, after prolonged tortures, were all tied to pillars and roasted alive at a slow fire.[10] The Dominicans made money out of the survivors. They compelled the Jewish community to pay them a perpetual fine which was exacted annually until the end of the nineteenth century. After a special drive for conversions, organized in 1453 by St. John of Capistrano at Breslau, some

Jews were accused of stealing a consecrated host. "A Jewess was torn to pieces with red-hot pincers. Ritual murder charges followed; and forty-one Jews were burnt alive." [11] Behind these barbarities the motive of greed was predominant. "Many Christians," wrote a contemporary observer, "grew rich with the money plundered from the Jews." These atrocities continued to disgrace the name of Poland long after such wickedness had been forgotten in Western Europe. Jews charged with murdering children to use their blood in the synagogues were flayed alive, only two hundred years ago.

Although a few English writers have shown a tendency to soft-pedal the history of Polish Judaeophobia, no one has shown more ingenuity than Hilaire Belloc, who endowed the Poles with a special credit of patience, toleration, and charity, during the long martyrdom which, he suggests, they have suffered for centuries at the hands of the Jews. "The Poles," he wrote, "after making themselves a city of refuge for all the persecuted Jews in Christendom, became the victims of their own generosity, and are today suffering for it." [12] There has not, however, been any example in Polish history of a Pole being flayed alive by a Jew; if such an event had been recorded, no doubt Hilaire Belloc would have mentioned it.

The story of Jewish sufferings, told by S. M. Dubnow in his *History of the Jews in Russia and Poland,* was not read very carefully by many people in England, although an English translation was published in 1916. These mediaeval tales, most people liked to think, belonged to days of ignorance and superstition which had long passed, never to return. Science and modern education had put an end to all that. Dubnow was not so optimistic. He ended his book with a question the Jews have been asking for centuries: "The martyred nation stood on the threshold of a new reign with a silent question on its lip: What next?" Forty years later, Dubnow, then over eighty years old, was shot by the Nazis.

One of the reasons why the Germans chose Poland as the

principal Jewish crematorium and sent Jews there from all over Europe, was the conviction, justified by the events, that, whatever they did to them, they could rely on the passivity of public opinion and a certain degree of local co-operation. Many Poles did indeed refuse to co-operate, and helped Jews to escape, or hid them in their houses, and Catholic priests preached sermons, always at the risk of their lives, urging their congregations not to hand them over to the Nazis. Yet the tradition of centuries could not be effectively checked even by these heroic preachers, and it is hardly surprising that people who had not been encouraged to love their Jewish neighbors in times of peace were not always prepared, when the crisis came, to make the sacrifice which love may sometimes demand.

The notion that Jews have not really been persecuted at all, or have not been persecuted more severely than other minority groups, may sometimes be due to ignorance. It has often provided a favorite argument for people who secretly approve of oppressing them, provided they are not oppressed too much. It is possible, in England, to be well read in history, even to take an honors degree, and yet know practically nothing about the history of the Jews in Europe. In many textbooks of European history, they are either not mentioned at all, or simply referred to, in passing, as usurers.[13]

Ignorance is the probable explanation of a remarkable sentence written in 1913 by Cecil Chesterton: "We are told that the Jews have been persecuted! Well, the Irish Catholics have been persecuted . . . more severely than the Jews."[14] G. K. Chesterton knew perhaps a little more history than his brother. Yet his reading had been confined within the same narrow limits. "To talk of the Jews always as the oppressed and never as the oppressors," he wrote, "is simply absurd; it is as if men pleaded for reasonable help for exiled French aristocrats or ruined Irish landlords, and forgot that the French and Irish peasants had any wrongs at all!"[15] The theory held by these

writers is probably that Jews may perhaps have been persecuted from time to time, but that they always deserved it:
Christians, irritated to the point of frenzy at the sight of people
who had more money than they had, turned upon them, and
righteously slaughtered them. French anti-Semites, who are
seldom humbugs, do not hesitate to express their sympathy
with such procedure in plain language. The late Georges
Bernanos frankly approved of the crimes committed by his
Christian forebears. "When the right moment came they
cleaned out the Jew, just as a surgeon cleans out an abscess." [16]

In Spain "the abscess" was cleaned out with cold-blooded
efficiency under Dominican guidance. Torquemada, the
master surgeon, prepared and supervised the operation. In
1492, the whole Jewish population—estimates of the number
vary from two hundred thousand to half a million—were
despoiled of their property and ordered to leave the country
at four months' notice. A few thousand saved themselves for
the time being by accepting baptism. Cecil Roth writes:

> The stalwarts who ventured forth were by no means at
> an end of their tribulations. Famine and pestilence dogged
> their footsteps to the end of the earth. Many were robbed
> and murdered at sea by unscrupulous ship masters. Those
> who landed on the coast of Africa had to face the terrors of
> fire and famine as well as the onslaughts of brigands. More
> unfortunate still were those who were cast ashore in Chris-
> tian Europe; and even contemporaries were shocked at the
> spectacle of zealous friars wandering among the famished
> groups on the quayside of Genoa, with a crucifix in one hand
> and loaves of bread in the other, offering food in return for
> the acceptance of the religion of love.[17]

Bartholomew Seneraga, who witnessed the desperate condition of these refugees, has recorded, with a hint of disapproval,
why the populace, and indeed the whole world of his time,
showed such complete indifference to their fate. This indifference, far from being a sign of inhumanity, was simply due
to the fact that Jews were not regarded as human beings, but as

creatures of a lower order, like animals. The suffering of these people, he said, "seemed praiseworthy, as regarding our religion; yet it involved some amount of cruelty, if we look upon them, not as animals, but as men, the handiwork of God." [18]

Jews were looked upon not merely as animals, but as animals whose destruction was profitable; good money could always be made by killing them; they were "fur-bearing" animals. Even the poorest of them always had something that could be appropriated. Jew baiting, said an English doctor in Palestine, a few years ago, has always been the sport of kings. It was a sport that paid.

The Spaniards who burnt Jews at the stake, the princes who drove them into exile, and the priests who framed ritual-murder charges against them and then tortured them to death, were all animated by the same profit-making motive. The excuse varied, but whether it was religious, political, or economic, the result was always the same: Jewish money went into the pockets of the hunters.

The technique of this sport was perfected by twentieth-century Germans, who showed how money could be made from Jews after they were dead. Tons of gold were collected and stored in a Berlin bank—melted down metal from rings hacked off fingers; gold tooth fillings pulled from dead men's mouths. Many sacks were filled with tresses shorn from the heads of dead women, flesh was used to make soap, and bones to make fertilizers, when the royal sport of Jew baiting became a popular sport in Germany. These things were done by men who were baptized Christians. They should be remembered by people who talk about the Jewish greed for gold. [19]

Jews in the fifteenth century were allowed the right to a grave. But while they were alive, while they had any money or property, they were hunted to death. Most of those who were driven from Spain, after being robbed of their possessions (some say as many as a hundred thousand), [20] escaped over the frontier into Portugal, where they found no friends. In 1496, King Manuel decreed the expulsion of all Jews and Moors who refused baptism, under pain of death, and of course, confiscation of all their property. Moreover, their children were to be taken from them and forcibly baptized. By this last proviso the Jews, who have always had great devotion to their children, were attacked where they were most vulnerable. The Portuguese did not remember that when Christ said, "Suffer little children to come unto me, for of such is the Kingdom of Heaven," he did not mean: "Drag Jewish babies from their mother's arms; break up families; tear the boys and girls away from their weeping parents, send them as far away as possible, to the other end of the country, and then baptize them in the name of the Father, and of the Son, and of the Holy Ghost; and above all, make sure that they never see their parents again."

Most of the Jews who had sought refuge in Portugal were reduced to despair by an almost immediate renewal of the terror. They had nowhere to go, no friends anywhere. The priests were determined on the mass salvation of Jewish souls. Dr. Cecil Roth writes:

> The expulsion from Portugal is, in fact, a misnomer. The number of those who were able to emigrate was so exiguous as to be negligible. What put an end to the residence of the Jews in the country was a general conversion of unexampled comprehensiveness, knowing almost no exceptions and carried out by means of an unbridled use of force. . . . In most instances they were not even afforded the alternative of martyrdom. They were literally forced to the font and, after the merest parody of the baptismal ceremony, were declared to be Christians.[21]

They were forced to the font. But the Moors were spared for fear of reprisals in Moslem territory; the Moors had an army, and a land of their own. The cruelty of Turks, Saracens and Moors of all kinds had become proverbial, and the Christians had sound reasons for fearing them. But the memory of their atrocities has faded, and no one today blames "the Arabs" for anything their ancestors did in the fifteenth and sixteenth centuries. No one remembers what happened to the venerable Archbishop of Otranto, when the Moslems landed there in August, 1480. More than half the inhabitants of the district were put to death by a variety of painful methods, and the rest carried off into slavery. The aged Archbishop was sawn in two.[22] At Constantinople, in 1453, the Turks had shown a similar disrespect for the Christian religion. In a report of their proceedings, Pope Pius II complained that:

> They had destroyed the images of the Mother of God and of the Saints; they had cast down altars, thrown the relics of the martyrs to swine, killed the priests, dishonored wives and daughters, and even consecrated virgins, and murdered the nobles of the city. At the Sultan's banquet the image of our crucified Redeemer was dragged through the mire and spat upon, while they shouted "this is the God of the Christians."[23]

During the Hungarian Crusade, in the year 1525, "Five bishops and two archbishops were left lying on the field of battle. Two thousand heads were ranged as trophies of victory before the tent of the Sultan. On the following day, fifteen hundred prisoners were slaughtered."[24]

These atrocities left no permanent tradition of hate. Even at the time, Jews ranked higher than Turks and infidels among the enemies of Christendom. In the passenger list of Sebastian Brandt's "Ship of Fools," they were given priority:

> The cursed Jewes despysynge Christis lore
> For theyr obstynate and unrightwise crueltie
> Of all these folys must be set before.

Turks, Moors and Saracens, have somehow passed into the British tradition as "gentlemen." "The public memory is notoriously short," wrote Sir Arnold Wilson, "and I am frequently surprised to find among the generality of Englishmen the belief . . . that the Turks behaved during the war as clean fighters." [25] Most people, if they ever knew, have long ago forgotten how the Turks and the Arabs treated our prisoners of war in Mesopotamia, about thirty years ago. British soldiers, dying of dysentery and cholera, were flogged along the roads by the Arabs; those who fell by the way were robbed of their clothes, tortured, and sometimes buried, while still alive, by the Arabs. The full story of that march can never be told "for those who could tell the worst did not survive the journey. Some, especially the younger men of the Hampshires and Norfolks, suffered repeatedly, at the hands of Turkish soldiers, the worst indignity that a man can inflict on the body of another; they were too weak to resist their captors . . ." On the battlefields of Mesopotamia, "the Arabs prowled round, tireless in their foul lust for property and human life." [26] Yet no one in England today thinks it right to blame the Turks, or the Arabs, for the conduct of their ancestors at Otranto, or of their fathers in Mesopotamia. No one remembers a particularly savage affair which took place in upper Egypt near Minieh on the 17th of March, 1919. A train was held up. Two British officers and eight men were murdered. They were cut to pieces. Hands and feet, bits of flesh, were hawked through a village street with cries of: "English flesh!" [27]

If Jews at any period of history had sawn in two an archbishop, or even a sub-deacon, the operation would never have been forgotten. If Jewish terrorists had cut up the bodies of British officers and sold the fragments in the streets of a Jewish village, all the Jews in the world would have been held responsible, and would be forever reminded of the atrocious deed. There seems, therefore, to be one law for "the Arabs" and another for "the Jews." An Arab may steal half a dozen horses from a field, and get off with a reprimand; but a Jew who merely looks over the hedge is arrested and put behind barbed wire.

Education, intelligence and learning provide little protection against this bias which can put to sleep the critical faculty of even professional historians. It is depressing to find, in Ludwig von Pastor's *History of the Popes*, a sentence which might have been written by the commandant of a German concentration camp. Even in the mind of this indefatigable scholar, there was one law for the Christian and another for the Jew. A Pope accused of weakness, folly or crime must be given the benefit of the doubt, or allowed to plead extenuating circumstance; but the Jew, and the Jew only, may be condemned without benefit of clergy. Pastor hardly ever mentions the Jews, and seldom makes any comment on their misfortunes or on their conduct. But his vindication of the Holy Inquisition might have been written by Torquemada himself, had Inquisitors thought it necessary to explain why they burnt people alive. Pastor's explanation would give a feeling of satisfaction to any German race murderer at the present day; it has the faint but distinct odor of a Nazi:

> Sixtus IV showed great firmness in regard to the question of the Spanish Inquisition. This tribunal . . . was created in the first instance to deal with the special circumstances of the Jewish community in Spain. No other European State had suffered, to the same extent that Spain was then suffering, from the unrelenting system of usury and organized extortion practised by these dangerous aliens. Persecutions were the natural consequence. . . . [28]

There was nothing economically abnormal about the Jewish community in Spain. They were, on the whole, industrious, and many of them were consequently prosperous; some of them were very poor, and a few were very rich. The part they took in banking and in acting as the king's taxgatherers was indispensable to the economy of a primitive capitalism. Some of them, no doubt, both in Spain and in Portugal, had acquired their wealth by an excessive usury—but in both countries the Christians had a worse reputation for usurious practice. Owing to the security which Jews enjoyed in Spain until the end of the fourteenth century, the official rate of interest, fixed at 20 per cent, was lower than anywhere else in Europe. [29]

Overhead religious charges in Spain were higher than the economic resources of the country could afford. The rents received by the secular Church, excluding the revenues of monastic establishments, are estimated to have amounted to 4,000,000 ducats, a sum equal to about $60,000,000 in modern money values. [30] Along with this great revenue—perhaps because of it—went ignorance and immorality. All this revenue was a tax on commerce and industry, "much of which was in Jewish hands." [31] These "dangerous aliens" were industrious and consequently prosperous. The Spanish clergy watched this Jewish prosperity with envious eyes. Jewish money, unlike Christian money, could not be directed, by any of the bloodless ecclesiastical methods, into the coffers of the Spanish Church. The nobles, idle and rich, when they had ruined themselves by their extravagance, were always ready to avoid payment of their debts by massacring a few Jews. To arouse hatred and envy among the common people was always a simple task. They were told by the clergy that all Jews were fabulously wealthy; that they had crucified Christ; and that they made a practice of kidnapping little children to kill them and drink their blood. It was reasonable enough, after such premises, to affirm that God would approve of any severe measures that might be taken against them. Persecution was the logical consequence of such teaching.

After the great massacre of 1391, when over fifty thousand Jews were slaughtered and many thousands saved their lives by accepting baptism, the arguments of Christian preachers continued to meet with an ever-increasing success. St. Vincent Ferrer's conviction that scores of thousands had been converted by his eloquence seems to suggest that a naïve conceit may not be an impediment to canonization. Some of these converts were no doubt sincere; but the majority, as their history, and that of their children, proves, had accepted Christianity to save their lives and their property. They did not realize that by submitting to baptism they had condemned their bodies, as well as their souls, to live in the shadow of the Holy Inquisition.

No one knew better than Pastor, who made no attempt to hide the facts, that at the very time when he alleged Spain was groaning under the financial oppression of the Jews, the whole of Christendom was beginning to revolt against the organized extortions of the Roman Curia. At the end of the thirteenth century, under the guidance of the Papacy, which had become the greatest financial power in the world, the greater part of Europe had moved from a modified system of barter to a gold standard. Financial supremacy became more and more necessary as a support for the system of temporal power planned, and achieved, by Innocent III. The constant preoccupation of the Curia was to raise enough money to meet unavoidable expenses and to pay the ever-increasing crowd of seemingly indispensable officials. "It was this grasping, conscienceless, all-powerful body of clerics in the Curia, who blocked every endeavour to introduce reformation, who grew fat and worldly on the income of the Church, who made the hierarchy little more than a mighty secular power, and who put every spiritual service of the Church on a financial basis." [32] John XXII (1316–1334) was the cleverest financier and the richest man in Europe. He left a fortune of nearly $4,000,000. The Avignon cardinals were not uninterested in money; one of them, who died in 1364, left 176,000 gold florins, equivalent to more than $1,000,000. [33]

The return of the papal court to Rome led to no improvement either in morals or in financial methods. During the pontificate of Boniface IX, "the Curia at Rome became a veritable stock exchange." Places in the papal court and benefices throughout the Church were openly sold to the highest bidder. The corruption of the whole administration, and the confusion caused by the Great Schism, culminated in the election, in 1410, of the anti-pope John XXIII, described by Creighton as "a grotesque and blasphemous incongruity." A contemporary bishop deplored the fact that "simony and greed for gold were so openly practised in the Papal Court that they were not even looked upon as sins." The contributions which the Papacy extorted from an increasingly reluctant Christendom were not always used to meet merely the unavoidable expenses of the ecclesiastical administration. The cause of religion was not benefited to any notable extent when Sixtus IV, "who showed great firmness in regard to the question of the Inquisition," bought for himself a tiara which cost nearly thirty thousand pounds. Owing to the increasing expenditure of the papal administration and the extravagance of such Popes as Leo X (1513–1521), it became necessary to adopt the common expedient of insolvent governments—the creation and sale of offices and dignities; and worse still, the sale of indulgences and the proclamation of jubilees, against which Luther made his effective protest.

When allowances have been made for exaggeration, the history of the Roman Curia during the fourteenth, fifteenth, and sixteenth centuries suggests that the Jews of those times were not the only people who were unduly interested in money.

Spain was ruined economically not by "the unrelenting system of usury and organized extortion practised by those dangerous aliens," but as a consequence of the wholesale expulsion of her most hardworking and productive citizens, the Jews and the Moors. The Spanish Inquisition, as Pastor must have known, was an instrument of loot; and it acquired enormous wealth which remained in unproductive hands. "No other single factor," writes Dr. Roth, "was so instrumental in draining the Peninsula of its accumulated wealth during the sixteenth, seventeenth, and eighteenth centuries." [84]

Pastor had no word of sympathy for the Jewish victims of Spanish greed. The kind-hearted Seneraga, who witnessed the arrival of a shipload of refugees at Genoa, has recorded his impressions of a scene which became a familiar one during the past decade, when it attracted little more attention or commiseration from bystanders, than it did at the end of the fifteenth century:

> It was sad to see their misfortune. Many were exhausted by utter destitution and by thirst. The roughness of the sea, and their lack of experience in navigation had led to the loss of an incredible number. I say nothing of the cruelty and the avarice of those who brought them; many were thrown into the sea on account of the avarice of the sailors, and those who had no money for their passage sold their children. Many of them came into our town, where they were not destined to remain for long because the established custom of the Republic limited their stay to three days. Yet permission was granted for them to rest for a few days to recover a little from their stormy passage, and for the ships upon which they had been transported to be repaired. One might have thought they were ghosts: emaciated, pale, with upturned eyes, they might have been taken for dead, had they not sometimes moved a little . . . many of them died on the wharf, in a sector near the market, set aside to receive the Jews; there was, however, no fear of plague. As spring drew near, ulcers, dormant during the winter, began to appear, and this evil, a long time busy in the town, caused an epidemic the following year.[35]

Had Pastor lived a few years longer he would have seen "these dangerous aliens" on the move again—haggard processions of them driven to their death. He would no doubt have said that they had all been engaged in an "unrelenting system of usury" aimed at the destruction of Germany. He would have seen, also, another exodus across the Mediterranean, and scenes more disgraceful to humanity than those that had aroused the sympathy of Seneraga. Jews who fled by sea from the German terror fared far worse than their forebears who were driven from Spain by Ferdinand and Isabella. Ships packed with refugees sailed the high seas for months, both in the Old and the New World, unable to find any port where they could discharge their unwanted cargo. In 1940, three thousand Jews, who had succeeded in reaching the coast of Palestine, were caught by the Royal Navy before they could beach their wretched hulks on the shore of their National Home. They were transferred to a British ship in the harbor of Haifa, which, by a strange chance, was called the *Patria*. They were told that Mauritius was to be their destination. By some agency not certainly known, probably by some of the desperate passengers, the ship was blown up. Two hundred and fifty Jews were killed. A few who were picked up in the sea were taken on shore and allowed to remain. The rest of the survivors were deported to Mauritius where they remained in concentration camps for five years.

The story of the *Struma*, an unseaworthy vessel of 180 tons, had an even more tragic ending. The 769 passengers, more than a third of them women and children, reached Istanbul, but were not allowed to land, because they had no transit visas for Palestine. The British government refused to grant certificates, even to the children—even when the mothers said they would let the children go alone. After waiting for two months, the *Struma* was compelled to return to her Nazi-controlled port of embarkation. But the 769 passengers did in fact escape from the torturers and the gas chambers. The ship struck a mine, five miles from the Turkish coast, and all on board, save one, were drowned. A senior official of the British Immigration Office, when informed of the disaster by phone from the Jewish Agency, impulsively expressed his relief that this particular Jewish problem had been solved. "How dreadful!" he said; "but it is perhaps the best thing that could have happened."

The story of the Haganah ship *Exodus* six years later was

the climax and almost the end of the maritime war between the Royal Navy and the refugee ships. The Navy won; and the refugees were taken back to their concentration camps in Germany.

From the end of the Middle Ages to the end of the eighteenth century the Jews, in the greater part of Europe, had almost no history other than a history of endurance, resistance and survival. They lived as permanently displaced persons—subject to the whims and the greed of Christian princes; outlawed by the Church; protected, not from oppression, which was their constant burden, but from too much oppression, only by the spiritual shield of the Papacy. For, by a strange paradox, they found in the Papacy, which had condemned them to unending degradation, the only champion of their right to live. During the darkest centuries, in territories where the Popes ruled, whether in France or in Italy, they were granted a security of tenure and a continuity of that security, which they were not allowed, except in Holland at a later date, anywhere else in Europe. In the Papal States, they never suffered from the disaster of wholesale expulsion; they were protected from pogroms, with rare exceptions, not only by papal authority, but by the humane temperament of the Italian people. Papal prohibition of physical violence was never, in Rome or in the Papal States, merely an academic pronouncement. Paul II (1534–1549), ordered the Passion Play, which had been regularly staged in the Colosseum, to be suppressed because, after the performances, the audience used to go out and beat up Jews.

They were protected from severe oppression; but little was done to relieve them from the degraded condition of life to which they had been condemned by Innocent III. The shameful Corso Race, held at Carnival time, for two hundred years —a race in which elderly Jews were compelled to run half naked down the main street of Rome—was abolished in 1668, some years after Montaigne, himself half a Jew, had wit-

nessed the show without condemning it. This concession to
human decency was not granted for nothing. The Jews had
to pay, by way of compensation for the loss of a popular
sport, an annual tribute of money. At least one member of
every Jewish family had to attend a weekly sermon in a
Catholic church. Those who failed to comply with this regulation were heavily fined. Robert Browning, in his poem on
"Holy Cross Day," has pictured the grotesque scene:

> Higgedly piggedly, packed we lie,
> Rats in a hamper, swine in a sty,
> Wasps in a bottle, frogs in a sieve,
> Worms in a carcass, fleas in a sleeve.
> Hist! square shoulders, settle your thumbs
> And buzz for the Bishop—here he comes!
> Aaron's asleep—shove hip to haunch,
> Or somebody deal him a dig in the paunch!

The Jews, of course, always had to pay the preacher's fee.
Moreover, a special tax was imposed upon them to provide
for the upkeep of the Converts' House, where lost sheep who
had entered the fold of their own free will, or had been driven
in by economic or other pressure, were instructed in the principles of Christianity. Jewish money was in fact used to bribe
Jews into baptism—or, as a French historian prefers to put it,
"for the benefit of converts who were sometimes in too great
a hurry to wait for God to provide the reward due for their
abjuration." [36]

Under papal rule the Jews lived, not by right as human
beings, but on sufferance. Yet on the whole they lived less
miserably than in any other part of Europe. During the
fifteenth and early sixteenth century, owing to the human-
izing influence of the Renaissance, oppressive regulations were
often relaxed. This was sometimes for financial reasons, when
the Curia, in need of money, realized that Jews, if allowed a
little freedom, had a productive and taxable value; and sometimes by the humanity of a Pope who refused to adhere strictly

to the mediaeval tradition. A contemporary chronicler, during
the pontificate of the warrior Pope, Julius II, has recorded
one incident which almost presupposes a background of cor-
diality. The Pope had invited the Jews of Rome to meet him
on his way to the Basilica of St. Peter. They came dressed
in their best clothes, carrying olive branches and chanting
their psalms in Hebrew. "The Pope was delighted to hear
them singing in this manner." [37]

Never again were they to be seen in the streets of Rome,
marching in procession to greet the Pope, singing their sacred
songs in Hebrew; this tacit recognition of equality on the level
of humanity could never happen again. Humanity and humanitarianism were both swept away, so far as Jews were concerned, by the Reformation which divided Christendom.
They suffered the penalty of their unavoidable neutrality.
The reaction against them which coincided with the Catholic
Counter Reformation resembled in many respects the anti-
Semitic campaign which began in real earnest when Hitler
promulgated the Nuremberg Laws in 1935. Cardinal Caraffa,
elected Pope in 1555, taking the name of Paul IV, enforced
the policy of degradation. Within two months of his accession to the Papal throne, he issued the Bull *Cum nimis absurdum*—which has been described by a modern historian as
"one of the landmarks in the history of human persecution
and of Jewish martyrdom." [38] The text of this document
repeats and emphasizes the doctrine of the mediaeval Papacy.
The Jewish people are once more declared to have been condemned by God to "eternal slavery." They are told once
again that they are "insolent" because they presume to the
same standard of life as other human beings. And they are
accused, in the mediaeval manner, of committing "divers misdeeds," which are not specified.

In no public document, until the advent of Hitler, have
Jews been addressed with more unseemly language than that
employed in this message to Christendom:

*Cum nimis absurdum.* Forasmuch as it is highly absurd and improper that the Jews, condemned by God to eternal slavery because of their guilt, should, on the pretext that they are cherished by Christian love, and permitted to dwell in our midst, show such ingratitude to Christians as to insult them for their mercy and presume to mastery instead of the subjection that beseems them; and forasmuch as we have been informed that in Rome and elsewhere their shamelessness is such that they presume to dwell among Christians in the neighborhood of churches without distinction of dress, and even to rent houses in the more elegant streets and squares of the cities, villages and places in which they live, to purchase and possess real property, to hire Christian maidservants and wetnurses and other salaried attendants, and to perpetrate divers other misdeeds to the shame and contumely of the Christian name; and considering that the Roman Church tolerates the Jews in witness of the true Christian faith . . . we do therefore order the following measures, which are perpetually valid. . . .

It should be noted that Pope Paul IV emphasized the perpetuity of Jewish slavery. Like St. John Chrysostom, he offered them no hope of salvation in this world or in the world to come, unless they submitted to baptism. They were condemned to "eternal slavery," and the degrading conditions of their existence were to be "perpetually valid." They were ordered, of course, to wear the "badge of shame," a rule which had seldom been consistently enforced. They were ordered to live like animals in a compound, known henceforth as the Ghetto; and they had to sell, at nominal prices, all the property they possessed outside the new Ghetto walls. Paul IV made sure that Jewish money would find its way into Christian pockets.

Papal legislation during the following centuries confirmed, and often added to, these oppressive measures. The Council of Milan, in the year 1565, recommended a boycott of Jewish trade, adopting apparently the theory that Christian trade was honest and Jewish trade corrupt. If Christian traders were dishonest, they had merely followed the bad example of the Jews. Christian princes, said the Council, must therefore "combat the fraudulent and insidious customs of the Jews in their commerce with Christians." Jews were debarred from practising medicine, were not allowed to teach in universities, or to hold any dignity or public office which gave them any authority over Christians. In trade, they were restricted to traffic in old clothes and second-hand goods. Sexual intercourse between a Christian and a Jew was regarded as a sacrilege or a form of bestiality. The ruling of Pope Paul IV forbidding Christians to address Jews with a term of respect was repeated in March, 1729, by Benedict XIII, who prohibited Christian servants from addressing their Jewish employers with the title of "Sir." From the sixteenth to the eighteenth century, papal decrees frequently repeated that the Jews were the serfs of Christendom. But the Papacy never departed from the principle that they were not to be killed, and that no violence of any kind should be used against them.

The Reformation brought no immediate relief. "The worst evil genius of Germany," wrote Dean Inge, "is not Hitler, or Bismarck, or Frederick the Great, but Martin Luther." This statement is now seen to be unbalanced, not because it exaggerates the evil influence of Luther, but because the Dean, when making his comparison, did not foresee—could not have foreseen—the high place that Hitler was destined to occupy in the history of wickedness. Luther's hatred was intensified by his intellectual vanity and the vigor of his faith, which, like that of many others before and since his time, was united to an equally unshakable conviction that anyone who did not agree with him was an obstinate enemy of the Holy Spirit who deliberately closed his eyes to the truth. Evidence and arguments that were good enough for Luther should be good enough for everybody else.

He was convinced that his amended version of the Christian message would be readily accepted by the Jews, and that they would at once join with him in his assault on the Catholic Church. He naturally attributed their refusal to take any notice of his new doctrine, not to any defects it might contain or to any deficiency in his own exposition, but to the obstinacy of the stiff-necked race. He therefore attacked them with the full blast of his hatred. "All the blood kindred of Christ," he said, "burn in Hell, and they are rightly served, even according to their own words they spoke to Pilate." He recommended that their synagogues should be destroyed, their property, of course, taken from them, and finally that they should all be expelled from the country. His doctrine provided many suitable texts for Hitler's program of extermination. "Verily a hopeless, wicked, venomous and devilish thing," he wrote, "is the existence of these Jews, who for fourteen hundred years have been, and still are, our pest, torment, and misfortune. They are just devils and nothing more." [39] Such teaching seems to invalidate the Protestant claim that Luther "championed the cause of spiritual freedom in the modern world." [40]

Although he shared the popular prejudice against "usury," Luther bore Jews no ill-will on that account, for he admitted that Christians drove a harder bargain in business and in banking. [41] He was indignant at the greed of Italian bankers who were making fortunes out of the luxurious Roman Court. "The Florentines who surround the Pope," he wrote, in 1518, "are the most avaricious of men, they abuse the Pope's good nature in order to fill the bottomless pit of their passionate love of money." [42]

Luther attacked his enemies, both Catholics and Jews, with that special brand of vulgarity which has always appealed to the German people. After he had translated the Bible into German, with the help of Jewish rabbis, he claimed that it was henceforth a German book. The only Bible you have any right to, he told the Jews, "is that concealed beneath the sow's tail; the letters that drop from it you are free to eat and drink." [43]

He accused the Jews of cursing Christ every Sabbath in their synagogues, of planning to rob, stab and murder Christians whenever they got the opportunity, and expressed his hatred in language which has served as a model for the modern German Jew baiters—language which sounds, even today, like the ravings of a lunatic:

> When Judas hanged himself and his bowels gushed forth, and, as happens in such cases, his bladder also burst, the Jews were ready to catch the Judas-water and the other precious things, and then they gorged and swilled on the merd among themselves, and were thereby endowed with such a keenness of sight that they can perceive glosses in the Scriptures such as neither Matthew nor Isaiah himself . . . would be able to detect; or perhaps they looked into the loin of their God "Shed," and found these things written in that smokehole. . . ." [44]

> The Devil has eased himself and emptied his belly again —that is a real halidom for Jews and would-be Jews, to kiss, batten on, swill and adore; and then the Devil in his turn also devours and swills what these good pupils spue and eject from above and below. . . . The Devil, with his angelic snout, devours what exudes from the oral and anal apertures of the Jews; this is indeed his favorite dish, on which he battens like a sow behind the hedge. . . ." [45]

Although Luther's indelicate prose did not always meet with the approval of his contemporaries, they accepted his thesis that the Jews were outcasts, sons of Satan, who were unfitted to live alongside the good German Protestants. "We ought not to suffer Jews to live amongst us, nor to eat and drink with them," wrote the Lutheran preacher Ehrhardt, in 1558, who recommended at the same time, following the precedent of St. Ambrose, that "their synagogues should be set on fire." And he did not forget the necessity of relieving Jews of their cash. "Let all their ready money and treasures of gold and silver be taken from them; such faithful counsels and regulations were given by our divinely enlightened Luther." [46] Luther's scatological style has often been adopted in Germany, and to a lesser extent in France, to express the special brand of hatred which bears the German hallmark. The Germans showed a proper appreciation of the continuity of their history when they declared that the first large-scale Nazi pogrom, in November, 1938, was a pious operation performed in honor of the anniversary of Luther's birthday.

The substance of this German hate, which has not changed since Rudolf the Monk preached his crusade on the Rhine in the twelfth century, was analyzed, about fifty years ago, by the novelist Jacob Wassermann. He met reality for the first time, and discovered what it meant to be a Jew in Germany, when he went to serve his term of duty in the German army:

> For the first time I encountered that dull, rigid, almost inarticulate hatred that has permeated the national organism. The word "anti-Semitism" does not suffice to describe it, for the term reveals neither the nature nor the source, neither the depth nor the aim, of that hatred. It contains elements of superstition and voluntary delusion, of fanatical terror, of priestly callousness, of the rancor of the wronged and betrayed, of ignorance, of falsehood, of lack of conscience, of justifiable self-defense and of religious bigotry. Greed and curiosity play their part here, blood lust, and the fear of being lured and being seduced, the love of mystery and deficient self-esteem. In its constituents and background, it is a peculiarly German phenomenon. It is a German hatred.[47]

It would no doubt be very nice for the nationals of other countries to be able to agree with Jacob Wassermann that anti-Semitism was a peculiarly German phenomenon. But such agreement could be entertained only by ignoring the history of European behavior. One of the most often forgotten characteristics of this peculiar hatred is the fact that it does not depend on actual contact with the object hated, but can and does flourish, and indeed grow vigorously, in countries where no Jews have lived for generations. "My happier co-religionists," wrote Herzl, "will not believe me till Jew-baiting teaches them the truth; the longer anti-Semitism remains in abeyance, the more fiercely will it break out." The saying that every Jew carries anti-Semitism in his knapsack does not therefore explain the ubiquity and the permanence of the infection; it would be near the truth to say that anti-Semitism is carried in the knapsack of every Christian.

After the Jews had been expelled from England and France, they were still hated in those countries, for many centuries, as vigorously as ever. Cromwell's unsuccessful attempt to legalize their return, over three hundred and fifty years later, seems to have been part of his plan to develop English trade. A petition had been presented to him by the Jews, wrote the French ambassador in Holland to his colleague in London, "to obtain that their nation may be received in England to draw the commerce thither." [48] The scheme met with general opposition on the old religious and economic grounds. William Prynne (1600–1669), the Puritan pamphleteer, opposed it for the pious reason that the Jews in England "had crucified three or four children at least, which were the principle causes of their banishment." [49] Mediaeval tradition had evidently left its mark on English minds. The opponents of Cromwell's policy said it was not right that "the Jews should be permitted to live amongst us to blaspheme Christ." A group of petitioners protested that the idea was "sinful," and that the synagogue was a "scandal to Christian Churches." [50] But the real objection seems to have been based on fear of commercial competition: "The inhabitants of London suggest that it [the return of the Jews] would be very injurious to trade." [51] A number of Jews, however, began to enter the country, as a contemporary newsletter states, "by connivance." Two years later, in 1660, King Charles II was presented with a "Remonstrance concerning English Jews" wherein they were accused of having tried "to buy St. Paul's for a synagogue," and a petition was made for "a commission to enquire into their state." [52] This is the first mention in English modern history of the familiar Commission of Enquiry which became, long after, a permanent instrument of British administration in Palestine.

The handful of Jews were treated liberally by Charles II and James II and, under both kings, were able to consolidate their position. Nevertheless, they did not attain full citizenship until the middle of the nineteenth century.

The return of the Jews to France at the end of the eighteenth century met with considerable clerical opposition. The Bishop of Nancy, speaking in the National Assembly, on December 23, 1789, said that "the people regarded them with horror; a decree granting them the rights of citizenship would set the whole country ablaze."

The mediaeval doctrine that the Jews are a people accursed had continued to be popular in France for nearly five hundred years after they had all been expelled from the country. Instead of decreasing, Jew-hatred became even more intense than it had ever been before. This fact has not been recognized, owing to its unpleasant implications, by people who attempt to explain, without offending national or religious susceptibilities, the sudden outbreak of anti-Jewish demonstrations which began to disturb the private peace of Western Europe in the fourth quarter of the nineteenth century. "A stirring of men's minds, something quite new," wrote the French philosopher and critic Emile Faguet, "absolutely unknown in France for *three centuries* [sic], became manifest from about the year 1885—it was anti-Semitism." [53]

Far from being "absolutely unknown" in France from 1585 to 1885, Jew-hatred during that period, with the exception of a brief interval at the time of the French Revolution, was a consistent characteristic of the French people and of their civil, ecclesiastical and intellectual leaders. France, as Péguy said, has always been instinctively anti-Semitic. In the century of Louis Quatorze—"*le grand siècle*"—it would have been difficult to find anyone who did not accept as axiomatic, as an unchallengeable article of religious and social belief, that Jews should be treated as outcasts and as the enemies of God and man.

Pascal, for instance, accepted the mediaeval doctrine without question. He never applied his mind to the Judaeo-Christian problem; he received the popular Christian tradition as an article of faith, fortified it, and handed it on. "The condition in which one sees the Jews," he wrote, "is, moreover, a great proof of the Religion. For it is an astonishing thing to see that people subsisting for so many years, and to see them always in a state of misery; it being necessary for the proof of Jesus Christ, both that they subsist as a proof, and that they be wretched, because they crucified him." [54] It would be difficult to find in the writings of anyone belonging to the intellectual level of Pascal a sentence containing so much that is bewildering to the modern mind. Why should the divinity and message of Christ require such a peculiar proof? Why should the miserable condition to which the Jews had been reduced by the political action of their enemies, and their survival in spite of repeated attempts to exterminate them, be regarded as a proof of anything except Christian ill-will and Jewish toughness? Why did Pascal declare that it was "an astonishing thing to see that these people [were] . . . always in a state of misery," as if this misery had something miraculous about it, and was not merely the inevitable consequence of a policy of persecution which had lasted for centuries? After the Jews had been subjected for centuries to every economic disability, every method of extorting money, that priests and politicians could devise, had been expelled by princes and prelates from almost every country in Europe, and condemned to wander, homeless and hated, over the face of the earth, then comes Pascal, one of the giant thinkers of the seventeenth century, astonished to find that they are "always in a state of misery," ascribing that misery to divine intervention, accepting it as "a proof of Jesus Christ." Was it necessary for the proof of Jesus Christ that Jews be kept in a state of misery at Auschwitz, or that little Jewish children be flung, sometimes while still alive, into the furnaces of a German prison camp? It is easy to reply that "Hitler went too far"; but some responsibility rests surely with people who showed him the way, even long ago, and were going in the same direction themselves.

Bossuet was one of the most voluble anti-Semites who had preached in France since the days of Agobard. His sermons were distinguished by a religious zeal comparable to the fervor of the early Fathers. But, unlike them, he did not need to instruct his congregations; they had been learning the lesson for generations. He merely expressed, with the great power of his eloquence, the prevailing sentiments of the whole of Catholic France where hatred of the Jews was taken for granted. His influence with the pen was more pernicious than his pulpit oratory. In his *Discours sur l'histoire universelle*, written, in the first intention, for the instruction of the Dauphin, he popularized a historical theory which had, for generations, a corrupting influence on French ecclesiastical thought and even on French historical literature.[55] He rejoiced in the unhappy state of the Children of Israel and he described them, with an almost sadistic satisfaction, as the victims of divine vengeance, "banished from the Promised Land, having no land of any kind to cultivate, slaves wherever they may be, without honor, without liberty, without any appearance of a people. They are," he continued, echoing the words of Peter the Venerable, "a laughing stock among the nations and the object of their aversion." Many centuries had passed since a notable Christian preacher had ventured to go so far and declare, as Bossuet did, that "the Jews are the object of God's hatred." Twelve centuries had passed since they had first heard these words, spoken by St. John Chrysostom—"God hates you."

French literature in the eighteenth century provides many proofs that a popular prejudice against the Jews was still active in France four hundred years after they had been driven out of the country. Emile Faguet must have forgotten that Jean-Jacques Rousseau had written that they were "the vilest of people," [56] and that Voltaire had described them as "an ignorant and barbarous people who for a long time have combined the most unworthy avarice with the most detestable superstition." In a letter to a Portuguese correspondent who had accused him of intolerance, Voltaire apologized for having "attributed to a whole nation the vices of a number of individuals"; but he accompanied this apology with a renewal of his profession of dislike for "the Law, the Books, and the superstitions of Jewry." [57]

In Catholic France the miserable condition of Jews throughout Christendom was still complacently attributed to a divine plan; hatred, or at least contempt, for them continued to be admired as if it were a Christian virtue. "It is today a matter of common belief," wrote a student of Jewish history, in the first half of the eighteenth century, "that the state of misery to which the Jews have been reduced, and the universal contempt that people have for them, are the consequences of the malediction which Jesus Christ formerly cast upon that unhappy nation. This opinion does honor to the Christian religion." [58]

How firmly such fantastic ideas were rooted in the minds of French Catholics may be realized when they are found expressed almost casually and as a matter of common agreement, in the writings of Lamennais (1782–1854), one of the most liberal-minded ecclesiastics of his time. This unheeded pioneer of Christian socialism did not extend his sympathy for the oppressed proletariat to the people of Israel. In one of his most popular essays, written shortly before his break with the Catholic Church, he placed Jews in a category lower than slaves: "For eighteen centuries the Father has not yet pardoned them, and they drag on their life of suffering throughout the world, and in all the world slaves have to stoop in order to see them." [59]

During the nineteenth century this opinion was still carrying on its honorable function, especially among Royalists and Catholics. One proof of the power of such prejudice to survive, dormant and often hidden, yet menacing and vicious, in the minds of educated and intelligent people, is revealed by one sentence in the writings of a famous literary critic, Barbey d'Aurevilly (1809–1889), who once occupied a high place in the world of letters. This distinguished writer who, according to some of his contemporaries ranked with Chateaubriand, Lamennais, and Sainte-Beuve, implicitly approved of the mediaeval massacres which had been condemned by Pope Gregory IX, in 1236 as "so unspeakably offensive to God." "The Jews," wrote Barbey d'Aurevilly, "had killed Jesus Christ . . . and for this deicide they paid dearly in the Middle Ages. They passed under the lance of the Christian knights, who loved Jesus Christ as he has never been loved since . . . except by the saints. . . ." [60]

The mediaeval tradition of hate had, therefore, remained as fierce and irrational as ever in France long after the expulsion of the Jews at the end of the fourteenth century, and it was after their return as competitors in the scramble for money and power that economic motives combined with religious zeal, as in the Middle Ages, to produce "a stirring in men's minds" which was called anti-Semitism; there was nothing new about it except the name.

*And the Lord said to Abraham, if I find
in Sodom fifty just within the city, I
will spare the whole place for their
sake. . . .*

GENESIS XVIII:26

# 7

. . . . . . . . . . . . . . . . . . . . . . . . . . . . . . . . .

# Godfathers of Belsen

EDOUARD DRUMONT, whose name is now almost forgotten, became famous during the last decade of the nineteenth century as the leader of French anti-Semitism. His early journalistic career was uneventful and showed no signs of the talent for invective which he afterwards employed with remarkable success at the time of the Dreyfus case. His first contact with Jews had been friendly, and useful. He was employed, and well paid, for ten years on the staff of *La Liberté*, a newspaper owned and edited by Isaac Pereire.[1]

Shortly after the death of his Jewish patron, Drumont was converted from a vague to a more definite form of Catholicism by Père Du Lac, a French Jesuit. At the same time, he decided that the social and economic distress of France was due to the machinations of international Jewry, and that his true vocation was to save his country from that peril. He published in 1886 a book which ultimately obtained an enormous circulation and earned for him the distinction of being one of the leading Jew-haters of modern times. The book was *La France juive*. This classic of polemics, as its title suggests, was written to prove that France had fallen into the clutches of the Jews, who were plotting to obtain world domination after they had succeeded in destroying Christianity. Drumont believed, or pretended to believe, that in striking at them he was engaged, like the Crusaders, in a campaign for the defense of Christendom, and he professed his readiness to suffer martyrdom at the hands of the unbe-lievers: "I have prayed to Christ," he said, "for resignation if the publication of this book resulted for me in suffering, and for humility if my efforts were crowned with success." And he assured his readers that "God had taken the book under His care, because He knew, no doubt, that it was in-spired by love of justice." Readers nowadays have learnt to be suspicious of authors who announce that God is on their side and that their motive for writing is love of justice. Such professions of high moral purpose often conceal an uneasy conscience. Even Hitler's mind was perhaps not quite at ease when he wrote in *Mein Kampf:* "I believe today that my conduct is in accordance with the will of the Almighty Creator. In standing guard against the Jews, I am defending the handiwork of the Lord."

But if Drumont had any misgivings about which side God was on, they were dispersed by the testimony he received from the Catholics of France. Among the many heartening mes-sages from readers of all political parties, what touched him most was "the joy of our country parish priests—*ah! les braves gens! quelles belles lettres!*" He was consoled, not by the ignorance of these priests, but by the inversion of history they had apparently learned in their seminaries. More than any other section of the French people, he said, the parish priests had "a clear conception of that characteristic persecution, without parallel in history, which is directed by the manipu-lators of gold against the poor, by the sons of Judas against the servants of Jesus Christ." He called upon the clergy of France "to denounce the plotting Semites and hand them over to the secular arm."

Drumont described Jewry as an alien body, an irritating sub-stance, introduced into France at the time of the Revolution and now animated with an unchanging purpose to destroy

France, a plan already half accomplished, in order to be able in due course to destroy or dominate (the two usual alternatives) the whole of Christendom. He gave his blessing to anyone who at any period of history had persecuted Jews, and he approved of the Inquisition—just as he would have welcomed the Gestapo if he had lived to see it in action. "The Spanish Dominicans," he said, "were ardent patriots such as we are, who did not hesitate to suppress all Jews." He went on to say, with his usual note of piety, that since many of these Jew-destroying monks had eventually been canonized, "we cannot do better than imitate their manly virtue and defend, as they did, our patrimony, our country, and our race." All means of "defense" were justified, provided the end was achieved. Drumont therefore commended the pogroms in Russia, where Jews were being treated with mediaeval savagery, and advised his readers to adopt similar methods for driving them out of France.

The main idea that inspired *La France juive* was summed up by Jean Drault, one of Drumont's colleagues, in words which explain its appeal to many French Catholics: "Drumont restated the point of view of the Middle Ages, who hated the Jew because he had crucified the Savior of the world." [2] But Drumont made use also of economic arguments, based on statistics which were seldom reliable, to feed the flame of religious hatred and to bring into his party of haters the increasingly great number of Frenchmen who had abandoned the Catholic tradition. He would have been content to live peacefully in his library, wrote Léon Daudet, one of his most fervent disciples, "if his soul had not been oppressed by the tyranny of goats with human faces, the manipulators of gold and dung." [3]

The French people, bewildered by the prevailing political corruption, were indeed looking for a scapegoat, and Drumont provided them with what they wanted. The crowd which followed him "was the victim of a prodigious mystification." [4]

The French were told that out of a total national wealth estimated at 150 billions, the Jews owned 80 billions, which meant that the average wealth of each French Jew would be about one hundred thousand francs; all this money had, of course, been acquired dishonestly. The number of Jews in France during the last quarter of the nineteenth century did not amount to more than one-fourth of one per cent of the population; most of them were poor and not interested in anything outside their personal struggle to keep alive. The prominence and influence of many rich Jewish families, some of German or Alsatian origin, and a vulgar display of wealth which, for no valid reason, was regarded as more objectionable in a Jew than in a Christian, aroused the envy of competitors in business and in finance, who were glad to divert the watchful indignation of the proletariat from Christian to Jewish monopolists.

Drumont united religious, economic and racial sentiments into one single hatred. His theory of economics was inherited from the Middle Ages and, if his premises had been true, the conclusion, although morally unsound, could have been justified by expediency. He was sure that if the Jews could be driven out of France, or crushed out of existence, then peace and prosperity would follow. This conviction was based, in reality, not on religious but on racial pride. In Drumont's opinion, wrote Georges Weill, "the natural goodness of the Aryan race would enable the Frenchmen of France to put an end to all social trouble; the government would then resume its normal function, which was to protect the poor; the war against the Jews meant the liberation of the proletariat." [5] Such are the arguments commonly used to justify oppression of minorities; in the world of practical politics, where the rule of expediency is accepted as axiomatic, they are unanswerable. "If it were certain," writes Bertrand Russell, "that without Jews the world would be a paradise, there could be no valid objection to Auschwitz." [6]

*La France juive* did not at first attract much attention, although it obtained from Ferdinand Brunetière a long analysis in the *Revue des Deux Mondes*. This eminent critic, although an avowed Jew-hater, demolished the Aryan racial theory which provided the only apparently logical foundation for Drumont's thesis. "If one should insist," he wrote, "that there is really a difference between the Jew and ourselves, it is not race which has produced it but history, and history only—that is to say, we ourselves, and our forefathers, and their laws, their prejudices and their persecutions." He thought the book was "dangerous," and would mislead many people. French Jews did not take it seriously; they were wrong. Isidore Loeb, in the *Revue des Etudes Juives,* said that the whole thing was *"une fumisterie"*—a piece of nonsense—which indeed it was.

Drumont obtained his publicity from the Catholic press, first from *Le Monde*, the semi-official journal of the French hierarchy, and *L'Univers*, a paper which had been invigorated by Louis Veuillot, and was edited, after his death in 1883, by his brother Eugène. *Le Monde* had only about three thousand cash subscribers and was being run at a considerable financial loss. "The life of the paper is assured for 1886," wrote Monsignor d'Hulst to Cardinal Lavigerie, on January 7. "We have acquired a new and very capable editor, M. Drumont, who will be a help and a credit to us." [7] Drumont naturally took advantage of his new post to introduce the author of *La France juive* to his readers. "All right-minded people," according to an editorial dated May 6, 1886, "will sympathize with the Sergeant of Jesus Christ, and will thank him for his intrepidity." A missionary priest explained in *L'Univers* (May 13) that Drumont's plan was "not the extermination of the Jews but the more or less violent expropriation of Jewish property." "The Jewish race," he added, "seems to be organized for lucre, for systematic and scientific pillage." A writer in *Le Figaro* pointed out, however, that a proposal to confiscate all Jewish property might easily be extended to include also the property of honest French Catholics. Drumont advocated the expropriation of all capital which in his opinion had been unfairly acquired.

"All these ideas and arguments of Drumont," Jean Jaurès wrote many years after, "were taken from certain clerical opponents of the French Revolution, who had tried to convince the populace that the property expropriated by the revolutionaries would be handed over to the Jews. At this time, also, a distinction was made between 'good' and 'bad' capitalists." [8] Having carefully made this distinction, Drumont recommended that the workers of France should be encouraged to help themselves to Jewish property. "On the day when the Catholics, weary of defending a society which has become exclusively Jewish, allow the hungry mob to march on the mansions of Jewish bankers . . . , these beggars of yesterday, now the tyrants of today, will be crushed, and their blood will not make a stain any redder than the Kosher meat which they eat."

In a later work, *La Fin d'un monde*, Drumont extended his program of pillage to include, not only Jews of German origin, whom he particularly hated, but those who had been settled in France for generations. He now proposed to seize all Jewish capital and hand it over to a National Workers' Bank. He introduced this idea with a pious reference to St. Louis, who used to lock Jews up in solitary confinement and keep them on bread and water, until they disgorged their money.

Let us imitate St. Louis . . . ; let us put under lock and key a hundred individual Jews, Catholic or Protestant by birth, but all of whom have enriched themselves by the Jewish method, that is to say by financial operations. Let us compel them to restore the billions they have taken from the common national stock, and then found an Economic Chamber, composed entirely of representatives of the workers, who will adopt a regime which will seem to them best suited to the interests of all.[9]

These ideas were not taken very seriously by anyone.

*La France juive* became a best seller and was eagerly bought by the most stalwart supporters of capitalism, the Royalists who welcomed it as a political weapon against the Republic, and by the clergy who found in it edifying matter for their Sunday sermons. Before the end of the year, a hundred thousand copies had spread the gospel of anti-Semitism throughout France. *Le Petit Journal*, at that time the most widely read newspaper in the country, published the book in installments and offered copies as contest prizes.[10] Within ten years, more than 140 editions were printed; a popular illustrated edition, containing a picture of the author as a bearded warrior attacking Moses and the Tables of the Law, was advertised all over Paris. "Can anyone," asked Léon Bloy, "quote a single Catholic protest at the display . . . of the appalling effigy of this sacrilegious buffoon, clad in armor as a knight of the Holy Sepulchre, trampling Moses under his feet?"

Drumont spread his piety all over Europe. He sold the Spanish rights of his book for a nominal fee. "This is the least I can do," he wrote, "for a country like Spain, which originated the tribunal of the Inquisition, a tribunal, patriotic and humane, which the Jews have attacked because it protected Christian honesty against the invading and exploiting Semite." To a Polish publisher he gave the rights of translation free, expecting, he said, that God would reward him for his generosity. "Please God that my work may revive in the soul of every Polish patriot hatred for those infamous Jews who have betrayed them." Drumont prayed a great deal; prayer was a special, and most successful, part of his technique.[11]

In Austria, where a right-wing politician had proposed that the government should "offer a premium for shooting Jews similar to that offered for shooting wolves,"[12] Drumont found many sympathetic readers. The editor of a Viennese newspaper wrote to him, in 1886:

We Austrian anti-Semites, keeping up the unequal fight against the omnipotent Jew, had scarcely ventured to hope for this help coming from a country which we believed almost safe from the sinister influence of those people. France, with fifty to sixty thousand Jews, seemed to us an Eldorado in comparison with our country which is exploited by one and three-quarter million individuals of that race.[13]

Although *La France juive* was praised by Georges Bernanos, in 1931, as "a masterpiece of observation, analysis and erudition,"[14] it was, in fact a masterpiece of mendacity. Drumont had neither the equipment nor the temperament of an historian. His research was a search for scandal. He found most of his material in the long-forgotten compilations of A. Toussenel[15] and Gougenot des Mousseaux[16] who, having collected evidence to prove the corrupt state of French society, drew the patriotic conclusion that the Jews were responsible. He also made use of material originating from German sources, notably from the Protestant anti-Semite Johann Andreas Eisenmenger,[17] and from other German writers whose books had not been translated into French. Drumont knew no German, and it is probable that he was helped by collaborators. Armed with a mass of scurrility, mostly of German invention, he developed his thesis with a fluency which appealed to uncritical minds; he had almost certainly been encouraged to begin by some of his clerical friends, probably by Père Du Lac and even by Monsignor d'Hulst—both of whom, however, expressed their disapproval of his subsequent buffooneries. "It would be astonishing," said *Le Figaro* (April 19, 1886), "if Drumont had not consulted his friends at the Archbishop's headquarters before publishing his work." Some people evidently did not believe the writer of an article printed in *Le Monde* of April 7, who had affirmed that the paper had not been informed of the forthcoming appearance of the book

until it was actually in print and about to be issued to the
public. The writer of this article declared that

> . . . in spite of some statements, false or insufficiently veri-
> fied, [the book] meets with editorial approval. . . . It is a
> tremendous kick into the antheap of Jewry . . . which is
> overrunning everything, undermining everything, fouling
> everything . . . ; the task was urgent; Drumont has com-
> pleted it with a *furia francese;* and one feels relieved, and
> there is something truly healthy in this vigorous hatred.[18]

*La Croix*, a daily newspaper owned and edited by the Fathers
of the Assumption, likewise supported Drumont with their
own healthy and vigorous hatred, which went on for many
years until at last, in 1899, they were suspended from their
editorial functions by the Holy See.

Some of these Catholic papers that so fearlessly reprimanded
the Jews for their greed and their organized pursuit of money
were not themselves without faults of the same kind. But to
their undue affection for money were added hypocrisy, and
something very near to simony. They carried on a lucrative
practice of money-grubbing under pretext of devotion—especially devotion to two particular saints, one of whom was a
Jew: St. Joseph and St. Anthony of Padua. The headquarters
of this remunerative commerce was in the offices of the Société
des Bons Livres et des Bons Journaux. Paul Viollet, of the
Ecole des Chartes, protested against the conduct of such newspapers as *Le Pèlerin*, *La Croix*, and many others, which not
only "encouraged anti-Semitism and accepted it as a doctrine,"
but at the same time were engaged in making money out of
the credulity of the faithful. Although the French bishops
approved of Viollet's protest, it seems to have had very little
effect in restricting the pious traffic. "The faithful," said
Viollet, "regarded God as head manager of the business, and
the saints as commercial brokers with an interest in His operations." [19] The promoters of the industry, however, were not
disturbed by this reprimand, and they continued, somewhat

unwisely, to draw public attention to themselves by preaching against the financial transgressions of the Jews. A French anticlerical pointed out that "Congregations who extort money from devout imbeciles by promising them Heaven in exchange have no right to speak of Jewish money-snatchers." [20]

Encouraged by his success, Drumont produced a number of other fantastic volumes with an ever-increasing confidence in the credulity of his readers. He assured them in 1890, on the authority of August Rohling (whose forgeries had recently been exposed in an Austrian court of justice), that the Jews do not regard Christians as human beings, since "the marriage of Christians, as the Talmud explains, cannot be recognized any more than the copulation of animals." In 1891, he reminded the parish priests who had written him such beautiful and consoling letters that ritual murder had been the regular practice of Jews in the Middle Ages, and warned them "that in every country at the present day where the Jew is his real self [*à l'état de nature*], such crimes are constantly recurring." [21] He told them that the Catholic Church had officially confirmed and ordained belief in these pious legends. "To ask a Catholic priest," he wrote, "to deny the fact of ritual murder is simply to ask him to admit that the Church, by beatifying poor little children whose throats were cut by Jews, has been guilty of the most hateful imposture and made cynical sport of the credulity of nations." [22] Drumont had relied too confidently on a series of articles attempting to justify charges of ritual murder both in mediaeval and modern times, which were published anonymously, with the approval of high ecclesiastical authority, in *La Civiltà Cattolica*, the semi-official organ of the Vatican. (See Appendix B.)

Many priests in France, bewildered by such propaganda, seem to have regarded hatred of the Jews as part of the Catholic faith. They did not consider it their duty to deny any story, even if they suspected it might be false, which helped to keep that hatred alive. "To venture to deny ritual

murder," said the Rev. Stephen Coubé, "requires the incredible
aplomb of the Talmudist and the Freemason, or the incor-
rigible ignorance of certain Christians." [23]   Father Herbert
Thurston, S.J., a fearless exposer of humbug, bigotry and
superstition, took every available opportunity of castigating
these clerical anti-Semites. "If the temper of Father Coubé's
writings," he said, "were really representative of the *âme chrétienne*, we confess that we should prefer to take a chance in
the next world with the *âmes juives* whom he reviles." [24]

In all his books, Drumont mixed falsehood and piety with
an audacity which no mediaeval chronicler had surpassed.
He compared himself to Christ: "Following the example of
my divine master, I took up the defense of the oppressed
against the thieves and exploiters of the poor." He claimed,
indeed, that he was inspired by God and that his books contained a new revelation for mankind. "Christ saw the integrity of my soul . . . he rewarded me by enabling me to
learn Total Truth [sic], and by drawing me little by little
towards the light. By this light I saw contemporary events
clearly, and helped men of my own time to see them clearly
too. A few rascals, very few in fact, disapproved of me, but
honest folk were satisfied, and were good enough to congratulate me and praise me." [25]   Drumont was indeed greeted as a
great Christian hero, not only by many of the clergy, but by
some of the leading literary Frenchmen of his time. He had
no talent for public speaking, yet in 1887 he began to give
anti-Semitic lectures in Paris—encouraged, the brothers Goncourt noted in their journal, by the advice of his ecclesiastical
friends, who assured him that he would be helped by the Holy
Ghost. Edmond de Goncourt said that Drumont "wrote
what everyone was thinking, and he alone had the courage to
write." [26]

Among the "honest folk who were satisfied," one of the
most eloquent was Léon Daudet, who described, twenty years
afterwards, the effect which had been produced upon him by

the publication of *La France juive:* "On Hebraic dung, Jacobinism was in full flower. . . . Suddenly, under the livid lowering sky, came a burst of thunder, and the horizon was slashed with the lightening of truth—the book of vengeance had appeared; a book of critical value, a book of history, resplendent with cold, clear anger . . ."[27] Léon Bloy was one of the "few rascals" who disapproved, and his explanation of Drumont's success is nearer to the truth than the rhetoric of Léon Daudet:

> To say to the man in the street, even to the shabbiest specimen of a rottenness beyond hope: "These perfidious Hebrews who bespatter you with mud, they have stolen all your money. Get it back from them, O Egyptian! Beat them up, if you have any guts, and chase them into the Red Sea!"—to keep on saying this, to say it everywhere, to bellow it in books and in newspapers, and even now and then to fight a duel,[28] so that the idea will echo nobly over the hills and dales, and above all *never to speak of anything else,* that is the prescription and the mystification, the established tactics of the big guns which will ensure a triumphant success. No one—God help us!—can resist all that. We must remember that this great man speaks in the name of Catholicism. Everyone knows, of course, the disinterestedness of our Catholics, their unchanging scorn of speculation and of the manipulations of finance, and the celestial detachment they profess. . . . It is easy therefore to understand the impetuosity of their zeal when the monkey paws of the anti-Semite begin to tickle them up with notions of justice. One might even say that on this occasion the scales fall from many eyes, and that the man Drumont appears as the apostle of the lukewarm who had not realized that religion could be so profitable.[29]

From the sale of his books Drumont was enjoying a comfortable income, and he began to realize that more money, much more money, might be made out of the popular passions he had stirred up. His hatred of the Jews gradually became less intense than his growing greed for gold. The notoriety he had already achieved opened the way, not only to political power, but to the acquisition of that wealth which he affected to despise when it was in the pockets of other people.[30] In 1892, he founded a daily paper to defend Catholic France against infidels, Republicans, Freemasons and Jews. Eight years had passed, he told his readers, since he had first been inspired by God: "A Will from above told me to speak. And I have spoken." The fortune he made out of his new venture, according to the testimony of one of his associates, Jules Guérin, was derived mainly from swindling and blackmail.

Because Guérin quarreled with his chief over a division of the spoils and started a rival paper, he is not an unbiased witness against Drumont; but to verify all his allegations of bribery and corruption would involve an amount of research which the subject does not warrant. He published his *Trafiquants de l'antisémitisme* in 1905,[31] and died soon after. The book contains enough evidence to prove, beyond all doubt, that Drumont had been involved in many shady financial transactions, and that for many years he was in close contact, to his own advantage, with swindlers who had been convicted in the French courts for a variety of financial misdemeanors. Most of the charges made by Guérin are supported with quotations from letters that are undoubtedly genuine, and with many photographs of incriminating documents. The unedifying story about the founding of *La Libre Parole* was never challenged by Drumont.

The paper was financed, not, as has been said,[32] by the Jesuits, but by a man named J.-B. Gérin, who, two years earlier, had been editor of a newspaper, *Le National*, which was devoted to defense of the Jews and to combating the calumnies contained in *La France juive*. On April 20, 1890, *Le National* sent out a circular to a number of rich Jews in Paris:

*Monsieur et Co-religionnaire:*

. . . The Israelites have been the object of most odious calumny in the Press, and certain distinguished Jews have thought it would be useful to take up their defense in a news-paper of importance. *Le National* is willing to open its columns for this purpose . . . and I have the honor of asking for your help in this work of propaganda. . . .

Gérin, however, was known to be a disreputable financier, and few Jews fell into the trap—so he went over to the other side. Two years later, he reappeared as owner and editor of *La Semaine Financière*, and after some obscure negotiations with Drumont, "saw a future in anti-Semitism." [33]

On April 14, 1892, therefore, Gérin, on behalf of *La Semaine Financière* sent out another circular, not to rich Jews, but to a number of rich anti-Semites:

. . . Monsieur Edouard Drumont, well-known author of *La France juive* and many other books which have had such a well known success, intends to continue with a newspaper the work he has so brilliantly begun with his books. . . .

Gérin recommended that his clients buy shares of the new paper at two thousand francs each ($320). The shares, he pointed out were "to bearer," and no publicity would be involved by becoming a holder. "Our company has agreed to undertake the financial organization of this paper, which will be called *La Libre Parole* and will defend our national interests. . . ."

According to an agreement drawn up between Gérin and Drumont, the former undertook to provide the company with the necessary capital: 300,000 francs ($60,000). Drumont was to get an editorial salary of 25,000 francs ($5000) and 10 per cent of the profits. Moreover Messrs. Drumont and Gérin presented themselves each with 150 shares, priced at 2000 francs per share. They thus divided equally between them, in paper, a sum of 600,000 francs ($120,000). This paper could be cashed by selling the shares to the public.

"On the wall of every room in the offices of *La Libre Parole*, there hung a crucifix." [34]

Soon after, Gérin was arrested on various charges of fraud.

This unfortunate incident was explained in *La Libre Parole* (February 3, 1893) as "an act of political vengeance." The financier was then replaced on the board of the paper by a man of straw named Wiallard. A rival journal announced that the new administrator was a Jew, and that his real name was Crémieux. Although Wiallard-Crémieux produced evidence that he had been baptized, his name was soon after removed from the list of directors. Jules Guérin explains how the financial column of *La Libre Parole* was used in co-operation with *La Semaine Financière* to conduct blackmailing operations on a large scale. The campaign opened with an attack on the Crédit Foncier, a bank which, it was alleged, was controlled by German Jewish financiers. Before very long, rumors began to circulate in Paris that many shareholders of the newspaper were Jews. Guérin explains how this happened. Drumont's object was to sell as many as possible of his 150-franc shares at their fictitious value of 2000 francs. In 1897, an article appeared in *La Libre Parole* about certain alleged illegal transactions of Baron Robert Oppenheim. The campaign against Oppenheim ceased shortly afterwards for no apparent reason. He had silenced Drumont by buying from him three shares for 6000 francs.

In 1900, circulars were sent around among wealthy anti-Semites offering them shares at 2000 francs. Drumont was unloading. For seven years the newspaper had boosted bogus companies, rotten shares, bankrupt gold mines and patent medicines, under the cloak of religious piety. The credulity of his readers could not stand much more. The paper struggled on for several years with Drumont acting as nominal editor. He sold out in 1910, at the age of sixty-six years. He lost the greater part of his fortune when a bank in which he had invested his money (not a Jewish bank) became insolvent. He died during the First World War.

Attempts have been made to justify the methods of his campaign against Jewry on the ground that he was actuated, as indeed he claimed to be, only by religious and patriotic motives. "The spectacle of this man," wrote Lecanuet, "inspired solely by love of his faith and of his country, attacking alone, with an almost extravagant intrepidity, an enemy strong, numerous and perfidious—that is a spectacle worthy of admiration." [35] Drumont, however, seldom allowed hatred of his "perfidious" enemy to interfere with the profits of business. Jews who were attacked in *La Libre Parole* with "an almost extravagant intrepidity" were often able to buy his silence at a substantial figure, and publicity for their commercial or financial affairs at the usual rates. Drumont's polemic was not merely extravagant, it was obscene; yet he knew what he was doing. He wrote for a public whom he knew would lick their lips over the foulest lie he could tell them about any member of the accursed race. His readers were delighted to learn in his *Testament d'un antisémite* that "the Jews had succeeded in infecting part of Russia with syphilis." [36] Not even Julius Streicher was able, in his most grotesque moments, to reach much lower than the degree of literary turpitude to which Drumont descended in his comment on the German-Jewish poet Heinrich Heine:

> This exquisite poet, the delicate-minded Parisien, is indeed the brother of the filthy Jew-boy, of the Jew-boys with corkscrew curls from Galicia, who, met together for some ritual murder, look at each other with merry glances while, from the open wound of their victim, issues pure and scarlet the Christian blood destined for their sweet bread of Purim. [37]

This exhibition of "extravagant intrepidity" seems to have escaped the notice, not only of Père Lecanuet, but of Father Sydney F. Smith, S.J., who imprudently included in an article on "The Jesuits and the Dreyfus Case" the following statement made by Drumont, then posing as a champion of his country against Jewish "international finance": "You will be told that our campaign against the Jewish speculators is a religious campaign. This is absolutely false. . . . I have never written a single line which could wound the faith of the last Jew from Galicia." [38] Léon Daudet was delighted with the description of "Jew-boys from Galicia with corkscrew curls, met together for some ritual murder." He told his readers, in 1904, that "Edouard Drumont had revealed quite clearly the nomadic-Jew aspect of Henri Heine." [39]

Among the young men who gathered around Drumont, the most talented, the most implacable hater was Léon Daudet, in whose prose can be distinguished the rasping, ruthless, threatening note which listeners heard forty years later in the broadcasts of William Joyce from Hamburg:

> Oh, race of Judas, you wretched people! Will you never understand those among whom you live, hated and stinking, but still enjoying yourselves? Will you not ever realize that this French good nature, which seems at times to be listless, is followed by terrible reactions, and that your influential friends, your business connections and your cheques will never save you from a just vengeance? [40]

Soon the ominous question began to be asked in France, and in Germany: What can be done with them? "One has to be logical," wrote a Frenchman in 1925; "since they have not been willing to become assimilated, to melt away, to disappear, what can be done about it? . . . Politics will settle the question, in the usual way, by force; gold will not prevent it." [41] Ten years later, the Nazis had also discovered the utility of this logic. Drumont himself repeatedly announced that he was merely a pioneer, that the results of his work would be revealed in the future, and that future generations would remember and be grateful for the warnings he had given. "What Drumont proclaimed," wrote Jean Drault, one of the last surviving members of his party, in 1935, "Hitler has achieved."

Albert Monniot, another of Drumont's young men, lived to see the triumph of his ideas in Nazi Germany, and to record

his own satisfaction in *La Libre Parole*, now revived as a
monthly periodical and edited by a notorious fascist: "When
we see a man arouse a people, rescue it from unhealthy in-
fluences, free it from the toils of the International, and restore
it to its destiny, accomplishing, in a word, the task of salvation
attempted among ourselves by Drumont . . . , we cannot do
otherwise than envy such a privileged people." [42]

An attempt to revive French interest in the anti-Semitic
writings of Drumont was made in 1931 by Georges Bernanos,
who knew nothing, perhaps, of Drumont's disreputable history, but honored him as an enemy of the Jews. When a
Jesuit priest, Père Albert Bessières, told the truth about Drumont at a public meeting, Bernanos came to the rescue of his
hero with an appropriate piece of scatological scurrility, for
which, however, he has been generously forgiven. "The death
at sixty of Georges Bernanos," says a writer in *The Tablet*
(July 10, 1948) "is a great loss to French and European letters.
. . . The exceptional power of his writing . . . made everything that he wrote impressive in the literal sense, unforgettable
and unforgotten."

The death of Georges Bernanos was no loss to the cause
of humanity. He ranks, after Charles Maurras, as the leading
French race-hater of his time. In 1938, when Jews in German
concentration camps were being beaten to death with steel
whips, Bernanos did not use "the exceptional power" of his
pen in *their* defense—but in defense of Hitler. "I do not believe," he wrote, in unforgettable words, "that M. Hitler and
M. Mussolini are demigods. But I merely pay homage to the
truth when I say that they are men without fear. They would
never tolerate in their own countries the organization of
massacres." [43]

According to an obituary notice in the *Times* of London,
literature was for Georges Bernanos a "kind of sacrament."
But the language he used in his controversy with Père Bessières
was neither literary nor sacramental. He wrote:

A clown named Bessières, one of those jobbing contractors of souls, with the naïve but not uncommon coarseness which, hidden by the purrings of devotion, sometimes turns to ferocity, denounced Drumont to the young men of *La Vie Catholique* as one of the most notorious renegades of the century.—Allow me a word, Bessières, I do not want to be rude, but you were ill advised to allow your filth to drop on his poor tomb, even if you had to relieve yourself, my friend. There was plenty of room, old chap, up against the wall. In any case you are wasting your time; the good man is now sheltered and secure, under a sufficient load of earth; he cannot hear you now. And the dear little French lads whom you take for such a purpose, to relieve nature in cemeteries, they will not listen to you either. It is the good man from the corruption of his grave, who will speak to them now.[44]

At the time when Georges Bernanos was defending Drumont with such an appropriate choice of expressions, the good man was indeed speaking from his grave, not only to French youths, but to the young men of Germany who, with their rubber truncheons, their steel whips and their technique of shooting in the back of the neck, were carrying on at Buchenwald, Dachau and Belsen, the job of saving the world from Jewry.

In 1894, two years after the appearance of *La Libre Parole*, Drumont found his supreme opportunity for making mischief. Captain Alfred Dreyfus, a Jewish officer on the general staff of the French army, was accused of selling military secrets to Germany. Had it not been for Drumont, the *affaire* would never have been heard of.[45] Even the unscrupulous Mercier, minister for war, was not at first convinced that the flimsy evidence concocted by members of his staff against Dreyfus was sufficient to warrant an inquiry. But his doubts were silenced when *La Libre Parole* appeared with the headlines "Jewish Traitor Under Arrest," and the editor announced, in a pious article, that "just as Judas had sold the God of pity and love, so Captain Dreyfus has sold to Germany the plans for mobilization."[46] Drumont had been secretly informed of what was brewing by the notorious Colonel Henry. This intelligence officer was eventually discovered to be the chief agent in a long story of forgery and intrigue, in which practically the whole military hierarchy of France became involved.

Dreyfus, wealthy, intelligent and a hard worker, living happily with his wife and two children, did not gamble, drink, or keep mistresses, and was therefore regarded with suspicion and dislike by his brother officers. They were unable to produce any motive to account for his supposed treachery. But this absence of motive did not impress the military jury; Dreyfus was a Jew, and therefore, with or without any obvious motive, considered a traitor.

The trial was held *in camera* for reasons of "public security." Dreyfus was sentenced to life imprisonment and sent to Devil's Island, one of the most unhealthy settlements in the French colonial empire, where he was treated with exceptional severity.[47] The judgment was based on a "secret dossier" which was not communicated to the defense. This illegality was not discovered until two years later, when the excuse was made that it had been necessary in the interest of national safety. Colonel Picquart, an officer of the intelligence section, discovered certain facts which pointed to the guilt, not of Dreyfus, but of Major Esterhazy, a disreputable and impoverished scoundrel who was not related to the distinguished Hungarian family of that name. Picquart was disgraced and Esterhazy acquitted. The day after this curious verdict, Zola wrote his memorable letter to the president of the republic, the letter to which Clemenceau gave the title "*J'accuse.*" In July, 1898, Cavaignac, then minister of war, produced from the secret dossier evidence hitherto unpublished, and his oration in the Chamber of Deputies, confirming the guilt of Dreyfus, was published by proclamation throughout France. A few weeks later, however, Colonel Henry went to see Cavaignac and confessed that the evidence taken from the secret dossier was a forgery, and that he himself, with the best of intentions, was the forger. Henry was put under arrest, and next evening committed suicide. *La Libre Parole* announced that he had been "assassinated by the Jews." Revision of the trial was now unavoidable. In September of the same year, 1898, the case was reopened at Rennes; Dreyfus was found guilty, with "extenuating circumstances," sentenced to ten years' imprisonment, and a few days later pardoned by presidential decree. In 1906, the verdict of Rennes was annulled. Dreyfus was rehabilitated, and decorated with the Legion of Honor on the same parade ground in Paris, where, eleven years before, he had been degraded amidst the uproar of a mob shouting "death to the Jew."

Dreyfus at Devil's Island became a symbol and a test— a symbol representing, in the eyes of practically the whole French nation, Jewish treachery; and a test of French patriotism and French religion. Anyone who dared to suggest that he might be innocent, or that his trial had been illegal, was at once regarded as an enemy of that formidable trinity, *la Patrie, l'Armée et l'Église.* "It was not a man who was being degraded for a personal fault," wrote Drumont in *La Libre Parole*, "but a whole race whose shame was being exposed." The Jew had been condemned in the minds of his judges and by the almost unanimous voice of public opinion, even before the evidence, such as it was, had been heard. "I don't need anyone to tell me," wrote Maurice Barrès, "why Dreyfus was a traitor . . . or that he was capable of treachery. I know that from his race."

Public opinion began to change after the publication of Zola's "*J'accuse.*" Men such as Clemenceau, Bernard Lazare, Scheurer-Kestner, vice president of the French Senate, and Anatole France, who were convinced that Dreyfus was innocent and knew that his trial had been illegal, were denounced as members of an imaginary *Syndicat Juif*, who had been bought with Jewish gold. Apparently all French consciences were for sale except those of the aristocracy, the army and the Church. Albert de Mun, leader of the French Catholic Party, who advocated "a return to the social conceptions of the thirteenth century," [48] was convinced that "some occult power was at work trying to create disorder throughout France." He refused to discuss even the possibility that a Jew might be innocent of treachery, and was opposed to a revision of the trial. Teyssonnière, one of the handwriting experts at the first trial, said that Dreyfus was guilty "because all Jews are traitors." A French deputy, Georges Berry, declared in the Chamber that "Dreyfus, whether innocent or guilty, must remain at Devil's Island"—a remark which Clemenceau thought "should be handed down through the centuries."

When Charles Maurras was told that even the destruction of society was preferable to the toleration of injustice, he replied that many societies had been known to exist without justice, but that justice had never existed without a society. St. Augustine of Hippo had to deal with this kind of claptrap in the fifth century. "Kingdoms without justice," he pointed out, "are nothing but great associations of brigands."

Péguy saw the danger. "A single injustice," he wrote, "a single crime, a single illegal act, if it is universally, legally, nationally accepted from a motive of expediency, is enough to dishonor a whole people. It becomes a focus of infection which corrupts the whole body." Society, said Rabbi Simeon Ben Gamaliel, "stands firm on three pillars: truth, justice and peace." Maurras and his anti-Semitic friends were trying to build a new world founded on untruth, injustice and war—our world today.

François Coppée, Ferdinand Brunetière, Léon Daudet, Maurice Barrès and Charles Maurras were among the most notable defenders of France against the Jewish peril. These men believed in the thesis of Drumont that Jews were all potential traitors and the chief cause of political, financial and social disorder in France. Yet they hated them not primarily as traitors or as usurers, but as Jews. In Christian France, as Péguy said, hatred of Jews was an instinct. This instinct expressed itself in the writings of Maurras and Léon Daudet with the same fury which had filled the sermons preached for the same cause, nearly a thousand years earlier, by Bishop Agobard and Peter the Venerable. Ferdinand Brunetière wrote with more restraint, in the English manner. "I have little use for Jews," he began, when reviewing *La France juive;* "in fact I have no use for them at all." François Coppée expressed in verse his desire, and the desire of all France, to insult the condemned Jew and the whole of his treacherous race: "Ah! Why do they not let us see the foul features of the traitor so that we may all of us, one after the other, spit into his face." The opportunity was provided at Rennes. Barrès went to the court to gloat over the misery of a Jew. He watched "the figure of Dreyfus sweating treason," and saw him "as if he were crime itself sitting before his judges." [49]

The heroes of the thirteenth century were not forgotten. "How right was St. Louis, King of France," wrote another French author, "when he recommended that no one should argue with a Jew, but should drive a sword into his belly as far as it would go." The blood legend was revived by Drumont whose "scholarly brain was full of the great memories of the thirteenth century." [50] He informed the readers of *La Libre Parole* that "a great religious sacrifice was being prepared for the feast of Purim."

Although these Frenchmen did not demand that Jews should be exterminated, either in the ancient or the modern meaning of the word, they were determined to make their lives miserable, to shut them into a moral Ghetto and to set them apart as a race unworthy of human contacts. An archbishop produced a new charitable reason for not driving them out of France. He said it would not be fair to spread the infection over the frontier: "To expel Jews from a country is to be

wanting in charity and justice towards the neighboring countries into which one unloads those gnawing worms. . . . It
would be sufficient, we believe, to forbid Jews the occupations
of banker, merchant, journalist, professor, doctor and apothe-
cary." [51] Such proposals met at this time with the general approval of French Catholics. Abbé Gayraud, a member of the
Chamber of Deputies, explained to the National Congress of
Christian Democrats at Lyons, that the Church had always
been anti-Semitic, and he called for "the expulsion of all social
excrement, particularly Jewish excrement." [52]

When Zola came to the rescue of Dreyfus with his memorable letter "*J'accuse*," Drumont threatened to have him burned
at the stake; but Jews, he added, should be thrown into the
Seine, and not burned alive, for "what an evil odor a roasted
Jew-boy would make!" [53] An aristocratic lady, who might
well have belonged to the same stock as the Crusader, Draconet
de Montauban, who, seven hundred years before, had ordered
the breasts of Jewish women to be torn off, expressed the hope
"that Dreyfus might be innocent, so that he would suffer
more." When Colonel Henry, the forger of the documents
which were used to condemn Dreyfus, was at last exposed
and thrown into prison, where he cut his throat, he was
honored by half of France as a martyr. "*Mon Colonel*,"
wrote Charles Maurras, "there is not a drop of your precious
blood which is not still smoking wherever the nation's heart
is beating. . . . Your unhappy forgery will be counted among
your finest military achievements." He explained that forgery
as a means was justified by the end: "He fabricated it for the
public welfare. . . . Our defective education, half-Protestant,
is incapable of appreciating such intellectual and moral nobility." [54] Drumont took up a collection through the columns
of *La Libre Parole* to commemorate the memory of the
"martyr." A sum of more than 130,000 francs was collected;
the subscribers included two princes, seven dukes, hundreds
of counts, viscounts and barons, thirty-two generals, more

than a thousand officers, and three hundred priests. An officer whose name became famous in the First World War, and who was not so successful in the second one, sent ten francs: Captain Weygand. After the Rennes court martial, which condemned Dreyfus a second time, although the evidence submitted to the court had convinced the watching world that he was innocent, the fury of the French press exceeded all previous records. Drumont said that the witnesses at Rennes had all been bought by Jewish gold. Newspapers published letters suggesting that "Jews ought to be whipped," "given enemas of vitriol," "skinned alive," "their eyes put out," and so on. One fanatic wrote that nothing would satisfy him "but a rug made out of the skin of a Jew." The Nazis, a generation later, preferred to make lamp shades.[55]

Amidst all this pandemonium many notes of a chauvinistic nationalism were prominent, inspired by fear of Germany and a desire for revenge—as well as by hatred and jealousy of the English, who had recently driven Marchand from Fashoda. Drumont himself had some hatred to spare for the English, whom he described as "a predatory people, made cannibals by nature, and turned into hypocrites by Protestantism." He was annoyed with Queen Victoria because she refused to believe in the guilt of Dreyfus, and called her "an old ogress with yellow fangs." One of his colleagues wrote a book to prove that all Englishmen were of Jewish descent, and that the God of the English is Lucifer. Scotland, also, was full of Jews. Lord Aberdeen was "a Jew of the dark Spanish kind." Copies of this book were presented as a free gift to readers of *La Libre Parole;* evidently it was not a best seller.[56]

Drumont was infuriated by his failure to make any impression upon English public opinion. He had not been able to find a publisher for an English translation of *La France juive,* and the English press, almost unanimously, refused to believe in the guilt of Dreyfus. W. Stead wrote an editorial in the *Review of Reviews,* after the Rennes verdict, in which many readers must have recognized a parody of Drumont's scatological style:

> Ideal France, the deathless and divine, which inspired the enthusiasm of the world fifty years ago, instead of soaring up to the empyrean, has been wallowing like some obscene harpy in the open sewer into which drain all the feculent droppings of religious fanaticism and the putrifying garbage of a corrupt and luxurious society. The nation is indeed in an evil case which has a Drumont of *La Libre Parole* as its prophet and Esterhazy as its hero.[57]

The orchestra of hate in France, during the last decade of the nineteenth century, was conducted by Drumont; its dominant theme was hatred of the Jew, the foreigner, the enemy of Christ, the manipulator of gold and dung—the permanent scapegoat. All Jews were potential traitors, and anyone who maintained the innocence of Dreyfus, or the illegality of the first trial, had been bought with Jewish gold. The virtual acquittal of Dreyfus at Rennes did not therefore disturb the convictions of people who believed that it was more likely that a Jew should be a traitor than that French officers had condemned him unjustly.

The Jesuit official journal, *La Civiltà Cattolica*, published an unsigned article on the Dreyfus case which might have been dictated by Drumont himself. It was in fact written by the editor, Raffaele Ballerini, with a bias which was perhaps more political than religious. France, he declared, had fallen into the hands of a republican government "more Jewish than French." The condemnation of Dreyfus, he said, had been a terrible blow to Israel, and cosmopolitan Jewry, already plotting for revision of the trial, had bought all the newspapers and consciences in Europe that were for sale. He supported the view that all Jews were potential traitors by quoting an alleged saying of Bismarck that "the Jew was created by God to act as a spy wherever treachery was afoot." Ballerini disapproved, however, of the proposal that all the Jews should be driven

into exile, first of all on the practical or humanitarian grounds
that they had nowhere to go, and secondly for the mediaeval
reason that they were a people accursed by God, who had
been scattered to the four corners of the earth in order that
they might testify by their ubiquity to the truth of Christianity. The experience of centuries, he concluded, had proved
that wherever Jews had been granted rights of citizenship
the result had been, either that the Christians had been
"ruined," or that they had proceeded to massacre the alien
race. The remedy he proposed was that they should be
allowed to remain in Christian countries but should be classed
as "guests" and not as citizens.

Although the article in *La Civiltà Cattolica* cannot perhaps
be taken to represent more than the personal views of the
writer, not involving the responsibility of the Jesuit Order,
it undoubtedly convinced most people who read it that individual Jesuits in France and in Italy were not immune against
the prevailing anti-Semitic prejudice. The accusation frequently brought against the Jesuit headquarters in Rome of
political interference in the Dreyfus case through the inter-
mediary of Père Du Lac is not based on any reputable evidence.[58]

Many French Catholics during the first quarter of the
present century, partly because of political reasons, still refused to recognize the innocence of Dreyfus. The new generation was often instructed by writers who did not want the
whole truth told. A characteristic example of this dialectic
was furnished by the Rev. Father Besse, a Benedictine student
of religious history, who summed up the *affaire* without taking
much notice of the facts that had come to light both during
and since the revision of the trial at Rennes:

> An officer has been guilty of treason: he is a Jew. The
> treachery has been carried out under such conditions that
> proof cannot be produced in broad daylight. Grave national
> interests are involved. In such a case every man of good sense

confidently accepts the decision of the court and carefully avoids causing trouble. . . . The accused, because he is a Jew, will easily pass for a victim of State necessity and a martyr of anti-Semitism. Money begins to flow. Politicians and professors preach, in Paris and in the provinces, a crusade for the liberation of Dreyfus. The rest is known.[59]

Such misleading brevity helped, no doubt, to crush in the minds of some pious readers, in the minds of some young seminarists preparing for the priesthood, all sympathy for the people of Israel, and ensured that the old tradition would be handed on.

In Anatole France's parody of the Dreyfus case,[60] Père Cornemuse, the monk, conversing with Père Agaric (Du Lac) makes an appeal to "authority" to justify his belief in the guilt of Pyrot (Dreyfus), in words similar to those which the Rev. Father Besse employed eight years later. Cornemuse had explained that he was so busy distilling his liqueurs that he had no time to read the papers:

> The pious Agaric asked anxiously: "You have no doubts about the guilt of Pyrot?" "I cannot have any doubts, my dearest Agaric," replied the monk; "it would be contrary to the laws of my country, which must be respected as long as they are not in opposition to the law of God. Pyrot is guilty because he has been condemned. As for saying anything more, for or against his guilt, that would involve substituting my authority for that of his judges, and I would not permit myself to do that. It would indeed be useless, since Pyrot has been condemned. If he was not condemned because he is guilty, he is guilty because he was condemned; it is the same thing. I believe in his guilt as every good citizen must believe in it; and I will believe in it as long as the established judicial authority orders me to believe it . . . and, in any case, I have great confidence in general Greatauk (Mercier), who is, I fancy, more intelligent, without appearing to be so, than all those who attack him."

Anatole France worked effectively to diminish anti-Semitism in his country by making the anti-Semites look ridiculous. *L'Ile des pingouins* was the French reply to *La France juive*, the only sort of reply the book deserved. But most French Catholics, who were not encouraged by their bishops to read the works of Anatole France, continued to believe in the respectability of Edouard Drumont and the guilt of Dreyfus.

Even after Dreyfus had been finally reinstated, in 1906, people who expressed belief in his innocence were regarded by many of the clergy as heretics and enemies of France. The prevailing confusion of religion with politics was expressed by Monsignor Montagnini, representative of the Vatican in Paris, who, in July, 1906, warned the Holy See against the *"mauvais esprit"* prevailing among certain seminarists who had "favorable inclinations towards Loisy, Dreyfus and disarmament." [61] The Bishop of Nancy, in 1916, suggested that belief in the innocence of Dreyfus was equivalent to apostasy. "It will be to the eternal honor of the French Catholics of that time," he said, "that there was not one, at least among those who did not betray their faith, who approved of traitors and did not reject with indignation those who cursed the Army." The Bishop did not explain why, at that time, so many Catholics approved of Esterhazy, who was a self-confessed traitor and had written letters, read at his trial, in which he cursed and insulted France and the French army. But Esterhazy was not a Jew; he was nominally a Catholic, and had served with the Papal Zouaves.

Few French Catholics, even at the present day, have written with the frankness of Père Lecanuet, who admitted that he had been wrong and that his prejudices about the guilt of Dreyfus had been shattered by an examination of the documents:

> Up to this time, we believed in the guilt of Dreyfus, because of the verdicts of two courts-martial and the testimony of five War Ministers. But during an examination, which lasted for months, of the complicated documentation of the

*affaire*, chiefly the judicial reports, the enquiries and proceedings of the Supreme Court of Appeal for the revision of
the Rennes trial, we felt our ideas were changing, and our
prejudices melting away. We became painfully aware of the
fact that we had been in the wrong. And we believe that it is
impossible to study this affair with proper care without
reaching the same conclusions as we did. But, having once
recognized the truth, could we, without betraying our conscience, do otherwise than proclaim it openly? This is what
we propose to do, at the risk, perhaps of offending the feelings of a great many people. We hope our readers will approve of our conduct, and will decide, as we did, to yield
to truth and justice.[62]

This recognition of the truth, coming from the pen of a
Catholic historian, must have had considerable influence in
French Catholic circles, especially in the seminaries; and it accounts to some extent for the decline of anti-Semitism in
France during the critical years that followed. Yet there are
still a number of people in France at the present day whose
feelings are hurt when they are told that Dreyfus was innocent.

The most powerful personality who fought for Dreyfus
was Georges Clemenceau, who wrote a series of articles in
his own newspaper. Compared with the venom of *La Croix*,
the obscenities of Drumont, or the political malice of *La
Civiltà Cattolica*, the prose of Clemenceau reads like the word
of a prophet, a philosopher or a saint. The following selec-
tions from his newspaper articles would provide profitable
subjects of meditation for a retreat, for any religious community, and even for the modern man whose views about the
meaning of religion need clarifying:

A nation without conscience is merely a herd on the road
to the slaughterhouse. . . .
One may find oneself in a situation where it is necessary to
make a sacrifice for one's country harder and more cruel
than to give up one's life: the sacrifice of prejudices. . . .
I allow myself to conceive that for man there may be an

ideal superior to that of killing his fellow-men, with or without danger. . . .

We now know that institutions, laws and dogmas are
powerless against the evil which is in each one of us, and
that the greatest urgency in social reform is to begin with
ourselves. . . .

There exists in each one of us a tremendous force, if we
know how to use it, for the victims of human oppression. . . .

Although Clemenceau often went very far in his abuse of
the clerical party, he sometimes taught them a lesson with a
genuine touch of that French wit which most politicians of his
time had forgotten how to handle. "The Apostles," he reminded his opponents, "were Jews":

I see, in the niches of our churches, statues of Jews before
whom people are kneeling in prayer. It must be my unconscious clericalism which keeps me from crying, "Death to
the Jews." I would be afraid of offending St. Joseph, St.
Peter, St. Matthew and many others, without mentioning the
Virgin Mary and her Son, who is God. All the places of importance in the Christian paradise are occupied by Jews.

Indeed, he added, with a chuckle which can almost be heard:
*"On se croirait sur la terre."*

Clemenceau believed that the sin of injustice cannot in any
way be qualified by the status of the victim. The guilt of the
judges at Rennes who condemned Dreyfus, knowing him to
be innocent, was not in any degree different from the guilt
of Pilate:

Five years have passed since we laid hold of a Jew and
put him upon a cross, just as the Romans, from whom we
descend, did, without knowing exactly why, nearly two
thousand years ago. We left him for five years upon his cross
. . . and we know very well why; it was because we hate,
with a sectarian hate, the chosen people of God. . . . We
hate the Jew, and we refuse to take him down from his cross
of infamy, after five years of crucifixion.

Although here and there a few French priests preached, and even wrote books and pamphlets in defense of Dreyfus, "the Catholics of France left chiefly to others the honor of fighting for the truth." [63] "The French Catholics," wrote Paul Viollet to the papal nuncio in Paris, "with rare exceptions, have supported the cause of falsehood and crime against truth, law and justice; the Court of Rome knows this as well as all the courts of Europe." But the Court of Rome, like St. Louis, had no sympathy for the misfortunes of a Jew. Rampolla, Cardinal Secretary of State, at a diplomatic reception in the Vatican expressed "his joy" at the condemnation of Dreyfus at Rennes. The innumerable *monsignori*, all the busy crowd of ecclesiastical functionaries, had no time to waste on listening to the complaints of an insignificant French Jew, condemned by the whole of Catholic France, whose cause was championed chiefly by enemies of the Church.

The efforts of Leo XIII to moderate the political passions of French Catholics were regarded by the Royalists and by many of the clergy as a betrayal of France. In 1892, after the Pope had published a letter calling upon all right-thinking men in France, including Protestants and Jews, to unite together against "the enemies of religion and society," Baron Alfred de Rothschild paid a visit to the papal nuncio in Paris, Monsignor Ferrata, to assure him that the French Jews would endeavor to co-operate with the Pope's policy. Ferrata included in his *Mémoires* an account of this meeting. The conversation was conducted with the courtesy of a fencing match; each side scored a hit; but the manners of the baron were better than those of the nuncio who, in relating the encounter, did not quite succeed in hiding his antipathy to Rothschild and his nation. Ferrata began by explaining that, since the Holy Father had invited all men of good will, including Jews, to fight together against those who were attacking religion and society, he expected in return that "the sons of Israel, who are not very numerous in France, but are very

powerful, would cease from supporting the Freemasons and
other sectarians against the Catholic Church." The nuncio did
not intend, he said, to incriminate all Jews; but he could not
avoid seeing that a considerable group of them were always in
the forefront of attacks on the clergy, the religious orders and
religious interests. "This attitude was bound to arouse among
the Catholics ill-feeling which it might be afterwards difficult
to modify . . . and would in the end turn against the beliefs,
and still more against the wealth, of the Jews." The baron
admitted that a certain number of Jews deserved such reproaches, but he insisted that they did not represent the
sentiments of a majority of the French Israelites. A minority,
he pointed out politely to the nuncio, were unwilling to submit to the instructions of their leaders, just as some Catholics
rebel against the authority of the Church. Monsignor Ferrata,
who felt no doubt the point of this riposte, brought the conversation to a lower level by insinuating that it was in fact
Rothschild himself who directed and controlled the action of
Jewish anti-clericals. "I then pointed out to him that the
House of Rothschild had many ways of bringing pressure to
bear on all the Jews, and he answered me, with great courtesy,
that he would not fail to act in accordance with the sentiment
of the Holy Father's instructions, which he recognized to be
timely and profoundly wise." [64]

Few French Catholics, as Rothschild tactfully suggested
to the nuncio, had shown much readiness to follow the
Pope's advice. In the provinces, innumerable obscure mar-
quises, counts, viscounts and barons, sulking in their decaying
châteaux, continued to pray for the return of royalty. Drumont, of course, was infuriated by the suggestion that Catholics should co-operate with Jews, and he called for some
French knight to use the iron gauntlet with which Nogaret
had slapped the face of Boniface VIII at Anagni. The Pope—
"the illustrious dupe," as Georges Bernanos described him—
was regarded with disapproval by the clerical and royalist

parties because he was known to hold views about the Dreyfus *affaire* which were very different from those of Cardinal Rampolla and of the Roman Curia. He did not, and could not, under the circumstances, make any public pronouncement on the subject. But in a private letter, which he allowed his correspondent to publish, he expressed, in a striking phrase, his sympathy for the sufferings of the innocent Jew: "Happy is the victim whom God has recognized as worthy to have his lot assimilated to that of His own Son crucified." [65]

Most Frenchmen regarded the publication of this letter as an "unwarrantable interference" in French politics, and few of them were able to appreciate the Pope's reference to the mystical doctrine of vicarious suffering. They suspected some Jewish trickery and waited for the Vatican to publish a *démenti;* but they waited in vain. Devout Catholics, consoled by the knowledge that the Pope's words had not been written within the margins of Papal infallibility, took refuge in prayer, and many masses were said for the Pope's return to French orthodoxy.

Leo XIII may have seen something of the pattern of history which now, at a distance of fifty years, is already more distinct. The sufferings of Dreyfus, in whose name the whole Jewish people were once more held accursed, had an influence on the course of events which no one at the time could have foretold. For no one noticed that a visitor to France, a man destined to become one of the great leaders of the Jewish people, was watching the rising tide of hate with a prophetic understanding. He came from Austria, a tall man of imposing appearance, at home and at ease in the Gentile world where he had lived happily and had always been made welcome; a Jew completely assimilated, yet a prophet of Israel. His name was Theodor Herzl. Drumont drove Herzl back to Israel. Herzl was the most active of the many Jews who recognized in the tragedy of Dreyfus a reproduction in miniature of their own history since they had first gone homeless into exile. He became the apostle of the Return; he convinced many of his people that for them the only road of salvation in this world was the road leading to a home of their own.

The revival of Judaeophobia in Germany, in Austria, in Russia, and in Poland, a few years before the publication of *La France juive,* had not disturbed the confidence of western Jewry in a security dependent on progress, education and the doctrines of nineteenth-century liberalism. Lucien Wolf was sure, in 1881, "that the paroxysms of anti-Semitism would weaken until they died away altogether." Rabbi Hermann Adler assured his people that "the time is probably not far distant when Germany will regard Jew-baiting as a hideous nightmare . . . and a blot and stain on the nineteenth century." And no one listened, in 1882, to Leo Pinsker, a Jewish doctor who had been shaken out of his comfortable confidence by what he had seen happen in Russia. He told the Jews not to rely any more on the sense of justice, or on the professed friendship of other nations, but to save themselves by their own efforts. Pinsker was the first Jew in modern times to rediscover the ancient solution of the Jewish "problem," a solution familiar to the elite of Jewry throughout the ages. He told them they would never have peace until they recovered their status as a nation. Only then would they be able to live without the badge of shame and to enjoy, anywhere in the world, the privileges of liberty, equality and fraternity. "For the mere fact of the existence of a Jewish State, where Jews are masters and their natural life develops on lines of its own in accordance with their distinctive spirit, will suffice to remove the stamp of inferiority." [66] Pinsker's *Auto-Emancipation,* known today to almost every Jew in the world, was hardly noticed by anyone in France at the time of its publication (1882). The editor of the French periodical *Revue des Etudes Juives* gave it three lines: "The persecution of Jews in Russia has inspired the author with the chimerical idea of looking for Jewish emancipation in the foundation of a Jewish State." [67]

The illusions of western Jewry were dispersed, for a time, by the crude realities of the ancient and ever-enduring hatred which had been revived by the Dreyfus trial. "We had all believed," wrote Achad Ha-Am, "that elementary justice had become an integral part of European life, one of the unshakeable foundations of the social structure; and now we see that we were wrong." It did indeed seem, for a moment, before the verdict of Rennes, that the country of liberty, equality and fraternity was destined to command the final holocaust of the Jewish people. But France was saved from this ignoble fate by a minority, by the "fifty Just" who had not been found in Sodom.

The Dreyfus affair, as Péguy realized, "was a notable crisis in three histories, in the history of Israel, in the history of France and in the history of Christianity." [68] France nearly succumbed to the virus of hate because she was "instinctively anti-Semitic on account of her Christian past." Traces of this instinct were visible even in the writings of the few Frenchmen who had the courage to stand up for the Jews. Zola defended them "not as Jews, but as human beings." Léon Bloy loathed the smug anti-Semitism of the Catholic bourgeois. His *Salut par les Juifs* contains, however, more than one sentence which might prevent any Jew who reads the book from regarding him as a friend.

Péguy defended the Jews because he loved them. Without love, he said, "justice and truth are merely plaster saints." What he admired most in the Jewish people was "their spiritual force which the world, the flesh and the Devil had never been able to destroy." "Everyone," he said, "has the Jews he deserves":

> Bourgeois anti-Semites know and hate only bourgeois Jews; anti-Semites who are in the fashion know and hate only Jews who are in the fashion; anti-Semites in business

know and hate only Jews who are in business. But we who are poor, as it happens, we know a great many Jews who are poor, and some who are even destitute. And these Jews I have always found to be true as steel, and to be steadfast in friendship.

Péguy knew what he was fighting for. "We were heroes," he wrote. "This must be said, in all simplicity, for I am sure that no one else will say it for us." And it is indeed difficult to say it as he said it, to see it as he saw it, the meaning of the fight, the mystical significance which he, almost alone in his own time, saw to be, and explained to be, the fight of a minority "not only for the honor of our own people at this time, but for the honor of our own people in history, for the honor in history of our whole race, for the honor of our ancestors and of our children."

The whole world was watching the drama of Israel, which was also the drama of France, the battle of a mere handful of upright men who withstood a population demented by hate. These gallant few were able in the end to awaken the national conscience and to save their country from the fate which, forty years later, befell the proud Germans—when the devils went into them also, but were not cast out, so that the whole herd ran down the steep slopes, and perished.

*The anti-Semite localizes in the Jew*
*all the evil of the universe.*

JEAN-PAUL SARTRE

# 8

..................................

# Workers of Iniquity

ONE OF THE MOST PROMINENT English teachers of race-hatred
in the nineteenth century, the historian Edward Freeman, is
remembered, or ought to be remembered, in the United States
for a remark he made when he visited that country in 1881:
"This would be a grand land," he said, "if only every Irishman
would kill a negro and be hanged for it."[1] This was not
meant merely as a foolish joke; Freeman was in fact one of
the early pioneers of Nazi doctrine. He found a few sympa-
thizers in America, for he has recorded how a friend of his in
Massachusetts had succeeded in infecting the mind of an
American child: "Mrs. Gurney has a small niece . . . who
says to her father, 'Good night, father; I hope you will sleep
well, and that everybody will sleep well, *except the Jews.*'"[2]
Freeman was annoyed with the English for making public
protests against the Russian pogroms. "I am furious at all this
Jew humbug," he wrote. "I do say that if any nation chooses
to wallop its own Jews 'tis no business of any other nation.
. . . There is Bulgaria bullied, and Finland threatened; what
can Jews matter besides either of these?" Although he did not
actually recommend the extermination of the Jewish people,
he expressed his sympathy with such a policy, in 1878, with
language which would have justified Hitler: "Water enough
to wash away the whole accursed den of Jewry . . . would
be a real blessing to the whole civilized world."[3]

English men of letters do not often write so frankly about what they mistakenly call the "Jewish problem," except in their private correspondence—which, in these days, is sometimes unobtrusively censored by their biographers before publication.

Little interest was shown by Englishmen at the beginning of this century in French internal politics, or in the revelations about a Jewish international plot which, as Hilaire Belloc assured his readers periodically in the columns of *The Eye Witness*, threatened to destroy Christian civilization, especially the English part of it. In order to avert this peril, he recommended that Jews should be compelled in every country to live as a community apart, under special legislation. This return to the Ghetto system was not an original idea. German anti-Semites were already suggesting, as early as 1850, that Jews should not be allowed to take part in public life, because "the German State is essentially a Christian State." [4] The same excluding principle was advocated by the Catholic journal *La Croix* during the French elections of 1898, when a manifesto was printed on behalf of the French Catholic Party, declaring: "We will vote only for candidates who will undertake to propose, support, and vote for a law forbidding Jews to vote, or to hold any military or civil office in the State." Such restrictions of civic rights lead logically, and historically, to extermination. Julius Streicher protested at Nuremberg that "he had always only propagated the idea that the Jews, because of their alien character, should be removed from German national and economic life and withdrawn from close association with the body of the German people." [5]

In 1922, Belloc expressed his matured ideas on the subject of Jewry in a book entitled *The Jews*, written, as he said, "as an attempt at justice." In a preface to the second edition (1928), he complained that the book had been "called by those who had not read it, anti-Semitic—that is, a book written in antagonism to Jews by a man who hated Jews." He was surprised by this criticism of his work, made, he suggested, by reviewers who had a personal grudge against him and had not bothered to read the book. To anyone who did read it the accusation of anti-Semitism would appear, he said, absurd. "I have no antagonism of this kind. So far from hating the Jewish people, I seek their company, and of my friends the proportion who are either wholly or partly of Jewish blood is as large, I think, as that in the acquaintance of any man I know." [6]

People who begin books by informing the reader that many of their best friends are Jews are now put without hesitation into the category to which they belong. One of the earliest examples of this dialectical device was exhibited by Daniel O'Connell in the House of Commons almost exactly a hundred years ago. "I have the happiness of being acquainted with some Jewish families in London," he began rather pompously, "and among them more accomplished ladies, more humane, cordial, high-minded or better educated gentlemen, I have never met. It will not be supposed that when I speak of Disraeli as the descendant of a Jew that I mean to tarnish him on that account. They were once the chosen people of God." After this preamble, O'Connell then proceeded to do the very thing he was pretending not to do:

> There were miscreants among them, however, and it certainly must have been from one of them that Disraeli descended. [Roars of laughter.] He possesses just the qualities of the Impenitent Thief who died upon the cross, whose name, I verily believe, must have been Disraeli. [Roars of laughter.] For aught I know, the present Disraeli is descended from him, and, with the impression that he is, I now forgive the heir-at-law of the blasphemous thief who died upon the cross. [Loud cheers and roars of laughter.]

A list of modern writers and orators who have used this kind of humbug would take up a lot of space. Albert Monniot, a former colleague of Edouard Drumont, who in 1933

became a leading French fascist, announced that "anti-Semites
. . . have, as Drumont said, the generous soul of the Aryan;
they nourish no hatred towards individual Jews and are
always ready to be on friendly terms with them." "I have
a considerable number of Jewish friends," wrote H. G. Wells
in 1939, and, on the same page, expressed the opinion that "the
raucous voice of the Nazi might after all be saying something
worth hearing." "I am proud to number amongst my friends
many Jews," declared the Marquess of Londonderry; but in
1936 he wrote a letter to Ribbentrop encouraging him with
the characteristic English understatement that "he had no
great affection for the Jews." Ten years later Ribbentrop
tried to save himself with this same trick. The tribunal at
Nuremberg has recorded his protest: "Many of my best
friends are Jews."

If Belloc, as he asserted, had "no antagonism to Jews," and,
so far from hating them, "sought their company," he did not
encourage readers of his book to follow his example. Hatred is
perhaps too strong a word: but hostility and contempt for an
inferior people stand out on almost every page. "The Jew
must remember," he writes, "that not only is his domination
very bitterly resented, but that his presence in any position of
control whatsoever is odious to the race among which he
moves." [7] A similar sentiment was expressed more concisely
by a literary friend of the Jewish novelist Jacob Wassermann,
who said to him, when the Liberal Party in Germany was
advocating the admission of Jews to administrative employment: "I like Jews, but I refuse to be governed by them."
Belloc affirmed, moreover, that "there is a national antagonism to the Jewish race felt by nearly all those who are not of
it and among whom it lives." He was sure that "the average
English soldier and citizen has no ties and no sympathy" with
Jews. A man who remarks that "rich Europeans, . . . in
their habit of . . . submitting to almost any indignity for the
purposes of obtaining more wealth, marry their daughters to

Jews," [8] ought not to be surprised when his readers suspect that he is anti-Semitic.

Since the early days of the Dreyfus affair, when Belloc lived for a time in France and there became familiar with the writings of Edouard Drumont, he has always believed in the existence of a Jewish international power which has for its object the destruction or, alternatively, the domination of what is still called Christendom. He has never discovered, or at any rate never revealed to his readers, the names of the people in control; all that is known about them is that they are Jews and that, in some way not clearly explained, they can do what they like with the press and with banks. There is indeed some mystery about this power, which is, he says, "a corporate and semi-organized power," although "the individual banker or financier" may not be aware of it. Yet though no one seems to know who these conspirators are, the existence of the conspiracy itself is one of those "well-known facts" for which evidence is superfluous. "All educated men, down to a comparatively low stratum of society, are fully aware of it and every man who is aware of it resents it." What the Englishman resented most, if he did not live below this comparatively low stratum, was the interference of these conspirators with English policies of social reform, such as unemployment insurance and old-age pensions, which had been a subject of discussion and legislation during the years when Belloc was watching the machiavellian machinations of "the Jews." It is surprising to read that "Jews who control international finance" interfered in England not to prevent but to support these measures of social reform. "They stand," wrote Belloc, "behind those great Industrial Insurance schemes which are so detestable to the mass of the people . . . batteners upon the lapsed premiums of the poor."

When Belloc went to America, many years ago, he invented, on his return, a new name for anti-Semitism, which fitted in with his theory of a Jewish plot; he called it "defense

organization." He wrote another book in which he explained
that "on account of the acute irritation caused by the Jews,
defense organization in New York is just beginning." [9] But
in that year, when Cardinal O'Connell spoke about the campaign which was just beginning, he condemned the "defense
organization" which Belloc had discovered during his few
weeks' visit to the country. "My attention has been brought,"
the cardinal said, "to what would appear to be an organized
campaign against the Jew in America":

> Such a campaign is entirely at variance with America's
> best traditions and ideals; and its only effect can be the intro-
> duction of religious tests to determine citizenship, and a
> reign of prejudice and hatred wholly incompatible with loyal
> and intelligent American citizenship. To discriminate against
> any race or religion is utterly un-American; and I therefore
> wish to register my protest against any campaign against the
> Jews, or any other religious groups constituting the great
> citizenship of this country. [10]

The cardinal's ideas were corrected by one of the faithful
"defenders," who wrote in the *Revue Internationale des
Sociétés Secrètes:* "One could respectfully answer, let the
Jews first cease from attacking the social order with Bolshevism and socialism, and the Church with Freemasonry, as they
are doing in the whole world; then anti-Semitism will have no
longer any reason to exist." [11]

The "defense organization in New York" discovered,
seventeen years later, the only effective method of reducing
the "acute irritation caused by the Jews" in that city. A leaflet
issued by the American Gentile Youth Organization reached
the logical conclusion to which anti-Semitism, however it may
be disguised, logically tends: "To have peace and prosperity
for ever, each nation must kill its own Jews." [12] A translation
of this leaflet was circulated throughout Germany in the
columns of *Der Stürmer* (1939) by one of the leaders of German "defense," Julius Streicher.

The war against the Jews, said the multi-murderers in the

dock at Nuremberg, was a measure of defense. Germany had to protect herself and the world against the Jewish peril. This was the explanation given by Rudolf Hess, commandant of Auschwitz from 1940 to 1943, who admitted that approximately 2,500,000 Jews had been exterminated under his direction.[18]

It is remarkable that Hilaire Belloc was able to see enough of America in a few weeks to cause him to write a book about the Jewish peril in that country, and that no one had told him that the "defense campaign" against Jews was directed, for the most part, by people who were conducting a similar campaign against Catholics. According to propaganda sheets issued, or fathered, by the Ku Klux Klan, "Jews and Roman Catholics owned 95 per cent of the big producing and distributing companies in America"; and most of the press was said to be controlled, not by the Jews, but by Rome. People were told by the leaders of the Klan that, "every time a Catholic child was born, an extra rifle was placed in the vaults of the local cathedral." Photographs were circulated of the Jewish hospital in Cincinnati, which was said to have been assigned as headquarters for the Pope, who was shortly leaving Italy.[14] There is just as much truth in these stories as in the tales about Jewish international finance which Belloc has persuaded quite a number of people to believe.

Although millions of words have been written during the past fifty years about this Jewish international plot, no one was able to produce evidence of its existence until, a few years ago, details of the whole conspiracy were revealed in documents known as the *Protocols of the Elders of Zion*.[15] Innumerable editions of these documents have been circulated, and are still being reprinted, in nearly all the countries of the world, and were frequently studied by German citizens under the direction of Hitler's propaganda office—regardless of the fact that the London *Times*, more than twenty-five years ago, published the proof that they were forgeries.

The origin and subsequent history of the *Protocols of Zion* is very similar to that of certain bogus texts published with the title *Monita Secreta* in the seventeenth century, about the machinations of the Jesuits, who at that time were a special target of popular hate. A Spanish manuscript, supposed to be an extract from the secret archives of the Jesuit Order, was "discovered" in Padua and, after various adventures and travels, translated into Latin and printed at Cracow in the year 1614. This document consisted of secret plans and rules of conduct to be entrusted only to certain specially chosen members of the Order, and were to be kept secret from all the other Jesuits. Three chapters are devoted to ludicrous instruction about how to get money out of widows. Jesuits who were old and good-tempered were to be selected for this operation; they were advised to supervise the widows carefully and "to keep them away from anything which might give them the idea of remarrying." Every procedure, however immoral, which might increase the wealth of the Order was not only permitted but enjoined as a duty—including, of course, fraud and lying. The forger of the original documents, who turned out to be a Jesuit priest who had been expelled from the Order, recanted and repented before he died. But the legend he had started continued to develop on the usual lines. Twenty-two editions of the pamphlet were printed in the seventeenth century and the output from anti-clerical printing presses continued to flow vigorously during the eighteenth and nineteenth centuries. It diminished in volume only when the Jew began to replace the Jesuit as a popular scapegoat. The modern vulgar attack on Jewry is often conducted with the same primitive stupidity as the vulgar attack on Jesuits.

In France, where the soil had been fertilized by Drumont, a crop of books and pamphlets proclaimed that "the Jews" were conspiring with Freemasons and Protestants, who, it was said, joined in the plot because they wanted to destroy the Catholic Church. "It is certain," wrote a Frenchman in 1899, "that the Jews, the Freemasons and the Protestants have formed an alliance against the Catholic nations in order to ensure [Jewish] supremacy over the whole world." [16] Belloc did not accuse English Protestants of taking any part in the international conspiracy, although he explains "that it was natural for the Protestant power to take sides against the Catholic tradition and therefore in favor of the Jews. . . . The English middle classes were steeped in reading of the Old Testament. The Jews seemed to them the heroes of an epic and the shrines of a religion." [17] Too much reading of the Old Testament can have, apparently, deplorable consequences. "For my own part," wrote Erasmus, more than four hundred years ago, "provided the New Testament remain intact, I had rather that the Old should be altogether abolished, than that the peace of Christendom should be broken for the sake of the books of the Jews." [18]

The "Jewish international conspiracy" was denounced in France by Père Constant Popot, who warned his readers that not only all the gold, but all the soil of the country would almost immediately fall into the hands of the enemy: "France would be a Jewish State, and thirty-nine million Frenchmen would be slaves of the Jews," [19] who were supposed to be conspiring with Protestantism, Freemasonry, capitalism, communism and socialism; all these movements were Jewish or Jewish-controlled. Jews in France who were reported to be supporting socialism were told that they did so in order to obtain control of France for sinister purposes of their own. Another ecclesiastical historian explained:

In order to strengthen his domination in France and to extend it over the rest of Europe, the Jew has chosen as his instrument socialism. When everything is in the hands of the State, the Jews will seize at one blow the whole agricultural and industrial wealth of France. The State will be the Jew; the Jew reigning and governing by the power of gold. . . . Socialism will be the triumph of Jewish finance. [20]

An article on Freemasonry in the *Dictionnaire apologétique de la foi catholique* contains some uncritical and indeed ridiculous commentary on Freemasonry and Jewry which must have escaped the eye of the editor, Père d'Alès, S.J., Professor at the Catholic Institute of Paris. The writer of the article states that the Jews now control and direct Freemasonry as if the union of the two forces had been the natural terminus "of the ancient pretensions and hatreds of the deicide people." He quotes what he calls the sorrowful warning—*un douloureux cri d'alarme*—uttered by a certain M. Doinel who knows, apparently, the secret thoughts and plans of the devil:

> In the mind of Satan, the synagogue has an immense, a preponderant place. He relies on the Jews to govern Freemasonry, as he relies on Freemasonry to destroy the Church of Jesus Christ. . . . The Jewish brain directs the action . . . against the Apostolic and Roman Church . . . and against her visible head the Pope, and against her invisible Head, Christ. Crucify Him! Crucify Him! [21]

In an official letter of approval, Cardinal Gasparri gave his blessing to this useful work of reference, which would, he wrote, "provide important weapons," not only against religious error, but also "against many historical prejudices which bad faith and ignorance never cease from spreading even among people of more than average culture." His Eminence was obviously referring only to historical prejudices about Catholics.

Father Besse, writing in 1913, thought that the long-sought secret of international Jewry might perhaps be concealed behind the Alliance Israélite in Paris.[22] He did not say so outright, but he cautiously made the suggestion. In any case, he explained, "this organization is merely an instrument in the hands of a hidden Sanhedrin which succeeds in putting into activity enormous powers. . . . We perceive also the existence of an all powerful oligarchy, which maintains an authority both financial and religious. . . ." He admitted, reluctantly, that it would be impossible ever to discover who the members of this oligarchy were: "Five or six men might run the whole affair, and no one knows who they are; their nationality, their place of residence do not matter. They are Jews. That is enough." [23]

This mysterious oligarchy was apparently busy, in 1912, with disruption, massacre and misrule, not only in Western Europe, but everywhere in the world where such things happened. Even in Turkey, according to a writer in an English literary periodical, the Jews were working the mystery of iniquity: "The true Mahomedan has nothing to do with this atrocity campaign at all. That whole campaign is the work of the Judaeo-Masonic organization which is at present the master of Turkey." "Turkey is dead," the writer of the article continues, with a vocabulary reminiscent of Drumont; but Turkey has been resurrected by the Jews: "An unclean spirit has galvanized the corpse into a horrible simulacrum of life. The dead body of the Ottoman Empire is possessed at this moment by a demon as malignant as Islam ever was at its worst, but a hundred times more cunning." [24]

Reports of the behavior of these "cunning demons" were often contradictory. When Drumont was telling the French people that French Jews were plotting with German Jews to destroy France, the munition firm of Ludwig Lowe in Germany was accused, by the German anti-Semites, of taking bribes from the Alliance Israélite, in Paris, to deliver guns of inferior quality to the German army, so that the French, when the day came, might win their war of revenge. Similar stories about the machinations of international Jewry were in circulation after the First World War. In 1919, a French newspaper stated that a mysterious power was working to restore Germany and prepare her for a war of revenge, the power of "international gold, the gold of the tentacled Judaeo-Germanic finance, the gold of Israel." [25] Hitler accused the international Jewish financiers of trying to "plunge the nations once more into war . . . in the hope of destroying the German people." [26] But Belloc was sure that the Jews were intriguing to clear Germany of her obligation to pay a war indemnity to Britain. The Englishman, he wrote, "will not submit to be told that, in order to suit the convenience of these alien bankers, he must forego the rights of victory. . . . Still more urgently will he deny the right of the Jewish bankers to interfere with the national reparation due to him for damage wantonly done in the course of hostilities." [27] About the same time, a French writer was "affirming without hesitation that Jewish International Finance is Germanophile and has sworn to save Germany for Jewish profit." The most obvious explanation of all these contradictions is the one suggested by the late Mr. Sidney Dark: "The truth is that there is no such thing as International Jewry." [28]

This legend of a Jewish international conspiracy to destroy Christianity has grown out of a hatred many centuries old; it has replaced, in Western Europe, the ancient accusations of ritual murder and host desecration, with a similar appeal to popular credulity and a similar indifference to the facts. "It is difficult for a Jew," wrote Paul Goodman in 1913, "to take seriously the naïve assumption that . . . Jewish financiers who, like their Christian confrères, are out for their personal gain, meet in secret conclave to hatch plots against the nation for the benefit of their race and creed." [29]

Belloc, however, had no difficulty in convincing himself that "the Jews" controlled all the machinery of modern capitalism, the big banks and most of the industrial and commercial combines, both in Europe and in America. He believed that they used, or intended to use, the power they had thus acquired for some evil but never clearly defined purpose which he called the destruction of our civilization. He also believed that they had inspired and organized the Russian revolutionaries, and had therefore conspired to destroy the source of power, the capitalism, which they were supposed to control.

In his preface to the second edition of *The Jews*, ignoring this contradiction in his beliefs, he simply states as a well-known fact that Bolshevism and Jewry are identical: "The Jewish Government in Moscow," he writes, "has taken root and is firmly established." [30] This identification of Jewry with communism was exploited many years later by Goebbels and Rosenberg, and adopted by them as the chief Nazi slogan at the party rally in 1936.

The establishment of communism could not possibly bring any special benefit to Jewry, either inside or outside Russia. And there is no evidence or antecedent probability that Lenin's theory of government or the present Russian system owes its conception or its fulfillment to a Jewish conspiracy. "If Stalin reigns in the Kremlin," wrote Sidney Dark, "as the result of Mr. Belloc's 'close organization of Jews,' then they have successfully contrived loss and suffering for their own people. But neither in theory nor in practice is Bolshevism Jewish. Its terrorism, its dictatorship of a minority, its adoption of force are all Lenin's addition to Karl Marx." [31]

Karl Marx not only renounced his religion and his people, but adopted the Christian tradition, including the current catch phrases, of anti-Semitism. He identified Jewry with capitalism; he thought that Judaism "would disappear with the disappearance of the Capitalistic Order." [32] Belloc, however, suggested that the Jews were responsible for the political program expounded in *Das Kapital*, which he described as "a Jewish book written in German." Yet when the ex-Catholic Adolf Hitler explained what the Nazi policy was, in a compilation called *Mein Kampf*, no one thought of calling it "a Catholic book written in German." Many of Hitler's gangsters were nominal Catholics. Von Papen was a Papal Chamberlain, and Goebbels is said to have been educated by the Jesuits. [32a] Stalin was born and brought up as an Orthodox Christian and he studied for the priesthood in an Orthodox seminary, but no one holds the Eastern Orthodox Church responsible for his political views. "To identify Judaism and Communism," wrote Jacques Maritain, in 1939, "is a classic theme of Hitlerite propaganda. The theme is echoed by the anti-Semites of all lands. . . . What is true is that in some countries a section of the Jewish youth may find itself driven to revolutionary extremism by the force of persecution. Those primarily responsible, in such cases, are those who make their life unbearable." [33]

There is an anecdote told by Nicholas Berdyaev which suggests that this habit of selecting as scapegoats people who are not in a position to defend themselves is a universal human failing, not confined to any particular cultural level or area. "I remember," he wrote, "when I was still living in Soviet Russia, that the owner of the house in which I lived, a Jew, often said to me: 'You will not have to answer for the fact that Lenin is a Russian, but as for me, I will be made to suffer because Trotsky is a Jew. Is not that very unfair?' " [34]

Although the most effective appeal after the First World War was to social and financial prejudices, the stream of religious hate flowed steadily on, from pulpits and from the press, where priests holding responsible positions continued, unchecked by episcopal or Papal authority, to preach anti-Semitism. "The Jew," said Monsignor E. Jouin, Prelate of His Holiness and parish priest of Saint-Augustin, Paris, "is always a Jew; his thoughts are Talmudic, his will despotic, and his arm deicide. Until he kneels down at the foot of the cross of Christ, he will remain the enemy of humanity." [35] Twenty years later, German Jews who had knelt down at the foot of the cross of Christ were put into gas chambers along with the rest.

In 1935, Drumont still had many fanatical disciples, wrote Père Joseph Bonsirven, S.J., and "everywhere reigns a latent anti-Semitism." [36] These disciples never missed an opportunity of keeping the theory of a Jewish international plot before the minds of the French public. *La Libre Parole*, revived as a monthly, was used solely for this purpose. All this propaganda had some effect—how much it is difficult to estimate—in weakening the morale of the French soldiers during the years before the outbreak of the Second World War. The doctrine preached in 1933 was that the Jews meant to use the French army as an instrument for reprisals against Hitler. War with Germany would therefore be a war in defense of the Jews, a war provoked by the Jews. The press of all political parties, Left and Right, wrote Henri Coston in an article entitled "Israel wants War," had been sold to the Jews and was stirring up world opinion against the Reich. Hitler, the French were told, did not want war; but there was a power, a nation, that wanted war, and sought it with avidity—the Jewish nation.[37] The war of 1914 had been started by the Jews, and so it would be again: "If Germany is beaten, the Jews will enter triumphantly"; once more "the Christian nations are being incited to destroy each other for the benefit of Jewry."

However fantastic all this sounds today, there can be little doubt that the unwillingness of some French soldiers to fight, when the war came, may have been partly due to the effects of such propaganda. A Jewish deputy in the French Chamber, who had asked the government to protest against the pogroms in Germany, was accused in *La Libre Parole* of attempting to provoke war by "a stupid intervention in the internal affairs of a neighboring country. . . . If this criminal maneuver is successful, Frenchmen will at least know what they are going to be killed for. . . ."

It would have been absurd, of course, to start a world war merely to prevent the cold-blooded massacre of six million people.

Belloc never ceased to believe that Jews sit in secret session, preferably in banks, and direct the fate of the world. Such practices create, of course, a certain amount of anxiety and a good deal of friction, which, he said, was "endured in America" with a tolerance akin to virtue. All this Jewish plotting made the English feel uncomfortable. With this sort of thing going on, said Belloc, "men get the feeling of a swarm. They also get the feeling of being tricked." He explained that most people

> . . . on being asked the cause of friction between the Jews and their hosts at this moment, will reply (in England at least) that it lies in the anti-social propaganda now running loose throughout industrial Europe. "Our quarrel with the Jew," you will hear from a hundred different sources, "is that they are conspiring against Christian civilization, and in particular against our own country, under the form of social revolutionaries." Such a reply, although the almost universal reply of the moment, is most imperfect.[38]

A Jewish conspiracy to destroy Christian civilization, and especially the English part of it, seems to be enough to account for any quantity of friction. But this explanation is "most imperfect," Belloc continues, because it does not take into account the fact that the Jews had been the cause of the same friction, for the same sort of reasons, for more than two thousand years; and he points out, in a few terse sentences, how this continuity of friction could be traced, from the end of the nineteenth century in France, back through the Middle Ages to the days of Imperial Rome. "The friction between the Jews and the nations among which they are dispersed" is not, he says, merely a consequence of their attempt to control at the present time the affairs of England and America:

> It is far older, far more profound, far more universal. For a whole generation before the present crisis arose, the comparatively small number of men who were hammering away steadily at the Jewish problem, trying to provoke its discussion and insisting on its importance, were mainly concerned with quite another aspect of Jewish activity—the aspect of International Finance, as controlled by Jews. Before that aspect had assumed its modern gravity, the reproach

against the Jews was that their international position warred against our racial traditions and our patriotisms.

Few people who read these smooth words would realize that the "men hammering away steadily at the Jewish problem" were Edouard Drumont and his scatological French disciples; nor would they remember that these "aspects of Jewish activity"—namely, international finance—and the Jewish war "against our racial traditions and our patriotisms" provided the main thesis of *La France juive*.

"Friction" in the Middle Ages is dealt with in a single short sentence. "Before that again there had been the reproach of a different religion, and particularly their antagonism to the doctrine of the Incarnation and all that flowed from that doctrine." The reproach in fact was that the Jews were "ungrateful, insolent and perfidious" because they refused to abandon their ancient religion. The reproachful attitude of Draconet is not mentioned, the gallant Crusader who tried to reduce friction by tearing the breasts off Jewish women; nor is anything said about the friction which impelled Christian ghouls to dig up Jewish bodies and make money out of them, or about the friction which led to the international accusation of ritual murder, with the consequent torture and cruel death of countless innocent human beings. Friction is a poor excuse for burning people alive, even if you do sometimes strangle them first, and even if it were true that they did not feel it as we would. And, finally, it was not only the poor Christians who suffered. For "even before that great quarrel," the Romans had good reason to complain of "friction."

This use of the phrase "great quarrel" to describe the oppression of a tiny Jewish minority by the Christian world of the Middle Ages, characteristic of Belloc's method of argumentation, is trick number 12 in Schopenhauer's list of common dialectical devices. To carry out this trick, you simply choose a metaphor which is favorable to your proposition. For instance:

> What an impartial man with no further purpose to serve would call "public worship" or "a system of religion" is described by an adherent as "piety" or "godliness"; and by an opponent as "bigotry" or "superstition." This is at bottom a *petitio principii*. What is sought to be proved is first of all inserted in the definition, whence it is then taken by mere analysis.[39]

So might a fascist historian write of the "great quarrel" between the Germans and the Jews under the rule of Hitler; and so might the tiger complain about the aggressive bleating of the tethered goat; and the wolf be righteously indignant at the attitude of non-cooperation taken up by the reluctant lamb.

"And there had been," continues Belloc, "even before that great quarrel, the reproach that they [the Jews] were bad citizens within the pagan Roman Empire, perpetually in rebellion against it and guilty of massacring other Roman citizens."

It is true that the Jews refused to submit without a long struggle to Roman imperialism. They created a great deal of "friction" when the Roman armies invaded their country. The legionaries were amazed and angered by the vigor of Jewish resistance, and had to fight a long and arduous campaign before they were able to subdue Israel; the Romans had a much easier task when they set out to conquer the British. St. John Chrysostom admired the Jews for one thing only, their stubborn resistance to the Roman conquerors. "Was not the Jewish nation," he said, "seen to arise and arm against the Romans, to resist their united strength and sometimes to overcome it, and to create for the Caesar of that time very serious difficulties? Such was their great energy and valor." They were sometimes accused of being "bad citizens within the pagan Roman Empire" because they were the only citizens within the empire who refused to worship idols. As a rule the Romans recognized their religious independence. When, however, Caligula proposed to erect a colossal statue of Jupiter within the Temple at Jerusalem, the Jews protested violently, and Petronius, the Roman governor of Syria, reproached them with planning rebellion. "We are not rebels," they replied, "but we will rather die than violate our Law." They revolted in A.D. 66 because they were driven to desperation by the tyrannical conduct of Florus, the Procurator of Judaea, who "scourged and crucified many of the most honorable among them." [40] Josephus said that whenever the disturbances seemed to have calmed down, Florus "endeavoured to kindle the flame again." [41]

Jews did not make a habit of "massacring other Roman citizens": on the contrary, they exercised within the empire a unifying and civilizing influence. It was for this reason that laws were passed granting them special privileges and praising them as "friends of Rome . . . faithful subjects . . . submissive to the laws." [42] "It seems to me here necessary," wrote Flavius Josephus in the fourteenth book of his *Antiquities*, "to give an account of all the honors that the Romans and their Emperors paid to our nation . . . so that all mankind may know . . . that they have been abundantly satisfied of our courage and fidelity." Tiberius Claudius granted privileges "to the Jews which are in all the Roman Empire . . . on account of their fidelity and friendship to the Romans." The emperor ordered his edict to be proclaimed throughout the whole Roman Empire "and exposed to the public for full thirty days in such a place whence it may be plainly read from the ground."

Cicero is often quoted as representative of the general Roman attitude towards the Jews. [43] His anti-Semitism has a Christian, and even slightly British, flavor. He claimed that Heaven was on the side of the mandatory power: "How little the immortal gods love the Jews," he said, "has been proved by their defeat and humiliation." This alliance with Heaven against the Jewish people was homologated by the early Fathers, who often complained to the civil power about Jewish "friction." St. Ambrose, carried away from the facts by pious zeal, assured the Emperor Theodosius that the Jews "did not consider themselves obliged to observe the Roman laws, and that, on the contrary, they looked upon obedience as a crime." [44] The modern German remedy for doing away with Jewish friction was first frankly recommended in France by Charles Maurras, who regretted that "the Roman Emperors did not take the opportunity to rid the world of those Semitic lepers." [45]

Thomas Witherby, who wrote in defense of the Jews more than a hundred and fifty years ago, has disappeared with his work into the bottomless pit of forgotten books. He deserves to be rescued, and even to be read. He had moments of prophetic inspiration and of talent. He answered conceits such as those of Hilaire Belloc and Charles Maurras with a few sentences of common sense:

> How greatly have those so-called heroes of ancient Greece been celebrated for their ardent struggles to preserve the independence of their states; their names have been handed down to posterity as the bravest of mankind; and yet the struggles of the Jewish nation to throw off the Roman yoke is seen in another light and is never dwelt on by these admirers of Greek patriotism. Never were there acts of greater heroism performed than by the Jews in their defense (you will remember that they were attacked and acted on the defense), and yet the Grecian name is respected and the Jewish nation is despised. My motive for mentioning this is to show you how partial mankind are in forming their opinions and, when formed, that they follow each other like a flock of sheep. . . .
>
> Roman patriots have been praised almost to adoration, and yet if those qualities for which they were celebrated were virtues, how greatly were they outdone even by those Jewish boys, as well as men, who endured all imaginable tor-

ments, and death at last, rather than confess Caesar for their
master! They would acknowledge no master but God, the
Creator of heaven and earth. I attribute this partially to that
rancorous hatred with which the Jews have been so unjustly
treated by the rest of mankind.[46]

To hold this or that view about the comparative courage
of Greeks, Romans and Hebrews is not an affair of great importance; but to accuse the Jews in our own time of plotting
to dominate the world brings a man into evil company, for
this is the charge which forms the whole substance of the
forgeries known as *The Protocols of the Elders of Zion*.
People who helped to spread such stories were condemned by
a German court in 1922, when the voice of German justice
had not yet been silenced by Hitler. In that year, the German Supreme Court of Justice spoke out frankly about the
propaganda which had been responsible for the murder of
Rathenau (and which was to be responsible, twenty years
later, for the massacre of millions):

> Behind the assassins and their accomplices, there stands
> the principal bearer of guilt . . . the irresponsible, fanatical
> anti-Semitism. . . . The scurrilous and libelous "Protocols
> of the Elders of Zion" *are but one example*, which slanders
> the Jew as such, irrespective of his person, and thus plants
> the instincts of murder in immature and unbalanced minds.[47]

According to Belloc's reading of history, the "Good European" has suffered for nearly two thousand years, sometimes
with admirable patience, from the constant presence of an
irritating minority belonging to a race inferior in morals,
philosophy, religion, culture and behavior to the nations of
Christendom, and consequently a source of friction which
impeded the smooth running of social machinery. It was
therefore inevitable that this minority should sometimes suffer
some form of persecution. If at any time Christians persecuted the Jews, they were, of course, justified by the right of
self-defense; they were, in fact, forestalling the aggressive

intentions of the tethered goat. This explanation, which could be used to defend the policy of Hitler, Lenin, Torquemada and most of the innumerable tyrants of history, opens with the usual assumption that the Jews were always the aggressors. "If indirect hostilities," Belloc explains, "are opened against the majority by a minority in its midst, they [the minority] may be repressed and punished. Still more important, insincere and pretended conversion, used as a cloak, may be repressed and punished." Here Torquemada has been given absolution. "But though a community has the right to determine its own life, and (if it thinks it possible) even to eliminate (with justice, not with cruelty, violence, or injustice in any form) an alien, a hostile minority; yet that minority has its own right to live, if not there, then elsewhere." [48] Majorities have always found it possible to eliminate minorities, without cruelty, violence or injustice. The modern formula is: "The prisoner was shot trying to escape." Jews never got much profit from their "own right to live, if not there, then elsewhere." They had no "elsewhere" to go to.

Belloc, however, recognized the possible existence of a point of view different from his own, and sometimes thought it would be interesting to hear, just out of curiosity, what the other side might have to say. "I could wish," he wrote, "that some learned Jew would produce a History of Europe from the point of view of his people: a short text book, I mean, intended for our consumption; to show us ourselves from a standpoint very different from our own." [49] Such a book, entitled a *Short History of the Jewish People*, has been written by Cecil Roth, who has recorded a number of facts unknown to many Englishmen. After reading this book, said Sir Philip Gibbs, "one is bound to admit that the treatment of the Jews is the blackest spot in the annals of Christendom, which betrayed the spirit of Christ, who was a Jew, by ferocious cruelties, a complete lack of pity for fellow human beings, and a meanness which is, or ought to be, detestable to modern minds." [50]

It was not necessary, however, for men who wanted to know the truth to wait for a Jewish historian to tell the story. This "blackest spot in the annals of Christendom" has not always been ignored by English historians, by the "official" historians whom Belloc presumed to despise. H. A. L. Fisher, in the first pages of his *History of Europe*, summarized the indictment of Christian behavior to the Jews with an impressive brevity:

> For many centuries the gates of mercy were closed upon them. They were regarded as outcasts, debarred from the most honorable callings and responsibilities, and constrained to the pestilential squalors of the Ghetto. Always despised, periodically plundered and, in times of public calamity or fear, exposed to the blood lust of murderous and ignorant mobs, the Jews of Europe endured through the Middle Ages unspeakable miseries. . . .

What is the meaning, the real motive, behind this persecution, continuous in every country, century after century, with the same sequence of religious, social, and economic pretexts? Nobody has been able to give a conclusive answer to such a question. "Even Freud, the clearest-seeing mind of his time," wrote Stefan Zweig, "with whom I often talked . . . was baffled, and could make no sense out of the nonsense." [51] There may be no better answer than the one proposed by Solomon Goldman: "The causes of anti-Semitism have no basis except in the bedeviled nature of man." [52] A specific, and, in fact, convincing explanation is hidden away in the too-little-known pages of that relentless mystic, Léon Bloy, who, like the prophets of Israel, repelled so many of his contemporaries by trying to show them the truth. "Explanation" is indeed hardly a word which should be applied to the prose with which the intuition of a prophet endeavors to convey, to those less inspired, his understanding of the pattern of motives which inform the substance of history.

Léon Bloy wrote:

> The anti-Semitism stirred up by Drumont and his associates is a vile business. . . . The question is not at all as they state it. What does the financial power of the Jews amount to in comparison with that of the Protestant millionaires? Ah! the Jewish question is indeed something else; something, in a far different fashion, profound, and of grave import.
>
> The conscience of Christians, burdened with a terrible debt, gives them some obscure warning of tremendous danger. Knowing nothing, understanding nothing, they feel coming towards them the Prodigal Son who remembers the house of his father. Instinctively they divine his return from that far-off country where for so long he had tended swine, and coveted the husks which those animals rejected. Something warns them that this return is infinitely fearful for them; and such is the real, although deeply hidden origin of their aversion for the Jewish people.[53]

That "terrible debt" has not diminished, nor is the "tremendous danger" so obscure or so far away as it must have seemed, fifty years ago, to most people who read Léon Bloy. More than a hundred years before his time, an English poet, William Cowper, saw that if Israel had indeed been punished for her sins, there was not much hope that other nations would escape retribution:

> Their glory faded and their race dispersed,
> The last of nations now, though once the first;
> They warn and teach the proudest, would they learn,
> Keep wisdom, or meet vengeance in their turn:
> If we escaped not, if Heaven spared not us,
> Peel'd scattered and exterminated thus:
> If Vice received her retribution due
> When we were visited, what hope for you?

"The vile business" stirred up by Drumont and his disciples found its way, twenty years later, into England and into

English literature, chiefly through the writings of Hilaire Belloc. It is often interesting to observe how historians have been influenced by other people's books. Everyone who writes or attempts to write history carries on a tradition of ideas originally acquired from some long-forgotten source. No one has ever told a completely original story. Even the first story which, according to Hebrew chronology, was told by Eve, was not entirely her own; she was prompted by a serpent. The serpent behind Belloc's book on the Jews was Edouard Drumont.

In his analysis of the Jewish character, Belloc borrowed his ideas and even his manner of expressing them from Drumont. Both writers expected everyone to believe that the Jews had always been far more interested than Christians in making money and that they have always controlled—and still control—banks, politics and the press. Both agreed that the Jews are cowards, in the European or Aryan sense—not in the Jewish understanding of the word. "According to the vulgar belief," wrote Drumont, "the Jew is a coward." But this belief, he says, requires some modification, because the Jews have a special courage of their own: "Eighteen centuries of persecution, supported with incredible resolution, testify that if the Jew has no fighting spirit, he has that other sort of courage called endurance." The Jew, however, has not got the courage "of the Aryan soldier who finds in war his true element, who enjoys danger, and faces death bravely."

Belloc expresses his contempt for Jewish courage with a similar selection of words. The Jews, he writes, have great powers of endurance under suffering; they have therefore courage of a sort—but it is not courage of the British kind. "You will hear the Jews arraigned by their enemies for three such vices as cowardice, avarice and treason, to take three of the commonest accusations. . . . The man who accuses the Jews of cowardice means that they do not enjoy a fight of his kind, nor a fight fought after his fashion." [54] Although the

Jews have a passive sort of courage, they know nothing of
the gallant spirit of our fighting men "the simple-faced soldiers
and sailors, whose trade is the most typical of our race." (But
the Jews have now learned that this "typical" British trade is
not invariably honorable, is not always something to be proud
of. They have watched the "simple-faced soldiers" of the
Sixth Airborne Division and the "simple-faced sailors" of
His Majesty's Royal Navy, fighting immigrant ships in the
port of Haifa, ships loaded with women and children.) The
courage of the Jew, Belloc concludes, "is of a Jewish kind,
directed to Jewish ends, and stamped with a highly distinctive
Jewish mark."

Belloc agreed with the French anti-Semites that the Jews
have no understanding of loyalty in the English and French
meaning of the word; they are loyal to one idea only—the
idea of money. Love of one's country, said Drumont, in the
meaning we attach to those words, has no sense for the Semite.
"The Jews," wrote Barrès, "have no *Patrie* in the sense we
understand. . . . For them it is the place where they find the
most advantage. . . . The Jews find their *Patrie* wherever
their best interests lie." [55]

Drumont and Belloc make the same comparison, in much
the same words, between European and Jewish ideas of
loyalty. The French writer says:

> We must not judge the Jews according to our ideas. . . . It
> is undeniable that every Jew betrays his employer. . . . The
> Jews cannot betray any country, for they do not possess
> one. . . . The mother country, in the sense we attach to the
> word, does not exist for the Semite. . . . The Jew regards
> every country . . . except Jerusalem as a place where he
> may find himself at ease, and may even find some profit for
> himself in rendering service . . .

And so on, for several pages, quoting a large number of in-
stances—whether true or false, it is now almost impossible to
discover—of how this or that Jew was disloyal to his employer, and making a great stir about the "betrayal" of France

by "the Jews" in 1870. Belloc says that it is simply nonsense to talk about Jewish loyalty because there is no such thing, according to our understanding of the word. The Jews are not interested in patriotism, but in money; that is what he means, and this is how he says it: "The conception of a national feeling must seem ridiculous to [the Jews] everywhere or, if not ridiculous, subsidiary to the more important motive of individual advantage." He suggests that all Jews are either traitors or potential traitors. Why does he not say so and be done with it? He does in fact say so, almost outright, on another page: "The Jew will serve France against the Germans, or the Germans against France, and he will do so indifferently as a resident in the country he benefits or the country he wounds; for he is indifferent to either."

These superficial judgments had been formulated, with even less understanding of realities, by a distinguished German philosopher at the end of the eighteenth century. Herder wrote:

> The situation of the Jew deprived him, almost from the beginning, of the virtues of the patriot. The people of God, to whom Heaven itself had once given a homeland, has been for many centuries, and indeed since its origin, a parasite growing on the branches of other nations; a nation of cunning usurers in almost the whole world, which, in spite of all persecutions, in no place continues to sigh for its own honor, its own home, its own fatherland.[56]

It is indeed odd that Herder apparently knew nothing about the great mass of European Jewry, oppressed and always miserably poor, whose only hope in life was, and had been for centuries, voiced in the ancient greeting: "Next year in Jerusalem!"

To all such ill-will and misreading of history, Herzl replied with words framed in a fuller knowledge and inspired by a vision of the future:

> We are a people—one people.
> We have honestly endeavored everywhere to merge our-

selves in the social life of surrounding communities and to preserve only the faith of our fathers. We are not permitted to do so. In vain are we loyal patriots, our loyalty in some places running to extremes; in vain do we make the same sacrifices of life and property as our fellow citizens; in vain do we strive to increase the fame of our native land in science and art, or her wealth by trade and commerce. In countries where we have lived for centuries we are still cried down as strangers, and often by those whose ancestors were not yet domiciled in the land where Jews had already made experience of suffering. . . . In the world as it now is, and for an indefinite period will probably remain, might precedes right. It is useless, therefore, for us to be loyal patriots, as were the Huguenots, who were forced to emigrate. If we could only be left in peace. . . .

But I think we shall not be left in peace.[57]

Anyone who takes the trouble to analyze the writings of Edouard Drumont will see that the part played by this French anti-Semite in the formation of the opinions which Hilaire Belloc has expressed in *The Jews* cannot be reasonably doubted. There is indeed one significant paragraph in this book where—although Drumont's name is not, of course, mentioned—Belloc describes the effect, on French thought and French action, of *La France juive*. He begins this paragraph with his usual dialectic, by suggesting to the English reader that the French Jews in the last quarter of the nineteenth century were the aggressors: "The first expression of reaction," against them, he wrote,

. . . was to be found in sundry definitely anti-Semitic writings appearing in Germany and France, most noticeably in the latter country. Their effect was at first slight, though they had the high advantage of extensive documentation. The great majority of educated men . . . passed such things by as the extravagancies of fanatics; but these fanatics, none the less, laid the foundation of future action by the quotation of an immense quantity of facts which could not but remain in the mind even of those who were most contemptuous of the new propaganda.[58]

None of the "sundry anti-Semitic writings" which appeared in France during the last quarter of the nineteenth century had "the high advantage of extensive documentation." Most of the stuff was mere ignorant invective. The only book which claimed to be documented, which pretended to be serious history, was *La France juive*; and this is the book which Belloc had in mind, for there is no other, when he wrote the above paragraph. Among the "immense quantity of facts" which Drumont provided for his readers and which "could not but remain in the minds, even of those who were most contemptuous of the new propaganda," the following are perhaps the most important; they will be found, not only in *La France juive*, but in many of the "sundry anti-Semitic writings" of that time:

> The Jews in the Middle Ages drained the blood of Christian children and crucified them. The Jews organized a conspiracy of lepers to poison the wells. In the fourteenth century the Jews continued their intrigues, their profanation of hosts, their strangling of children on Good Friday.

Drumont explained that these "facts" "are contradicted by official science at the moment . . . because authentic documents have no value at all at the present time, when they displease the Jews." He pretended to believe in the existence of an agreement among French scholars to declare "that all documents not favorable to the Jews are apocryphal." French historians had all been bought with Jewish gold.

"The new propaganda" directed against the Jews in the last quarter of the nineteenth century was merely the same old story of ignorance, stupidity and hate that had been told throughout Christendom for a thousand years. By repeating these fables, which in the imagination of Hilaire Belloc became "an immense quantity of facts," Drumont did indeed help to lay the foundations of future action. On these foundations Hitler built his factories of death.

*But Ah! What once has been shall be no more!*
*The growing earth in travail and in pain*
*Brings forth its races, but does not restore,*
*And the dead nations never rise again.*

LONGFELLOW
*Verses written in the Jewish*
*cemetery at Newport*

# 9

...............................................

# The "Inevitable Failure"

WHEN HERZL TOLD THE JEWISH PEOPLE that the time had come to throw off their chains, to escape from the servitude in which they had lived for more than eighteen hundred years, and to establish themselves in some corner of the earth as an independent nation, his signal of revolt attracted little attention in the Western world, where the inferior status of Jews had long been accepted as a natural and therefore permanent feature of social order.

Ernest Renan believed that the Semitic race represented "an inferior combination of human nature." [1] The superior moral and intellectual quality of the European Aryan, explained to the Germans with a show of science by Houston Stewart Chamberlain, was accepted almost everywhere as proved by the fact of Aryan domination. Leaders of Catholic thought continued to believe that the Jews, still pursued by the wrath of God, had no inclination or capacity for any other occupation than moneylending.

In the first half of the nineteenth century this tradition had been confirmed by the writings of a Spanish theologian, Jaime L. Balmez, who, according to the *Catholic Encyclo-*

*pedia*, "has a universally admitted place amongst the greatest philosophers of modern times." The year 1948 was the centenary of his death. "The work of Balmez," writes the *Times Literary Supplement*, "has a quality of temperate persuasiveness, a willingness to discuss very fully every point, and a wealth of information. . . . His countrymen have today more need of the spirit of Balmez; of his passion for facts about men and society, and his refusal to be content to reproduce the old textbooks and demand their acceptance." [2] These admirers of Balmez do not, apparently, notice—perhaps they do not think it important—that his passionate interest in facts about men and society did not include interest in facts about the Jews; that when he wrote about the Jewish people he was content to reproduce the old textbooks; that his contempt for them gives him an important place, important because of his greatness in a limited field, in the long procession which leads from St. John Chrysostom to Edouard Drumont. In his most widely read work, translated into English with the title *Protestantism and Catholicity in Their Effects on the Civilization of Europe*, Balmez wrote a paragraph which belongs to the century of Torquemada:

> This singular people, which bears on its forehead the mark of proscription, and which is found dispersed among all nations, like fragments of insoluble matter floating in a liquid, seeks to console itself in its misfortunes by accumulating treasures, and appears to wish to revenge itself for the contemptuous neglect in which it is left by other nations, by gaining possession of their wealth by means of an insatiable usury. [3]

The ideals of Zionism, the attempt to escape from this "contemptuous neglect," and, above all, the Return to the Land, were regarded by many Catholics at the end of the nineteenth century, and for long after, as contrary to the will of God. Although the doctrine of permanent Jewish degradation has no place in the official teaching, it has long been embodied in

the devotional practice of the Church. The following sample
of this practice is taken from Dom Prosper Guéranger's guide
to the Church's liturgy: [4]

> For eighteen centuries, Israel has been without prince or
> leader. . . . After all these long ages of suffering and hu-
> miliation, the justice of the Father is not appeased. . . . The
> very sight of the chastisement inflicted on the murderers pro-
> claims to the world that they were *deicides* [sic]. Their
> crime was an unparalleled one; its punishment is to be so
> too; it is to last to the end of time. . . . The mark of Par-
> ricide here fastens on this ungrateful and sacrilegious people:
> Cain-like, they shall wander fugitives on the earth. Eighteen
> hundred years have passed since then: slavery, misery and
> contempt have been their portion: but the mark is still upon
> them. [5]

The English, perhaps because of their familiarity with the
Bible, have usually taken a more optimistic view of the future
of the Jewish people. In the eighteenth century many of them
were convinced that the time was at hand for the Return.
The Bishop of Rochester was indeed rash enough to name a
date. He announced that "the restoration of Israel will happen
about the year 1866." He found in the Book of Isaiah evidence that Great Britain had been chosen to act as the instrument of Providence: "Surely the Isles shall wait for me . . .
to bring thy sons from afar." "What Briton reads this passage," exclaimed Thomas Witherby, "without anxiously de-
siring . . . that the British Isles (to whom it has pleased
God in his providence to give such pre-eminence in maritime
power and commerce) may have the high honor . . . to
contribute to the ease and advantage of Israel?" [6] Witherby
himself made a good forecast of what actually happened in
1917 and in 1947, when he wrote:

> Previous to the great and most conspicuous Return of the
> Jews to their own land (which will be effected by the zeal
> of all nations), there will be a Partial Restoration of many
> of them to their own Land, which will probably be effected

by the Piety of the Protestant Powers, who may renounce their prejudices against them.[7]

There are many references in English ecclesiastical literature of the early nineteenth century to a general expectation of an imminent Return. The Rev. Edward Bickersteth, in 1840, gave the world some excellent advice (which unfortunately did not gain much publicity) about how to handle this enterprise. "There is no small national danger," he wrote, "in unrighteously meddling with their restoration and using them as a tool for selfish ends. . . . Any aid that we can nationally render to their peaceful return . . . will be graciously accepted by the God of Abraham, Isaac and Jacob, and will bring down blessings on the country rendering such aid." [8]

History has now confirmed the right of George Eliot to rank among the prophets. The vision of "Mordecai" in *Daniel Deronda*, which few readers, especially in recent years, have thought worthy of serious attention, has now become a reality:

> There is a store of wisdom among us to found a new Jewish polity, grand, simple, just, like the old—a republic where there is equality of protection, an equality which shone like a star on the forehead of our ancient community, and gave it more than the brightness of Western freedom amid the despotisms of the East. Then shall our race have an organic centre . . . the outraged Jew shall have a defence in the court of nations . . . and the world will gain as Israel gains. For there will be a community in the van of the East which carries the culture and the sympathies of every great nation in its bosom; there will be a land set for a halting place of enmities—a neutral ground for the East. . . . Difficulties? I know there are difficulties. But let the spirit of sublime achievement move in the great among our people, and the work will begin.[9]

George Eliot knew that what the Jews most urgently needed was the "equality of protection" which they had never known during the centuries when they were subject to the Christian princes, and which they could secure only when they had achieved national independence.

Although prospects for settlers were at that time far from attractive, practical schemes for the return were taking shape in many minds. Sir Moses Montefiore (1784–1885), during his second visit to Jerusalem in 1839, made plans for forming a company to acquire and cultivate land in the vicinity. "I hope," he wrote, "to induce the return of tens of thousands of our brethren to the land of Israel." [10]

During the four centuries of Turkish rule in Palestine, from 1517 to 1917, the few Jews who lived there suffered from hardly any disabilities which were not shared by other Turkish subjects. Until 1865, however, Turkish land laws restricted the sale of property and afforded no security of tenure to agricultural settlers. Then, when large areas of derelict but potentially fertile land could have been bought for a few shillings an acre, there was no organization ready to embark on large-scale development. But the idea was growing. "The feeling seems everywhere abroad," wrote a missionary in 1877, "that the time has arrived to restore the desolation of Zion. . . . The very existence of the Syrian and Palestine Colonization Society, which is but a year old, constitutes a striking expression of such a sentiment." [11] This society had been formed "to promote the colonization of Syria and Palestine, by persons of good character, whether Christians or Jews." The plan could not be carried out because of the insecurity of Turkish rule and the unhealthy condition of the country. German colonists who attempted to settle in the Vale of Esdraelon were unable to survive. Most of them died of malaria.

Many of the Western Jews in Europe and America at the beginning of the present century, including most of those who had plenty of money, were opposed to the ideas of Herzl and showed no inclination to follow a new Moses into the desert. With a few notable exceptions, the millionaires have

confirmed the prophetic observation made by Thomas Witherby in 1800: "It is to be feared," he wrote, one hundred and
fifty years ago, "that too many of the wealthy Jews are luke-
warm in their national expectations, and care not whether
their tribes ever go up to Jerusalem again." [12]

Opposition to Zionism was seldom well informed. An American Jew wrote a book in which he explained that the soil of
Palestine had never been very fertile, that no water was available and that the land had probably never been cultivated at
all. It was absurd, he said, to take Jews to such a place in
order to make farmers of them.[13] Some of the most distinguished Jewish scholars in Europe expressed their disapproval with a great confidence in their own judgment.
Lucien Wolf, in an article entitled "The Zionist Peril,"
stated that "Zionism was an attempt to turn back the course
of modern history." [14] Israel Abrahams described it as "a
conception which has no roots in the past and no fruits to
offer for the future." [15] And Israel Zangwill said, in 1910, that
"as a practical solution of the Jewish question in Palestine,
Zionism is already bankrupt."

Assimilated Jews in Germany were afraid that by showing
sympathy with Zionism they might incur a charge of dis-
loyalty to the country where they had been living for centuries. "The German Jew," wrote one of these deluded
optimists in 1905, "must look to Germany alone as his
Fatherland. . . . Any desire to form, together with his co-
religionists, a people outside Germany, is downright ingratitude towards the nation in whose midst he lives." [16] A
few years later, in 1913, an influential German Jewish association—the Central Society of German Citizens of the Jewish
Faith—adopted a strongly anti-Zionist resolution:

> They declared: on the soil of the German Fatherland, we
> wish, as Germans, to co-operate in German civilization, and
> to remain true to a partnership that has been hallowed by
> religion and by history. . . . We must sever ourselves from

the Zionist who denies German national [racial] sentiments, feels himself to be a guest among a strange people, and only feels nationally [racially] as a Jew.[17]

Here and there a few men were able to interpret the vision of Israel. Paul Goodman wrote in 1909 that Palestine would some day provide "a rallying center for the Jews, which will raise their morale all over the world, where their spiritual genius, once more in touch with its native soil, may be quickened into a new birth."[18] Michael Davitt, the Irish Nationalist leader, became, after the Russian pogroms of 1903, "a convinced believer in the remedy of Zionism." In that year the whole civilized world was shocked by the terrible news from Kishinev. But the whole civilized world has a short memory when Jews are the victims. Nothing more brutal than usual happened in 1903 at Kishinev. The story is both mediaeval and modern—mediaeval because the massacre originated with the finding of a dead body, and modern because every massacre, however savage, finds its counterpart in modern German history. Michael Davitt, who went to Russia to investigate, has recorded some details:

> From their hiding places in cellars and garrets the Jews were dragged forth and tortured to death. Many mortally wounded were denied the final stroke and left to perish in their agony; in not a few cases nails were driven into the skull and eyes gouged out. Babies were thrown from the higher stories to the street pavement; the bodies of women were mutilated, young maidens and matrons dishonored. . . . Jews who attempted to beat off the attackers with clubs were quickly disarmed by the police. . . . The local bishop drove in a carriage and passed through the crowd, giving them his blessing as he passed. . . .

The system employed at Kishinev, it will be noticed, resembles in many points the modern technique. The Jews, if they have any weapons, are always first disarmed by the police. But the episcopal blessing is an extra. The bishop probably did not know exactly what was happening and he may have been trying to pacify the crowd. Bishops of the Orthodox Church used to distribute their blessings, right and left, whatever the circumstances, everywhere they went.

After their experience at Kishinev, Russian Jews were naturally attracted by the idea of going to Palestine. But the anti-Zionists said then, in 1903—and they were still saying it forty years later—that Jews who went there would inevitably be massacred by the Arabs and that they were much safer in Europe. Davitt answered this objection with a page which has not grown old:

> One ground of objection to the Zionist movement for the repatriation of the Jews is that the Hebrews, who are not a military people, would be shut off from European help, while being at the mercy of Turkish rule and of Arab hostility in Palestine. The record of the Turks in the matter of modern anti-Semitism compares more than favorably with that of the tender feelings of European Christianity. . . . The Arabs might be trusted to show no more savage propensities towards their Israelitish kindred than Russian Seminarists or Roumanian Christians have done in recent years. Two or three millions of Jews in Palestine would, however, develop a national sentiment and ideal that would soon nourish a spirit of patriotism capable of defending them from possible Arab aggression. The Jews of the world would be their foreign friends and allies, while the civilized nations, inhabited by the scattered Hebrews, could not in reason neglect to take a sympathetic interest in the protection and welfare of one of the oldest peoples in the world, restored again to the Promised Land of Israel.[19]

At the end of the nineteenth century, the notion that Israel could ever recover nationhood was regarded by most Frenchmen as fantastic. Drumont thought that, if Jews were to be allowed to live anywhere, they should be sent to some desert where they could do the least amount of harm. "The Jewish race cannot live in an organized society; it is a race of nomads and Bedouins. When it installs its camp anywhere, it destroys everything near it, cuts down trees, dries up springs, and one finds nothing but ashes on the spot where it has put up its tents." [20] He explained, in an interview published by the *Review of Reviews* in 1898, that France had been almost completely ruined by Jewish financial exploitation and that French anti-Semitism was merely a form of self-defense. "If their immoral sources of income are cut off," he said, "the Jews may begin to listen to the sensible advice of Herzl, and decide to return to Palestine en masse."

Anatole Leroy-Beaulieu, who defended the Jews at the time of the Dreyfus case without for a moment ceasing to despise them, was convinced that they would never go to Palestine, a country where few opportunities were available for financial trickery. "Even if we gave back to the ten tribes the territory of Israel," wrote this French philosemite, "it would be necessary, in order to attract them to Jerusalem, to construct on Mount Zion a stock exchange, banks, chambers of commerce, and everything needful for those business operations of which they are always trying to secure a monopoly." He knew something about the beginnings of practical Zionism, for he added in a footnote: "Within recent years the Jews have founded a few settlements which have not done too badly, but this does not change the situation to any extent." [21] Nor was the situation changed to any extent when "the ten tribes," instead of building banks and chambers of commerce on Mount Zion, built on Mount Scopus a Hebrew University; an English writer, many of whose best friends were Jews, described this institution as "the Temple of Mammon." [22] A similar pessimistic view of Jewish enterprise was expressed about the same time by the English Dominican, Father Bede Jarrett, in the abusive manner which the Nazis adopted ten years later:

> The Jew has always specialized in money. . . . Industrial labor has no interest for him, and agricultural labor even less. Therefore he will never go back to Palestine where the

wealth is almost entirely in agriculture. Indeed, why should he worry over Palestine, when he has the whole world at his feet? Yes, the world is at his feet, for he controls the complete social scale, ruling at one end of it and revolting at the other.[23]

Everyone agreed that, whatever the Jews might be able to do, they were incapable of real work; they would never be able to undertake any task involving physical labor, such as tilling the soil. "The Israelite is never seen to take a spade in his hand," said William Cobbett (1762–1835), "but waits, like the voracious slug, to devour what has been produced by labor in which he has no share."[24] Even G. F. Abbott, a sympathetic student of Jewish history, wrote that "although the Jew can excel in most pursuits, there is, apparently, one thing beyond the reach of his versatility. He cannot dig."[25] When the French journalists Jérôme and Jean Tharaud, more than a quarter of a century later, made a tour of Palestine, they could not help seeing that someone in that country had been digging; but they continued to repeat, for the benefit of their French readers, the old story that Jews can live only on the work of other people. "I don't like ploughing," they made the Jew say, "I have long lost the habit; and all Israel is the same . . . unless one calls ploughing to make others plough, as during all my life I have seen we always did."[26]

When, at last, the time came, the time to which the words of Isaiah can be so impressively fitted, when "the least shall become a thousand and a little one a most strong nation," the world had to admit that the end for which Israel had watched for nearly two thousand years had been achieved, not by Jewish gold, but by the manual labor of Jewish men and women. A plentiful supply of money was not the deciding factor. "The land becomes Jewish," Dr. Weizmann had said in 1917, "not through the act of buying it, but through the act of holding it and working it."

Few political pronouncements in the present century have

led to more complicated controversies and conflicts than the Balfour Declaration—a document composed with a diplomatic ingenuity which apparently endeavored to imply far more than the text itself was permitted to express:

> His Majesty's Government view with favor the establishment in Palestine of a National Home for the Jewish people, and will use their best endeavors to facilitate the achievement of this object, it being clearly understood that nothing shall be done which may prejudice the civil and religious rights of existing non-Jewish communities in Palestine or the rights and political status enjoyed by Jews in any other country.

The ambiguities in the declaration were cleared up by the text of the mandate as finally approved by the Council of the League of Nations, where the duties of the mandatory power are clearly specified. Whereas His Majesty's government had "viewed with favor," and were prepared to use "their best endeavors to facilitate," the mandatory power undertook to act in a specific way: "The Mandatory shall be responsible for placing the country under such political, administrative and economic conditions as will secure the establishment of the Jewish National Home." The administration, moreover, undertook "to facilitate Jewish emigration under suitable conditions" and to "encourage close settlement of Jews on the land, including State lands and waste lands not required for public purposes."

It cannot be said that the mandatory power was entirely successful in carrying out either of these obligations, or that they were undertaken by the British administration with any notable appearance of enthusiasm. Nor can much weight be allowed to the reason often given for administrative reluctance, namely that the Palestine Arabs had not been consulted before the declaration was issued; for, as Lloyd George pointed out, "We could not get into touch with the Palestinian Arabs as they were fighting against us." [27] The opposition of Arab nationalism, even where it was most genuine, proved ineffective in the long run because it was not based on a rational economic foundation. If the Palestinian Arabs had a valid reason for objecting to the prospective arrival of Jewish immigrants, the remedy was in their own hands. There was nothing to prevent them, under the British mandate, from setting to work and developing the country themselves, on both sides of the Jordan.

And this in fact was what at least one Englishman, who knew the Middle East intimately, confidently expected they would immediately do. At a public meeting held in Manchester (December 9, 1917) to enlighten the British public about the meaning of Zionism and the Balfour Declaration, Sir Mark Sykes made a forecast about the future of the Middle East which history soon proved to be too optimistic. He was not completely wrong; the events he foretold did actually take place, but in a way which completely contradicted his expectation. He was sure that an immense and immediate economic revival would be accomplished, not by Jews, but by Arabs, who, freed at last from Turkish domination, would shortly astonish the world:

> There were seven or eight millions of them; they were prolific. There was a combination of man-power, virgin soil, petroleum and brains. What was that going to produce in 1950? The inevitable result was that the seven or eight millions would turn to twenty millions; the Mesopotamian canal system would be reconstructed; Syria must become the granary of Europe; Bagdad, Damascus and Aleppo would be each as big as Manchester; Universities and a great Press must arise. Arab civilization was coming there; no Sultan or Kaiser could prevent it, and when it came, no imperialists and financiers would be able to control it.

Sir Mark then explained why the Arabs feared the prospective arrival of Jewish immigrants. He made no reference to Arab nationalism. A warlike population of seven to eight millions had nothing to fear from Jewish guns; what they feared, he said, was Jewish gold—the power of Jewish international

finance, the stock exchanges, the banks, and all the financial
machinery which Leroy-Beaulieu had thought it would be
necessary to establish on Mount Zion to attract the Semitic
usurers. "What did the Arab fear?" asked Sykes, and answered:

> He feared financial corporations, pivoted on Palestine, con-
> trolling Syria and Mesopotamia. He feared the soil of Pales-
> tine would be bought by companies, and that he would be-
> come a proletarian working on the soil for alien masters.
> He feared the Palestinian colonists might drop their colonies
> and drift into Syria and Mesopotamia as middlemen, and
> crush him out of existence. It was essential that Zionists
> should realize and face these dangers. He dared say these
> things because he believed in Zionism, and he knew it was an
> idealistic and not a financial manoeuvre.

Mark Sykes, like many of his contemporaries, evidently believed that financial corporations, companies and middlemen,
were "dangers" only when they were Jewish. Financial corporations were indeed already watching the Middle East, and
waiting for opportunities they knew that the end of the war
would bring. But Palestine was not to be the pivot of their
activities. They were not Jewish corporations. Like vultures,
they had already marked down their prey; they arrived on
the scene almost before the ink had dried on the Balfour
Declaration; and the power has remained in their hands until
now.

Sykes would have been horrified to read a report on the
effects of the oil monopoly on the development of the Middle
East, a report published in 1946 by the American Council
on Public Affairs:

> Palestine has very meager fuel resources within its own
> frontiers. But it has the natural advantages of location near
> the Iraqian, Iranian, and Arabian oil fields. This natural ad-
> vantage has not been converted into an economic advantage.
> The British Government has allowed a monopolistic group
> of oil companies to establish prices that constitute a severe

drag on economic development. The progress of Palestine has counted less than the profits of the petroleum monopolists. . . . A favorable natural resource position has been dissipated by . . . tender considerations for vested interests.[28]

The Arabs still have their man power, their virgin soil, their petroleum and their brains. But their men have remained idle, their soil has retained its virginity and their brains have been employed in getting as big royalties as possible out of the sale of their petroleum to English and American financial corporations—money which could have provided water, housing, education, hospitals and medical service for every Arab family, and still have left a margin to pay for harems and luxury motor cars. Meantime, the Arab peasants continued to live in appalling conditions of poverty, disease and illiteracy. "I find it hard to believe," wrote St. John Irvine, in 1936, "that a ruling race can spring from a people whose infants' first articulate cry is not 'Allah,' but 'Baksheesh.' That whine, from the moment we reached Capharnaum to the moment we left Haifa, was continually in our ears." [29]

When G. K. Chesterton visited the country in 1920, he looked at everything Jewish from the point of view of a man who believed, as he wrote in his notes while in Jerusalem, "that the Jews wield colossal cosmopolitan power"; that they are, and always have been, more interested than Christians in the pursuit of money; and that their principal occupation everywhere is, and always must be, usury. He had a quick eye for usury anywhere, when it was practiced by Jews, but he was blind to usury practiced by Arabs. "In the politics of Palestine at this moment," he wrote, "the question of usury is the primary question." He was right. But like Mark Sykes, he was also completely wrong. Palestine, he discovered, "has a peasantry to be oppressed, and especially to be oppressed, as so many peasantries have been, with usury and forestalling." He did not stay long enough to make the still more important discovery that the peasants had been oppressed for centuries

and were still being oppressed; but not by Jewish usury.
More than a million acres of land in that tiny country were
"owned" by about two hundred and fifty families who had
often acquired their estates by lending money on landed
security at extortionate rates and foreclosing when payment
became overdue. In 1920, Arab peasants who still owned land
were heavily in debt to Arab moneylenders. "These local vultures," according to a modern traveler, "appear to be more
rapacious in Palestine than in any other country, for they
charge a hundred per cent for a three months' loan. If at the
end of that period the debtor cannot pay, the interest is
doubled, so that it becomes three hundred per cent for six
months, or six hundred per cent for a year." [30] Norman Bent-
wich, however, states that the interest charged by the Arab
moneylenders, who were generally rich traders or landlords,
did not as a rule exceed one hundred per cent. [31] There was
little improvement in the financial situation of the peasants
under the British mandate, until high war prices for agricultural produce enabled some of them to pay off their debts.
In 1936, sixty per cent of the peasant population of Palestine
were still handing over a fifth to a third of their gross produce
to the Arab owners of the land, and were "deep in permanent,
usurious debt to the effendis." They were virtual serfs. [32]

Chesterton shared with Mark Sykes the Western notion
that the word Jew was inseparable from the idea of usury.
He told his English readers, just as Sykes had told his audience
in Manchester, that the Arab peasants were hostile to the
arrival of Jewish immigrants because they were afraid of
Jewish usury, and Jewish exploitation:

> The Syrians and Arabs, and all the agricultural and pastoral
> populations of Palestine, are, rightly or wrongly, alarmed
> and angered at the advent of Jews to power: for the perfectly
> practical and simple reason of the reputation which the Jews
> have all over the world. . . . Rightly or wrongly, certain
> people in Palestine fear the coming of the Jews as they fear

the coming of locusts; they regard them as parasites that feed on the community by a thousand methods of financial intrigue and economic exploitation.[33]

Whatever reasons the agricultural and pastoral populations of Palestine may have had, rightly or wrongly, for objecting to the entry of Jewish immigrants, it is certain that fear of their usurious practices was not one of them. The policy of the Arab landowners, like that of French anti-Semites at the end of the nineteenth century, was to divert from themselves, and direct against the Jews, the threatening revolt of the oppressed proletariat. This policy with its accompanying program of loot effectively united, while the prospects of loot were promising, nearly the entire Arab population against the Jews, not only in Palestine, but throughout the whole Middle East.

"What the Arabs need," said Dr. Weizmann, "is our knowledge, our experience and our money." To Chesterton this truism sounded like the ravings of a lunatic, or the childish belief of an idealist who was completely out of touch with reality. "There is not the smallest difficulty," he replied, "in stating in plain words what the Arabs fear in the Jews. They fear in exact terms their knowledge, their experience and their money. . . . Men bar themselves into their houses, or even hide in their cellars, when such virtues are abroad in the land." Nearly twenty years later, these words were gratefully remembered by another journalist whose writings on Middle Eastern politics had a considerable influence on public opinion in England: "I think that on the whole these are the truest, most enlightening, most potent and pointed words ever uttered upon the Palestine Question. They ought to be carried, emblazoned on a banner or printed a foot high upon a placard, into the House of Commons when next that Question is debated there." [34]

Yet Dr. Weizmann was right. What the Arabs needed was Jewish knowledge, Jewish experience and Jewish money. The

Arab states possessed an immense source of wealth, comparable to the coal upon which Britain in the nineteenth century had built her industrial and commercial superiority. This wealth has not been used, as Sir Mark Sykes expected it would be used, to create a new civilization in the Middle East. The Arabs, as Dr. Weizmann feared, have fallen among sharks.

The Jews brought to Palestine, not stock exchanges and banks, but an industry, a tenacity and a creative spirit which triumphed not only over sand and swamp, but over administrative obstruction. Men have recently come from far countries, from countries which have been long under British rule, from India and from West Africa, to study at first hand the achievements of Zionism. Such men do not bar themselves into houses or hide in cellars, when the virtues which can grow peaches in the Negev are abroad in the land.

In spite of his anti-Semitic prejudices, Chesterton, as a result of his visit, became for a moment a convert to Zionism. He foresaw what the Jews would achieve, but characteristically he was a prophet who did not believe in his own prophecy. The theory of Zionism, he said, "was on the face of it perfectly reasonable. It is the theory that any abnormal qualities in the Jews are due to the abnormal position of the Jews. They are traders rather than producers because they have no land of their own from which to produce." This obvious fact had been recognized more than a hundred years earlier by William Hazlitt who, in his "Essay on the Emancipation of the Jews," pointed out that "they could not devote themselves to the pursuit of agriculture when they were not allowed to possess a foot of land." Chesterton saw as clearly as the Zionist leaders themselves—and it is by some of them that he must have been instructed—what the conditions were which would make possible the return of Israel. He himself did not believe that such a return was possible. He was attracted by the poetic aspect of the ideal, and he had, almost alone amongst English visitors at that date, the courage to express his admiration.

In 1920 very little had yet been done. Tel Aviv was a village containing only 2,084 inhabitants.[35] Here and there throughout the long abandoned and neglected land, a few Jewish settlements were struggling to keep alive, and few of them were entirely self-supporting. The administration, the bystanders and the pilgrims, the Christian communities, the military, all the British world of Palestine regarded Zionism with indifference or contempt. But Chesterton saw the vision and the poetry of a plan which was already on the move. He wrote:

> A Jewish State will be a success when the Jews in it are scavengers, when the Jews in it are sweeps, when they are dockers and ditchers and porters and hodsmen. . . . It is our whole complaint against the Jew that he does not till the soil with the spade; it is very hard on him to refuse him if he really says "give me a soil and I will till it; give me a spade and I will use it. . . ." It seems rather indefensible to be deaf to him if he really says "give me a land and I will love it. . . ." If he asks for the spade he must use the spade, and not merely employ the spade, in the sense of hiring half a hundred men to use spades. If he asks for the soil, he must till the soil; that is, he must belong to the soil, and not merely make the soil belong to him. . . . There can be no doubt of the patriotism and even poetic spirit in which many of them hope to make their ancient wilderness blossom like the rose. They at least would still stand among the great prophets of Israel, and none the less though they prophesied in vain.[36]

This vision of a future where Jews would plough and dig, and would not merely sit in banks to plot the destruction of Christendom, was not what the British public wanted to hear about. It was suppressed in the English newspaper which published Chesterton's articles. "A difference of opinion which divided the writer of the book from the politics of the newspaper," he wrote in his preface, "prevented the complete publication of the chapter on Zionism in that place."

When Hilaire Belloc wrote in *The Jews* that it was "highly probable" that Zionism would be a failure, most of his readers naturally hoped that he was right, because he told them that one of its chief functions was "the expropriation of the local landowners." He did see, however, with more understanding than Mark Sykes or Chesterton, and from a different angle, what would have to happen—and what he was certain would never happen—before Zionism could be successful:

> If the Zionist experiment is necessary or advisable, then let it be made in such a fashion that it can be dependent on a Jewish police and a Jewish army alone. . . . If it be answered that the Jews are not capable of producing such an army, or such a police, that they would inevitably be defeated and oppressed by the hostile and more warlike majority among whom they would find themselves, then let them make the experiment elsewhere. But it is certain that the present form of the new Protectorate is the most perilous form which could have been chosen for it, so far as the Jews themselves are concerned. I appeal confidently to the near future to confirm this judgment.[37]

It seemed absurd to anyone who was convinced that Jews were "capable" only in banks and business offices to suppose that they could ever produce an army or a police force, or could ever defend themselves against "the hostile and more warlike majority" of Palestinian Arabs who were described as late as 1946, by a contributor to an Information Paper issued by the Royal Institute for International Affairs, as "members of a fighting race." [38]

The Arab upper and professional classes, the natural leaders of the Arab nationalist movement, were opposed to Zionism, not on economic grounds, which would have been absurd, but for farseeing and respectable political reasons. They realized that Zionism "threatened to impose upon them the political sacrifice of giving up the seats of power in a Palestinian State." [39] George Antonius, leader and chronicler of the Arab nationalists, had a better understanding of political possibilities than most of his colleagues. He was a man of culture, integrity and intelligence, whose death was a great loss to the Middle East. Yet he also foretold, but with a certain hesitation, the failure of Zionism. He was not, perhaps, quite sure that the Palestinian Arabs would fight: "It is not possible," he wrote, "to establish a Jewish State in Palestine without the forcible dislodgement of a peasantry who seem readier to face death than give up their land. On that ground alone, and without taking the political issues into account, the attempt to carry the Zionist dream into execution is doomed to failure." [40]

The English hoped, and the experts were certain, that the Jews would fail. The Zionist movement, according to the Pritchett Report of the Carnegie Institute for International Peace

> . . . was unfortunate and visionary. . . . The inherent pov-
> erty of the country, its lack of resources, the absence of an
> industrial life, operate to make futile the economic success
> of such an effort. The enterprise is an artificial one, having
> its chief justification in the enthusiasm of well-meaning men
> who apparently do not appreciate the difficulties of their
> problem nor the interests of the existing native population.[41]

Meantime the work went steadily on, in spite of intermittent economic setbacks, misunderstood by the non-Jewish world, ignored by many of the wealthy Jews in the West and scarcely noticed at all by the stream of tourists and pilgrims to the Holy Land. Owing to the indifference, and often to the obstructive legislation, of the mandatory power, the settlers during the early years had a hard struggle to keep going. Tourists who had heard of the adventure and inquired how it was progressing were told that it had failed. Very little help was offered, very little sympathy was expressed, by anyone outside the Jewish community, anywhere in the world. Very few people, outside the Jewish community, wanted the experiment to succeed. These pioneers lived and worked in an atmosphere of acid disapproval. But their faith in the future of the Land never faltered.

The brothers Tharaud, suspected most unfairly of being Judaeophile, were sorry for these misguided people, and reported in 1927 that the whole enterprise was practically at an end:

> All these social experiments of which these poor people are so proud cast the mantle of Noah upon a miserable reality. Whether they are organized in a communist, socialist, co-operative or family way, they all subsist thanks to outside help. Like the wailers at the Wall, they also live on the charity of the whole Jewish people. Not one of these colonies is self-supporting. . . . Every one of the *Halouzim* is a Jewish luxury (*un luxe d'Israël*). Ah! How far away one is from the romantic imagination of Herzl! . . . A great many have already left, and how many of those that still remain will be here if I come back in ten years time? [42]

The two French anti-Semites had been well coached by their English friends in Palestine, and Sir Ronald Storrs, military governor of Jerusalem, paid them a suitable tribute. "Few writers have written more beautifully or more sympathetically about the Jewish people." [43] These Frenchmen, however, often had a strange way of showing their sympathy. "A first-rate persecution, a first-rate massacre, a first-rate injustice," they wrote in 1920, "flatters always the taste of Israel for groaning and complaining." [44] During their visit to Palestine they had probably professed the genteel variety of anti-Semitism, but in France they made no attempt to conceal their real sentiments. "They supplied," wrote Jean Drault in 1935, "a link between what Drumont proclaimed and what Hitler has realized." [45] They were glad to hear in Jerusalem that Zionism was doomed, and they passed the good news on to their French readers. The movement had been bolstered up, they wrote, "with oriental exaggeration and misplaced vanity"; and because "the Jew by nature is averse to all labor," they were convinced that Israel "will soon be merely directing another enterprise, with all the real work done by the Arabs, and the Zionists will have failed in their great effort to rejuvenate their nation by contact with the soil." [46]

English tourists who, after a brief stay in Palestine, went home and put into books their ideas about the Jewish people no doubt wrote less beautifully than the two Frenchmen; they seldom pretended to be sympathetic, and indeed were sometimes very fierce. An unusually frank and violent commentary was written by a woman:

> With the arrogance for which this stiff-necked people has always been noted, [the Zionists] always try to persuade the world that Islam and the Arab do not count, and that the Jews belong to a peculiar and privileged race, and own a private and only true God. . . . Are these spoon-fed workers going to wrestle with agricultural problems when the first enthusiasm of the "backers" begins to slacken? . . . Surely it is not enough to give material prosperity to a country. . . . Mere luxury is not civilization! [47]

The possibility had begun to occur to some Englishmen that these stiff-necked people might actually succeed in their plans for restoring to Palestine its ancient repute as a land of milk and honey. They were therefore advised by Sir Arnold Wilson in 1936 to abandon their plantations and their scientific institutes, and concentrate their activities on the Wailing Wall. They were told to go elsewhere, to some less sacred land, if they wanted to dig:

> Will not Zionism as now conceived prove to be the grave of Jewry? Will not true Zionists come to realize that for them, too, the Promised Land has a spiritual rather than a material connotation, which is consistent with a symbolical home in Palestine, such as, I believe, Lord Balfour contemplated, supplemented by colonial settlements in other lands? [48]

Consider for a moment the meaning of Sir Arnold Wilson's words. He hoped that all good Jews would follow the example of the good English, and that they "too" would learn to look upon Palestine as a religious museum. He offered them a home in "other lands," when he knew that the doors of every country in the world were barred against them. And at the very time when he was hoping, but pretending not to hope, that Zionism would be the grave of Jewry, the plan of extermination in Germany had already begun to take shape. A few years later bodies were boiled down to provide soap for German women, and bones were crushed to make fertilizers for German gardens.[49] Jewry was denied even the last privilege which Byron thought they would always be allowed:

> Tribes of the wandering foot and weary breast,
> How shall ye flee away and be at rest!
> The wild dove hath her nest, the fox his cave,
> Mankind their country—Israel but the grave.

Ecclesiastical writers, with Jesuits sometimes giving a lead, have been remarkably consistent in forecasting the failure of the Jews in Palestine. And they have seldom taken much trouble to find out for themselves what was going on in that country so long as the rumors which reached them seemed to suggest that failure was inevitable. The Rev. Joseph Bonsirven, S.J., contributed to the sixth volume of Eyre's *European Civilization* (1937) an essay on modern Jewry in which he included a brief summary of the situation of Zionism. His account of Jewish activities outside Palestine does not inspire confidence, especially when he declares that it "is certain that all the big banks are affiliated to Jewish houses [*sic*] . . . and that the Jews control, to a great extent, the traffic in money." After such an unpromising start, it is not surprising to find that his information about what the Jews were doing in Palestine is considerably out of date. "In a few years a modern town has arisen, Tell-Aviv. It counts 40,000 inhabitants." In 1936, Tel Aviv "counted" some 148,000 inhabitants. His statistics about Jewish agricultural development are equally misleading: "Zionist farmers hardly exceed 7,000." The expression "Zionist farmers" is, of course, inaccurate. The Zionist system of agriculture excludes "farmers" in the English sense of the word. It was not difficult, surely, to discover that the total number of Jews gainfully employed in agriculture, according to the figures supplied by the Jewish Agency, "rose from about 4,000 in 1922, to 12,300 in 1931." And in 1936–37, the number of "Zionist farmers" not only exceeded seven thousand, but had increased to about five times that figure. It was also a mistake to write in 1936–37 that "farms of the communistic [sic] type do not pay, are not self-supporting, and are kept worse than the holdings which accept the law of private property."

The facts about the growth of Jewish agricultural settlement in Palestine during the decade 1927–37, were available at any time from the publicity department of the Jewish Agency. The progress reported in 1934–35 seems to have escaped the notice of Father Bonsirven. Most of the communal settlements were already self-supporting: "In none of the older *Kvutsot* was there a loss; in fourteen of the newer *Kvutsot* there was a profit, in two only was there a loss." [50] In spite of the difficulties created by an unsympathetic British Administration, the Zionists were able to establish in Palestine an agricultural system which, even as early as 1930, had proved its stability, its power to survive both local and world-wide economic depressions. Yet Father Bonsirven concluded that the experiment had failed; "Zionism seems for some time to be paralysed if not arrested in its development." [51]

At no time did Jewish agriculture in Palestine show any symptoms of paralysis; nor did Jewish industry, during the decade which preceded the printing of Father Bonsirven's essay, show any signs of arrested development. A table of comparative statistics shows that the number of Jews employed in industry increased from 4,750 in 1921, to 28,616 in 1937; the value of the annual output rose from $2,000,000 to $34,104,-

ooo.[52] According to Father Bonsirven, one of the causes of the alleged paralysis and arrested development was the fact that the Zionists, "by their first seizure of lands and government, irritated the Arabs." He assured his readers, however, that there was now no cause for alarm; these attempts at domination have been checked: "Zionism is retarded in its progress and reduced to proportions that render the fulfilment of its dream of nationhood and national civilization out of the question." [53]

These "dreams of nationhood and national civilization" were, of course, under the Mandate the clearly expressed obligations of Great Britain. It is difficult to discover any sense in the statement that the Zionists "had seized lands and government." They were allowed no effective part in the administration of Palestine, which was completely autocratic and, at times, despotic.[54] No Jew ever acquired any land from an Arab in Palestine without buying it and without paying a high price:

> Jewish payments to Arab landowners have been on so lavish a scale as to permit the Arab to sell part of his land, eliminate his debts, improve his farm equipment and intensify his cultivation of the remaining land. . . . Jewish land purchases would have been even more stimulating had not so large a share of the sellers been absentee owners, in many cases living abroad in Syria and Lebanon.[55]

Moreover, the administration, which was under the obligation (according to article 6 of the Mandate) "to encourage close settlement of Jews on the land, including State lands and waste lands not required for public purposes," made the mistake of presenting large tracts of marsh and waste areas to Bedouins who promptly sold portions of it to Jews at an exorbitant figure and made no attempt to reclaim the rest. It should be noted that the money used by Zionists to buy land was not supplied by "the big banks affiliated to Jewish houses." Although the soil of Palestine had to be covered with Jewish gold, "that gold, for many, many years, came out of the pockets, not of Jewish millionaires, but of the poor." This is the testimony of President Weizmann, and he ought to know where the money came from; he collected a great deal of it himself.[56]

Father Bonsirven must have obtained his information about the paralysis of Zionism from people who were unwilling to recognize to what a surprising extent, working without government assistance or sympathy, the Zionists had been successful.

In England, Father Joseph Keating, editor of *The Month*, gave his readers the impression that the whole thing was a swindle; under Sir Herbert Samuel, he wrote, ". . . money was lavishly expended to expropriate the indigenous inhabitants from their land . . . nothing was done to mitigate the Jewish exploitation of Palestine." He accused the British government of "letting loose in Palestine the Jewish remnant which cannot make good elsewhere." He also suggested, choosing his phrases carefully, that the attempted "exploitation" of the country was directed by Jewish international finance, and that everything would have fallen into the clutches of the Jews, had not a great international authority intervened just in time: "It needed the intervention of the Permanent Court of International Justice to prevent the establishment of the Rutenberg monopoly whereby almost all the economic development of Palestine was sought to be entrusted to a Jewish financial group." This account of what happened is incorrect. The Court of International Justice was asked by the British Government to decide a dispute about the validity of concessions for various public works in Palestine alleged to have been granted by the Turks, prior to the outbreak of war in 1914, to a Greek subject. The court rejected all the claims of this Greek, except the concession to supply electric power to the city of Jerusalem, and confirmed the validity of the concessions which the British government had granted in 1921 to Mr. Pinchas Rutenberg, founder and managing director, until his death in 1942, of the **Palestine Electric Corporation.** The Permanent Court of International Justice did not intervene, and was not asked by anyone to intervene, "to prevent the establishment of the Rutenberg monopoly." The concessions, "whereby almost all the economic development of Palestine was sought to be entrusted to a Jewish financial group," were implemented by the British government in 1923.

The consequences were not so disastrous as Father Keating—and, no doubt, most of his readers—would have expected. Mr. Rutenberg did not waste any time; he started to work at once. Three years later, in 1926, the greater part of his plan for the electrification of Palestine had already been accomplished, and the whole country was provided with the opportunity of obtaining electric power and light. As a result of this "Jewish exploitation" the total number of units sold by the corporation in 1926 amounted to 2,344,000 (kilowatt-hours); in 1944 the total had increased to 184,000,-000. During the first fourteen years, industry and irrigation have accounted for more than half of the total sales.[57] Such rapid economic development in a land where neither Turk nor Arab nor Briton had made any practical attempt to use the available water power would have surprised readers of *The Month* who, having been told in 1922 that the Rutenberg concession was "preposterous" and "monstrous," were assured in 1925 that "the only result [of Zionism], according to credible reports, had been to flood the land with the scum of various ghettoes to the scandal and demoralization of the inhabitants."[58]

This "scum" did, in fact, create considerable alarm in British administrative circles during the early years of the mandate, and consequently Mr. Rutenberg did not meet with much encouragement from Palestinian officials, many of whom obviously did not want any enterprise to be successful if it was a

Jewish one. "It will be interesting," wrote C. R. Ashbee, civil adviser of the mandatory administration, in 1922, "to watch . . . the inevitable failure of the Rutenberg scheme." [59] What these Palestinian officials were watching for was not merely "the inevitable failure of the Rutenberg scheme"—but the inevitable failure of Zionism.

# 10

........................................

# Pride, Arrogance, and Hate

CHRISTIAN WRITERS IN GENERAL have looked with suspicion at every attempt which has been made, at any time, to fertilize the soil and raise the standard of living in Israel. Many of them believed that God had condemned the land, along with the people, to perpetual impoverishment. When a French writer in the seventeenth century accounted for the sterility of the country by explaining that "God had punished the soil of Palestine on account of the crimes of its inhabitants," Basnage, with his usual common sense, pointed out that, although Judaea was a desert and almost abandoned, the hypothesis of Divine intervention was unnecessary—"since lands become sterile when people cease to cultivate them." [1]

Not only do such lands become sterile, but erosion spreads over the whole countryside; the soil is washed away from the hillsides; the surface of the valleys under stress of wind and water breaks up, changes its formation, and, amidst deep rifts and stony hillocks, and often stretches of malarial marsh, a few goats and camels, tended by half-starved shepherds, struggle to find a miserable pasturage. An American traveler who went to Palestine nearly fifty years ago observed that erosion was threatening to ruin what little fertile land remained: "If the process goes on long enough, the entire plain of Sharon will be buried under a slowly creeping desert." [2] If the process had not been arrested by the energy of the Jews, the whole country would now be as derelict as the greater part of Syria and Transjordan; one more new desert would have been marked on the map of the world.

Englishmen who visited the country in the eighteenth century were often more liberal-minded and more observant than the hurried traveler of the present day. Dr. Thomas Shaw (1694-1751), Principal of St. Edmund's Hall, Oxford, went to the Near East more than two hundred years ago; he was interested chiefly in botany. But he has recorded some facts about the conditions of the land of Israel and its inhabitants, conditions which remained unchanged until the British took over the mandate. If his book had been read by cabinet ministers at any time during the last twenty-five years, Britain might have been saved the trouble and expense of sending out so many fact-finding commissions. Dr. Shaw was impressed by the absorptive capacity of the country. He did not, of course, employ this phrase, which, of recent coinage, was gratefully included by the officials of the Palestinian administration in their dictionary of convenient catchwords. He wrote at a time when Englishmen, including English dons, tried to say what they meant and usually meant what they said. His report is much more informative, and much shorter, than any of the findings of the slightly ridiculous committees of experts who were sent out to Palestine almost annually during the first twenty years of the British mandate. Shaw summed up the economic possibilities of the country in a few sentences which express nearly all that needed to be said on the subject, either in 1738 or in 1938:

The Barrenness or Scarcity rather, which some Authors malignantly or maliciously complain of, does not proceed from the Incapacity or natural Unfruitfulness of the country, but from the Want of Inhabitants, and the great Aversion there is to Labour and Industry in those few who possess it. . . . The Land is a good Land, and still capable of afford-

ing its Neighbours the like Supplies of Corn and Oil, which
it is known to have done in the Time of Solomon.[3]

An American explorer of a puritanical turn of mind, who
conducted an expedition in 1848 to the Jordan and the Dead
Sea, described Palestine as "a land scathed by the wrath of an
offended Deity." He did not, however, believe that the Jews
had been condemned forever to be separated from their
country. His forecast of the future was remarkable, for he
announced that, before they could return, not only the power
of Turkey, but the power of "the worshippers of Thor,"
would have to be destroyed:

> It needs only the destruction of that power [Turkey]
> which, for so many centuries, has rested like an incubus upon
> the Eastern world, to ensure the restoration of the Jews to
> Palestine. The increase of toleration, the assimilation of
> creeds, the unanimity with which all works of charity are
> undertaken, prove to the observing mind that ere long, with
> every other vestige of bigotry, the prejudice against this un-
> happy race will be obliterated by a noble and Godlike sym-
> pathy. . . . Many a Thor with all his Eddas must first be
> swept away; but a time will come.[4]

A Scottish missionary, Dr. James Smith, at the end of the
nineteenth century recognized the potential fertility of the
land, "were it cultivated by a peasantry less poverty-stricken,
incapable and slothful than the present tillers. . . . If only
the long stopped up wells could be re-opened, and the water,
where it is to be found, be better distributed, a new era of
prosperity might dawn upon the once smiling but now unhappy country."[5] Under Turkish rule the inhabitants had
been reduced to a condition of indescribable destitution.
James Smith wrote with dismay about the "appearance and
odor of the streets" and the almost complete lack of lighting
and sewerage. The population of Jerusalem, he wrote, num-
bered 70,000, including about 40,000 Jews, many of whom
lived "in the rocks and caves outside the city." The German

consul stated that poor Jews in Jerusalem "used to buy, and not cheaply, water that had been used by the wealthy for washing or bathing; I have seen this done as late as the year 1900." [6]

Among the literary celebrities who have visited and commented on Palestine in modern times, not one—not even Chateaubriand—was able to combine lack of vision with a poetic romanticism so movingly as Pierre Loti. Although his profession of Christianity was nominal, his melancholy skepticism did not weaken his inherited contempt for the people of Israel. After visiting the Wailing Wall, he expressed this contempt in almost the identical words which Balmez had used a generation earlier: "There is no doubt that a special mark is impressed on their foreheads, the mark of reprobation which is stamped upon that race." He would have been inclined "to weep along with them . . . had they not been *Jews*, and if one did not feel one's heart strangely chilled by their abject appearance." The Land was included in the curse. Pierre Loti traveled through Galilee in the springtime and found it "silent under an immense shroud of flowers." He mourned over the "irremediable desolation of Samaria," and saw "death brooding over Judaea." He pitied the efforts of a few old Jews in Tiberias who were dreaming of "a past which had gone for ever." The Arabs, always dignified and stately, had come, long ago, "to implement the threat of the Biblical prophecies, to depopulate slowly, to destroy slowly, to spread a strange torpor over all the land." Without any doubt, as Chrysostom and Bossuet had said, there was no hope. The ruins still remaining of the ancient glory would be "immovable for all time," and the "melancholy of abandonment which broods over all the Holy Land is something final, doomed to last for ever." Here was the befitting and inevitable end. It was better, indeed, that "the sacred soil of Galilee should remain thus closed and dead to the world," so that a "Christian" who did not believe in Christ could still come to weep in comfort over the distress of the land and its ancient people. This was no place for men to live and work. "Not altars of gold, not basilicas built by emperors, would be so worthy to mark the place of such a memory, as this abandonment, this reign of silence, this kingdom of weeds, this end of all human time."[7]

The general opinion of visitors at the beginning of the present century was that the technical agricultural difficulties of recovery were insurmountable. An American who spent some time in the country in 1903 was particularly impressed by the apparent futility of trying to reclaim the Dead Sea area, where the Jews have since established a chemical industry and several agricultural settlements. He wrote:

> The Zionists, who are trying to repeople Palestine with Jews, talk fluently of the possibility of establishing a large and profitable colony in this unnatural and repulsive sink . . . , but they fail to consider certain conditions. . . . No power can induce workmen to stay in a region where the summer heat is intolerable, where mosquitoes and other insect pests are often unendurable, and where poisonous miasma fills the atmosphere.[8]

This traveler, like so many others before and since, not only was convinced that such plans for economic development were impracticable, but thought that they were contrary to the will of God. He was one of the first to express in print the opinion that the country should be kept for all time to come in its desolate condition as a sacred place for pilgrims. "If Palestine could be preserved and protected as a great religious and Biblical museum, it would be a blessed undertaking."[9] In those days, the "museum" preserved a deplorable exhibit, viewed by most pilgrims as an inevitable part of the establishment. "Beggars were almost as necessary in Jerusalem," noted Sir Frederick Treves in 1913, "as the altar, the relic and the clouds of incense." Visitors to the city had been accustomed for generations to bestow alms upon the hordes

of mendicants who guarded the entrance to every Christian
shrine and plied their most profitable traffic in the lane leading
down to the church of the Holy Sepulchre. Sir Frederick
Treves wrote a vivid description of the scene:

> As the way is steep, it is cut into steps and paved. On
> either side is a blank wall. On the steps where they touch the
> wall the beggars lie, huddled close together in a brown,
> damp, feebly writhing mass. They seem to have been blown
> into the gutter and to have become heaped up there against
> the wall, as are leaves and litter after a wind. . . . They
> seem to ooze down the steps in a thick continuous mass,
> made up of inharmonious human ingredients. Here is a
> cinder-grey hand stretched out. All the fingers are gone, but
> there is a thumb left which keeps moving to and fro. Spread
> out on the flags are paralyzed limbs looking like shrivelled
> tree branches, although it is difficult to say to which bundle
> of tatters any two belong. Here is a club foot dangling over
> a stone. It is so livid with cold as to resemble a purple root.
> Faintly seen under the shade of a cowl is a face without
> a nose and without eyes. Nearby a bony knee projects with
> a fungating tumour on it like a crushed tomato. There are
> horrible sores, too, effectively displayed, as if they were
> possessions of great price. Above all there comes ever from
> this medley of maimed folk a low monotonous sound, as
> dreary as the moaning of a winter wind around a lonely
> house.[10]

Although most of these horrors were swept away five years
later when the Allies entered Jerusalem, the suggestion that
the inhabitants should be provided with some better occupation than begging did not meet with universal approval. In
many minds the notion still prevailed that the introduction of
modern industry anywhere, and especially in or near the Holy
City, would be almost a sacrilege. This sentimentalism, this
idolatry of the locus, was endangered by the practical energy
of the Zionists.

The Christian communities, united for the time being by a
common interest, drew up a memorandum for an American

commission which visited Palestine in 1920; in it they expressed the fear that the Arabs were threatened by the danger
of "excessive colonization," and some Christian Arabs made
the somewhat sinister suggestion that they should be allowed
to deal with this peril "in their own way." Zionism was denounced, moreover, by most sections of the Christian Church
as a threat to Christian security. The Rev. Dr. Ewing, a Pres-
byterian minister who had lived for many years in Palestine,
dreaded the power of Jewish gold. He thought the Moslems
might eventually "suffer a measure of Jewish intrusion *at a
price*," and that the Christian population would then "be
crushed between the upper millstone of Islam and the nether
millstone of Jewry." [11] Catholic opposition was almost invariably ill-informed. Cardinal Bourne, at the Liverpool Catholic Congress of 1920, called attention to the working of a
process by which the expropriation of the original inhabitants
was being carried out by Jewish syndicates; and Pope Benedict XV, misled by his representatives on the spot, protested
that the condition of Christians in Palestine was now worse
than it had been under Turkish rule, and called upon "the
governments of Christian nations, even non-Catholics," to
make a joint protest to the League of Nations. [12]

The brothers Tharaud suggested that "the Jews, who consider themselves to have suffered persecution for two thousand
years, might, as soon as they got any power, immediately start
taking revenge on the Christians." [13] Twenty-five years later,
the weekly bulletin of the Congregation for the Propagation
of the Faith (*Fides*, May 9, 1949), expressed the view that
Zionism might be "spiritually inspired in a 2000-year-old revenge against Christianity." The Holy Land, from the ecclesiastical point of view, was a land where control of the
"Holy Places" seemed of more importance than the material
welfare of the people who lived there. "There exists in Palestine at the present time," wrote a French cleric in 1923, "a
Protestant peril, the almost inevitable consequence of English

influence, and a Jewish peril, resulting from Zionist aspirations, and the combined efforts of all Catholics will be required to fight against this double peril." [14]

The "Jewish peril" threatened to interfere with the devotional practices of pilgrims who, for sentimental but unhistorical reasons, wanted the land to remain forever desolate, and thought that agricultural tractors were out of place in a religious museum. St. Benedict would not have agreed with a monk of his Order who visited Palestine in 1930 and then wrote a book.[15] This pilgrim felt that work and prayer were incompatible in holy places; and he could not pray in comfort if people were to be allowed to disturb, with the noise of their agricultural machinery, the silence of the derelict lands in the valley of Gennesaret. He found that "the comparative desolation which reigns for the best part of the year in this stifling valley enables the Christian pilgrim to recapture more easily the atmosphere of the days when the Word of Life dwelt here among men." If this monk had been acquainted with the works of Josephus, or had ventured to read Ernest Renan, he would have known that in the days of Christ this valley had been one of the most populous districts in Israel, covered with plantations and celebrated for its fertility, until the seventh century, when the process of Moslem destruction began. Renan wrote:

> The horrible state to which Galilee has been reduced, especially near Lake Tiberias, ought not to create a wrong impression. This district, now scorched, was in olden time a celestial paradise. The baths of Tiberias, which are today a hideous sight, were once the beauty spot of Galilee, and Josephus praises the beautiful trees in the plain of Gennesaret, where now not one is left.[16]

Like so many others who visited the Holy Land during the period of the British mandate, this pilgrim did not show much interest in the welfare of either Jews or Arabs: he was more attracted to places than to people, and his first view of Jeru-

salem was disappointing: "Jews everywhere; the shop signs
are in Hebrew." He was not surprised to find that his British
friends were worried about the presence of these Jews, who
had already proved to be a difficult problem, long ago, for the
greatest of all legislators. "Moses had been responsible to
God," he said, "for as hopeless a set of people as anyone could
be entrusted with." [17]

While this "hopeless set of people" were draining the
marshes and turning rocks and sand into vineyards and or-
chards, the English community watched their work from a
distance with indifference or contempt. Many of the army
officers and civil personnel of the Palestinian administration,
who were predominantly town-minded, had been brought
up in English public schools to regard the country as a place
which afforded opportunities for sport and recreation—in England, hunting, fishing and shooting; in India, polo and pig
sticking; in Palestine, wild-duck shooting in the marshes and
jackal hunting in the desert. H. V. Morton has drawn a picture of the Englishman in the Middle East with a few simple
sentences:

> An Englishman in breeches, golf stockings and a tweed
> coat. "Good morning," he said pleasantly, "looking round?"
> "Yes," I said. "Do you think we could raise a drink in the
> hotel?" "We could try. Hot isn't it? I've been in the Jordan
> marshes looking for quail. They come over in thousands
> just about this time." . . . "Do you live here?" I asked.
> "I've been here since 1921. I came over with the 'Black and
> Tans' to join the police. I'm still in the police. It's a good
> country,—at least it suits me. I get plenty of shooting." [18]

Twelve years later, another visitor was being shown round
a Jewish settlement in the Negev, a desert where nothing had
been grown for two thousand years—a desert without water.
Now, after five years work, the settlers had achieved a vine-
yard, an orchard and several acres of wheat and roots. In a
few years, the eucalyptus trees they had planted would be

providing one more thing the desert had forgotten—shade. A young Jew from central Europe acted as guide, tall, slim, blonde, wearing khaki shorts and shirt—he looked like an Englishman, except that he was not sun-tanned. His skin had baked to a deep brown that was almost black. A few hundred yards from the whitewashed settlement fort, built on a high mound, fenced with barbed wire, a reservoir had been dug, about fifty yards square and fifteen to twenty feet deep, to catch the flood of water which rushed, two or three times a year, down the nearby wadi. The reservoir had sprung a leak, and was now being repaired by a squad of about thirty men who were laying strips of tar along the cement flooring. "It would be hot down there," said the guide, "but the job will soon be finished." "Your job," replied the tourist somewhat fatuously, "is never done." The young man smiled: "When we have time," he said, "we are going to build a tennis court."

During the early years of the mandate, inquiring pilgrims, who had heard vague rumors about pioneers with tractors threatening to disturb the peace of the Holy Land, were told that there was no cause for alarm. "The project is failing," wrote the Rev. Reginald Ginns, in 1924, who spent three years in Jerusalem, "as indeed it was bound to fail. Palestine is the last place on earth they should have chosen. . . . Palestine is to prove the death of political Zionism." This Dominican friar came to the country with an open mind; he had no prepossessions against Zionism or against the Jews; but he found no traces of such impartiality in the English colony. He wrote:

> One was frequently shocked by the apparent lack of elementary Christian sentiment towards the Jews, even among those whose lives were dedicated to God. The impression was sometimes given that the Jew was excluded from the law of charity, outside the pale and beyond redemption. Nowhere indeed would it be harder to work for the conversion

of the Jews than in Jerusalem. *"Sales juifs"* is a phrase that
one often heard. . . . The moral atmosphere in Jerusalem
during the last few years became a little infected, and one
was almost imperceptibly influenced by it. Christian feeling
was almost universally on the side of the Arabs.

The extent to which Father Ginns himself was influenced by
the local propaganda is revealed by a story he tells of his own
fears and fancies. He was walking one day in the Jewish
quarter of Jerusalem and met some Jewish boys, who followed
him, apparently out of curiosity. He was afraid that they
wanted to spit on the crucifix he was carrying.[19]

None of the politicians, commissioners and committeemen
who have reported on the Palestine problem have referred to
the main reason why the British mandate has proved (as they
all agree) "unworkable"; but the reason was given by Father
Reginald Ginns—the anti-Semitic infection of "the moral atmosphere." Not only was Christian feeling almost invariably
on the side of the Arabs, but there was an almost universal
sentiment of hostility to the Jews, not merely "among those
whose lives were dedicated to God," but among those whose
lives, for the time being, were dedicated to carrying out the
mandate. From the record of administrative officials, the
reports of pilgrims and tourists, and especially from the conduct and conversations of army officers stationed in the country, it is evident that from the very beginning the English colony did not appreciate the social value of Zionism, or take the
least interest in the constructive work that was being carried
on. In 1920, Dr. Weizmann had already reported to the London Zionist Conference that "the military Administration of
Palestine was anti-Zionist and perhaps anti-Jewish." [20]

The riots of Eastertide in 1920 were the direct consequence
of the notorious anti-Semitic attitude of the British military
administration. When the Jewish Self-Defense Corps, which
had been organized by Lieutenant Jabotinsky with the knowledge and grudging consent of the military authorities, at-

tempted to rescue the Jews in the Old City, they found the gates closed against them and held by British troops. Murder, rape and looting continued unchecked for nearly three days. When the pogrom was at last put to an end, the British proceeded to arrest a few prominent leaders of the Jewish Self-Defense Corps. Jabotinsky was sentenced by a military court to fifteen years of penal servitude, a sentence later annulled by orders from London. Colonel J. H. Patterson, British commander of the Jewish Battalion in Palestine, wrote:

> The whole history of this atrocious outrage is a foul stain on our fair name. . . . Jabotinsky was cast into prison, clothed in prison garb, had his hair cropped, and was marched, in company with two Arabs convicted of rape, through Jerusalem and Kantara, places where he was well known as a British officer. Even the worst Hun that we have read of could hardly have exceeded the savagery and tyranny shown by the military authorities of the E.E.F. towards Jabotinsky, an officer who fought stoutly for us, and helped England and her cause in every possible way to the full extent of his power during the war.[21]

Responsibility for this miscarriage of justice, which in many details of procedure resembles the Dreyfus case, ought not to be confined to individual anti-Semites among the military staff. It is difficult to see how the commander in chief, Lord Allenby, can be acquitted of all blame for the disgraceful behavior of the officers under his command.

The anti-Jewish sentiments to which Dr. Weizmann referred were not confined to regimental officers and the staff, but were shared, and expressed openly, by a majority of civilian visitors and residents. These people had a curious and irrational confidence in the potential industrial and military qualities of the Palestinian Arabs; many of them agreed with the view, first popularized by Mark Sykes, that nothing could now prevent these hitherto unsuccessful workers from going ahead and building up a new Palestine. This conviction was expressed with characteristic confidence by a writer who had lived in Palestine for many years in a position which enabled her to acquire an intimate knowledge, not of the people, but of local English society. The daughter of the Anglican bishop in Jerusalem wrote:

> Now, under British rule the Arab peasant has a chance, almost for the first time in history, one might say. He can labor, and the fruit of his labor will not be stolen from him. . . . In the fellah himself . . . England had the finest material she could desire, to train and to use, for the building up of Palestine now, and for its future defense.[22]

For more than a quarter of a century, the problem of Palestine has been confused, and made to appear insoluble, with all this verbiage about the building up of the Near East by Arabs. In 1917, Mark Sykes was sure that they would immediately start to create a new civilization. Twenty-seven years later, Mr. Cordell Hull, head of the American State Department, expressed "strong hope" that they would begin "soon." In his *Memoirs* he wrote:

> As I left office [in 1944], I entertained strong hope that the Arab states of the Near East would soon begin to take the economic, social and cultural steps we believed necessary as an approach toward political unity, that they would be able to compose the conflicting ambitions of various of their leaders, and that, not too many years after the conclusion of the war, they would be able to bring stability, unity, and economic development to that historic corner of the world.[23]

Sir John Hope Simpson had thought that the Arab cultivators might improve their position "if they got the chance of learning better methods, and the capital which is a necessary preliminary to their employment."[24] Something more than instruction and capital is needed to enable cultivators to raise crops on land which has been derelict for a thousand years.

The revival of an Arab civilization is a long-term proposition which the mandatory power made no serious attempt to tackle. No effective campaign was undertaken against disease and illiteracy, or to weaken the dominating feudalism which kept the Arab proletariat in a condition of helpless poverty. An equal level of Arab and Jewish prosperity could be attained under the British Mandate only by restricting the work of the Zionists, who were therefore not encouraged to make any progress until the Arabs were ready to follow them. It soon became impossible to deny any longer that while the Arabs remained idle the Jews, in spite of official discouragement, could not be prevented from working. Moreover, these "fragments of insoluble matter floating in a liquid," as Balmez had called them, were beginning to coalesce, and the process, if permitted to continue, might eventually lead to inconvenient results.

The growth of Zionism was therefore regarded by the British administration as a political danger, a form of socialism, a protest of people who unreasonably denied the right of "the Squire and his relations, to keep them in their proper stations." The proper state of these people, according to an English journalist who had, on behalf of a section of the English popular press, made a visit to the Middle East, was the state of dispersion to which Christendom had always believed they had been condemned by God:

> The Jews most manifestly have the quality of an essence, which requires to be distributed and disseminated. It can only be used to good purpose in solution, like some ingredient amalgamated into a thousand products of pharmacy, everywhere the same and yet everywhere different. In bulk it is overwhelming, useless, and very possibly dangerous.[25]

Jews "in bulk" were undoubtedly dangerous. In Palestine, the "fragments" had formed a community which threatened to upset the balance of power in the Middle East.

British officials, even those who were doing their best to carry out the terms of the mandate, were irritated by the "arrogance" of young Jewish immigrants who were often seen marching arm in arm along the streets of Tel Aviv or

Jerusalem, singing patriotic songs, and thus demonstrating
their claim—recognized by British statesmen—to be in the
country by right and not on sufferance. The fundamental
opposition of Englishmen in Palestine to Zionism was due to
the fact that Zionists had rebelled against an established order
of Western society, which had existed for nearly two thousand
years, and were behaving, as the mediaeval Popes would have
expressed it, "with insolence and ingratitude." Although the
words *"sales juifs"* were often heard in Jerusalem, as Father
Ginns had noted in 1924, they were not so often heard, at least
in public, during the last two years of the British mandate. In
1946, a young English officer went into a café in Tel Aviv.
He was perhaps a little drunk, and gave the waiter an order:
"Hurry up, you dirty Jew!" The waiter, who was a member
of the Haganah, took the customer by the scruff of his neck
and the seat of his trousers and deposited him gently in the
street. That is why the English hated Zionism.

Not only did the attempt of the Jews to escape from
Gentile domination give new vigor to anti-Semitism, but it
revealed the presence of the microbe in unexpected places,
sometimes in the blood of Englishmen, reputed to be liberal-
minded, who were probably unconscious of the infection. H.
H. Asquith thought that the ideas of political Zionists were
"fantastic"; he did, however, admit that Jews seemed to be
happier in Palestine "than in the wretched places from which
they were exported." He had no sympathy with the notion
that "the scattered Jews would in time swarm back there
from all quarters of the globe." [26] For Asquith, these were
people who did not emigrate, or travel from place to place,
like human beings: they were "exported" like cattle or they
"swarmed" like locusts. After visiting Palestine in 1924, he
wrote to a friend that "Tiberias swarms with Jews, unlike
Nazareth which is full of Christians." [27] His unfavorable impressions of Jewry were probably acquired from his social and
political contacts with some of the assimilated English Jews,

who did not resent—and therefore deserved—the contempt
with which they were sometimes treated by their Gentile
friends. "I have had," wrote Margot Asquith, "and still have,
devoted friends among the Jews, but have often been reminded
of the saying 'A Jew is round your neck, at your feet, but
never at your side.'" She thought that the highest compliment
that could be paid to one of her "devoted" Jewish friends was
to compare him to an Englishman. "Rufus Isaacs," she wrote,
"is one of the best fellows that ever lived. . . . By race a Jew,
he is British to the core, neither touchy, nor restless, nor suspicious, but combines wisdom with caution, and has the laugh
of an English schoolboy." [28]

C. R. Ashbee, an official of the British administration in
Palestine, tells a story which shows what the English ex-
schoolboy laughed at in Jerusalem twenty-five years ago.
"An English officer, one of the red efficient sort that gets
things done, turned up at the wailing place, but on the wrong
day, and found nothing doing. Quickly drawing a shilling
from his pocket he seized on the nearest Haluca, and shouted:
'Here—wail you blighter!' And he wailed." [29] The contempt
of the English for the Children of Israel is revealed even more
strikingly in another story, told by the same writer, of a young
British-born Zionist who said that he could imagine no nobler
death than at the head of a Jewish battalion defending this
country from the Arabs. An Englishman who heard these
words and repeated them to Ashbee, added laconically: "My
God! Fancy having once been an Englishman, and wanting
to become"—then after a pause, and a dropping of the voice to
unutterable depths—"a Levantine." [30]

Arab opposition to Zionism was encouraged by the uncon-
cealed Judaeophobia of practically the entire personnel of the
British administration. "We had to be seemingly harsh and
unfriendly," wrote Douglas Duff; "it did not pay for one's
seniors to think that one had any undue sympathy for the returning Jews." [31] Ashbee records scraps of a conversation at an

official banquet, conversation which might have been heard
at Government House, or in an officers' mess, at any time
from the beginning to the end of the British mandate. "For
the moment the Jews are in disgrace and not invited to our
banquet. But said one of the officials who sat on my left,
'We don't talk about that just now. . . . The business of the
moment . . . is raising an army; and the Arabs are good fighters!'" [32] British officers seldom had any illusions about the
fighting qualities of the Arabs. When they said that the Arabs
were good fighters, what they really meant was that the Jews
were bad fighters. However incapable the Arabs might be—
and their incapacity in the field had been obvious to every
general who had known them since the days of Napoleon—
they were believed to be good enough, even the Palestinian
Arabs, to make short work of the Jews. "If you English would
withdraw your army," a Zionist is reported by Ashbee to have
said in 1920, "we could quite well manage by ourselves . . .
at least in a year or two." "Rot," replied John Smith, the
Englishman. [33] This was the right thing to say at Government
House dinner parties.

The Arabs were good fighters, and the Arab was a gentleman; both assertions carried the implication that the Jew was
neither. "The Arab," wrote Ashbee, "is so much more of a
gentleman." In the category of "gentleman" he included Haj
Amin Husseini, [34] who, after inciting his fellow Arabs to murder a few Jews in the riots of 1920, was chosen by Sir Herbert
Samuel to be Mufti of Jerusalem; he became a frequent
and almost familiar visitor at the High Commissioner's table,
where his picturesque attire provided the popular Oriental
coloring. It has been said, no doubt with some truth, that
many of his best friends were British officers. Twenty-three
years later, this dignified Arab gentleman was in Berlin, advising Hitler how to complete the extermination of the Jews
in Europe.

It was difficult, but not altogether impossible, for a Jew to attain the distinction of being recognized by the British as a "gentleman." The appointment of Sir Herbert Samuel as High Commissioner of Palestine was regarded with suspicion, wrote the Rev. Dr. Ewing, by both Arabs and Christians, who were not completely reassured when they were told "that although of Jewish race, Sir Herbert was really an honorable and upright English gentleman." [35] "Why are you pro-Arab and anti-Jew?" a tourist in 1936 asked an English officer who was in a very responsible position. "Because the Arab is a gentleman and the Jew is not," he snapped. [36] No one has described more concisely than Horace Samuel the attitude of the average British officer during the period of the mandate: "They regarded the Balfour Declaration as damned nonsense, the Jews as a damned nuisance, and the Arabs as damned good fellows." [37] Representing the more literate personnel of the administration, C. R. Ashbee wrote a paragraph which has a bias both mediaeval and modern, and as a criticism and a forecast is a fair sample of the views held by officials under the mandate twenty-five years ago:

> I have not met one Zionist yet whom I would really trust for a wise and sure constructive policy. . . . The wise Jews are lukewarm or hostile. There is something factitious, journalistic, about the whole movement. . . . Walking down the streets of Jerusalem, an American friend pointed to the anaemic slum population drifting past us, and said to me, "These people haven't got the proper material for the making of a State." Further, the Jew is unthinkable without the bargain, he bears the brand of that mean fellow Jacob upon his brow, and with all the nobility of his convictions, and the grandeur of his Messianic idea, one would not trust him, *qua* Zionist, not to exploit the Holy Land commercially in his own and his tribe's interest. [38]

The tragic consequences of all this ill-will are not often referred to by pilgrims and tourists, or by the journalists who write books about the Holy Land. The murder of a Jew, or indeed of an Arab, was seldom regarded by the administration as a crime on a par with the murder of an Englishman. During the riots of 1929, the administration not only failed to protect the Jewish population, but actually forbade them to defend themselves and made sure, by disarming them, that they would *not* be able to defend themselves.[39] The conduct of the British authorities convinced the Arabs that Jews could be killed with impunity. No serious effort was made to search for the killers, and those who were caught were usually acquitted "owing to lack of evidence." "Clashes have taken place between Arabs and Jews"—this was the phrase invariably used by the administration to describe the murderous attacks on people they had disarmed, people for whose safety they had undertaken to be responsible. Such verbal evasions provide merely a brief and localized immunity, a temporary escape from the facts. "There were constant clashes," said one of the criminals at Nuremberg, describing the German pogroms of 1938. Himmler used the same trick: "It is not the task of the police," he declared, when German civilians were murdering Allied airmen who had bailed out over Germany, "to interfere in clashes between the Germans and the English and American terror-fliers." [40]

The commission which came from England to inquire into the causes of the "disturbances" reached the conclusion that the administration had, as ever, done its best to sustain the high reputation of British fair play. In England, public opinion was fed with stories about the gallant and glamorous Arabs.

But foreigners were not so easily fooled. "The wholesale murder and plundering in the riots of 1929," wrote J. N. Kann, who was consul of the Netherlands at the time, "will always remain a blot on the British Administration." [41] Mr. Kann was shocked by the behavior of the Palestine police who frequently connived at murder, and even, it was alleged, took part in it—and by the bias of the court which repeatedly declined to convict the murderers. He gives a brief account of the farcical judicial proceedings which followed the massacre, on August 24, 1929, of a family of Russian origin named Macleff, who had lived for many years on a settlement at Motza, about four miles from Jerusalem. They were warned two days before the attack and asked for police protection, which was refused. Macleff, two daughters and a son, were killed outright, and Mrs. Macleff was mortally wounded.[42] Haim, an eighteen-year-old son, then killed the leader of the assassins with the butt end of an old Turkish rifle, jumped from a back window with his brother Mordecai, aged nine, and ran to the main road, three hundred yards away, to look for help. At that moment, an R.A.F. convoy of armored cars stopped opposite the farm and watched the smoke and flames issuing from the outbuildings which had just been set on fire. Haim asked the British officer in charge of the convoy to come and save his mother who had been stabbed in a dozen places and was still alive. The officer refused to give any help and the convoy passed on. Next day, British justice took prompt action. Haim was arrested and charged with murder, detained in prison for a few days and then released. Some of the Arabs who had taken part in the attack were subsequently arrested, and were identified by Haim, by a young sister who had also managed to escape, by young Mordecai, and by two neighbors. The accused were all acquitted "owing to insufficient evidence."

On being told of their acquittal, the astonished Arabs and their friends were convinced that the British secretly approved of the massacre. They exclaimed in court: "The Government is with us: The English are on our side." "These are the cries," wrote a leading Hebrew daily paper, "with which the first murders were committed. They are the same cries that were heard in the streets of Jerusalem during the riots of ten years ago. They are the cries that mean: Jews may be killed with impunity." It is not surprising, concluded the Dutch consul, that "the Jewish population lose their confidence in the administration of justice. When Arabs who have taken part in attacks on Jews can be identified by name, it need not be first proved that they dealt the mortal blow. Their presence alone is sufficient. Complete acquittal is in such a case a piece of rank injustice." [43]

The consul noted that the British in Palestine "were anti-Jewish, and still more anti-Zionist." "It is considered good form," he wrote, "to look down upon the Jewish community." [44] It was apparently not considered good form, however, to prevent Arabs from murdering Jews. Decorations were given by the Government to soldiers and policemen for gallant conduct in towns where scores of disarmed Jews had been massacred. Police officer Cafferata, stationed at Hebron when eighty Jews were murdered and many of the corpses mutilated, was given a police medal for "gallantry." But, as a Palestinian lawyer pointed out, "no decoration was given to Mr. Riggs, the Jaffa officer who . . . prevented a violent massacre in Tel Aviv by firing on the Arabs." [45]

Twenty years after the murder of the Macleff family, the town of Haifa was captured from the Arabs by 240 soldiers of the Haganah, armed with fifty rifles and a few machine guns. They were commanded by Mordecai Macleff.

After Holland was invaded by the Germans in 1940, Mr. J. N. Kann, his wife and all the members of his family, except one daughter, were taken away and murdered in a Nazi concentration camp.

Few English writers have expressed their contempt for the Jewish people more subtly and in a more popular form than H. V. Morton. In his most widely read book, first published in 1934 (an eleventh edition was printed in 1941), entitled *In the Steps of the Master*, Christ and His Apostles are almost the only Jews who are mentioned without some hint of malice or condescension. Solomon is presented to the reader as "the first great Jewish financier." The Arabs are obliquely represented as the present-day heirs of the people who lived in

Palestine during the time of Christ; this effect is usually obtained by omitting essential facts. For example, Morton
writes: "When Jesus had raised the daughter of Jairus, He
said, '*Talitha cumi*,' translated in our Bible as 'Damsel, I say
unto thee, arise!' . . . The word '*cumi*' is still regularly used
by the Arabs today for 'get up.'" English readers were not
reminded that "*cumi*" is a Hebrew verb, used in 1934 by Jews
all over the country—and used long ago, by Solomon, in a
context which has nothing to do with finance:

> My beloved spoke, and said unto me;
> Rise up, my love, my fair one, and come away.
> For lo, the winter is past,
> The rain is over and gone.
>
> The flowers appear on the earth;
> The time of singing is come,
> And the voice of the turtle is heard in our land.
>
> The fig tree putteth forth her green figs,
> And the vines in blossom give forth their fragrance.
> Arise, my love, my fair one, and come away.

In 1934, among the most noteworthy people in Palestine
found by H. V. Morton to be following in the steps of the
Master were picturesque Arabs, the peerless Arab Legion, and
wonderful British policemen. "The British passion for justice," he wrote without a blush, "is stamped on the ancient face
of Bethlehem in the form of a new building—the Bethlehem
Police Station." The Arabs were indeed picturesque; but
they had an infant mortality rate which would be a disgrace
to any white controlling power anywhere in the world. The
reader is not told about this. He is asked to admire "the wonderful prestige of the Arab Legion." He is told what a Belgian
is reported to have said to an Englishman, "Things like the
Arab Legion justify your colonization." Arabs are picturesque, even when they have committed murder. Morton

visited a prison in Transjordan where he saw ninety convicted murderers "happily and busily engaged in a laundry." He does not seem to have met any Jewish murderers; in Palestine, if a Jew committed murder, he was not sentenced to do laundry work, but was hanged. According to Palestine criminal law, the penalty for harboring a murderer was five years; but any Jew found guilty of harboring his wife or mother or daughter who had escaped from the Nazis and had taken refuge in Palestine was liable to be sent to prison for eight years.[46]

English anti-Semitism has nearly always been an underground movement, protected by the pretense that it does not exist. This pretense is facilitated by a proficiency in the art of innuendo which has been perfected by the severity of the English libel law. Journalists have become as expert in avoiding the charge of anti-Semitism as they are in dodging the law of libel. This law is supposed to have purified journalism. It has also created a technique of abuse which is not actionable, favors the attacker, evades controversy and often leaves the victim without defense. A libel may often be covered, by a clever writer, with a transparent veil of humbug which intensifies its venomous effect on the reader. Many visitors to Jerusalem during the decade before the Second World War must have heard someone say from time to time, at English social meetings, in the officers' mess or at the cocktail bar of the King David Hotel, that "the Jews crucified Christ, and would crucify him again if they got the chance." This saying was widely accepted as a profound and terrible truth; it caught on and became fashionable, but not, of course, in public or in print. In print it was repeated by H. V. Morton, with an artistic disguise; many of his readers, in Palestine and in England, could not help seeing what he meant and were probably delighted with his tactful way of putting it:

This high city [Jerusalem] perched above ravines . . . seemed to be the dwelling place of ruthless emotions, such as Pride, Arrogance and Hate. . . . I thought to myself "This is undoubtedly the place that crucified Jesus." Like an echo to my thought came the terrible reply: "And it would probably do it again."

"A Jewish National Home," said Sir Herbert Samuel, "requires a solid foundation of good-will to be secure." No such foundation was possible under a mandate administered by officials who regarded the Jews with a contempt they seldom troubled to conceal, and spoke of friendship with a Jew as "letting down the side" or "not playing the game." "It is most unfortunate," wrote a chief inspector of the Palestine police, "that a British official rarely visits a Jewish family. Should he do so, it is almost invariably as a duty, and then only in the form of patronage." [47] Newcomers who at Government House dinner parties, or in the officers' mess, showed any sign of interest in a Jewish settlement, or said a word in defense of the Jewish point of view, were immediately put in their place and instructed in the rudiments of anti-Zionism. Brigadier F. H. Kisch told the O'Donnell Commission in 1931 that "the Administration could not be expected to function effectively so long as the head of the government and a number of senior officials appeared to be definitely out of sympathy with the conception of the Jewish National Home as interpreted in the mandate." Senior officials did not hesitate to proclaim that their hostility to the law which they were paid to administer amounted to something more than lack of sympathy. One of them hinted that the League of Nations had been bribed by the Jews. He described the mandate as "an iniquitous document," which had been "imposed" upon the League "by International Jewry." [48] The cost of buying the consciences of the states who were members of the League of Nations is unfortunately not mentioned; prices had probably slumped since the good old days when the French Jews were accused of buying the conscience of an archbishop.

Western Judaeophobia played an important part in the es-

tablishment of political partition in Palestine. Copies of the
*Protocols of the Elders of Zion* circulated openly among
British and Arabs; extracts were printed by an Arab daily
paper in Jerusalem. The *Brown Book of the Hitler Terror*
was banned by the British censor. But the Administration
sanctioned in silence the sale of *Mein Kampf* in English and
in Arabic. The Nazis of Berlin had their prototypes in Palestine. Three American senators who visited the country in
1936 stated that "the prolongation of terror in the Holy
Land was due to a manifest sympathy for the vandals and
assassins displayed by many [British] officers." [49] "The vast
majority of the Palestine civil service," writes an eyewitness
of those days, "showed from the beginning a degree of personal sympathy for the Arabs, and personal antipathy for the
Jews, which is very difficult to reconcile with the duties that
had been imposed on them by the mandate." [50]

There is something to be said, and a great deal has been
said, on the other side. Humphrey Bowman, for instance, has
recorded his opinion, after long service as chief education
officer, that "there were few, if any, British residents in
Palestine who did not reckon many Jews among their
friends." [51] A few officials did their best to carry on with
their work in the spirit of the mandate, and their names are
not forgotten. Among the "notable exceptions" in early
days, President Weizmann mentions "Wyndham Deedes and
Gilbert Clayton, and the Commander in Chief [Allenby] himself." [52] He points out, however, that "the man in daily contact with the population . . . men of lower rank in the military hierarchy . . . were, almost without exception, devoid
of understanding, or vision, or even of kindness." Yet the
three most efficient High Commissioners under the mandate
were all soldiers. The strong hand of Plumer, who stood no
nonsense from anyone, ensured peace, and indeed progress,
during his term of office. The premature death of Gort
was a disaster. If he had lived only a few months longer, he

might have been able to repair some of the damage done to the good name of Britain by his cold-blooded predecessor, Sir Harold MacMichael.

To Palestinian officials, and indeed to most Englishmen, a Jewish nation, a Jewish army, Jews on a parade ground, Jews who were not afraid, were notions which always had been and always would be merely fantastic. An English evangelical who in 1828 had enough sense to see that, if the Jews ever returned to Israel, they would have to fight was just as certain then as the men of the Palestinian administration were to be a hundred years later, that the despised race could never face the test of war: "Either the Jews themselves, or themselves in league with others, must be the warriors to subdue. . . . If the former, the change in their habits, their resources, their relative consequence among the nations, must be so great, that credulity itself would be tasked to believe it." [53]

A hundred years later few Englishmen anywhere believed that Jews could ever become warriors to subdue anyone. The general opinion, openly expressed in Palestine, was that most of them were cowards. The Jewish policy of restraint, known as *Havlagah*, which prohibited all reprisals, was taken by both Arabs and British as an additional proof of Jewish timidity. When Arab raiders attacked settlements in the Vale of Esdraelon and the settlers refrained from raiding Arab villages, they were contemptuously referred to by their neighbors as the "Children of Fear." The Arabs had indeed succeeded in creating, in British minds and throughout the whole of the Middle East, the mirage of a Holy War; and they themselves had acquired a belief in their own prowess which had never been put to a real test. English readiness to accept this belief may have been partly due to the myth of Arab battle scenes, created by admirers of Lawrence; yet the prevailing contempt for Jewish poltroonery was more often the natural reaction of the English variety of anti-Semitism—the instinc-

tive inclination to sneer at the Jew which so many Englishmen ten years ago, even those of the intellectual upper class,
were seldom able to suppress. J. N. Schofield, who wrote with
the responsibility of an historian, fell into the traditional error
of fact and judgment. "Judas Maccabeus," said this teacher
of Hebrew history in 1938, "was a fierce fighter of the kind
that has often appeared in Palestine, and is more akin to the
Arab tribesmen from the desert than to the modern Jew." [54]

Most of the innumerable books written by tourists, pilgrims
and retired administrators during the years of the Mandate
express—sometimes emphatically, more often discreetly—contempt for Jewish cowardice and admiration for Arab valor.
An English writer who visited the country in 1933 had the
good fortune to meet a number of "charming and educated
Arabs." He appreciated the dignified confidence of these
desert warriors and their contempt for the money-grabbing
Jews. "A nation does not begin by being rich," explained
one Arab. "It begins with war. . . . The Jews must fight for
their earth. It is not enough that they should buy it. . . .
The Jew naturally prizes safety more than valor." And another son of the desert remarked: "The Jew is a coward—a
physical coward." The Englishman agreed: "The hideous
nightmare in Zionism," he wrote, "comes with the recollection
that they are *buying* their land instead of fighting for it. And
no great nation has ever bought its earth. . . . Zionism has
enlisted too many scholars and too few farmers and soldiers." [55]

Another English tourist, who came during the "disturbances" in 1936 and was, as he said, "trying to be fair," admitted that "most certainly all Jews are not physical cowards."
But he was quite sure that most of them lived in a perpetual
state of terror and were incapable of defending themselves
against the fierce Arabs. "I cannot help remembering one
evening in Jerusalem," he wrote. "I was walking abroad with
two Arab acquaintances, both speaking a little English. And
somewhere we picked up two Cameron Highlanders." The

two soldiers were both drunk. One of them entered a Jewish café to look for more drink. The English tourist asked his Arab friends to go in after the drunkard and bring him out:

> There may have been forty or fifty stalwart young Jews in that café, but as the two Arabs stalked grimly into the place those Jews shrank back in what seemed to me a frightened silence. It is a poor and an insulting simile, but it is the one which struck me at the moment. You turn a stoat into a cage of rabbits and watch what happens! Rightly or wrongly that point made the stock English joke through the Palestine of those days. . . .[56]

A few days later, the same writer reports, an English corporal, who was not drunk, summed up the whole situation in words which expressed what most Englishmen in Palestine firmly believed: "The Arabs had no sense and the Jews had no pluck."

The Palestinian administration, which had looked on Arab terrorists with passive disapproval as long as they confined their activities to murdering Jews, was compelled to take action when it became clear, in 1937 and in 1938, that the rioting had developed into an organized rebellion directed, not merely against the idea of a Jewish National Home, but against British power in the whole Middle East. The strength of the British army in Palestine, which at that time amounted to about two divisions, proved insufficient to intimidate the rebels or to protect the vulnerable pipe line.

In the spring of 1938, an officer attached to the army intelligence section, Captain Orde Wingate, succeeded in convincing one of his seniors that the situation called for a change of plan, and he was reluctantly permitted to put his own ideas to a practical test. The immediate success of his tactics created considerable alarm, not only among the Arabs, but among officials of the Palestinian administration. Unlike a famous predecessor in the Middle East, Wingate was not provided with an ample supply of golden sovereigns. "I was given," he wrote, "three officers and thirty-six men." He operated against thousands of Arab rebels with a force, which he had trained himself, of Palestinian Jews, "more or less selected at random," never more than two to three hundred strong. Yet in less than five months, during the summer of 1938, the Arabs of northern Palestine were driven from their strongholds and the safety of the pipe line was assured. The success of the operation, Wingate reported, "was due to the special quality of the Jewish troops." He taught his Jewish comrades his own theory of war, and they have since proved, in wider fields, how well they had profited from his instruction. Many of them are now leaders in the army of Israel.

A completely peaceful Palestine, or a Palestine where peace was enforced with the help of Jews, did not apparently suit the policy of the administration. Wingate's organization was broken up. He received from Colonel (later Field Marshal) Montgomery the order to disband his special night squads. His own commentary on this order is illuminating:

> The authorities viewed at this time the employment of Jews in active measures for stopping the rebellion with deep repugnance, and the experiment was gradually brought to an end. I am sorry to have to confess that the Jews who fought with such devotion and gallantry were later (and in some respects at all times) treated in an exceedingly shabby manner by the authorities.[57]

In a letter to *The Times* of London, dated July 21, 1938, Josiah Wedgwood summed up in three sentences the truth about the riots: "For two years murder and destruction of Jewish property have gone unpunished under British rule. The administration continues to be strictly impartial between the murderers and the murdered. I have not known of such a black page of incompetence and hypocrisy in British history."

Most of the rioters, many of whom were in the pay of the Axis powers, were given free pardons; a few, however, had to be shot. Their ringleader, the Mufti of Jerusalem, had, as usual, no difficulty in keeping out of British hands. The whole affair ended, for the time being, as most people expected: the Arab nationalists were given all, and more than all, they had asked or hoped for. In 1939 the British government issued a document known as the MacDonald White Paper, in which all pretense of carrying out the duties imposed by the mandate— the only legal justification for the presence of the British in the country—was frankly abandoned. The mandatory power had undertaken to "facilitate Jewish emigration under suitable conditions" and to "encourage close settlement of Jews on the land." These promises were broken by two enactments which were declared by the mandatory commission to be illegal. The first put an end to all Jewish immigration after a period of five years, except with Arab consent. The second prohibited the purchase of land by Jews in practically the whole country.

Whether the terms of the mandate were equitable or not was never the question at issue. The British government was committed to the mandate, governed Palestine in virtue of the mandate, and had no rights at all in that country except under the mandate. An administration which did not rule in accordance with the terms of this mandate was exercising arbitrary power—no doubt with the best intentions, and following the example of Hitler and Mussolini. The British government, committed to the establishment of a National Home for the Jewish people, subject to the proviso that "nothing should be done which might prejudice the civil and religious rights of existing non-Jewish communities in Palestine," declared in fact, when they issued the MacDonald White Paper, that this proviso had made the establishment of a Jewish National Home impossible. They proceeded therefore to cancel a public contract and to set up in its place a new contract, private and unilateral, which the authority behind the mandatory power, the League of Nations, refused to sanction. The politicians responsible for this blunder were saved, for the

time being, from the consequences of their unconstitutional
decision by the outbreak of the Second World War, which
provided them with a reasonable excuse for not following the
honorable course and immediately announcing their intention
to hand back to the League of Nations a mandate which
they had already in practice repudiated.[58]

Thus the destiny of Israel, for the moment, was decided,
not by legal arguments about the meaning and validity of a
declaration or a promise or an obligation, but by force, or
rather by a threat of force—a threat which the mandatory
power seemed to welcome. One question, however, still remained unanswered. What was to be done with the Jews?
During the following decade various answers were given. But
at that time no one, with the exception of the Jews themselves,
worried very much about the question, or about the answer
which came from Germany.

*If you wait for other people to come and set everything right for you, said the black girl, you will wait for ever.*

BERNARD SHAW

# 11

..............

# Epilogue

THE WORLD WAS NOW READY for the massacre. In every country, soldiers were standing on the frontier, eager to repel any helpless, homeless man or woman who had been able to escape from the terror. Every door was closed, every loophole watched, every emergency regulation in the interests of "security" strictly enforced to make sure that the Jews should remain huddled inside the land where millions of them lived, still lived, in the shadow of death. From 1939 to 1943, the British and American governments in close co-operation discussed what steps, if any, could be taken to save them. When the truth was published to the world that the Germans were planning to exterminate them all, men, women and children, with women and children and old men first on the program, "the American government and people, especially the Jewish people," writes Cordell Hull, Secretary of the American State Department, "gave the most serious attention to the problem of thwarting Hitler's designs. . . . We sought places of rescue for them ranging from Madagascar, Cyrenaica, Palestine and French North Africa, to the Dominican Republic and Ecuador." The search was unsuccessful; and even if a place of refuge had been found, the problem of getting them out of Germany had still to be solved.

In the spring of 1943, a decision was made to hold a formal meeting, known as the Bermuda Refugee Conference. The results achieved by this meeting were not impressive. The delegates announced at the outset that they were concerned not with the fate of Jews, but with the sufferings of "refugees." It would be unfair, they said, to put nationals who professed the Jewish faith on a priority list for relief. The Conference was asked by representatives of the World Jewish Congress to enter into negotiations with the Axis to obtain the release of the Jews in Europe, and to promote the dispatch of food parcels to ghettoes and concentration camps where they were being systematically starved to death. The delegates refused to discuss these proposals. The United States declined to relax American immigration laws. Great Britain would not permit Jewish children to enter Palestine. The only result of the Bermuda Refugee Conference was to strengthen Hitler's conviction that the world did not really care very much what happened to the Jews, and to fortify his resolution to exterminate them.

The British Foreign Office and the American State Department knew how the Jews could be saved. They knew that the Germans could be bribed, that they were willing to sell Jewish lives for allied money. But the Allies would not pay the price, the comparatively trifling sum the Germans were ready to accept—two to ten dollars for a life. The children, hundreds of thousands of children, could have been redeemed at any time, at the cost of a few million dollars and a little departmental good will. But the American State Department had no money; the American State Department had no personnel to carry out such negotiations. And so the children, packed like sheep into railway trucks, were sent away, alone, to their death. Hull writes:

> The Germans permitted Jews to leave only when they were amply paid to do so. We were reluctant to deposit sums of money to the credit of the Nazis, even though the deposits were to be made in Switzerland, were to be liquidated only after the end of the war, and apparently could

not be used by the Nazi leaders. Moreover the State Department did not have the large amounts of money and the personnel needed to carry out a plan of reaching and bribing the German officials in charge of the extermination program.[1]

The British Foreign Office shared the reluctance of the American State Department. Even when the objections by the British Ministry of Economic Warfare to the dispatch of funds—with precautions ensuring that the money would not help the enemy, had been overcome—months of delay elapsed before a final license could be issued. The license was held up, writes Henry Morgenthau, in spite of the cables from Berne which had disclosed the specimen fact that "four thousand children between the ages of two and fourteen had been taken from their parents in France and deported in sealed trains, locked in windowless box cars, sixty to a car, without adult escort, without food, water or hygienic provisions . . . but worse was to come." Nothing worse, no news more hideous, could come from Germany; what horrified Morgenthau was the news from London:

> On December 17, 1943, the State Department received a cable from London quoting a Ministry of Economic Warfare letter to the Embassy. The Foreign Office, this letter said, is concerned with the difficulty of disposing of any considerable number of Jews should they be released from enemy territory. For this reason they are reluctant even to approve of the preliminary financial arrangements; though these were now acceptable to the Ministry of Economic Warfare.[2]

Such indifference to the fate of Jewry among officials in key positions, both in Britain and in America, obstructed and fatally delayed every attempt at rescue. Marie Syrkin records that on one occasion, "a British official, when discussing the Brandt proposal [for a large-scale rescue], so far forgot himself as to exclaim: "But what shall we do with them?"[3] "Where should we be," Mr. Randall of the Foreign Office asked Mr. Shertok, "if the Germans should offer to dump a million Jews on us?" [4]

These, therefore, were the three objections raised against every plan to save millions—or to save a few hundred thousand children out of the millions who had been condemned to death: (1) We have no money (the war was costing more than $40,000,000 a day). (2) We have no personnel. (3) We have no place to put them when they are saved from the slaughterhouse. The only way we can save them, people said, is to win the war. But when the war was won, six million Jews were dead.

While the "life-and-death struggle" in which the Germans were engaged made it necessary to murder more than a million children, the Allies explained that any attempt to rescue some of them might "weaken the war effort." The House of Commons stood in silence for two minutes; letters were written to *The Times;* public meetings were held in England and in America; but nothing, or almost nothing was done. For nearly eighteen months after the Nazi plan of extermination had been published to the world, in August, 1942, "the American State Department did practically nothing. Officials dodged their grim responsibility, procrastinated when concrete rescue schemes were placed before them, and even suppressed information about atrocities in order to prevent an outraged public opinion from forcing their hands." [5]

It is not surprising that the apparent reluctance of the Allies to take any action to help the Jews until they had nearly all been murdered encouraged the Germans to believe that their own method of dealing with the Jewish problem met with the secret approval of humanity. These fragments of a people, despised and hated everywhere for a thousand years, were not wanted by anyone. No country would take them in. They were non-adaptable. They did not fit into the world of the Allied powers. There was no place for them in the new world that Hitler was making and intended to control. Might not

Hitler's plan, scientific and comparatively painless, prove to be, in the long run, the most logical, the most merciful solution? What else could be done with them?

A young soldier from the north-east of Scotland, one of the first rescuers to arrive at Bergen Belsen in 1945, was walking to a nearby German village the day after the camp had been liberated. He saw by the roadside the dead bodies of three civilians; all three had been shot in the back of the neck. He asked a German woman at the village inn who these three people were. She replied: "They are men who fell out from the convoy which passed here a few days ago; they were unable to keep up." "Why were they shot?" enquired the soldier. "What else could be done with them?" asked the woman; "they were Jews."

What else could be done with them? What else could be done, people asked, with the remnant which remained in Europe after the Germans had been defeated? While that question was being debated, for months, for years, the survivors were left behind the barbed wire. They were given medical attention and food; but they were told by the English foreign minister not to push to the head of the queue. They were not submissive; some of them were "insolent" and "ungrateful." They objected to the barbed wire and to German guards. Here and there, in England, people were heard to say that it was a pity Hitler had not finished off the job. The Jews were told that it was their duty to stay and help in the building up of Germany, to assist in the economic revival of Poland. For them Palestine remained the forbidden land. Thousands of them escaped from their prisons, struggled across Europe and crowded into unseaworthy hulks. But the sea was watched by the Royal Navy.

The hostility of both Jews and Arabs to the presence of a costly and idle army, and the growth of Jewish terrorism, made the British position in Palestine untenable. The British government, in 1946, having agreed to abide by the findings of an Anglo-American commission, wriggled out of their promise when the commission unexpectedly recommended the admission of one hundred thousand Jewish refugees.

In November, 1947, the General Assembly of the United Nations, meeting at Lake Success, decided by an ample majority—the Anglo-Arab group dissenting—to sanction in part of Palestine the establishment of a Jewish State. The British had previously renounced their mandate; they now disarmed the Jews, armed the Arabs, inside and outside the country, and ordered the Royal Navy to watch the coast. They then withdrew all their troops and waited to see what might happen.

The record of British action and inaction during the period immediately preceding the establishment of the State of Israel has been concisely summarized by Hans J. Morgenthau, professor of political science in the University of Chicago:

> The words and actions of the Arab countries left no doubt that the Arabs inside and outside Palestine would oppose partition by force of arms. Great Britain declared in advance of the vote and repeatedly since that she would not assist in the execution of any plan which was not acceptable to Arabs and Jews alike. In view of the Arab opposition, this was tantamount to saying that Great Britain would not cooperate at all in carrying out the recommendations of the General Assembly.
>
> Great Britain has, however, gone beyond mere non-cooperation. It has done what it was able, short of taking up arms, to make the execution of the recommendations of the General Assembly impossible. To that end Great Britain continued to send arms to the Arab states adjacent to Palestine, while at the same time preventing arms from reaching · Palestine. Furthermore, it refused to recognize the right of the Palestinian Jews to arm themselves and to establish a military organization during the transition period from British rule to actual partition. Finally, Great Britain did not allow the General Assembly to make on-the-spot preparations for an orderly and peaceful transition and to establish provisional agencies of government before the actual end of British rule. All these measures were bound to favor the Arabs and to

work to the disadvantage of the Jews. If it had been the avowed purpose of the British Government, to make the change from British to the new rule chaotic and violent instead of peaceful and orderly and to assure victory of the Arabs in the ensuing civil war, it is hard to see what more Great Britain could have done.[6]

To most spectators outside the ring it seemed inevitable that the soldiers of the six Arab States, armed with modern weapons of war, some of them trained and led by British officers and German Nazis, would immediately drive the trembling Jews into the sea. The invaders attacked with tanks and artillery. They were held on all fronts—held at Daganiah by a hundred settlers, armed with a few rifles and home-made hand grenades. A shipload of modern weapons, which slipped through the British blockade, arrived by night at Tel Aviv in the nick of time. That night the arms were unloaded and next morning sent to the front.

It was a near thing. Had the line of almost unarmed men not held at Daganiah, at Gesher, at Mishmar Ha-Emek, at Negba and in a dozen other places, the story of two thousand years might have ended in a final massacre.

The Return of Israel is accomplished. A hope which never weakened during the weary centuries of exile has been fulfilled. The light, awaited with confidence by so many generations, has come with a dramatic suddenness, after the darkest night:

> Happy is he that waiteth, that cometh nigh and seeth the
>     rising
> Of thy light, when on him thy dawn shall break—
> That he may see the welfare of thy chosen, and rejoice
> In thy rejoicing, when thou turnest back unto thine olden
>     youth.

No people has ever had to pay so fearful a price for freedom—the uncounted, unrecorded dead: an exceeding great

army. Only a remnant has escaped from the contempt and
hatred, from the toleration and patronage of the Western
world. But the question asked by the German woman at
Belsen will never be asked again. No more conferences will
be held to decide what is to be done with the Jewish people.
The Gates of Israel are open to all who wish to enter; the
Shield of David will protect them, and their children.


Thus saith the Lord God: Come from the four winds,
    O Breath,
And breathe upon these slain that they may live.
So I prophesied as he commanded me,
And the breath came into them, and they lived,
And stood upon their feet, an exceeding great army.
Then he said unto me, Son of man,
These bones are the whole house of Israel:
Behold they say, Our bones are dried, and our hope is lost.

Therefore prophesy and say unto them:
Thus saith the Lord God,
Behold, O my people, I will open your graves,
And bring you unto the land of Israel.
I have opened your graves, O my people,
And brought you up out of your graves,
And I shall put my spirit in you, and ye shall live,
And I shall place you in your own land.

# Appendix

## A

### "THE JEWS" IN ST. JOHN'S GOSPEL

St. Augustine, commenting on the text "Salvation is of the Jews," explains that these words must not be taken in the literal sense: "In the person of the Jews, indeed, this is said, but not of all Jews, not of the reprobate ones; but of such as were the Apostles, of such as were the Prophets." [1]

It is a pity that this explanation was not used, *mutatis mutandis*, by St. Augustine to clarify the meaning of many other texts in the Fourth Gospel where references to "the Jews" are uncomplimentary and misleading. Modern commentators have sometimes recognized the anti-Semitic tendency of these texts. The alleged "polemical aims" of St. John were discussed by E. F. Scott.[2] Père Thomas Calmes wrote:

> The Fourth Gospel is the most anti-Jewish book of the New Testament. . . . The Jews are represented in it, from beginning to end, as enemies of Jesus. . . . In the mind of the author of the Fourth Gospel, the Jews are not only foreigners but enemies. From reading certain passages one might be inclined to believe that not a single Jew had accepted the teaching of Jesus. This, however, was not the meaning of the Evangelist.[3]

# B

## THE RITUAL-MURDER CHARGE IN MODERN TIMES

*A man has no right . . . to make himself the medium of propagating scandalous and defamatory accusations, unless he himself believes them to be true, and his belief is not an honest belief if it is formed in a reckless and inconsiderate manner.*

C. G. ADDISON, *The Law of Torts*
(4th ed., London, 1873), p. 787.

The blood accusation was first introduced to the Near East from Europe in 1840, when a charge of ritual murder was brought against the Jewish community of Damascus by the Capuchins in that city. Half a dozen Jewish citizens were accused of kidnaping and murdering a Capuchin friar, Father Thomas Calangiano. The affair was taken up with enthusiasm —if it was not actually framed—by the French consul in Damascus. Many Jewish residents were thrown into prison and tortured. Two of them died under the bastinado.

In the same year a similar charge was brought against the Jews of Rhodes; they were accused of murdering a Greek boy in order to use his blood for the Passover. "Amongst the bitterest accusers of the persecuted Hebrews were the British consul, Mr. Wilkinson, and his son." [4] The French government, represented by Thiers, refused to take any action; but Lord Palmerston called for a public inquiry. The acquittal and liberation of the Jews at Rhodes and Damascus were due to the protests of the British government and the energetic efforts of Sir Moses Montefiore.

At the present day this blood legend has not, as many people think, ceased to obtain credit; its center of activity has merely shifted to the East. "In Central and Eastern Europe," writes Dr. James Parkes, "among both Roman Catholics and Eastern Orthodox Christians . . . there are almost more examples of the accusation in the years between 1880 and 1945 than in the whole of the Middle Ages." [5] It is now not generally known that the credulity of these Catholics in Central and Eastern Europe was encouraged by the apparently authoritative propaganda of an ecclesiastical anti-Semitic faction in Rome.

Although Pope Innocent IV in the thirteenth century had decreed that no one was to accuse the Jews of using human blood in their religious rites, this prohibition did not prevent the publication of the old calumnies by the semi-official journal of the Vatican, *La Civiltà Cattolica*, in a series of unsigned articles written by Giuseppe Oreglia de San Stefano, S.J.; they appeared between February, 1881, and December, 1882. The following extracts will show that these articles merit a more prominent place than they have hitherto occupied in the literature of modern anti-Semitism:

> The practice of killing children for the Paschal Feast is now very rare in the more cultivated parts of Europe, more frequent in Eastern Europe, and common, all too common, in the East properly so called. [In the West, the Jews] have now other things to think of than to make their unleavened bread with Christian blood, occupied as they are in ruling almost like kings in finance and journalism. [Aug. 20, 1881, p. 478.]

> It remains therefore generally proved . . . that the sanguinary Paschal rite . . . is a general law binding on the consciences of all Hebrews to make use of the blood of a Christian child, primarily for the sanctification of their souls, and also, although secondarily, to bring shame and disgrace to Christ and to Christianity. [Dec. 3, 1881, p. 606.]

> Every year the Hebrews crucify a child. . . . In order that the blood be effective, the child must die in torments. [Jan. 21, 1882, p. 214.]

> Opinions of the Hebrew casuists in the Middle Ages differed, as they do now, not about the substance but about the accidents of the sanguinary Paschal rites. . . . Some hold that the blood of a child is essential, others, as we shall see, think that the blood of an adult is sufficient. [Jan. 21, 1882, p. 226.]

In the century which invented printing, discovered
America, revived literature and science, half of Europe was
full of . . . Masters in Israel who bought and sold and made
use of Christian blood for their piety and devotion. But now
the light has been thrown on these deeds which we know even
more about than our ancestors did. [Feb. 4, 1882, p. 362.]

In Hebrew Jubilee years, the fresh blood of a child is
essential; in ordinary years dried blood will do. [Feb. 18,
1882, p. 472.]

Every practising Hebrew worthy of that name is obliged
even now, in conscience, to use in food, in drink, in circum-
cision, and in various other rites of his religious and civil life
the fresh or dried blood of a Christian child, under pain of
infringing his laws and passing among his acquaintances for
a bad Hebrew. How all this is still true and faithfully observed in the present century, we shall see, God willing, with
all the evidence, in the next installment of our correspondence. [March 4, 1882, p. 613.]

Although these articles were read by prominent ecclesiastics not only in Rome, but also in the whole Catholic world,
and although they could surely not have remained unknown
to Leo XIII, no protest made itself heard, no public objection
was raised. There is, however, in Purcell's *Life of Cardinal
Manning* a carefully constructed sentence which reveals that
at least one distinguished prelate had made a protest behind
the scenes. Manning paid his last visit to Rome in 1883. "He
never failed," wrote Purcell, "to manifest a partiality for the
Jewish race, and in Rome itself he vindicated the Jews from
the fantastic charges of cruelty imputed to them in the
practice of their religious rites." [6]

It is a pity that the cardinal did not give to his vindication
of the Jews the publicity and the semi-official sanction which
these "fantastic charges" against them had obtained from the
intellectual headquarters of Catholic Christendom.

The construction of the articles in *La Civiltà Cattolica* suggests that the scavenging for material was not done by the

author himself. Most if not all the matter may have been taken from German sources supplied by Abbé Sebastien Brunner (1814–1893), who was in Rome during the year before the articles were printed. Abbé Brunner, editor of the *Kirchenzeitung*, and author of a number of articles on "ritual murder" in that paper, was a frequent visitor to Rome and was highly esteemed by many notable Roman ecclesiastics. He had the reputation of being an accomplished historian and was the acknowledged leader of anti-Semitism in Austria-Hungary. His activities were sympathetically reported by Abbé A. Kannengiesler in a series of articles in *Le Correspondant* (1895, Vol. CXLV, pp. 62ff.) entitled: "Le père de l'antisemitisme autrichien, l'Abbé Brunner."

# C

## Letter to Edouard Drumont

Monsieur!

C'était une surprise, ce livre "la France juive"! Nous "Antisemiten" en Autriche soutenant le combat inégal contre les juifs omnipotents nous n'avons guère pu espéré à ce secours provenant d'un pays qu'on croyait presqu'à l'abri de l'influence sinistre de ces gens. La France avec ses 50–60,000 juifs nous paraissait un Eldorado en comparaison avec notre patrie qui est exploitée par 1 ¾ millions individus de cette race. Il paraît maintenant que c'était une grande erreur de notre part, quoique nous ne savons pas autre chose du contenu de votre livre, que ce qu'indique le titre. Les grands journaux de Vienne, tous à l'exception d'un seul appartenants aux juifs, se sont bien gardés, d'éclairer le public là-dessus. C'est donc pour remplir notre devoir envers les lecteurs de notre journal hebdomadaire que nous souhaitons vivement, que vous ayez la complaisance de nous permettre de publier dans notre journal des extraits de votre livre et de nous accorder pour ce but une copie.

En échange, si tel vous plaîrait, nous serions enchantés de pouvoir vous remettre une année entière de notre journal lequel est d'ᵉdié exclusivement à la guerre contre ces ennemis acharnés de tout peuple non-"sémitique."

Espérant une réponse favorable nous vous prions, Monsieur, de vouloir agréer l'assurance de notre considération distinguée.

Dr. L. Psenner
Rᵉdacteur des
OESTERR. VOLKSFREUND
Wien, VIII.,
Piaristengasse 48.

Vienne, Mai 31, 1886.

## D

JEWISH CHILDREN AND THE NAZIS

A child is of greater value and nearer to God than all the fiery vapors of all the suns.

ALFRED NOYES

What happened to the Jewish children who could not get certificates? Here are some of the answers to this question which were given at the trial of the war criminals at Nuremberg:

> They killed them with their parents, in groups, and alone. They killed them in children's homes and hospitals, burying them alive in graves, throwing them into flames, stabbing them with bayonets, poisoning them, conducting experiments upon them, extracting their blood for the use of the German army, throwing them into prison and Gestapo torture chambers and concentration camps where the children died from hunger, torture, and epidemic diseases. [*Trial of the Major War Criminals*, I, 50.]

> Very frequently women would hide their children under their clothes, but of course when we found them we would send the children in to be exterminated. [I, 251.]

Mothers in the throes of childbirth shared cars with those infected with tuberculosis or venereal disease. Babies when born were hurled out of these cars' windows. [III, 439.]

At that time, when the greatest number of Jews were exterminated in the gas chambers, an order was issued that the children were to be thrown into the crematory ovens, or into the crematory ditches, without previous asphyxiation with gas. . . . The children were thrown in alive. Their cries could be heard all over the camp. [VIII, 318, 319.]

# Bibliography

Abbot, G. F. *Israel in Europe*. London, 1907.

Abrahams, Israel. *Jewish Life in the Middle Ages*. London, 1896. New ed., 1932.

Achad Ha-Am (Asher Ginzberg). "Pinsker and Political Zionism." 1902. In *Essays and Letters and Memoirs*. Tr. from the Hebrew and ed. by Leon Simon. 1947.

Ademarus of Chabannes. *Chronicle*. In J. P. Migne, *Patrologia latina*, Vol. CXLI.

*Analecta Bollandiana*. Vol. LXVIII. "Mélanges Paul Peeters." Brussels, 1950.

Anchel, Robert. *Les Juifs en France*. Paris, 1946.

Antonius, George. *The Arab Awakening*. London, 1938.

Arnoulin, S. *Edouard Drumont et les Jésuites*. Paris, 1902.

Ashbee, C. R. *A Palestine Notebook, 1918–1923*. London, 1923.

Asquith, H. H. *Memories and Reflections*. London, 1928.

———. *Letters to a Friend*. 2nd series (1922–27). 1934.

Asquith, Margot. *Autobiography*. London, 1923.


Balfour, Arthur James. *Essays, Speculative and Political*. London, 1920.

Balmez, Jaime. *Protestantism and Catholicity in Their Effects on the Civilization of Europe*. London, 1849.

Barbey d'Aurevilly, Jules. *Les Oeuvres et les hommes*. Paris, 1887.

Barbier, Emmanuel. *Le Progrès du libéralisme catholique en France sous le Pape Léon XIII*. Paris, 1907.

Barrès, Maurice. *Scènes et doctrines du nationalisme*. Paris, 1902.

Basnage, Jacques. *History of the Jews*. Tr. by Thomas Taylor. London, 1708.

———. *Antiquitez judaïques, ou remarques critiques sur la republique des Hébreux*. Amsterdam, 1713.

Batault, Georges. *Le Problème juif*. Paris, 1921.

Baudrillart, Alfred. *Vie de Mgr. d'Hulst*. Paris, 1914.

Bayle, Pierre. *Dictionnaire historique et critique*. Amsterdam, 1730.

Bell, Harold Idris. *Jews and Christians in Egypt*. London, 1924.

Belloc, Hilaire. *The Jews*. 2nd ed. London, 1928.

———. *The Contrast*. London, 1923.

Berdyaev, Nicholas. *Le Christianisme et l'antisémitisme*. Tr. from the Russian by Princess Theodore. Pub. by the Académie Religieuse et Philosophique Russe de Paris. No date.

Berger, E. *Les Registres d'Innocent IV*. Paris, 1884.

Berzin, A. Z. *Izcor Am Israel Et Kedoshei Av Tharpat*. Jerusalem, 1930.

Bernanos, G. *La Grande peur des bien-pensants: Edouard Drumont.* 23rd ed. Paris, 1931.

———. *Les Grands cimetières sous la lune.* Paris, 1938.

Bernard of Clairvaux. *Works.* In *Monumenta Germaniae Historica, Scriptores,* Vol. XXVI.

———. *The Life and Works of St. Bernard.* Ed. by J. Mabillon. Tr. by S. J. Eales. London, 1889–1896.

Bernstein, Victor H. *Final Judgment: The Story of Nuremberg.* London, 1947.

Besse, R. P. *Les Religions laïques.* Paris, 1913.

Beugnot, A. *Les Juifs de l'Occident.* Paris, 1924.

Bickersteth, Edward. *The Restoration of Jews to Their Own Land.* 2nd ed. London, 1841.

Bloch, J. S. *My Reminiscences.* 1923.

Bloy, Léon. *Le Salut par les Juifs.* Paris, 1905.

———. *Le Vieux de la montagne.* Paris, 1910. 6th ed., 1919.

Blumenkranz, Bernhard. "Die judischen Beweisgründe im Religions-gespräch mit den Christen in den christlich-lateinischen Sonderschriften des 5. bis 11. Jahrhunderts." In *Theologische Zeitschrift,* March–April, 1948.

Blyth, Estelle. *When We Lived in Jerusalem.* London, 1927.

Boncour, J. Paul. *Entre deux guerres.* Paris, 1945.

Bondy, Louis W. *Racketeers of Hate.* New York, 1946.

Bonsirven, Joseph. *Juifs et Chrétiens.* Paris, 1936.

———. "The Jews in the European System." In Vol. VI of *European Civilization, Its Origin and Development,* by various contributors, under the direction of Edward Eyre. London, 1937.

Bosch, Firmin van den. *Vingt années d'Egypte.* 2nd ed. Paris, 1932.

Bossuet, J. Bénigne. *Discours sur l'histoire universelle.* Paris, 1724.

———. "Good Friday Sermon." In Vol. II of *Oeuvres.* 1841.

Bolitho, Hector. *Beside Galilee.* London, 1933.

Bourquelot, F. "Etudes sur les règles du commerce aux xii–xiv siècles." In *Académie des Inscriptions et Belles Lettres.* 2nd series. Paris, 1865. Vol. V.

Bowman, Humphrey. *Middle East Window.* London, 1942.

Brandt, Sebastian. *The Ship of Fools.* Tr. by A. Barclay. Edinburgh, 1874.

Broadbent, Joseph. *From Vine Street to Jerusalem.* London, 1936.

Burns, C. D. *The First Europe.* London, 1947.

Buzy, Denis. *Les Paraboles.* Paris, 1932. 16th ed., 1948.


Calmes, Thomas. *L'Evangile selon Saint Jean.* Paris, 1904.

Capéran, Louis. "La Légende de l'intervention du Gesù dans l'affaire Dreyfus." In *Mélanges offerts au R. P. Cavallera.* Toulouse, 1948.

Chagny, Louis-Martin. *L'Anglais est-il Juif?* Paris, 1895.

Chaine, Léon. *Les Catholiques français.*

Chapman, C. E. *A History of Spain.* New York, 1931.

Chateaubriand, F. René de. *Itinéraire de Paris à Jérusalem.* Paris, 1839.

Chesterton, G. K. *The New Jerusalem.* London, 1920.

Clemenceau, George. *Injustice militaire.* Paris, 1902.

Clerke, R. F. "The Continuity of Catholicism." In *The Nineteenth Century,* Feb., 1900.

Cobbett, William. *Rural Rides*. London, 1853.
Constant (Popot). *Les Juifs devant l'Eglise et l'histoire*. Paris, 1897.
Coubé, Stephen. *Ames juives*. Paris, 1907.
Crispinus, Gilbertus. *Disputatio Judaei cum Christiano de fide Christiana*. In J. P. Migne, *Patrologia latina*, Vol. CLIX. Paris, 1854.
Curtis, W. Eleroy. *Today in Syria and Palestine*. New York, 1903.

D'Alès, A. *Dictionnaire apologétique de la foi catholique*. 4th ed. Paris, 1925.
Daniel-Rops. *Histoire sainte: le peuple de la Bible*. Paris, 1947.
Dark, Sidney. *The Jew Today*. London, 1933.
Daudet, Léon. *La France en alarme*. Paris, 1904.
Davitt, Michael. *Within the Pale*. London, 1903.
Debidour, A. *L'Eglise catholique et l'État sous la Troisième République*. Paris, 1909.
Delitzsch, Franz. *Jewish Artisan Life in the Time of Christ*. London, 1902.
De Smedt, Charles. *Principes de la critique historique*. Brussels, 1883.
Desportes, Henri. *Le Mystère du sang chez les Juifs de tous les temps*. Paris, 1889.
Drault, Jean. *Edouard Drumont, "La France juive," et "La Libre Parole."* Paris, 1935.
Drumont, Edouard. *La France juive*. Paris, 1886.
———. *La Fin d'un monde*. Paris, 1889.
———. *La Dernière bataille*. Paris, 1890.
———. *Le Testament d'un antisémite*. Paris, 1891.
Dubnow, S. M. *History of the Jews in Russia and Poland*. Tr. by I. Friedlander. Philadelphia, 1916.
Duchesne, Louis. *Early History of the Christian Church*. London, 1912.
Duff, Douglas. *Palestine Picture*. London, 1936.
———. *Sword for Hire*. London, 1934.
Dulaure, J.-A. *Histoire civile, physique, et morale de Paris*. 3rd ed. Paris, 1826.

Eisenmenger, Johann Andreas. *Entdecktes Judenthum*. Königsberg, 1711.
Eliot, George. *Daniel Deronda*.
*Epistolae Obscurorum Virorum*. Ed. by F. G. Stokes. London, 1909.
Ervine, St. John G. *Journey to Jerusalem*. London, 1936.
Esposito, Mario. "Un procès contre les Juifs de la Savoie en 1329." In *Revue d'Histoire Ecclésiastique*, Vol. XXXIV, 1938.
Eusebius. *Historia ecclesiastica*. Tr. by C. F. Cruse. London, 1842.
Evans, Joan. *Life in Mediaeval France*. London, 1925.
Ewing, W. *Paterson of Hebron*. London, n.d.

Ferrata, Dominique. *Mémoires*. Rome, 1920.
Fishberg, M. *The Jews*. New York, 1911.
Fisher, H. A. L. *History of Europe*. London, 1936.
Fleury, Claude. *Histoire ecclésiastique*. Paris, 1732.
Flick, Alexander Clarence. *Decline of the Mediaeval Church in the Fourteenth and the Fifteenth Centuries*. 1930.
Forbes, Rosita. *Conflict*. London, 1931.

France, Anatole. *L'Ile des pingouins*. Paris, 1908.
Frescobaldi, Lionardo di Niccolo. *Viaggio in Egitto e in Terra Santa (1384) con un discorso dell' editore sopra il commercio degl' Italiani nel secolo XIV*. Rome, 1818.
Friedlander, G. *Shakespeare and the Jew*. London, 1921.

Gabirol, Solomon ibn (Avicebron, Avencebrol). *Selected Religious Poems*. Philadelphia, 1923.
Gheradacci. *Historia di Bologna*. In Muratori, *Rerum Italicarum Scriptores*, Vol. XXXIII.
Gibbons, John. *The Road to Nazareth*. London, 1936.
Gibbs, Philip. *Across the Frontier*. London, 1939.
Gilbert, G. M. *Nuremberg Diary*. London, 1948.
Ginsberg, M. *Reason and Unreason in Society*. London, 1947.
Glaber, Rodolphus. *Chronicle*. In J. P. Migne, *Patrologia latina*, Vol. CXLII.
Goldman, Solomon. *Crisis and Decision*. New York, 1938.
Goncourt, Edmond de. *Journal des Goncourt*. Paris, 1894.
Goodman, Paul. *The Synagogue and the Church*. London, 1909.
Gougenot des Mousseaux. *Le Juif, le judaïsme et la judaïsation des peuples chrétiens*. Paris, 1869.
Goyau, Georges. *St. Bernard*. Paris, 1927.
Graetz, H. *History of the Jews*. London, 1891–92.
Graf, Ernest. *In Christ's Own Country*. The Catholic Book Club. London, 1937.
Grayzel, Solomon. *The Church and the Jews in the Thirteenth Century*. Philadelphia, 1933.
Gregory of Nyssa. "Oratio in Christi resurrectionem." In J. P. Migne, *Patrologia graeca*, Vol. XLVI.
Grisar, Hartmann. *Luther*. Tr. by E. M. Lamond. London, 1913–16.
Guéranger, Prosper. *L'Année liturgique*. 14th ed., 1894. Tr. by L. Shepherd as *The Liturgical Year*. Dublin, 1868–1870. Westminster, Maryland, 1949.
Guérin, Jules. *Les Trafiquants de l'antisémitisme: la maison Drumont "and Co."* Paris, 1905.

Ha-Cohen, Joseph. *Emek Ha Bakha*. London, 1881.
Halevi, Jehuda. *Selected Poems*. Tr. by Nina Salaman. Philadelphia, 1946.
Hall, W. P. *Empire to Commonwealth: Thirty Years of Imperial History*. London, 1929.
Hanotaux, Gabriel. *Mon Temps*. Paris, 1933–47.
Hazen, N. H. "Agriculture in Palestine and the Development of Jewish Colonization." In *Foreign Agriculture*, Vol. I, No. 3. U. S. Department of Agriculture. Bureau of Agricultural Economics. Washington, March, 1947.
Heine, Heinrich. *Hebrew Melodies*.
Herder, Johann Gottfried von. (*Ideen zur Geschichte der Menschheit*. 1787.)
Herzl, Theodor. *The Jewish State*. Tr. by J. de Haas. New York, 1904.
*Histoire Littéraire de la France*, by the Benedictines of St. Maur. 1733–1906.
Hosmer, James K. "*The Jews, Ancient, Mediaeval, and Modern*." In *The Story of the Nations*. London, 1885. 5th ed., 1891.
Hull, Cordell. *The Memoirs of Cordell Hull*. 1948.

Infield, Henrik F. *Co-operative Living in Palestine.* International Library of Sociology and Social Reconstruction. 1946.

Inge, W. R. *The Jews.* London, 1923.

Isaac, Jules. *Jésus et Israël.* Paris, 1948.

d'Israeli, Isaac. *The Genius of Judaism.* London, 1833.

Jacobs, Joseph. "Little Saint Hugh of Lincoln." In *Transactions of the Jewish Historical Society of England.* 1893–94.

Janssen, Johannes. *History of the German People at the close of the Middle Ages.* London, 1896–1910.

Jaquemet, G., ed. *Catholicisme hier, aujourd'hui, demain.* Paris, 1947.

Jarrett, Bede. *Social Theories of the Middle Ages.* London, 1926.

Jaurès, Jean. *Histoire socialiste de la Révolution française.* Paris, 1922.

Jefferies, J. M. N. *Palestine the Reality.* London, 1939.

Jessop, A., and James, M. R. *Life of St. William of Norwich.* Cambridge, 1896.

Job, Charles de. *De l'influence du Concile de Trente sur la littérature et les beaux-arts chez les peuples catholiques.* Paris, 1884.

Joseph, Bernard. *British Rule in Palestine.* Washington, 1948.

Josephus, Flavius. *The Works of Flavius Josephus.* Tr. by William Whiston. Edinburgh, 1826.

Julian of Norwich. *Sixteen Revelations of Divine Love* (1373). Ed. by Grace Warrack. London, 1909. 9th ed., 1927.

Juster, Jean. *Les Juifs dans l'empire romain.* Paris, 1914.

Kann, J. N. *Some Observations on the Mandatory Government of Palestine.* 1930.

Kay, J. W. *The Administration of the East India Company: A History of Indian Progress.* 2nd ed. London, 1853.

Kempe, Margery. *The Book of Margery Kempe.* Early English Text Society. 1940.

Kisch, F. H. *Palestine Diary.* London, 1938.

Klausner, J. *Jesus of Nazareth.* Tr. from Hebrew by Herbert Danby. New York, 1925.

———. *From Jesus to Paul.* London, 1942.

Lagrange, M.-J. *L'Evangile selon Saint Jean.* 8th ed. Paris, 1947.

———. *Le Judaïsme avant Jésus-Christ.* Paris, 1931.

Lamb, Charles. *Essays of Elia.*

Lamennais, F. de. *Paroles d'un croyant.* Paris, 1838.

Langlois, Charles. "Le Procès des Templiers." In *Revue des Deux Mondes,* Vol. CIII.

Lea, Charles. *History of the Inquisition of Spain.* New York, 1906–07.

Lecanuet, E. *L'Eglise de France sous la Troisième République.* Paris, 1910.

Leroy-Beaulieu, Anatole. *Israël chez les nations.* Paris, 1893.

Lifschitz-Golden, Manya. *Les Juifs dans la littérature française du moyen âge.* New York, 1935.

Lingard, J. *History of England.* Ed. by Lingard and Belloc. London, 1912.

Livermore, H. V. *History of Portugal.* London, 1947.

Loeb, Isidore. "Le Juif de l'histoire et le Juif de la légende." In *Revue des Etudes Juives,* Vol. XXI. 1890.

———. "Le Juif devant l'opinion romaine." In *Revue des Etudes Juives,* Vol. II. 1885.

Loti, Pierre. "Jérusalem," and "La Galilée." In Vol. VII of *Oeuvres Complètes.* Paris, 1894–1911.

Lowenthal, Marvin. *The Jews of Germany.* Philadelphia, 1935.

Luchaire, A. *Histoire de France jusqu'à la révolution.* Paris, 1901.

Lunt, W. E. *Papal Revenues in the Middle Ages.* London, 1934.

Luther, Martin. "Vom Schem Hamphoras und vom Geschlecht Christi." In Vol. LIII of *Werke.* Weimar, 1920.

Lynch, W. F. *Narrative of the U. S. Expedition to the River Jordan and the Dead Sea.* London, 1849.

Maimonides, Moses. *The Guide for the Perplexed.* Tr. by M. Friedlander. 2nd ed. London, 1947.

Mann, Horace K. *Lives of the Popes in the Middle Ages.* London, 1902–10. 2nd ed., 1925.

Maritain, Jacques. *Anti-Semitism.* London, 1939.

Marlowe, John. *Palestine Rebellion.* London, 1947.

Maxe, Jean. *L'Anthologie des défaitistes.* Paris, 1925.

Meurin, Léon. *La Franc-maçonnerie synagogue de Satan.* Paris, 1893.

Meyer, Arthur. *Ce que mes yeux ont vu.* Paris, 1911.

Michaud, J. F., and Poujoulat, J. J. F. "Le Journal d'un bourgeois de Paris." In *Nouvelle collection des mémoires pour servir à l'histoire de France depuis le 13e siècle jusqu'à la fin du 18e.* Paris, 1850.

Milman, H. H. *History of Latin Christianity.* London, 1854.

———. *The History of the Jews.* 3rd ed. London, 1863.

Minder, Robert. *Allemagnes et Allemands.* Paris, 1948.

Mirabaud, Jean-Baptiste de. *Opinions des Anciens sur les Juifs.* Londres (Paris), 1769.

Modder, Montague Frank. *The Jew in the Literature of England to the End of the Nineteenth Century.* Philadelphia, 1944.

Mollat, G. *Les Papes d'Avignon.* 7th ed. Paris, 1930.

Montefiore, Moses. *Diary of Sir Moses Montefiore and Lady Montefiore.* Ed. by L. Loewe. London, 1890.

Moore, George. *Hail and Farewell.* London, 1925.

Moore, G. F. *Judaism in the First Centuries of the Christian Era.* Cambridge, Mass., 1927.

Morgenthau, Hans J. *Politics Among Nations: The Struggle for Power and Peace.* New York, 1948.

Morgenthau, Henry. "The Morgenthau Diaries." In *Collier's.* Nov., 1947.

Morison, J. C. *Life and Times of St. Bernard.* London, 1863.

Morris, W. B. *The Divinity of Christ.* London, 1898.

Mortier, D. A. *Histoire des Maîtres généraux de l'Ordre des Frères Prêcheurs.* Paris, 1903.

Morton, H. V. *In the Steps of the Master.* London, 1934.

Mosheim, J. L. *Institutes of Ecclesiastical History.* London, 1863.

Nathan, Robert P., Joss, Oscar, and Creamer, Daniel. *Palestine: Problem and Promise.* American Council of Public Affairs. 1946.

Neander, J. August W. (David Mendel). *Life and Times of St. Bernard.* Eng. tr. London, 1843.

Neuman, Abraham. *The Jews in Spain.* Philadelphia, 1944.
Newman, J. H. *Historical Sketches.* London, 1872–73. Vol. II.
Newton, Thomas. *Dissertation on the Prophecies.* London, 1765.
Nichols, Beverley. *No Place Like Home.* London, 1936.

O'Neil, James. *Palestine Re-peopled.* 1877.

Paassen, Pierre van. *The Forgotten Ally.* New York, 1943.
Paris, Matthew. *Chronica majora.* Ed. by Luard. London, 1872–73.
Parkes, James. *The Conflict of the Church and the Synagogue.* London, 1934.
——. *A History of Palestine from 135 A.D. to Modern Times.* London, 1949.
——. *Judaism and Christianity.* London, 1948.
Pascal, Blaise. *Pensées sur la religion, et sur quelques autres sujets.* Paris, 1754.
Pastor, Ludwig von. *History of the Popes.* Eng. ed. London, 1910.
Patkin, A. L. *The Origins of the Russian Jewish Labor Movement.* Melbourne, 1947.
Patterson, J. H. *With the Judaeans in the Palestine Campaign.* London, 1922.
Paul-Boncour, J. *Entre deux guerres.* Paris, 1945.
Peers, E. Allison. *Spain.* London, 1930.
Péguy, Charles. *Notre jeunesse.* Paris, 1910.
Peruzzi, S. L. *Storia del commercio e dei banchieri di Firenze dal 1200 al 1345.* Florence, 1868.
Pike, L. O. *History of Crime in England.* London, 1873.
Pirenne, H. *Economic and Social History of Mediaeval Europe.* London, 1936.
Petit de Julleville, L. *Les Mystères.* Paris, 1880.
Puech, Aimé. *St. Jean Chrysostome.* Paris, 1902.

*Rapports présentés à la première conférence européenne des commissions historiques et des centres de documentation juifs.* Paris, 1947.
Reinach, Joseph. *Histoire de l'affaire Dreyfus.* Paris, 1901–11.
Reinach, Salomon. *Cultes, mythes et religions.* Paris, 1923.
Renan, Ernest. *Histoire générale et système comparé des langues sémitiques.* 5th ed. Paris, 1878.
——. *Vie de Jésus.* 3rd ed. 1863.
Renault, E. *Le Péril protestant.* Paris, 1899.
Rhodes, W. E. "Italian Bankers and Their Loans to Edward I." In *Owen College Essays.* 1902.
Robertson, J. A. *Royal Commission on Historical Monuments.* London, 1924.
Rohrbacher, R. F. *Histoire universelle de l'Eglise catholique.* 1832–47. New ed., 1851.
Rosen, F. *Oriental Memoirs of a German Diplomatist.* London, 1930.
Roth, Cecil. *History of the Jews in Italy.* 1946.
——. *History of the Marranos.* 1932.
——. *Magna Bibliotheca Anglo-Judaica.* London, 1937.
——. *Mediaeval Lincoln Jewry and Its Synagogue.* 1934.
——. *The Ritual Murder Libel and the Jew.* London, n.d.

————. *Short History of the Jewish People*. (An abbreviated American edition has been published under the title *A Bird's-Eye View of Jewish History*.)

Rousseau, J.-J. *Emile, ou de l'éducation*. Paris, 1898.

Rowan-Hamilton, N. *Both Sides of Jordan*. London, 1928.

Royal Institute for International Affairs. Information Paper No. 20: *Great Britain and Palestine*. 3rd ed. 1946.

Ruppin, Arthur. *Jewish Fate and Future*. Tr. by E. W. Dickes. London, 1940.

Russell, Bertrand. *Philosophy and Politics*. London, 1947.

Saige, Gustave. "De la condition des Juifs dans le comté de Toulouse avant le XIV⁰ siècle." In *Bibliothèque de l'Ecole des Chartes*, Vol. XXXIX.

Samuel, Herbert. *The Unknown Land*. London, 1942.

Samuel, Horace. *Unholy Memories of the Holy Land*. London, 1930.

Sampter, Jessie. *Modern Palestine*. 1933.

Sartre, Jean-Paul. *Portrait of the Anti-Semite*. 1948.

Schapira, Israel. *Der Antisemismus in der französischen Literatur: Edouard Drumont und seine Quellen*. 1927.

Schofield, J. N. *The Historical Background of the Bible*. London, 1938.

Scholem, Gerschom G. *Major Trends in Jewish Mysticism*. Jerusalem, 1941.

Schopenhauer, A. *The Art of Controversy*. Tr. by T. Bailey Saunders, 1896.

Scott, E. F. *The Fourth Gospel*. London, 1906.

Seneraga, Bartholomew. "De Rebus Genuensibus, 1488–1514." In Muratori, *Rerum Italicarum Scriptores*. Vol. XXIV.

Shaw, Thomas. *Travels or Observations Relating to Several Parts of Barbary and the Levant*. Edinburgh, 1738.

Slosson, Preston William. *The Great Crusade and After*. Vol. XII in *A History of American Life*, ed. by Arthur M. Schlesinger and Dixon Ryon Fox. 1914–28.

Smith, Goldwin. *The United Kingdom*. London, 1899.

Smith, James. *A Pilgrimage to Palestine*. 1895.

Stafford, R. S. *The Tragedy of the Assyrian Massacre*. London, 1935.

Steed, H. Wickham. *The Hapsburg Monarchy*. London, 1913.

Stephens, W. R. W. *Saint Chrysostom*. London, 1872.

————. *The Life and Letters of Edward A. Freeman*. London, 1895.

Storrs, R. S. *Bernard of Clairvaux*. London, 1892.

Storrs, Ronald. *Orientations*. London, 1937.

Strack, Hermann L. *The Jews and Human Sacrifice*. New York, 1909.

Swaine, Edward. *Objections to the Doctrine of Israel's Future Restoration to Palestine. . . .* London, 1828.

Symonds, John Addington. *Renaissance in Italy*. London, 1886.

Tharaud, Jérôme, and Tharaud, Jean. *L'An prochain à Jérusalem*. Paris, 1924.

————. *La Jument errante*. Paris, 1933.

————. *Petite histoire des Juifs*. 26th ed. Paris, 1927.

————. *Quand Israël n'est plus roi*. Paris, 1933.

Thibaudet, Albert. *Les Idées de Charles Maurras*. Paris, 1919.

Thurston, Herbert. "The Ritual Murder Trial at Kiev." In *The Month*, 1913.
Toussenel, A. *Les Juifs, rois de l'époque*. Paris, 1848.
Tovey, D'Bloisier. *Anglia Judaica, or History and Antiquities of the Jews in England*. London, 1738.
Tractenberg, Joshua. *The Devil and the Jews*. New Haven, 1943.
Trail, H. D., and Mann, J. S. *Social England*. London, 1901.
Treves, Frederick. *The Land That Is Desolate*. London, 1913.
Trevor, Daphne. *Under the White Paper*. 1948.
*Trial of the Major War Criminals before the International Military Tribunal*. Nuremberg, 1947-48.

Ullman, S. *Histoire des Juifs en Belgique*. Anvers, n.d.

Vacandard, E. *Vie de Saint Bernard*. Paris, 1895.
———. *Etudes de critique et d'histoire religieuse*. 3rd series. Paris, 1912.
Valentin, Hugo. *Antisemitism*. Tr. from Swedish. London, 1936.
Valois, Noël. *Guillaume d'Auvergne, évêque de Paris (1228-1249)*. Paris, 1880.
Van der Bosch, Firmin. *Vingt années d'Egypte*. 2nd ed. Paris, 1932.
Vermeersch, A. *La Tolérance*. Louvain, 1922.
Venard. "Voyage de Mgr. Baudrillart en Orient." In *La Revue des Amitiés Catholiques Françaises à l'Etranger*.
Viollet, Paul. *Histoire des institutions politiques et administratives de la France*. Paris, 1890-1903.
———. *Abus dans la dévotion: avis d'évêques français et étrangers*. (Author's name not given.) Published by the Comité Catholique pour la Défense du Droit. 1903.
Vitry, Jacques de. *Histoire des croisades*. In *Collection de mémoires relatifs à l'histoire de France, depuis la fondation de la monarchie française jusqu'au treizième siècle*. Ed. by F. Guizot. Paris, 1823-27.

Wasserman, Jacob. *Mein Weg als Deutscher und Jude* (1921). Tr. as *My Life as German and Jew*. London, 1934.
Weill, Georges. *Histoire du mouvement social en France*. Paris, 1924.
Weizmann, Chaim. *Trial and Error*. London, 1949.
Williams, A. Lukyn. *Adversus Judaeos*. Cambridge, 1935.
Wilson, Arnold. *Loyalties, Mesopotamia 1914-1917*. London, 1930.
Wilson, Thomas. *A Discourse upon Usury* (1572). Ed. by R. H. Tawney. London, 1925.
Witherby, Thomas. *An Attempt to Remove Prejudices Concerning the Jewish Nation*. London, 1804.
———. *Observations on Mr. Bicheno's Book entitled The Restoration of the Jews, The Crisis of all Nations. . . .* London, 1800.
Wolf, Lucien. *Sir Moses Montefiore*. London, 1884.

Zevaes, Alexandre. *L'Affaire Dreyfus*. Paris, 1931.
Ziff, W. *The Rape of Palestine*. 1938.
Zuckerman, Nathan. *Wine of Violence*. New York, 1947.
Zweig, Stefan. *The World of Yesterday*. London, 1934.

## Additional Documentation

*Page 89, line 27:*

In 1959 Pope John XXIII personally struck out from the Catholic liturgy the Latin words " perfidis " and " perfidiam " (unbelieving) referring to the Jews. The Pontiff, according to a Vatican source, decided against the use of the words because of the meaning of the modern derivations in Italian, French, English and other languages from the Latin.

*Page 127, line 6:*

In October 1959 the Dean and Chapter of Lincoln Cathedral decided to remove the notice concerning the legend of Little Saint Hugh and replace it with a new notice which reads: " Trumped up stories of ' ritual murders ' of Christian boys by Jewish communities were common throughout Europe during the Middle Ages and much later. . . . Such stories do not redound to the credit of Christendom and we pray ' Remember not, Lord, our offences nor the offences of our forefathers.' "

# Notes

For further details about place and date of publication, see the Bibliography.

## Chapter 1.

### THE GOLDEN MOUTH

1. *Trial of the Major War Criminals* (Nuremberg, 1947), I, 248.
2. Arthur Ruppin, *Jewish Fate and Future*, p. 52.
3. W. Ziff, *The Rape of Palestine*, p. 487.
4. *Trial of the Major War Criminals*, III, 538.
5. Marie Syrkin, *Blessed is the Match* (1948), p. 68.
   The excuse that German spies were sure to come in disguised as Jews is not valid. Refugees could have been screened and suspects interned. Moreover, young children and babies could not be spies. Palestine was open to Polish refugees, *if they were not Jews*, and thousands of them were allowed in during the war. See also Appendix D.
6. Daphne Trevor, *Under the White Paper*, p. 86.
7. Associated Press report from Nuremberg, July 2, 1948. In the Paris *New York Herald Tribune*, July 3, 1948.
8. According to *The Palestine Post*, April 3, 1948: "A memorial grove for the 1,250,000 Jewish children who died under the Nazi persecution is to be planted soon in Galilee on behalf of the children of the Congregational Church of Milton, Massachusetts."
9. *Trial of the Major War Criminals*, VII, 494.
10. *Portrait of the Anti-Semite*, p. 115.
11. In a lecture given in Paris, Feb. 5, 1939.
12. *Judaism and Christianity*, p. 167.
13. Jules Isaac, *Jésus et Israël*, p. 572.
14. *The Forgotten Ally*, p. 45.
15. Juster gives a total of six to seven million Jews in the whole Roman Empire—7 per cent of the population. Klausner estimates the population of Palestine to have been about three million Jews and a half million Syro-Canaanites, Greeks, Arabs and Romans. (*From Jesus to Paul*, p. 33.)
16. "Sermon for Good Friday," *Oeuvres*, II, 628. Chateaubriand is one of many modern Christian writers who have made God responsible for the massacre of Jews. "The people," he wrote, "had cried out—'His blood be upon us and upon our children'—God listened to this vow of the

Jews . . and answered their prayer." (*Itinéraire de Paris à Jérusalem*, II, 17.)

17. See Appendix A.

18. "Il semble bien que Jo. ait forgé cette nuance du mot pour ne pas répéter 'les grands-prêtres et les Pharisiens.'" *L'Evangile selon Saint Jean*, p. cxxxi.

19. *De Principiis*, IV, 8.

20. H. A. L. Fisher, *History of Europe*, p. 3.

21. Jacques de Vitry (1180–1244), *Histoire des croisades*. Pious hatred of the Jews was frequently invigorated by a crude misrepresentation of the Gospel text. Matthew of Edessa (962–1136), for instance, referred to the lance discovered by crusaders at Antioch, and believed by some of them to be the one used at the crucifixion by a Roman soldier (John XIX:34), as "the weapon with which the impious nation of Jews pierced the side of Christ." (Steven Runciman, "The Holy Lance Found at Antioch," in *Analecta Bollandiana*, Vol. LXVIII, Brussels, 1950, II, 204–05.)

22. Julian of Norwich, *Sixteen Revelations of Divine Love*, chap. xxxiii, p. 68. The coupling of hatred and devotion was not confined to Western Christendom. Father Mouterde, S.J., of Beyrouth, has translated a thirteenth-century religious poem, written in Syriac, which contains the following verse addressed to the Blessed Virgin Mary:

> "When with Him thou wert at Cana
> Thou didst intercede with Him for troublesome people,
> The Jews sons of vipers.
> Thou didst say to Him 'They have no wine,'
> And out of water He made wine for them."

The beauty of this poem, as Father Mouterde points out, "is quite spoilt [*bien gâtée*] by its crude antisemitism." (*Analecta Bollandiana*, 1950, II, 305–09.)

23. *The Book of Margery Kempe*.

24. *Epistolae Obscurorum Virorum*, p. 295.

25. "Passiontide and Holy Week" in *The Liturgical Year*, p. 251.

26. S. M. Dubnow, *History of the Jews in Russia and Poland*, II, 379.

27. Albert Thibaudet, *Les Idées de Charles Maurras*, p. 175. The words are taken from *Chemin de Paradis*, a work which, with all the writings of Maurras, was put on the *Index* in 1914, by order of the Pope.

28. Pierre Bayle, *Dictionnaire historique et critique* (1730), I, 75.

29. *Jesus of Nazareth*, p. 348.

30. *The Guide for the Perplexed*, p. 51.

31. Homily viii, "On the Gospel of St. John."

32. Jacques de Vitry, *Histoire des croisades*, p. 11.

33. Fleury, *Histoire Ecclésiastique*, I, 32. The British in Palestine were following a precedent more than nineteen hundred years old when, in the summer of 1946, they searched Jewish settlements for arms, and during these operations often acted with unnecessary brutality, beating up Jewish women and ex-service men.

34. *Historia Sacra*, Book II, chap. xxx.

35. Part 2, chap. xxi.

36. Guilliman et Le Ster, *Histoire de France* (1947), cited by Jules Isaac, *Jésus et Israël*, p. 372.

37. *In the Steps of the Master,* p. 40.
38. *Ibid.,* p. 55.
39. Isidore Loeb, "Le Juif de l'histoire et le Juif de la légende." Jews who had settled in Alexandria and in Egypt were engaged for the most part in business and in trade. They were prosperous and consequently unpopular for the usual economic, political, and religious reasons. The assumption has often been made by writers who are insufficiently equipped and have no time for research that this Jewish prosperity was a product, not of business ability and hard work, but of a specifically Jewish traffic in money. "Jewish money-power," according to Hilaire Belloc, "was everywhere felt, through the action of their great bankers, who had a sort of financial centre in Alexandria." (*The Battle Ground,* 1936, p. 261.) Contemporary documents do not support this hypothesis. Sir Harold Idris Bell, who in 1924 published the result of his researches into the social history of the Jews in Alexandria, found no evidence of their "money-power." "They were not, apparently, to any great extent bankers or money-lenders, as we might expect. . . . There is only one instance of an imputation of usury against the Jews, and this dates from a time when the anti-Semitic feeling was peculiarly intense." (Harold Idris Bell, *Jews and Christians in Egypt: Jewish Troubles in Alexandria and the Athanasian Controversy,* London, 1924, p. 11.)
40. Louis Duchesne, *Early History of the Christian Church,* III, 300.
41. "*Foedum taetrumque Judaeorum nomen.*" In *Codex Theodosianus,* 16. 8.19.
42. "Preface to Memoirs of Richard Cumberland," *Observer,* No. 38.
43. Thomas Newton, *Dissertation on the Prophecies,* p. 101.
44. Book I, chap. i.
45. Book I, chap. i.
46. *Ecclesiastical History,* Book III, chap. xx.
47. *Ibid.,* Book VII, chap. xvi.
48. Letter X (A.D. 338).
49. *Treatise on the Incarnation,* 40, 7.
50. Letter XI, to the Emperor Theodosius.
51. *Israel in Europe.* St. Simeon Stylites, the Elder (388–459).
52. "Oratio in Christi resurrectionem," p. 685.
53. *History of the Jews,* Book VI, chap. xv, p. 553.
    Jacques Basnage, minister of the Reformed French Church at Rouen, was driven out of France after the Revocation of the Edict of Nantes in 1686, and went to Amsterdam where he wrote his *Histoire des Juifs.*
54. R. S. Storrs, *Bernard of Clairvaux,* p. 357.
55. *Historical Sketches,* II, 234.
56. Aimé Puech, *St. Jean Chrysostom,* p. 97.
57. Dom Prosper Guéranger (Abbot of Solesmes), "Passiontide and Holy Week," in *The Liturgical Year,* p. 105.
58. *Saint Chrysostom,* p. 133.
59. The Jewish people, wrote Bossuet, were "driven *without hope* from the land of their fathers." *Discours sur l'histoire universelle,* chap. xx.
60. *Early History of the Christian Church,* I, 52.
61. Jean Juster, *Les Juifs dans l'empire romain.*
62. "Sixth Homily Against the Jews."

Chapter 2.

## THY BROTHER'S BLOOD

1. Article "Agobard" in Vol. I of the encyclopedia *Catholicisme hier, aujourd'hui, demain*, edited by G. Jaquemet.
2. *Monumenta Germaniae Historica, Epistolarum*, V, 200–201.
3. Robert Anchel, *Les Juifs en France*, p. 94. The Jews in the Middle Ages were numerically an insignificant minority. "If Rome had wished to do so," wrote S. Reinach, "she could have exterminated them, or converted them by force." *Revue des Etudes Juives*, XL (1900), p. lv.
4. Pope Gregory VII, Regesta, IX, 2.
5. Charles Lea, *History of the Inquisition of Spain* (1908), I, 82.
6. Ademarus of Chabannes, *Chronicle*, III, chap. lii.
7. *Ibid.*
8. Radulphus Glaber, *Chronicle*, III, 7.
9. J. A. Robertson, *Royal Commission on Historical Monuments*, Vol. I. Bernhard Blumenkranz, "Die judischen Beweisgründe im Religionsgespräch mit den Christen in den christlich-lateinischen Sonderschriften des 5. bis 11. Jahrhunderts," in *Theologische Zeitschrift*, March-April, 1948.
10. Joseph Ha-Cohen, *Emek Ha-Bakha* (French tr., London, 1881).
11. A. L. Poole, in *Cambridge Modern History*, V, 277.
12. J. A. W. Neander, *Life and Times of St. Bernard*, p. 217.
13. H. Graetz, *History of the Jews*, III, 355.
14. Ep. 363, "Ad orientalis Franciae clerum et populum," in Migne, *Patrologia latina*.
15. St. Bernard had good reasons for affirming that the Jews were not the only people interested in money. "Trade crept within the cloister," and nearly forty years after his death, the chapter general, in 1191, said: "The Congregation does not cease from acquisition, and the love of property has become a scourge." Similarly the *Bible Guiot* (1203) states:
    "They buy livings and churches, and cheat in many ways,
    They know how to buy and sell, how to wait for settling day,
    And the best sale of their corn.
    And I have certainly heard and proved
    That they lend money to the Jews."
    Joan Evans, *Life in Mediaeval France*, p. 89. ("Bible" was used as a title for a certain type of religious and satirical verse. Guiot de Provins, a wandering minstrel, traveled to Palestine and ended his days at the Abbey of Cluny.)
16. J. P. Migne, *Patrologia latina*, Vol. CLXXXII, "De laude novae militiae ad milites Templi," chap. v, 10.
17. *Chronica majora*, III, 373, 374.
18. *Acta Conciliorum*, VII, 71–78. Quoted by W. E. Lunt in *Papal Revenues in the Middle Ages* (1934), II, 90.
19. *Patrologia latina*, epistle 365, "Ad Henricum Moguntinum archiepiscopum."
20. Ep. 158 (A.D. 1133). "Ad Dominum Papam Innocentium super inter-

fectione Magistri Thomae Prioris S. Victoris Parisiensis." In Migne, *Patrologia latina*, Vol. CLXXXII.

21. According to eighteenth-century usage, the word "zeal" was generally employed by ecclesiastical writers on the side of virtue. Jean-Baptiste Massillon defined it as "a holy desire to make oneself useful to one's neighbors," *Pensées sur differens sujets de morale et de pieté tiré des ouvrages de feu M. Massillon, Evêque de Claremont* (Paris, 1751), p. 80.

22. Maisie Ward, *Gilbert Keith Chesterton* (1944), p. 377.

23. *The New Jerusalem.*

24. *St. Bernard*, p. 210.

25. Lingard, *History of England*, II, 250.

26. Sermon lx, "De incredulitate Iudaeorum, qua compleverunt mensuram-patrum suorum occidendo Christum," in Migne, *Patrologia latina*, Vol. CLXXXII.

27. Ep. 149.

28. Sermon lx, "De incredulitate Iudaeorum."

29. Sermon xxix, in Migne, *Patrologia latina*, Vol. CLXXXII.

30. *Trial of the Major War Criminals*, XXII, 548.

31. J. C. Morison, *Life and Times of St. Bernard.*

32. *Vie de St. Bernard*, I, 100.

33. "St. Bernard and Peter the Venerable," explained Father A. Vermeersch, "shrank from extreme measures." *La Tolérance*, p. 89.

34. "Tractatus adversus Judaeorum inveteratam duritiem," in Migne, *Patrologia latina*, Vol. CLXXXIX.

35. Lea, *History of the Inquisition of Spain* (1908), I, 81.

36. Achille Luchaire, *Histoire de France jusqu'à la Révolution*, Vol. III.

37. *Le Salut par les Juifs* (1905), p. 42.

38. "For centuries, Gabirol marched through the philosophic schools of mediaeval Europe, some taking him for a Christian, and some for a Mohammedan, none suspecting that he was a Jew." *Selected Religious Poems of Solomon ibn Gabirol*, p. 32.

39. Heinrich Heine, "Romancero," in *Hebrew Melodies*, Book III.

40. Ignorant of both Arabic and Hebrew, St. Bernard could have known nothing of the Jewish spiritual writer Bahya Ibn Paquda, a contemporary of Gabirol, whose work on the "interior life" has recently been translated into French (*Introduction aux devoirs des coeurs*), and published in Paris with an introduction by Jacques Maritain. For an account of Jewish spirituality in the Middle Ages, see Gerschom G. Scholem, *Major Trends in Jewish Mysticism* (Jerusalem, 1941).

41. E. Vacandard, *Vie de St. Bernard*, II, 101.

42. "There are few Jews who, without the influence of propaganda, would genuinely prefer to be the Founding Fathers of their new State rather than business men in New York." (*The Tablet*, May 29, 1948.)

43. *Les Oeuvres et les hommes* (1899), p. iii.

44. Article "Judaism," in *Catholic Encyclopedia.*

45. Denis Buzy, S.C.J., *Les Paraboles* (1932), p. 127.

46. A list of authorities quoted by Dr. Jules Isaac (*Jésus et Israël*, pp. 324-328), includes: L.-Cl. Fillion, *Vie de Notre-Seigneur Jésus-Christ* (1929), A. Reville, *Jésus de Nazareth*; D. Buzy, *Les Paraboles* (1932); A. Brassac, *Manuel Biblique à l'usage des séminaires* (12th ed., 1912); P. Battifol,

*L'enseignement de Jésus* (1905); Karl Adam, *Jésus-Christ* (Fr. tr., 1941);
F. Prat, *Jésus-Christ* (1933).

47. *Rationalist Criticism* (1925).
48. Denis Buzy, *Les Paraboles* (16th ed., 1948), p. 127.
49. *The Divinity of Christ*, p. 57.
50. *The Month*, Sept., 1921.
51. Jules Isaac, *Jésus et Israël*, p. 381.
52. *Hail and Farewell*, II, 421.
53. Ep. 761. March 15, 1518.
54. *Petite histoire des Juifs*, p. 55.
55. *Vie de St. Bernard*, II, 165.
56. *Histoire littéraire de la France* (1789), XIII, 139.


## Chapter 3.

## WANDERERS UPON THE EARTH

1. *Cambridge Modern History*, VII, 634.
2. Horace K. Mann, *Lives of the Popes*, XII, 286.
3. Soames, in J. L. Mosheim, *Institutes of Ecclesiastical History*, II, 238, note.
4. *Constitutio pro Judaeis*, Sept. 15, 1199. A collection of the papal documents which show the relation between the Church and the Jews from 1198 to 1254 is printed, with an English translation, in *The Church and the Jews in the Thirteenth Century*, by Solomon Grayzel.
5. *De Fide*, 81.
6. C. D. Burns, *The First Europe*, p. 591.
7. Ep. 2, 38. To Peter, *rector patrimonii*, in Sicily.
8. Ademarus of Chabannes. *Chronicle*, chap. xlvii.
9. Sept.–Oct., 1201.
10. Basnage, *History of the Jews*, Book VII, chap. xi, p. 639.
11. Canon VIII.
12. Basnage, *History of the Jews*, Book VII, chap. x, p. 637.
13. The mediaeval prohibitions forbidding Jews to employ Christian servants were revived in Germany in 1935, by the "Law for the Protection of German Blood and German Honor," which decreed: "Jews may not employ in domestic service female nationals of German or kindred blood under the age of 45 years."
14. *Essays, Speculative and Political*, p. 262. "We throw in the teeth of the Jews," wrote William Hazlitt, "that they are prone to certain sordid vices. If they are vicious we have made them so." (*The Tatler*, II, 701.)
15. Jan. 16, 1205.
16. *Cambridge Modern History*, VI, 8.
17. Joseph Bonsirven, *Juifs et Chrétiens*, p. 47.


## Chapter 4.

## THE BADGE OF SHAME

1. "Non est pro ipsis vehementer orandum." Durand de Mende (died 1296), cited by L. Canet, *Revue des Etudes Juives* (1911), p. 221.

2. The reference must be to John XIX:2–3. "And the soldiers platting a crown of thorns, put it upon his head: and they put on him a purple garment. And they came to him and said: Hail King of the Jews." These soldiers were, of course, not Jews, but Romans.

3. *Les Juifs devant l'Eglise et l'histoire.* By Rev. Père Constant (Popot), O.P., Doctor of Theology and Canon Law (Paris, 1897). The book was printed with an imprimatur from the Provincial Prior, Fr. Raym. Boulanger, O.P.; read and approved by Fr. B. Hebert, O.P., and Fr. Dalm. Sertillange, O.P.; printed at the Imprimerie Salésienne, Paris (Director: Abbé L. Beissière); and published by Gaume et Cie, a well-known firm of Catholic publishers.

4. "Passiontide and Holy Week," in *The Liturgical Year,* p. 484.

5. *Les Juifs devant l'Eglise et l'histoire* met with the vigorous disapproval of Herbert Thurston, S.J., in *The Month,* June, 1898.

6. The Pope's greeting seems to have been, and undoubtedly became, on such occasions, a mere formality.

7. Gregory IX. Sept. 5, 1236.

8. Paul Viollet, *Histoire des institutions politiques,* III, 202.

9. F. Bourquelot in *Académie des Inscriptions et Belles-Lettres,* 2nd series (1865), V, 152.

10. Le Grand d'Aussy, "La Patenotre de l'usurier," in *Fabliaux ou contes du XIe et du XIIIe siècle* (Paris, 1781), III, 411.

11. *A Discourse upon Usury,* p. 252.

12. Matthew Paris, *Chronica majora.*

13. *An Attempt to Remove Prejudices Concerning the Jewish Nation,* p. 27.

14. *Economic and Social History of Mediaeval Europe,* p. 133.

15. S. L. Peruzzi, *Storia del commercio e dei banchieri di Firenze,* p. 154.

16. W. E. Rhodes, "Italian Bankers and Their Loans to Edward I," p. 133.

17. *The United Kingdom,* I, 108. Goldwin Smith was Regius Professor of History at Oxford.

18. "Un procès contre les Juifs de la Savoie en 1329," in *Revue d'Histoire Ecclésiastique,* XXXIV, 790.

19. April 6, 1233.

20. Bourquelot, *op. cit.,* p. 143.

21. G. F. Moore, *Judaism in the First Centuries of the Christian Era,* II, 145.

22. March 5, 1233.

23. S. M. Dubnow, *History of the Jews in Russia and Poland,* I, 49.

24. H. H. Milman, *History of Latin Christianity,* III, 202.

25. The *auto-da-fé* of Hebrew books commanded by the King of France in the thirteenth century was repeated, on a smaller scale, in 1947, when all Hebrew and Yiddish books, including copies of the Bible, sent to refugees who had been taken off the S.S. Exodus, were burnt by order of a British officer, on the pretext that they might contain "Zionist propaganda." The soldiers explained that, since they could not read Hebrew, they were unable to distinguish between the Bible and any other books written in Hebrew characters.

26. *Histoire universelle de l'Eglise catholique,* XVI, 406. The Bollandist, Charles De Smedt, drew attention to the fact that the popularity of the works of Rohrbacher was regarded by Catholic critics at the end of the nineteenth century as significant evidence of the decadence of his-

torical studies among the French clergy. (*Principes de la critique historique*, p. 285.) Barbey d'Aurevilly, however, maintained that "the thirty volumes of Rohrbacher were of more importance," to any man who can think, "than Guizot's *History of Civilization*." (*Les Oeuvres et les hommes*, p. 123.)

27. Noël Valois in *Guillaume d'Auvergne, évêque de Paris (1228–1249)*.
28. M. Ginsberg, *Reason and Unreason in Society*, p. 200.
29. Gautier de Coinci, *Le Miracle de S. Hyldefonse*.
30. Matthew Paris, *Chronica majora*, V, 136.

## Chapter 5.

## THE MURDEROUS LIE

1. "But what saith the Scripture: Cast out the bondwoman and her son, for the son of the bondwoman should not be heir with the son of the freewoman."
2. R. P. Mortier, *Histoire des maîtres généraux de l'Ordre des Frères Prêcheurs*, I, 428.
2a. A well-known Dominican, R. P. Marie-Joseph Ollivier, wrote, in 1883, that the use by Jews of Christian blood for their religious services is not merely a hypothesis, "but a certainty, unless history is to be denied." The "history" which must not be denied includes "the ritual murder accomplished in France at Valréas de Vaucluse on March 26, 1247." (*Le Correspondant*, 1883, Vol. XCVII, pp. 637–38, "L'Affaire de Tisza-Eszlar.")
3. E. Berger, *Les Registres d'Innocent IV*, I, 424.
4. *Monumenta Germaniae Historica, Scriptores*, XVI, 178.
5. The practice of desecrating Jewish cemeteries still continues, and was reported from eighteen places in Germany between March and October, 1947. "We record the fact," comments the *Jüdisches Gemeindeblatt für die Britische Zone*, Sept. 24, 1947, "that the great majority of these reports come from the British zone. We recall only one such incident in the French zone, which was never repeated, thanks to the immediate intervention of the French authorities." *Der Weg*, Nov. 7, 1947, writes: "We know that these anti-Semitic hooligans derive a great deal of encouragement from the exaggerated leniency with which these shameful acts are frequently regarded."
6. H. H. Milman, *The History of the Jews*, III, 198.
7. A. Jessop and M. R. James, *Life of St. William of Norwich* (1896), p. xiv.
8. R. P. Constant [Popot], O.P., *op. cit.*, p. 246.
9. *Histoire ecclésiastique*, XVI, 507–508.
10. H. V. Livermore, *History of Portugal*, p. 216.
11. "Imperfect Sympathies," in *Essays of Elia*.
12. Isidore Loeb in *Revue des Etudes Juives*, XV, 203–232. Charles Lea in *English Historical Review* (1889), IV, 239–250.
13. Lea, *History of the Inquisition of Spain* (1908), I, 134.
14. Vacandard, *Etudes de critique et d'histoire religieuse*.

15. *Ibid.*, p. 367.
16. 11th series, VII (August 1881), 476, 478.
17. H. D. Trail and J. S. Mann, *Social England*, I, 579.
18. Quoted in *Jews Court and the Legend of Little Saint Hugh of Lincoln* (n.d.), a guidebook to the Jew's House at Lincoln. The Corporation of Lincoln has published a new guidebook in which the falsity of the legend is emphasized. Cf. *Mediaeval Lincoln Jewry and Its Synagogue* by Cecil Roth.
19. R. F. Clerke, S.J., in *The Nineteenth Century*, Feb., 1900, p. 247. Father Clerke's views on beatification would not, at the present time, meet with the unanimous approval of Catholic theologians.
20. *History of the Jews in Russia and Poland*, I, 177.
21. Alban Butler, *Lives of the Saints*, ed. H. Thurston, III, 390.
22. The report is given fully by Hermann L. Strack in *The Jews and Human Sacrifice*. A witness at Nuremberg described how the Germans used the mediaeval method of torture by hanging: "The patient's hands were handcuffed behind his back. A hook was slipped through his handcuffs and the victim was lifted up by a pulley. At first they jerked him up and down. Later they held him suspended for varying, fairly long, periods. The arms were often dislocated. In the camp I saw Lieutenant Lefevre [a Belgian officer] who, having been suspended for more than four hours, had lost the use of both arms." (*Trial of the Major War Criminals*, VI, 173.)
23. *Social Theories of the Middle Ages.*
24. Charles Langlois "Le Procès des Templiers," in *Revue des Deux Mondes*, CIII, 382–421.
25. In the third volume of his *Aegyptiaca*.
26. *The Genius of Judaism* (1833), p. 213. This book is by Isaac D'Israeli, author of *Curiosities of Literature*, and the father of Benjamin Disraeli.
27. E. Drumont, *Le Testament d'un antisémite*, pp. 321, 324.
28. *The Jew Today.*
29. *The Ritual Murder Libel and the Jew.* The report by Cardinal Lorenzo Ganganelli (Pope Clement XIV), London, n.d., p. 17.

Chapter 6.

"MONEY WAS THEIR GOD"

1. J. W. Kay, *The Administration of the East India Company: A History of Indian Progress*, p. 64.
2. Georges Batault, *Le Problème juif*, p. 160.
3. Daniel-Rops, *Histoire sainte: le peuple de la Bible*, p. 367.
4. H. Samuel, *The Unknown Land*, p. 130.
5. *History of Crime in England*, p. 184. The English historian Edward Freeman wrote that the best thing to do with the Jews was "to kick them out altogether, like Edward Longshanks of famous memory." (*Life and Letters of Edward Freeman*, II, 428.)
6. H. Graetz, *History of the Jews*, IV, 48.
7. *Ibid.*, IV, 106.

8. *La Vengeance de nostre Seigneur* (a mystery play dedicated to Charles VIII). In Petit de Julleville, *Les Mystères* (Paris, 1880), II, 453.

9. V. A. Dulaure, *Histoire civile, physique, et morale de Paris*, III, 82. Petit de Julleville, *Les Mystères* (Paris, 1880), II, 103. *Le Journal d'un bourgeois de Paris*, in J. F. Michaud and J. J. F. Poujoulat, *Nouvelle collection des mémoires* (1850), Vol. III.

10. S. N. Dubnow, *History of the Jews in Russia and Poland*, I, 55.

11. *Revue des Etudes Juives*, XI, 59. St. John of Capistrano (1385–1456) was a Franciscan orator whose main mission field was in Italy. The Queen of Naples, Jeanne II, a niece of St. Louis of France, of whom Brantôme said that "she was always in love with someone," encouraged him to preach against the Jews. "It was probably to expiate her scandalous amours," wrote Jean de Sponde (Spondanus), "that she did good to the Church and allowed Capistran to worry the Jews." (Bayle, *Dictionnaire historique et critique*, III, 461.)

12. *The Contrast*, p. 199.

13. For instance, in *La Chrétienté médiévale (395–1254)*, by A. Fliche (Paris, 1929), the word "Jew" will not be found, and there is no reference of any kind, in 497 pages, to the Jewish people.

14. *British Review* (1913).

15. *The New Jerusalem*, p. vi.

16. *Les Grands cimetières sous la lune*, p. 42.

17. *Short History of the Jews*, p. 247.

18. "De Rebus Genuensibus, 1488–1514," in Muratori, *Rerum Italicarum Scriptores*, Vol. XXIV.

19. The Germans did not always wait till people were dead before collecting the gold from their teeth. A report to Rosenberg, read at the Nuremberg trials, states: "In the presence of an S.S. man, a Jewish dentist has to break all the gold teeth and fillings out of the mouths of German and Russian Jews *before* they are executed." (*Trial of the Major War Criminals*, II, 125.)

20. The statement of Salomon ibn Virga that "three hundred thousand Jews were compelled to leave the States of His Catholic Majesty in one day" is clearly an exaggeration. (Bayle, I, 30.)

21. *History of the Marranos*, pp. 60, 61.

22. Ludwig von Pastor, *History of the Popes*, IV, 334.

23. *Ibid.*, III, 90.

24. *Ibid.*, X, 179–180.

25. *Loyalties, Mesopotamia 1914–1917*, p. 129.

26. "The Turk," wrote Dr. W. Ewing, "is, in his own queer way, a gentleman." (*Paterson of Hebron*, p. 201.)

27. Firmin van den Bosch. *Vingt années d'Egypte*, p. 40.

28. *History of the Popes*, IV, 398.

29. Abraham Neuman, *The Jews in Spain*, p. 201.

30. C. E. Chapman, *A History of Spain*.

31. E. Allison Peers, *Spain*, p. 53.

32. Alexander Clarence Flick, *Decline of the Mediaeval Church in the Fourteenth and Fifteenth Centuries*, I, 91.

33. *Ibid.*, I, 65. See also G. Mollat, *Les Papes d'Avignon*, p. 345.

34. *History of the Marranos*, p. 122.

35. Bartholomew Seneraga, "De Rebus Genuensibus Commentaria," in *Rerum Italicarum Scriptores*, XXIV, viii, 24, 25.
36. Charles de Job, *De l'Influence du Concile de Trente sur la littérature et les beaux-arts chez les peuples catholiques*, p. 20.
37. Gheradacci, *Historia di Bologna*, in Muratori, *Rerum Italicarum Scriptores*, XXXIII, i, 2, 356.
38. Cecil Roth, *History of the Jews in Italy*, p. 295.
39. Hartmann Grisar, *Luther*, IV, 286. This phrase, "The Jews are our misfortune"—erroneously believed to have been coined by Treitschke (1834–96)—was adopted as a slogan by Adolf Stocker, leader in 1878 of the Christian-Socialist party in Germany; and it became one of the most popular mottoes of the Nazis.
40. John Addington Symonds, *Renaissance in Italy*, VI, 254.
41. *Table Talk*, IV, 266.
42. Grisar, *Luther*, I, 348.
43. *Ibid.*, IV, 285.
44. "Vom Schem Hamphoras," quoted by Grisar, in *Luther*, V, 406.
45. *Ibid.*, p. 406.
46. Grisar, VI, 78. See also Jansen, *History of the German People at the Close of the Middle Ages*, XV, 49.
47. *My Life as German and Jew*, p. 53.
48. *Thurloe State Papers*, II.
49. M. F. Modder, *The Jew in the Literature of England*, p. 36.
50. *Calendar of State Papers, Domestic*, Nov., 1655.
51. *Ibid.*, 1658–1659.
52. *Ibid.*, Nov., 1660.
53. In Preface to *Ce que mes yeux ont vu* by Arthur Meyer, p. x.
54. *Pensées*, 16, v.
55. Bossuet did not scruple to manipulate Scripture to suit his thesis; for instance, he interpolated a word of his own into Mark XIII:8 in order to apply the text to the Jews: "These things are the beginning of [their] sorrows." (*Discours sur l'histoire universelle*, Part II, chap. xx.)
56. J.-J. Rousseau, *Emile* (Paris, 1894), p. 370. On the same page Rousseau, following the popular tradition, stated that Christ died on the cross, "cursed by a whole people." There is no warrant for such a statement in any of the Gospels. The Jewish people as a whole did not know anything about the crucifixion.
57. *Lettres de quelques Juifs portugais, allemands, et polonais, à M. de Voltaire* (4th ed.; Paris, 1776), p. 45.
58. Jean-Baptiste de Mirabaud (1675–1760), *Opinions des anciens sur les Juifs*, p. 1.
59. *Paroles d'un croyant* (1834), p. 95.
60. *Les Oeuvres et les hommes*, p. 260. The critical faculty of Barbey d'Aurevilly was often obscured by his irrational respect for papal authority. For instance, when he heard that Pope Pius IX wanted to canonize Columbus, he described the discoverer of America as "after the divine Redeemer, the second redeemer of humanity" (*Philosophes et Ecrivains*, p. 263).

Chapter 7.

## GODFATHERS OF BELSEN

1. Isaac Pereire, political economist and social reformer, wrote and worked
   for the improvement of education among the working classes and for the
   suppression of poverty. He advocated reforms of French finance which
   included a partial capital levy and the imposition of an income tax. He
   corresponded with Pope Leo XIII, urging him to effect a reconciliation
   between the Church and modern civilization. Georges Weill, *Histoire
   du mouvement social en France*, p. 211.
2. Edouard Drumont, *"La France juive,"* et *"La Libre Parole."*
3. *La France en alarme*, p. 201.
4. S. Arnoulin, *Edouard Drumont et les Jésuites*, p. 7.
5. Georges Weill, *op. cit.*, p. 416. "The Roumanians would be perfectly
   happy," wrote Drumont, "and so indeed would be the French, if the
   Jews did not exist." (*La France juive*, I, 451.)
6. *Philosophy and Politics*, p. 25.
7. Alfred Baudrillart, *Vie de Mgr. d'Hulst*, II, 27.
8. *Histoire socialiste de la Révolution française*, II, 82, 84.
9. In 1246, when the Jews of Carcassonne had been thrown into prison,
   St. Louis ordered them to be kept in duress and squeezed for money.
   He asked for a report on the amount they could pay. (*Bibliothèque de
   l'Ecole des Chartes*, XXXIX, 274.)
10. *Jewish Social Studies*, Vol. X, No. 2 (April, 1948), R. F. Byrnes,
    "Edouard Drumont and *La France juive*." Several editions of a scurril-
    ous paraphrase, partly a translation, of *La France juive* were published in
    America, anonymously, with the title *The Original Mr. Jacobs*. (The
    Minerva Publishing Company, New York, 1889.)
11. "Let us pray," he wrote, "to the little martyred children of olden time
    . . . asking them to intercede on behalf of their comrades of today who
    are the victims of Jewish Freemasonry." *La France juive*, II, 390.
12. Article "Judaism," in *Jewish Encyclopaedia*.
13. Dr. L. Psenner of the *Oesterr. Volksfreund*. This letter dated May 31,
    1886, was recently found inside a book which had belonged to
    Drumont's own library. See Appendix C.
14. *La Grande peur des bien-pensants: Edouard Drumont*, p. 185. An
    obituary notice (*Manchester Guardian*, July 7, 1948) states that Georges
    Bernanos, "one of the most distinguished and independent French
    writers of the twentieth century, . . . was a Roman Catholic with a
    mediaeval vein of mysticism and deeply preoccupied with the problem
    of evil.
15. *Les Juifs, rois de l'époque* (Paris, 1848).
16. *Le Juif, le Judaïsme et la judaïsation des peuples chrétiens* (Paris, 1869).
17. *Entdecktes Judenthum* (Königsberg, 1711): "Judaism Unmasked: or a
    thorough and true account of the way in which the Stubborn Jews
    frightfully blaspheme and dishonor the Holy Trinity, revile the Holy
    Mother of Christ, mockingly criticize the New Testament, the Evange-
    lists, and the Christian Religion, and despise and curse, to the uttermost
    extent, the whole of Christianity."

18. Cited by S. Arnoulin, in *Edouard Drumont et les Jésuites*. Drumont was dismissed from his post as editor of *Le Monde* after his duel with Arthur Meyer, a converted Jew, editor of the Royalist paper, *Le Gaulois*. Monsignor d'Hulst was, no doubt, glad of an excuse to get rid of him.

19. *Abus dans la dévotion: avis d'évêques français et étrangers*. Published anonymously, but written by Paul Viollet.

20. S. Arnoulin, *Edouard Drumont et les Jésuites*, p. 159.

21. Drumont had previously expressed, with the same confidence, his belief in the ritual-murder myth in a preface he wrote for *Le Mystère du sang chez les Juifs de tous les temps* (1889), by Henri Desportes, who a few years later edited an acidulous periodical called *Le Clergé Contemporain*.

22. *Le Testament d'un antisémite*, p. 325.

23. *Ames juives*.

24. "The Ritual Murder Trial at Kiev," in *The Month* (1913).

25. *La Dernière bataille*, p. 321.

26. *Journal des Goncourt*, VII, 283.

27. *La France en alarme*.

28. The reference is to the much-advertised duel between Drumont and Arthur Meyer, editor of *The Gaulois*.

29. *Le Salut par les Juifs*, p. 18.

30. His first four anti-Semitic books had brought him a profit of 550,000 francs (about $90,000). (Maurice Vanikoff, "Documents sur les débuts d'Edouard Drumont," *Evidences*, Aug.–Sept., 1949, p. 16.)

31. *Les Trafiquants de l'antisémitism: La Maison Drumont "and Co."*

32. By Hugo Valentin, *Antisemitism*, p. 70; and S. Reinach in *Cultes, mythes et religions*, V, 436.

33. Jean Drault (Alfred Gendrot), *Edouard Drumont, "La France juive," et "La Libre Parole."*

34. *Ibid.*

35. *L'Eglise de France sous la troisième République*, II, 338.

36. *Ibid.*, p. 126.

37. *La Fin d'un monde*, p. xv.

38. *The Month*, Jan., 1899.

39. *La France en alarme*, p. 119.

40. *Ibid.*, p. 201.

41. Jean Maxe, *L'Anthologie des défaitistes*, I, 560.

42. *La Libre Parole*, new series, 1933. Albert Monniot acted as one of Drumont's seconds in his duel with Clemenceau, in Feb., 1898.

43. *Les Grands cimetières sous la lune*, p. 126.

44. *La Grande peur des bien-pensants*, p. 174. Bernanos recognized, too late, the tragic meaning of the breach between Christianity and Judaism. See *L'Honneur est ce qui nous rassemble* by Georges Bernanos, unpublished text edited by Albert Beguin in *Evidences*, June–July, 1949, p. 17.

45. "It was set alight," wrote Gabriel Hanotaux, "by heated political passions and by the fierce fury of Drumont." (*Mon Temps*, II, 116.)

46. *La Libre Parole*, Nov. 3, 1894. "*La Libre Parole* simply gave the facts," remarked Georges Bernanos, misleadingly, "without any injurious commentary." (*La Grande peur*, p. 304.)

47. "A summer residence, monotonous but comfortable . . ." Bernanos, *La Grande peur*, p. 308.
48. *"Discours de réception à l'Académie française,"* March 10, 1898.
49. *Scènes et doctrines du nationalisme*, p. 209.
50. G. Bernanos, *La Grande peur des bien-pensants*, p. 133.
51. Léon Meurin, S.J., Archbishop of Port Lewis, in *La Franc-maçonnerie synagogue de Satan.* A reviewer, in *Etudes Religieuses*, LIX (1893), 489, recommended "this learned work" to his readers.
52. *Compte rendu du Congrès National de la Démocratie Chrétienne à Lyon* (1897), p. 78.
53. *La Libre Parole*, Feb. 12, 1898.
54. *Gazette de France*, Sept. 5, 1898.
55. Sir Bernard Spilsbury, British government pathologist, identified as human skin a piece of tanned hide, found at Buchenwald, which had been, apparently, part of a lampshade. A photograph of this exhibit was published in the *New York Herald Tribune* (Paris edition), Dec. 15, 1948.
56. Louis-Martin Chagny, *L'Anglais est-il Juif?*
57. *Review of Reviews*, March, 1898.
58. Louis Capéren, "La Légende de l'intervention du Gesù dans l'affaire Dreyfus," in *Mélanges offerts au R. P. Cavallera*, pp. 497–522.
59. R. P. Besse, *Les Religions laïques*, pp. 199–200.
60. *Penguin Island.*
61. Alexandre Zevaes, *L'Affaire Dreyfus*, p. 210.
62. *Histoire de l'Eglise sous la troisième République*, III, 140.
63. Léon Chaine, *Les Catholiques français*, p. ix.
64. Dominique Ferrata, *Mémoires*, II, 312–13.
65. Cited by Joseph Reinach in *Histoire de l'affaire Dreyfus*, V, 37.
66. Achad Ha-Am, "Pinsker and Political Zionism" (1902), in his *Essays and Letters and Memoirs*, translated from the Hebrew and edited by Leon Simon.
67. *Revue des Etudes Juives* (1882), V, 298.
68. *Notre jeunesse*, p. 54.

## Chapter 8.

## WORKERS OF INIQUITY

1. Dec. 4, 1881.
2. Oct. 30, 1881.
3. W. R. W. Stephens, *Life and Letters of Edward A. Freeman.*
4. *The Eye Witness*, Vol. I (1911); *Revue des Etudes Juives*, Vol. XXVII, p. 2.
5. *Trial of the Major War Criminals*, XVIII, 197.
6. *The Jews*, p. xvi.
7. *Ibid.*, 2nd ed., p. 193.
8. *Ibid.*, p. 88.
9. *The Contrast.*
10. Cited by Nathan Zuckerman, in *Wine of Violence*, p. 25.

11. July, 1921, p. 411
12. Quoted by Louis W. Bondy in *Racketeers of Hatred*, p. 239.
13. *Nuremberg Diary*, p. 156; by G. M. Gilbert, formerly prison psychologist at the Nuremberg Trial.
14. Preston William Slosson, *The Great Crusade and After*, XII, 310, 313.
15. First published in England by Eyre and Spottiswoode.
16. E. Renault, *Le Péril protestant*.
17. *The Jews*.
18. Ep. 673. (Louvain, Nov. 3, 1517.)
19. Rev. Father Constant (Popot), O.P., *op. cit.*, p. 37.
20. Emmanuel Barbier, *Le Progrès du libéralisme catholique en France sous le Pape Léon XIII*.
21. Gustave Gautherot, article "Franc-maçonnerie," in *Dictionnaire apologétique de la foi catholique* (1929).
22. The Alliance Israélite Universelle was founded in 1860 "to defend the honor of the Jewish name." According to the statutes, this association, which is non-political, has the following aims:
    (1) To work everywhere for the emancipation and moral progress of the Jews.
    (2) To give effectual support to those who are suffering persecution because they are Jews.
    (3) To encourage all publications calculated to promote these ends.
23. R. P. Besse, *Les Religions laïques*, p. 110.
24. *The British Review*, April, 1913.
25. *Le Rappel*, October 6, 1919.
26. *Mein Kampf*.
27. *The Jews*, p. 95.
28. *The Jew Today*, p. 120.
29. *British Review*, 1913.
30. *The Jews*, p. xi.
31. *The Jew Today*.
32. A. L. Patkin, *The Origins of the Russian Jewish Labor Movement*, p. 173.
32a. Robert Minder, *Allemagnes et Allemands* (1943), I, 57.
33. *Anti-Semitism* (1939), pp. 7, 8.
34. *Le Christianisme et l'antisemitisme*, p. 31.
35. *Revue Internationale des Sociétés Secrètes*, April, 1921. Mgr. Jouin's chief contribution to the literature of his favorite subject was a work entitled *Le Péril Judéo-maçonnique* (Paris, 1920–21).
36. *Juifs et Chrétiens*, p. 7.
37. A. Monniot, in *La Libre Parole* (1936).
38. *The Jews*, p. 69.
39. A. Schopenhauer, *The Art of Controversy*, p. 25.
40. *Eusebius*, II, 30.
41. *Ibid.*, 401.
42. J. Juster, *Les Juifs dans l'empire romain*, I, 220.
43. E.g., by Houston Chamberlain in *Foundations of the Nineteenth Century*, and by H. V. Morton in his contribution to *Query*, 2 (1939).
44. Epistle 29.
45. Albert Thibaudet, *Les Idées de Charles Maurras*, p. 98.

46. *An Attempt to Remove Prejudices Concerning the Jewish Nation* (1804), p. 88.
47. From the judgment of the German Supreme Court of Justice in the trial of the accomplices of the Rathenau murders in 1922. Quoted by Karl Brammer in *Das Politische Ergebnis des Rathenau Prozesses* (Berlin, 1922), p. 22.
48. *The Jews*, p. 210.
49. *Ibid.*, p. 284.
50. *Across the Frontier*, p. 298.
51. *The World of Yesterday*, p. 322.
52. *Crisis and Decision*, p. 31.
53. *Le Vieux de la montagne*, p. 315.
54. *The Jews*, p. 73.
55. *Scènes et Doctrines du Nationalisme*, p. 153.
56. Johann Gottfried von Herder, *Ideen zur Geschichte der Menschheit* 1787), Vol. XII, chap. 3.
57. *The Jewish State* (1896), tr. into English by J. de Haas (New York, 1904)
58. *The Jews*, 2nd ed., p. 49.

Chapter 9.

## THE "INEVITABLE FAILURE"

1. *Histoire générale et système comparé des langues sémitiques*, p. 4.
2. Oct. 16, 1948.
3. *Protestantism and Catholicity*, p. 74.
4. *L'Année liturgique*, by Dom Prosper Guéranger, Abbot of Solesmes and Superior General of the Benedictines of the Congregation of France. More than thirty editions have been published, the last French one in 1930. The English edition, translated by Dom Lawrence Shepherd, monk of the English Benedictine Congregation, was published in 1868–70. The first three volumes of a new American edition were issued in 1949 by the Newman Press, Westminster, Maryland.
5. *Ibid.*, pp. 152, 450.
6. *An Attempt to Remove Prejudices Concerning the Jewish Nation* (London, 1804), p. 296.
7. *Ibid.*, p. xii.
8. *Restoration of Jews to Their Own Land.*
9. *Daniel Deronda*, Book VI.
10. *Diaries of Sir Moses Montefiore and Lady Montefiore*, I, 167.
11. James O'Neil, *Palestine Re-peopled*, p. 34.
12. *Observations on Mr. Bicheno's Book*, p. 30.
13. M. Fishberg, *The Jews.*
14. *The Jewish Quarterly Review*, XVII.
15. *Jewish Life in the Middle Ages*, p. 9.
16. L. Geiger, *Stimmen der Wahrheit* (1905). Cited by Fishberg.
17. *Neue Freie Presse*, March 31, 1913. Cited by H. Wickham Steed in *The Hapsburg Monarchy*, p. 177.
18. *The Synagogue and the Church*, p. 80.

19. *Within the Pale*, pp. 243, 244.
20. *La Dernière bataille*, p. xvi.
21. *Israël chez les nations.*
22. *The Nineteenth Century* (1925), XCVII, 782.
23. *The Month*, Sept., 1921, p. 194.
24. Quoted by J. K. Hosmer in *The Story of the Nations*, and by many others. Cobbett seldom mentioned the Jews without adding the adjective "blaspheming," except when he called them "Jew-devils" or "blaspheming and bloody Jews." (*Rural Rides*, II, 183, 315.) The religious basis of his hatred is shown by a pamphlet he published in 1830 with the title *Good Friday, or the Murder of Jesus Christ by the Jews.*
25. *Israel in Europe*, p. 364.
26. *La Jument errante*, p. 148.
27. *The Truth about the Peace Treaties*, II, 1140.
28. *Palestine: Problem and Promise: An Economic Study*, by Robert P. Nathan, Oscar Joss, Daniel Creamer, published by American Council on Public Affairs (1946), pp. 182, 183.
29. *Journey to Jerusalem*, p. 301.
30. Rosita Forbes, *Conflict*, p. 40.
31. *Palestine*, p. 172.
32. Henrik F. Infield, *Co-operative Living in Palestine*, p. 100.
33. *The New Jerusalem*, pp. 288–89.
34. J. M. N. Jefferies, *Palestine the Reality*, p. 707.
35. *Palestine: Problem and Promise*, p. 119.
36. *The New Jerusalem*, pp. 293–296.
37. *The Jews*, p. 244.
38. Information Paper No. 20: *Great Britain and Palestine* (3rd ed., 1946), p. 130.
39. *Palestine: Problem and Promise*, p. 66.
40. *The Arab Awakening*, p. 410.
41. Cited in *Empire to Commonwealth: Thirty Years of Imperial History*, by W. P. Hall, 452.
42. *L'An prochain à Jérusalem*, pp. 163, 172.
43. *Orientations*, p. 363.
44. *Un Royaume de Dieu*, p. 273.
45. *Edouard Drumont, "La France juive," et "La Libre Parole,"* p. 328.
46. *Petite histoire des Juifs*, p. 255.
47. Norah Rowan Hamilton, *Both Sides of the Jordan*, pp. 145–149.
48. Douglas Duff, *Palestine Picture*. Preface by Sir Arnold Wilson.
49. "From 1943 the Germans, in order to utilize the bones which were not burned, started to grind them and sell them . . . for the manufacture of superphosphates. In the camp there were found bills of lading . . . of 112 tons and 600 kilograms of bone meal from human corpses. The Germans also used for industrial purposes the hair shorn from women who were doomed for extermination." (*Trial of the Major War Criminals*, VII, 587; report on Auschwitz.)
50. *Bulletin of the Audit Union of the Jewish Agricultural Labor Co-operatives in Palestine, 1934–35.*
51. *European Civilization*, VI, 853.
52. *Palestine: Problem and Promise*, p. 222.

53. *European Civilization*, VI, 853.
54. "Whatever sovereignty over Palestine may reside in law, the Mandatory for Palestine exercises in practice, virtual sovereign powers since it is answerable to nobody. It legislates in complete disregard of the provisions of the Mandate." (Bernard Joseph, *British Rule in Palestine*, p. 50.)
55. *Palestine: Problem and Promise*, pp. 183–89.
56. *Trial and Error*, p. 316.
57. *Palestine: Problem and Promise*, pp. 179, 180.
58. The *Month*, May, 1925, CXLV, 452. "Scum" is the traditional word. Bossuet, in 1681, described the Jews of the fourth century as the "scum of the earth." A similar metaphor was used in 1948 at the Belsen trial when a British officer, defending Kramer, appealed for a lenient sentence on the ground that "the concentration camps came to contain the dregs of the Ghettoes of Central Europe." This observation has been omitted from the official record of the proceedings. (*War Crimes Series*, 1949, Vol. II, ed. by Raymond Phillips.)

A pessimistic forecast of the future of Zionism was expressed, in the mediaeval manner, by a Catholic writer who visited Palestine in 1926: ". . . The infamous Rutenberg concessionaires pursue their plans. . . . It is still possible that . . . the whole thing may in the long run fizzle out. . . . Distrust and dislike of the Jew are universal. . . . It seems an intolerable lapse from *pietas* that the Jews, of all people, should be encouraged to overrun the country which to Christians is holy beyond words. From being the Chosen People, they became the accursed people; they were popularly regarded as such throughout the Middle Ages, and are so looked upon by many even to our own day. And not without reason. . . . If there is one thing that seems to stand out in history as part of the punishment of this race, it is their exile from the Promised Land. . . . If this movement [Zionism] solidifies into a Zionist State, it appears that the land of Jehovah and Jesus will present an organised synthesis of modernist heresies: materialism, nationalism, financierism, communism, sicklied over with humanitarianism and sentimentalism, and bolstered up by every mechanical and intellectual fad of the twentieth century." (Donald Attwater, "Religious Conditions in Palestine," in *The Month*, Oct., 1926, CXLVIII, 347–57.)
59. *A Palestine Notebook*, p. 214.


## Chapter 10.

## PRIDE, ARROGANCE, AND HATE

1. *Antiquitez judaïques* (1713), I, 19.
2. W. Eleroy Curtis, *Today in Syria and Palestine*, p. 333.
3. *Travels or Observations Relating to Several Parts of Barbary and the Levant* (1738), pp. 365, 366.
4. W. F. Lynch, *Narrative of the United States Expedition to the River Jordan and the Dead Sea* (1849), p. 319.
5. *A Pilgrimage to Palestine*, p. 27.
6. F. Rosen, *Oriental Memoirs of a German Diplomatist*, p. 7.
7. "Jérusalem, la Galilée," in *Oeuvres complètes de Pierre Loti* (Paris, 1894–1911), Vol. VII.

8. W. Eleroy Curtis, *Today in Syria and Palestine*, p. 510.
9. *Ibid.*, p. 162.
10. *The Land That Is Desolate*, p. 63.
11. *Paterson of Hebron*, p. 201.
12. *Acta Apostolicae Sedis*, June 18, 1921, XIII, 282–83.
13. *L'An prochain à Jérusalem*, p. 125.
14. A. Baudrillart, *Lettres d'un Pèlerin Français dans le Levant et en Terre Sainte* (Paris, 1924). (In Appendix: "Le voyage de Monseigneur Baudrillart en Orient," article by M. l'Abbé Venard published in *Revue des Amitiés catholiques françaises à l'étranger*, p. 105.)
15. Ernest Graf, *In Christ's Own Country*.
16. *Vie de Jésus*, I, 64.
17. Ernest Graf, *In Christ's Own Country*, p. 236.
18. *In the Steps of the Master*, pp. 97, 98.
19. *The Month*, Aug., 1924.
20. Bernard Joseph, *British Rule in Palestine*, p. 11.
21. *With the Judaeans in the Palestine Campaign*, p. 272.
22. Estelle Blyth, *When We Lived in Jerusalem*, p. 295.
23. *The Memoirs of Cordell Hull*, II, 1547.
24. *Hope Simpson Report* (1930), p. 66.
25. J. M. N. Jefferies, *Palestine the Reality*, p. 709.
26. *Memories and Reflections*, II, 219, 220.
27. *Letters to a Friend*, p. 112.
28. *Autobiography of Margot Asquith*, p. 272.
29. *A Palestine Notebook*, p. 6.
30. *Ibid.*, p. 171.
31. *Sword for Hire*, p. 118.
32. C. R. Ashbee, *A Palestine Notebook*, p. 9.
33. When the British Government relinquished its mandate in Iraq in 1933, without first solving the Assyrian problem, the Iraqis promptly solved it by massacring most of the Assyrians. The Tharaud brothers were sure that history, if given a chance, would repeat itself; they were confident that if the British left Palestine, "there would not be a single Zionist left in the ancestral land twenty-four hours after their departure." *Quand Israël n'est plus roi*, p. 194.
34. Page 148.
35. *Paterson of Hebron*, p. 218.
36. Beverley Nichols, *No Place Like Home*, p. 254.
37. *Unholy Memories of the Holy Land*, p. 39.
38. *A Palestine Notebook*, p. 65.
39. "Shortly before the Rebellion all the colonies had been disarmed, their sealed armories removed by a government bowing before the Arab agitation." (Douglas Duff, *Sword for Hire*, p. 258.)
40. *Trial of the Major War Criminals*, XIII, 115; IV, 49.
41. *Some Observations on the Mandatory Government of Palestine*, pp. 36, 57.
42. A. Z. Berzin, *The People of Israel Will Remember the Martyrs of Ab*, 5680. (Jerusalem, 1930.) In Hebrew.
43. *Some Observations on the Mandatory Government of Palestine*, pp. 47, 49.
44. *Ibid.*, p. 57.

45. Horace Samuel, *Unholy Memories of the Holy Land*, p. 306.
46. Bernard Joseph, *British Rule in Palestine*, p. 219.
47. Joseph Broadbent, *From Vine Street to Jerusalem*, p. 250.
48. E. T. Richmond in *The Nineteenth Century* (1925), XCVIII, 49.
49. *The Rape of Palestine*, p. 415.
50. John Marlowe, *Palestine Rebellion*, p. 47.
51. *Middle East Window*, p. 330.
52. *Trial and Error*, p. 276.
53. *Objection to the Doctrine of Israel's Future Restoration to Palestine* (1828), p. 118.
54. *The Historical Background of the Bible*, p. 253.
55. Hector Bolitho, *Beside Galilee* (1933), pp. 98, 115.
56. John Gibbons, *The Road to Nazareth*, pp. 76, 77.
57. Wingate Report, June 6, 1939.
58. The Permanent Mandates Commission of the League of Nations was always well informed about the situation in Palestine. In 1930, the representatives of the mandatory power had to listen, at Geneva, to some very unwelcome comments. One of the Commissioners, M. Rappard, remarked that: "The Government's method of encouraging immigration was to limit it. . . . They had done practically nothing concrete . . . to encourage close settlement by Jews on the land. The Government had not prevented it, but he did not see that they had taken any positive action to encourage it, and that was why he understood the protest of the Jews who declared that the mandate was not being carried out. The Arabs, of course, were discontented also, but they were discontented primarily owing to the existence of the mandate. The Mandates Commission, however, was not competent to discuss the existence of the mandate, but only its application." (Minutes of the Seventeenth [Extraordinary] Session, tenth meeting, June 9, 1930.)

Chapter 11.

EPILOGUE

1. *Memoirs*, II, 1539.
2. "The Morgenthau Diaries," *Collier's*, Nov. 1, 1947.
3. *Blessed Is the Match.*
4. Daphne Trevor, *Under the White Paper*, 121.
5. Henry Morgenthau, "The Morgenthau Diaries."
6. *Politics Among Nations: The Struggle for Power and Peace*, p. 357.

APPENDIX

1. Homilies on St. John's Gospel, xv, 26.
2. *The Fourth Gospel* (1906), pp. 65–103.
3. *L'Evangile selon St. Jean* (Paris, 1904), pp. 60–65.
4. Lucien Wolf, *Sir Moses Montefiore* (1885), p. 82.
5. *Judaism and Christianity*, p. 12.
6. *Life of Cardinal Manning* (1895), II, 652.

# Index